Political Gender

Political Gender

Texts and Contexts

edited by

Sally Ledger, Josephine McDonagh
and Jane Spencer

preface by

Maud Ellmann

HARVESTER
WHEATSHEAF

New York   London   Toronto   Sydney   Tokyo   Singapore

First published 1994 by
Harvester Wheatsheaf
Campus 400, Maylands Avenue
Hemel Hempstead
Hertfordshire, HP2 7EZ
A division of
Simon & Schuster International Group

Typeset in 10/12pt Galliard
by Dorwyn Ltd, Rowlands Castle, Hants

Printed and bound in Great Britain by
T.J. Press (Padstow) Ltd

British Library Cataloguing in Publication Data

A catalogue record for this book is available from
the British Library

ISBN 0–7450–1562–X

1   2   3   4   5   98   97   96   95   94

Contents

List of Figures

Preface

A Matter of Style

Maud Ellmann

In her recent book *The Alchemy of Race and Rights*, Patricia Williams, a black American law professor, gives a harrowing account of being turned away from Benetton's in New York's Soho. 'Buzzers are big in New York City,' she writes. 'Favored particularly by smaller stores and boutiques, merchants throughout the city have installed them as screening devices to reduce the incidence of robbery: if the face at the door looks desirable, the buzzer is pressed and the door is unlocked. If the face is that of an undesirable, the door stays locked' (p. 44). On the occasion in question, when Williams pressed her 'round brown face' to the window, the white teenager at the desk, his cheeks bloated with chewing gum, took one look at her and mouthed, 'We're closed,' blowing a pink bubble in her face. It was two Saturdays before Christmas, at one o'clock in the afternoon, and there were several white people browsing in the shop. The united colours of Benetton, it seems, don't stretch to brown. (For a full account of this incident, see Joseph Bristow's note 24, p. 222).

In her fury, Williams wrote an article for a law review, describing how it felt to be excluded, to be told her money wasn't wanted in a world where purchasing power is usually regarded as an open sesame. When her manuscript was edited, however, she discovered that every vestige of her 'rushing, run-on rage' had been removed. In the second edit, all reference to Benetton's had been deleted, the editor claiming that Williams's unverified account might be regarded as defamatory. In the final page proofs, all mention of race had been eliminated too, because it was 'against "editorial policy" to permit descriptions of physiognomy'. When Williams protested, the editor replied that her article, though ' "nice and poetic" ', didn't ' "advance the discussion of any principle. . . . This is a law review, after all." ' Infuriated, she accused him of censorship; but he replied, in a voice 'gummy' with condescension, ' "This is just a matter of style." '[1]

This anecdote reveals that style, far from being a superfluous adornment, plays a crucial role in the dynamics of exclusion. In 1792, Mary Wollstonecraft was already grappling with the problem of style in *Vindication of the Rights of*

Woman. Both Wollstonecraft and Williams establish a close analogy between style of dress and style of address: Williams, deprived of the sweater that she wished to buy in Benetton's, was then deprived of the style of argument in which she wished to tell her story in the law review. The shop assistant, with his gummy face, and the editor, with his gummy voice, both locked the door. Whereas Williams clings to style, Wollstonecraft vows to strip it from her prose, just as she demands that women strip their dress of frippery: 'wishing rather to persuade by force of my arguments than dazzle by the elegance of my language', she writes, 'I shall try to avoid that flowery diction . . . pretty superlatives, dropping glibly from the tongue, vitiate the taste, and create a kind of sickly delicacy that turns away from simple unadorned truth. . . .' Women's persons, she declares, should be pure and unadorned as truth itself, for 'the whole mischief of trimmings, not to mention shopping [and] bargain-hunting', vitiates the brain. If men and women both 'took half as much pains to dress habitually neat as they do to ornament, or rather to disfigure, their persons, much would be done towards the attainment of purity of mind'.[2]

By denuding her argument of style, traditionally regarded as the dress of thought, Wollstonecraft lays claim to the universal voice of the free citizen, renouncing the 'pestiferous purple' associated both with the dress and with the language of the aristocracy, of which class bourgeois women are the tawdry imitators.[3] As Barbara Taylor has pointed out, it was impossible in Mary Wollstonecraft's society for women to speak as citizens without speaking against their womanhood: 'So clearly gendered was the concept of the free citizen that Wollstonecraft's attempts to employ it on women's behalf constantly drew her away from a discourse of humanity to one of masculine identification.'[4]

However, Wollstonecraft also punctures the authority of men through a series of cunning comparisons, in which she smuggles back the rhetoric she has ostensibly forsworn. She likens women, in the first place, to the aristocracy: both, deprived of vital action, sink into luxurious debility, living only for the hollow finery of style. Lavished with 'regal homage', women grow vain and enervated as the aristocracy; whereas aristocrats, in turn, are feminised by power, growing narcissistic and corrupt as women.[5] Wollstonecraft then draws a daredevil analogy between women and a standing army: like the *'fair* sex', she argues, the business of soldiers' lives is gallantry; they show a feminine attention to their dress, for they are 'taught to please, and they live only to please'. 'Where then is the sexual difference', she demands, 'when the education has been the same?'[6] This analogy boldly repudiates the error that we now inelegantly term 'essentialism': that is, the view that 'sexual difference' is innate, rather than the consequence of 'education'. Instead, Wollstonecraft suggests that femininity is drag, whether donned by women, soldiers or aristocrats; while freedom and enlightenment, she feels, can be attained only when everyone gives up pretending to be women. Renouncing style, coded feminine, is the forfeit everyone must pay in order to become a free citizen, a condition that presents itself as style-less and gender-less.

To deny style is to deny difference: this is what Wollstonecraft and Williams both reveal, though Wollstonecraft denounces style as the trappings of despotism, whereas Williams struggles to preserve her style from the specious neutrality of legalese. Difference, however, is an awkward term to use these days, since its meanings have become confounded through excessive use. It would be difficult to count the titles in which 'difference' has appeared in the last decade, but they include some of the most important work in gender studies: *In a Different Voice, The Future of Difference, A World of Difference* – just to name a few. Why has this abstract, even boring, word attained the status of a shibboleth? Its blandness masks the differences raging in the term itself, the rivalries of its promiscuous associations.

Difference, according to the *Oxford English Dictionary*, means the condition of dissimilarity, distinction or diversity, denoting the relationship of non-identity between two things, or more. In mathematics, the difference is the remainder left over after subtracting one quantity from another. Difference, however, also means a disagreement of opinion, as well as the estrangement or hostility produced by such a clash. In the current rhetoric of race and gender politics, 'difference' embraces all these meanings: it signifies the variance dividing blacks from whites, women from men, lesbians from heterosexuals; and it also signifies the enmities that keep those groups distinct and self-enclosed. Thus difference comes to represent a kind of trademark or heraldic sign that certifies a group's identity and its resistance to assimilation into other groups. However, difference in the sense of mathematical remainder also features prominently in contemporary theory: difference is what is left out after race and class and gender are subtracted from the body politic; difference is what the law review omitted when it whitewashed Williams's impassioned prose. The idea that Western culture is haunted by the difference that it debars has become a truism of current thought.

In all these usages, difference serves to reinforce the identity of groups, rather than to undercut their insularity: difference functions as a border guard preventing the contamination of one term, one tribe, or one tradition by another. Jacques Derrida, however, uses the term difference precisely to discredit the idea that an identity could ever be complete or sufficient to itself. In his lexicon, difference bespeaks miscegenation rather than autonomy, and implies that all identities are tainted by the otherness that they exclude. To borrow Barbara Johnson's economical formulation, deconstruction is concerned not with the difference *between*, which holds identities apart, but with the difference *within*, which confounds identities together, and undermines the very notions of the same, the integral, the unadulterated.[7]

This form of difference has been welcomed by the French feminist psychoanalyst Luce Irigaray, who claims that female speech and sexuality perpetually differ from themselves, thus exceeding masculine conceptions of the one, the proper, or the self-identical. She condemns psychoanalysis for reducing women to the Other of the Same, castrated shadows of a monosexual identity, and insists instead upon the need to devise new forms of discourse to express the specificity of womanhood:

> what a feminine syntax might be is not simple nor easy to state, because in that 'syntax' there would no longer be either subject or object, 'oneness' would no longer be privileged, there would no longer be proper meanings, proper names, 'proper' attributes. . . . Instead, that syntax would invoke nearness, proximity, but in such an extreme form that it would preclude any distinction of identities, any establishment of ownership, thus any form of appropriation.[8]

This conception of female discourse could be summed up, in the words of Cole Porter, as 'the urge to merge with the splurge'. If masculine thought represses differences in favour of identity, Irigaray dissolves them into indistinguishable goo; in her ethics of 'mucosity', she promotes primeval slime as the feminine alternative to the constipated fixities of 'male' philosophy.[9] By positivising difference, however, Irigaray transforms it into an identity, as homogeneous as the 'male' truths that she sets out to undermine: in her view, difference is opposed to sameness as female is opposed to male, and each remains inviolate within its separate sphere. Thus Irigaray's usage of 'difference' takes us full circle back to the definitions in the *OED*, in which difference means identity in contestation.

In literary studies, the call for difference, while emphasising gender, has led to the virtual collapse of genre: for instance, in a bookshop the other day, I discovered *Daniel Deronda* shoved up against a guide to home remedies for thrush, both works having been classified under the single rubric – WOMEN. But feminists have now progressed beyond asserting their difference from men to proclaiming their difference from one another, in an effort to prevent the specificities of race and class and sexuality from being swallowed up into a new consensus, dominated by a white straight middle-class 'femocracy'. For at least a decade, feminist conferences have been punctuated by the tedious refrain: 'You haven't paid enough attention to difference!' – as if the mere reiteration of the word could automatically absolve its user of essentialism, the cardinal sin of gender politics. Unfortunately, essentialism cannot be defeated by a magic word: to insist upon the absolute uniqueness of every social group – its one and only, incorruptible particularity – is just as essentialist as the opposing tendency to universalise at the expense of difference. Challenging in its inception, this chorus of difference has grown so pious and so punitive that it often creates ghettos within ghettos, reinforcing the very racial, economic and sexual divisions that feminism should be striving to eliminate (among its other definitions, difference means 'discrimination'). In this context, to plead for common bonds is often more abrasive than to champion diversity.

Of course, it is important that the voices of minorities be heard, rather than appropriated by the privileged; yet there is a danger on the other side, when differences ossify into identities, that only those belonging to the club in question, be it gender, race or class, may claim the authority of experience. Conceived in this way, difference is more likely to issue in confession than in any form of political organisation – particularly in a culture that fetishises authenticity, and markets 'true stories' as ruthlessly as any other article of merchandise. Witness the Oprah Winfrey show, where victims of oppression, illness and abuse bare their souls to viewers mesmerised by prurience. In current politics, moreover, the celebration of diversity conceals the fact that difference is the burden, as well as the resource, of the oppressed. A black student told me of a survey conducted at his American high school, in which respondents were asked to name what they saw as most important to their own identities. Predictably, all the blacks declared their blackness, whereas no whites declared their whiteness; being the norm, their whiteness was no colour; the blacks embodied 'colour' for the whole community. If the blacks felt their identities constricted by their skin, however, they could at least perceive their colour; unlike their white peers, whose obtuseness vindicates Lacan's idea that the place of power is the place of blindness and the place most likely to be ambushed unawares, like the proverbial ostrich with its head in the sand.

Yet Patricia Williams points out that even as a black person, condemned to 'carry' difference for the whole society, her colour comes and goes according to the motivations of her interlocutors:

> A man with whom I used to work once told me that I made too much of my race. 'After all,' he said, 'I don't even think of you as black.' Yet sometime later, when another black woman became engaged in an ultimately unsuccessful tenure battle, he confided to me that he wished the school could find more blacks like me. I felt myself slip in and out of shadow, as I become nonblack for the purposes of inclusion and black for the purposes of exclusion; I felt the boundaries of my very body manipulated, casually inscribed by definitional demarcations that did not refer to me.

Such demarcations, Williams argues, must be recognised for the 'rhetorical gestures' they are; this complicates 'the supposed purity of gender, race, voice, boundary'. While granting 'the utility of such categorizations for certain purposes', we must also acknowledge 'the necessity of their breakdown on other occasions'.[10] In other words, identity is not an essence but a strategy: while there are contexts in which it may be crucial to assert one's race or class or gender, there are other contexts in which it may be more effective to expose the artificial nature of those terms. Without this vigilance to context, words like difference harden into orthodoxies, so that we forget the ambiguities they conceal.

Each of the essays in this volume tackles the question of difference, addressing all the warring meanings of the term. Kadiatu Kanneh defends the notion of difference as identity, attacking deconstruction for dissolving the identities of race and class before they have been understood in their historical reality. Gargi Bhattacharyya points out that as an Asian woman, identity is thrust upon her even if she tries to deconstruct its terms: it is almost impossible, she argues, 'for a black person to talk about "race", and not be read as saying, in however veiled a manner, "see, it happened to me" ' (see below, p. 86). Laura Marcus, with great dexterity, exposes the pitfalls of the current vogue for 'personal criticism', in which the critic, suspicious of impersonality and objectivity, brings her own predicament into the foreground of the argument. The advantage of this strategy is that it avoids appropriating the experience of others; the risk, however, is that it lapses into narcissism and irrelevance, as well as reinforcing the convention that women be restricted to the personal, domestic sphere of life.

Many writers in this volume take up the notion of difference as remainder: Rita Felski, for example, shows how women are subtracted from the history of modernity; Lawrence Normand, how homosexuality is omitted from Irigaray's analysis of gender; Christine Battersby, how female transcendence is excluded from accounts of the sublime; Joseph Bristow, how anal sexuality returns as the repressed in a culture dominated by the cant of family values. Derek Duncan examines the difficulties faced by gay novelists in their attempts 'to plot a gay trajectory as anything other than gender pastiche' (see below, p. 159); while Lynnette Turner argues that anthropology, since its inception, has been predicated on the notion of the Other as ' "a threat to be reduced, as a potential same-to-be, a yet-not-same" ' (see below, p. 99). Terry Lovell shows how feminist accounts of Charlotte Brontë, by reducing her heroines to 'everywoman', have disregarded the importance of anti-papism and xenophobia in constructing British Protestant identity. Elisabeth Bronfen, in a fascinating essay, argues that the phallus, which Lacan exalts as the 'signifier of signifiers', masks the more disturbing message of the 'omphalos' or navel, the mark of our maternal origin and hence of our facticity, our historicity and our mortality.

Other contributors use difference in the deconstructive sense to dispute the very notion of identity; Jane Moore, for instance, agreeing with Derrida that 'There is no such thing as the essence of woman' (see below, p. 78). Linda Williams, in a deft and provocative essay, argues that feminist attacks against pornography misunderstand the nature of fantasy. She endorses the psychoanalytic argument that ' "fantasies are marked by multiple and fluid identifications on the part of the subject" '; they ' "constitute scenarios with multiple points of entry" '. For this reason, she argues, 'pornography could offer a site upon which individuals could challenge their own sexual identities . . .' (see below, p. 197). There is much appeal in the idea that fantasy provides a kind of smorgasbord of possible identities, each of them experimental, ludic, uncongealed. Yet this is to ignore the 'compulsion to repeat' exemplified in fantasies which, although they offer multiple identifications, regularly reproduce the same scenarios. Freud attributed the compulsion to repeat to the power of the death drive, which he defined as the 'impulse to return to an earlier state of things', and ultimately to the chill repose of inorganic matter.[11] Clearly, pornography partakes of this repetitive, demonic character of fantasy; and to be sceptical about the liberating powers of pornography is not to opt for censorship but to recognise the grim conservatism of the libido.

Vivien Jones brings us back to Mary Wollstonecraft, where the politics of gender necessarily begin. She discusses how Wollstonecraft, while adopting a masculine discourse in the *Vindication*, attempted to refashion the sentimental novel for the purposes of female emancipation. Forced to choose between the 'feminine' domain of sensibility and the 'masculine' domain of sense, Wollstonecraft remained marooned, without a country. Sadly, her dilemma was not so very different from the choice that Patricia Williams, two centuries later, was obliged to make between the neutralising discourse of the law review and another discourse – metaphorical, impertinent, and often indiscreet – which insists upon its difference from the voice of the academy, yet always runs the risk of being snubbed or marginalised. Wollstonecraft is frequently criticised for selling out to masculine authority; yet on the other hand, attempts to fabricate a 'female' style often end up reaffirming the inveterate ideas that women are poetic, irrational, subjective, gossipacious, enigmatic, fluid, mucous or incontinent. It is clear, in any case, that the slogan of difference cannot rescue us from the problem of style, any more than it can insulate us from the idioms and the identities of others. Difference is not the answer. Difference is the question.

Notes

1 Patricia Williams, *The Alchemy of Race and Rights* (1991; London: Virago, 1993), pp. 44–8.
2 Mary Wollstonecraft, *Vindication of the Rights of Woman*, introd. Barbara Taylor (London: Everyman, 1992), pp. 4, 81, 139.
3 Wollstonecraft, *Vindication of the Rights of Woman*, p. 19.
4 Barbara Taylor, Introd. to *Vindication of the Rights of Woman*, pp. xviii, xvii.
5 Wollstonecraft, *Vindication of the Rights of Woman*, p. 23. For an excellent discussion of this point, see Anna Wilson, 'Mary Wollstonecraft and the Search for the Radical Woman', *Genders* 6 (1989), p. 93.
6 Wollstonecraft, *Vindication of the Rights of Woman*, pp. 26, 25.
7 Barbara Johnson, *The Critical Difference: Essays in the Contemporary Rhetoric of Reading* (Baltimore, MD: Johns Hopkins University Press, 1980), p. x.
8 Luce Irigaray, *This Sex Which Is Not One*, trans. Catherine Porter with Carolyn Burke (Ithaca, NY: Cornell University Press, 1985), p. 134.
9 See Luce Irigaray, 'The Limits of the Transference', in *The Irigaray Reader*, ed. Margaret Whitford (Oxford: Blackwell, 1991), esp. pp. 109–17.
10 Williams, *The Alchemy of Race and Rights*, pp. 9–11.
11 *Beyond the Pleasure Principle* (1919), in *The Complete Psychological Works of Sigmund Freud*, trans. James Strachey (London: Hogarth, 1953–74), vol. 18, p. 36.

Acknowledgements

Most of the essays in this volume were presented at the 'Feminist Criticism in the 90s' conference at Exeter University in April, 1992. The editors wish to thank the many people who supported and assisted them in the organisation of this event, in particular Inga Bryden, Richard Crangle, Patricia Dowse, Joanne Hill, Colin Jones, Samantha Moore, Patricia Moyer, Gareth Roberts, Jacqueline Rose, Helen Taylor and Michael Wood. The conference was made possible by funding awarded by the British Academy, the University of Exeter Research Fund, the School of English and American Studies of the University of Exeter, and Bristol LTP group, for which the editors express their gratitude. Finally, the editors would like to thank Jackie Jones of Harvester Wheatsheaf for the care and expertise with which she has assisted in the production of this volume.

Chapter 8, Elisabeth Bronfen, 'From Omphalos to Phallus', was previously published in *Women: A Cultural Review* 3, 2 (1992) © Oxford University Press. The editors gratefully acknowledge permission to reprint this essay.

Figure 8.3 is reproduced from Jane Ellen Harrison, *Epilegomena to the Study of Greek Religion and Themis: A Study of the Social Origins of Greek Religion* (New York: University Books, 1962). Figure 14.3 was printed in *The Pink Paper*, 5 April 1992 and is reproduced here with the permission of the photographer John Campbell. Figure 14.1 and Figure 14.2 are reproduced with permission of The Estate of Robert Mapplethorpe.

Introduction

Sally Ledger and Josephine McDonagh

When Virginia Woolf embarked on her study of women and fiction, in *A Room of One's Own* (1929), she paid a visit to the British Library. Her observations concerning the ordering and production of knowledge were pertinent: in the monumental scheme of the library catalogue, 'woman' existed as an obscure subcategory of male universalising knowledge. As a consequence, the study of women took on random and diverse forms, constituting a bizarre mishmash of unconnected perceptions, representing, *in toto*, the embodiment of self-enhancing male fantasies and the effacement of women's lives and experiences.

In at least one important respect, things have changed since then. Now, Elaine Showalter has noted in her introduction to the collection *Speaking of Gender*, in the world of publishing and academic research, everyone is speaking about gender.[1] In recent years gender has been taken seriously as a critical category in the production of knowledge, and this, at least in part, is thanks to the impact of writers such as Woolf. As feminist scholars have charted the particularities of the lives, desires, anxieties and ambitions of different women, they, like Woolf, have noticed the ways in which the forms of knowledge, the modes of criticism and investigation, themselves frequently replicate the social inequalities they seek to address. The consequence of this feminist endeavour has been the dismantling of the possibility of a universal knowledge, and a reformulation of modes of enquiry – in short, a revitalisation of the humanities as a place in which women and men, their fragmented and disparate lives, can be both the subjects and objects of knowledge.

But not all has changed. While Showalter's optimistic view of the prominence of gender issues in academic work accurately reflects the buoyancy of interest in these issues in some circles, it also obscures the situation within academic institutions where the same inequalities and exclusions that persist in broader society are perpetuated both in the curricula and also in the hierarchies of the institution. Showalter takes her evidence from academic conferences and debates in the United States, where there has been widespread coverage of gender issues. In Britain the situation is similar. In April 1992, for instance, more than six hundred delegates attended three different conferences over the same few days, on closely related topics: 'Feminist Criticism in the Nineties', held at

1

Exeter University; a conference on women and philosophy at Cambridge University; and another on women and early modern literature at Liverpool University. The essays in this book are, in fact, largely drawn from the first of these occasions, which was a celebration of the bicentenary of another important landmark in the history of feminist scholarship: the publication of Mary Wollstonecraft's *Vindication of the Rights of Woman*. In addition to this, the widespread development of women's studies and related courses in higher education, the explosion of feminist titles in academic publishers' lists in the humanities and social sciences, and the success of feminist publishing houses such as Virago and The Women's Press, prove not only that women are a formidable presence in the book market, but that they are reading and writing, talking and listening, enrolling as students, teaching and publishing at an extraordinary rate. Nevertheless, this situation is a hard-won achievement. We know from experience as feminist teachers in British universities that women still constitute a minority and often marginalised group among staff members, and that the resistance to gender issues on mainstream syllabuses, even on such basic points as the inclusion of women writers, is still regrettably strong. The high profile of gender in particular areas of academic activity does mark a heightened awareness of oppression and discrimination, and it is welcome. But it cannot be seen to signal the end of gender-related discriminations and oppressions, or the necessity for feminist struggle.

Gender studies presents one academic context in which this struggle can be fought. All the essays in this collection deal with issues and approaches in gender studies, and show quite emphatically how gender studies derives from a feminist critique and feminist politics. Since the 1970s there has been a strong tradition of feminist criticism, pioneered by women within higher education, which has insisted on the importance of gender as a crucial factor in all forms of cultural and critical analysis. More recently this has been extended and reinvented in order to explore, in fruitful juxtaposition to the consideration of more familiar women's issues, other socioculturally determined positions of difference. This, we would claim, has increased the influence of the project of feminist criticism, enabling the discussion in this volume of issues relating to 'race' and nation, male homosexuality and the discourse of AIDS, and the exploration of feminism's own trouble spots: for instance, its divisions over questions of sex and censorship, and its difficult relation, since poststructuralism, to the 'personal'. The key concern of the collection is the operation of gender in the formation of representations and in the production of knowledge, and the essays are loosely grouped around four topics: identity, epistemology, aesthetics and repression. Not all the essays deal with literary texts, although they all share an interest in texts, and all of them utilise the insights of contemporary critical theory, making radical interventions in current critical debates.

This volume asserts the place of gender studies within a tradition of feminist criticism. However, by no means all feminists are entirely happy with this assessment. The feeling in some quarters is that the move to gender studies represents a dilution and depoliticisation of feminist criticism rather than its enlargement. Gender studies is regarded by some as a leech on the back of feminism, draining its political lifeblood. Tania Modleski, for instance, has argued that gender studies is in the business of marginalising feminism. In *Feminism Without Women*, she chastises exponents of gender studies, and Elaine Showalter in particular, for what she regards as a political sell-out; 'what's in these new developments *for feminism* and for women?' she insists. For Modleski, gender studies is admissible only 'according to the contributions it can make to the feminist project and the aid it can give us in illuminating the causes, effects, scope, and limits of male dominance'.[2] It seems to us, however, that there is a political problem both with Modleski's conception of 'the feminist project' – which, it is implied, is unproblematically homogeneous – and with the unspecified 'male dominance' to which she refers. In an age in which the diversity of forms of female oppression has been highlighted, and when attention by various sections of the late-twentieth-century feminist movement to adjacent forms of oppression based on class and 'race' has expanded the perimeters of – and, at the same time, problematised – 'the feminist project', there is surely a political as well as an intellectual imperative to identify much more clearly both the 'women' whom Modleski confidently posits as her subject, and their oppressors.

The politics of feminism in the 1970s was predicated on women's shared identity. With the ascendancy of poststructuralism in literary and critical theory in the 1980s, 'identity' has become a problematic term, so that a politics based on identity becomes at best difficult. One issue which the essays in this volume tackle is whether a feminist identity politics remains viable in the 1990s, or whether the attention of feminist critics and theorists should be turned to the ways in which gender is *constructed*, to an analysis of the technology of gender and to the processes through which we *become* women and men. Only then, arguably, can women be freed from forms of oppression which have become internalised in the gendering process. Modleski's fear is that to relinquish a feminist identity politics in favour of such an approach would be to lose what political clout is left to feminism in the late twentieth century. Judith Butler, in *Gender Trouble*, recognises Modleski's position when she reflects that 'Contemporary feminist debates over the meanings of gender lead time and again to a sense of trouble, as if the indeterminacy of gender might eventually culminate in the failure of feminism.'[3] Arguing that it is no longer straightforwardly the case that feminism needs to settle the question of primary identity in order to enable political action, Butler claims that feminists should, more positively, be attempting to determine the new political possibilities to be born of a radical critique of the categories of identity, now that identity as a common ground 'no longer constrains the discourse on feminist politics'.[4]

While we are broadly supportive of Judith Butler's position, we also recognise, with Modleski, the political problems associated with the loss of a stable concept of identity, as do several of the contributors to this book. However, we wish to suggest that at the level of praxis it is surely possible – and, indeed, necessary – to accept the provisionality of 'woman' as a construct, while at the same time quite properly basing forms of feminist activism on 'woman' as a category of oppression, given that all women – however they *became* women – are indeed oppressed in various aspects of social and economic life. Moreover, as the essays in this book demonstrate, the insights of poststructuralist theory attacked by Modleski can, rather than dissolving identities, provide a way of thinking about how identities are formed, and understanding the discursive mechanisms of oppression.

Questions of identity, then, provide the focus for many of the essays in this collection. Laura Marcus goes to the heart of the debate over the possibility of a feminist identity politics in her overview of the autobiographical drift in contemporary criticism and theory. She questions whether the 'return of the subject' in recent criticism constitutes a positive reclamation of agency, identity and subjectivity for feminists in a postmodern age, or whether in fact such a return is born of a sense of crisis, doubt and uncertainty about 'identity'. Marcus remains sceptical about the autobiographical drift within feminist criticism, and notes that 'there seems to be little value in the discourse of an "I" which declares that it speaks only for itself to an "us" or "we" constituted in and by the safety of a like-minded professional group'. In the context of racial oppression, however, 'the discourse of an "I"' carries a greater political urgency than it lacks in the circumstances Marcus invokes. Kadiatu Kanneh and Gargi Bhattacharyya both argue that for Black feminists it is vital to place oneself within a historical narrative of identity. Thus Bhattacharyya will use personal anecdotes to mount a critique of the construction of Asian women in British ideation. But, like Marcus, she and Kanneh are also worried by the dangers of an essentialism which depends on an unsophisticated notion of the authentic (Black) self – being part of a 'Black' community, for instance, can involve as much prescription as description. Manoeuvring her way between these problems, Kanneh focuses on the way in which women of mixed race experience the contradictory demands of different racial identities, but she demonstrates the persisting compulsion towards narratives of belonging and inheritance: the structuring forces of identity, she claims, 'as yet cannot be reinvented in total, flagrant abandonment'. Terry Lovell also asserts the importance of attending to narratives of identity, but this time in the voices of an imperial nation. Her case study of the critical reception of Charlotte Brontë's *Villette* reveals a consistent blindness to the jingoistic sense of national identity that is displayed in this text, and shows the way in which even feminist critics have half-vindicated the novel's nationalist bearings as no more than displaced forms of more honourable feminist motifs. Lovell shows the need to confront questions of identity when these are obscured within the discourse of the oppressor.

Lawrence Normand reveals another repression in some feminist work as he takes up the question of identity in relation to male homosexuality. Normand challenges Luce Irigaray's designation of male homosexuality as the epitome of phallocentrism and as 'the actual male self-love which the detour of heterosexuality tries to disguise'. He contends that such a conflation of male self-love and male homosexuality is a false rhetorical move which assumes that sexual difference is the difference which has priority over all others, and fails, in its representation of maleness as a single Other, to perceive the splits and exclusions within the masculine. In an arresting move, Normand turns Irigaray's critique on itself, for he shows how – if, as Irigaray eloquently demonstrates, femininity is Freud's 'blind spot of an old dream of symmetry' – male homosexuality functions similarly in her own work. He then analyses Marlowe's *Edward II* and Thom Gunn's *The Man with Night Sweats* to render visible what Irigaray's essentialising and ahistorical construction of homosexuality would leave invisible – that is, the historical contingency of the concept, and the widely different discursive formations in which it appears.

All four essays in Part II stage challenging critiques of familiar models of enquiry. Jane Moore engages with arguments within feminism itself. Troubled by a return in recent feminist work to a notion of essence – formulated, she claims, as a response to the perceived excessive abstraction and antifeminism of poststructuralist models of critique – Moore argues that feminism does not *need* a concept of essence, which would not facilitate, but only block change. On the contrary, Moore makes a case for a feminist appropriation of deconstruction as a politically enabling model; moreover, she sees a continuity between the work of Mary Wollstonecraft and that of Jacques Derrida in their shared critique of Enlightenment rationality.

Elisabeth Bronfen's essay 'From Omphalos to Phallus' proposes a feminist revision of the Freudian psychoanalytic model whose phallocentrism has long troubled feminists. Observing Freud's virtual ellipsis of feminine death in his account of *Oedipus Rex* in *The Interpretation of Dreams*, she argues that in his formation of the oedipal model Freud represses a prior desire of matricide. Gargi Bhattacharyya and Lynnette Turner scrutinise another psychoanalytically in-formed concept, the Other, which is used in cultural analysis as a tool for understanding issues of 'race'. Bhattacharyya demonstrates how the Other is primarily concerned with the repressions and fantasies of white subjectivity, and ignores the day-to-day experiences of oppression. Her concern is to find the terms in which, as she puts it, 'Black might mean "disadvantaged" without being "exotic"'. Turner extends this critique into the realm of ethnography. She argues that the Other, as an anthropological category, always effaces sexual difference: the legacy of late-Victorian ethnography in contemporary critical discourse, she suggests, is that the Other is simply rendered as the 'not-us'; this leads to a prioritisation of the wholly cultural over and above the simultaneity of sexual and cultural difference. Turner explores the semantics of anthropological knowing in the late nineteenth century, a transitional stage in the development of anthropology as an academic subject, to show how anxieties about the limits of its epistemology are displaced on to femininity – or, more specifically, the 'Aboriginal Woman'. She thus shows the way in which the development of this discipline is bound up both with a failure to see the ethnically different woman, and with a repudiation of sexual difference as an operative category in the production of knowledge.

The work of gender in the formation of aesthetic forms and movements is the concern of Part III. In an essay that complements Elisabeth Bronfen's discussion of feminine death, Christine Battersby's 'Unblocking the Oedipal' is a timely reminder of the need to rethink aesthetic categories from a feminist point of view, and to judge women's artistic achievements on their own terms. Battersby takes up the question, formulated most notably by Patricia Yaeger,[5] of the possibility of a feminine sublime, and shows, through a reading of a poem by the German writer Karoline von Günderode, that feminist revisions of this aesthetic have been constrained by the dominance of an oedipal model in current the-orisations of the sublime. Battersby makes a useful intervention in the burgeon-ing critical literature on the Romantic discourse of the sublime. On a similar tack, Rita Felski challenges the traditional masculine gendering of modernity, and boldly locates 'woman' as the central motif within early modernist writing. She reassesses both the moment of modernity and the aesthetic movement of modernism, invoking Baudelaire's lesbian 'heroine of modernity' as well as women sex-workers and actresses as central figures within the 'modern' matrix. Finally, Derek Duncan pursues the implications of feminist work on narrative and plot in his discussion of the strategies which have been deployed to articu-late the AIDS 'story'. Duncan is concerned with the way in which political agendas are prescribed – and in some cases seriously limited – by particular aesthetic categories, traditions and cultural forms. He sharply turns the question 'how has the experience of AIDS affected the gay novel?' into a more complex and disquieting question about the interactions between narrative forms and material possibilities.

Repression, in the form of censorship, is the final thematic focus of this volume of essays. Vivien Jones addresses the guilty feelings and the self-censorship associated with heterosexual desires. She looks back to the Enlightenment, and pinpoints there a dichotomy between rationality and feel-ing as a crucial source of the difficulties faced by heterosexual feminists in their attempts to formulate a politics that does not involve the repression of their sexuality. She suggests that this dichotomy was already being challenged in the feminist novels of Mary Wollstonecraft and Mary Hays. Jones links these prob-lems with the current debate on pornography, an issue further developed in the remaining essays. Feminism's problematic involvement with the censorship of pornography frequently polarises the women's movement in the late twentieth century. While anti-pornography feminists are accused of aligning themselves with the moral Right, anti-censorship feminists are themselves blamed for a complicity with pornography's objectification of women. Linda Ruth Williams explores the way in which, ironically, the strong feelings produced by porno-graphy themselves perform a kind of censorship, at once consolidating feminist opinion at a time of fragmentation and backlash, but also blotting out oppo-sitional feminist voices and blocking discussion of other issues. Joseph Bristow shifts the ground to focus on the consistent censorship of the homosexual body that he observes in contemporary culture. In a wide-ranging essay, he pursues the implications of this repression for a homosexual community stricken by AIDS. Against Elisabeth Bronfen, he argues that the unrepresentable body-part is in fact the anus, and follows the effects of this repression. Bristow's conclusion is that the censoring of representations of the male homosexual body seriously inhibits any attempt to promote safer sex, and that this silence in the discursive and representational spheres leads quite literally to death.

Bristow's essay is perhaps the most controversial in a collection characterised by its pursuit of issues and agenda which, in more consoling contexts, would be circumvented. A diverse range of topics is negotiated, and critical approaches are employed; and there are unresolved differences between contributors on key points. Yet the essays share a belief that issues of social import cannot be understood outside their own historical and cultural contexts, any more than they can be comprehended apart from the discursive mechanisms that frame them.

Notes

1 Elaine Showalter (ed.), *Speaking of Gender* (New York and London: Routledge, 1989), p. 1.
2 Tania Modleski, *Feminism Without Women: Culture and Criticism in a 'Postfeminist' Age* (London and New York: Routledge, 1991), p. 5.
3 Judith Butler, *Gender Trouble: Feminism and the Subversion of Identity* (New York and London: Routledge, 1990), p. viii.
4 *ibid.*, p. ix.
5 Patricia Yaeger, 'Toward a Female Sublime', in *Gender and Theory: Dialogues on Feminist Criticism*, ed. Linda Kauffman (Oxford: Blackwell, 1989), pp. 191–213.

Part I

Identities

Chapter 1

Personal Criticism and the Autobiographical Turn

Laura Marcus

My starting point is the recent development in feminist theory of what has been called 'personal criticism' (along with 'political correctness' and the personal computer, the other variety of PC in North America today). Personal criticism is both less and more than the claims made for it. It may be something of a chimera, since the term is applied to and in the work of a very small number of (mainly) American critics, who would comfortably fit in a yellow cab or on an MLA panel. But the interest in 'personal criticism' – the very coining of the term – is also part of larger and more general questions and concerns about – among other themes – identity, subjectivity, and the state and status of theory. I want to tease out these issues, beginning with 'personal criticism' as it is being defined by its practitioners, and broadening out to more general concerns.

A brief list of the most salient shifts in thinking about identity which form the background to current debates would include the decline of older deterministic positions and, more generally, suspicion – if not the end – of grand narratives (Lyotard), a focus on the imaginary (Castoriadis and Irigaray), and a growing awareness of ethnic diversity and specificity. Despite – or because of – all these changes, we seem close in many ways to the concerns of the 1960s: with whatever qualifications and added precision, there has been a 'return of the subject'. This may be seen as a positive reclamation of agency, identity and subjectivity – or as reflecting, as Kobena Mercer has argued, a sense of crisis, doubt and uncertainty about 'identity' – a defensive response to 'the sheer difficulty of living with difference'.[1]

'Personal criticism' is part of the move to reclaim agency and subjectivity. Nancy Miller's recent collection of essays, *Getting Personal*, both defines and enacts what is variously called 'personal criticism', 'autobiographical criticism' and 'narrative criticism'.[2] 'Personal criticism', in Miller's account, has developed in part out of recent feminist interest in autobiography, and a more general feminist concern with the personal. An autobiographical moment is made central to the activity of criticism, thus both foregrounding the identity of the critic and reconceptualising the nature of criticism itself; in Miller's words, it 'entails an explicitly autobiographical performance within the art of criticism. Indeed, getting personal in criticism typically involves a deliberate move toward self-figuration, although the degree and forms of self-disclosure of course vary widely.'[3] Miller gives a number of examples of this critical genre:

> Personal criticism continued: there is self-narrative woven into critical argument, like Adrienne Rich's reflection on going to visit Emily Dickinson's house in Amherst, Alice Walker's revision of Woolf through her daughter's eye in 'One Child of One's Own', and Cora Kaplan's interleaving of political and autobiographical argument in *Sea Changes*; or the insertion of framing or interstitial material – like Jane Gallop's recontextualized self-productions (lovers and outfits) in *Thinking Through the Body*. Personal criticism can take the form of punctuating self-portrayal like Carolyn Heilbrun's account in *Writing a Woman's Life* of inventing Amanda Cross; Barbara Johnson's thirdperson cameo in 'Gender Theory and the Yale School'; the appearance of Stephen Heath's sick mother at the end of 'Male Feminism'; Frank Lentricchia's invocation of working-class Italian parents in 'Andiamo!' (the coda to his polemic – with photos of the author – against Gilbert and Gubar's 'essentialist feminism'); the coda to D.A. Miller's 'Cage aux folles' about the author's shoulder muscle spasm; and structurally discrete anecdote like Stephen Greenblatt's airline encounter that forms an epilogue to *Renaissance Self-Fashioning*. All function as a kind of internal signature or autobiographics.[4]

Miller's list continues with examples of 'self-representation as political representativity', experiments in form, intellectual autobiography, and collections of cultural criticism articulated through personal narrative. She adds: 'The spectacle of a significant number of critics getting personal in their writing, while not, to be sure, on the order of a paradigm shift, is at least the sign of a turning point in the history of critical practices.'[5]

The challenge by women of colour and ethnic minorities to the exclusions and universalisms of white feminisms seems to have led, particularly in North America, to a wariness of collectivist claims and claims to general representativity – what Nancy Miller calls the incantatory recital of the 'speaking as a's' and the imperialisms of 'speaking for's'. The 'speaking as a's' stem also, however, from an identity politics which, while it challenges 'bourgeois self-representation', produces, in Miller's view, an equally problematic concept of representativity. She is troubled by the demand that we should speak in the name of the group or groups we are said to represent in terms of class, gender, colour, and so on. Autobiographical discourse is thus closely linked to (or arises from) an anxiety about 'speaking for others' as well as the problems of representativity – an 'identity politics', in this view, may also subordinate the individual.

Personal criticism is also said to go along with an increasing suspicion of the 'impersonality' and 'objectivity' of theoretical discourse; this is viewed as a pseudo-objectivity, in that it conceals the first person and denies the 'situatedness' of the person theorising. This call for a recognition of the subjectivity of the theorist is not, of course, a new one – in both philosophy and literary criticism there seems to be a cycle whereby subjectivity and objectivity are invoked in turn to compensate for each other's shortcomings. The current climate – at least in Anglo-American criticism – appears to have moved strongly towards the subjective pole: 'I prefer the gossipy grain of situated writing to the scholarly sublime,' writes Miller.[6] The particularity of 'the autobiographical act – however self-fictional' resists 'the grandiosity of abstraction that inhibits what I've been calling the crisis of representativity'. Autobiographical or 'personal' criticism – like the study of autobiography – 'has in part to do', Nancy Miller writes, 'with the gradual and perhaps inevitable waning of enthusiasm for a mode of Theory whose authority – however variously – depended finally on the theoretical evacuation of the very social subjects producing it'.[7] This, of course, relates to the broader issue of whether or not deconstruction hindered the attempts of feminist thinkers to construct new identities. Personal criticism is in part an expression of the sense that – as Nicole Ward Jouve puts it – 'you must have a self before you can afford to deconstruct it' – though she adds that 'it is no easier to say "I" than to make theory'.[8]

Two primary emphases emerge in discussions of 'personal criticism': first, metaphors of the dramatic and corporeal; and second, representations of 'conversation' and dialogue. Extensively and wittily employing the former, Miller writes:

> the autobiographical act – however self-fictional – can, like the detail of one's (ageing) body, produce this sense of limit as well: the resistance particularity offers to the grandiosity of abstraction that inhabits what I've been calling the crisis of representativity.[9]

Miller uses the work of Roland Barthes to call attention to the importance of the bodily self, but her particular admiration is reserved for an essay by Jane Tompkins, 'Me and My Shadow', in which 'thinking about going to the bathroom. But not going yet' is seen to mark the risks taken by the feminist critic of embarrassing the self or the reader.[10] Tompkins's essay shares the emphasis on writing as a process much emphasised by Nicole Ward Jouve, and it is striking that the situation of the writer is now being emphasised by critics for whom the role of the reader, and of reading, were formerly so important. Some of the emphasis on writing as a process also recalls earlier emphases, in *écriture féminine*, on women's writing as subversion, and it is undoubtedly important that women bring the personal into places in which it is constituted as inappropriate. The attempt to erase the gap between 'body' and 'writing' in 'personal criticism', in part through versions of the performative utterance, may also, however, be a more anxious gesture – a claim to an 'authenticity' which is linked to the forms of identity claim or identity crisis with which I began. The 'performative' (I am using the term loosely for the moment) becomes both an 'embodiment', a speaking-out of selfhood, and an enactment of 'situation' and 'position' which exploits the spatial and substantive metaphors of political affiliation ('this is where I stand on this issue') while insisting upon the singularity of the self or body occupying a particular space.

The risks and dangers of personal criticism may, of course, be other than those feared or desired by the critic engaged in an act of self-exposure. D.A. Miller's

'Secret Subjects, Open Secrets', in *The Novel and the Police*, offers a nice take on the issue of embarrassment, a word that frequently occurs in personal criticism:

> We are all well acquainted with those mortifying charges (sentimentality, self-indulgence, narcissism) which our culture is prepared to bring against anyone who dwells in subjectivity longer or more intensely than is necessary to his proper functioning as the agent of socially useful work. (It is bad enough to tell tales out of school, but to tell them in school – or what comes to the same, in a text wholly destined for the academy – would be intolerable.) And those envious charges have at least this much truth in them, that the embarrassing risk of *being too personal* all too often comes to coincide with its opposite in the dismal fate of banality, of *not being personal enough*. Nothing, for instance, is more striking than the disproportion between the embarrassed subject and the occasion of his embarrassment: while the former imagines his subjectivity on conspicuous and defenceless display, the latter has usually been rendered all but invisible by its sheer mundaneness, its cultural or physiological predictability. Rarely does anyone even think to watch the spectacle we assumed we were making of ourselves. We say truly, 'I could have died of embarrassment', but nearer than one's fantasized murder at the hands (the eyes, the tongues) of the others is the danger lest such worldly homicide prove embarrassingly unnecessary, the subject who fears extinction having already died out on his own. The painfulness of embarrassment, which at least ought to have guaranteed its subject's vitality, instead betokens a mountainously agitated subjectivity that refuses to acknowledge its mousy stillbirths.[11]

In this passage D.A. Miller elides the embarrassments of personal confessions and the public performance – he also makes the mortified subject masculine. (Nancy Miller's list of 'personal critics' includes both men and women.) Performance anxiety, in the context of public speaking, has, perhaps, been theorised more often as a woman's problem in the twentieth century. Hélène Cixous writes of the woman speaking at a public gathering: 'She doesn't "speak", she throws her trembling body forward' – although this manifestation of fear is interpreted positively by Cixous as a bodily inscription of speech and a physical materialisation of thought.[12] In the late 1920s, the psychoanalyst Joan Riviere gave an account of the forms of anxiety experienced by women speaking out in public. In her essay 'Womanliness as a Masquerade', Riviere describes the responses of two intellectual women to giving public lectures.[13] The first delivered lectures in a wholly 'professional' way, but after her performance she suffered 'misgivings whether she had done anything inappropriate', and sought reassurance of a sexual kind by flirting with her male colleagues. Riviere writes: 'the extraordinary incongruity of this attitude with her highly impersonal and objective attitude during her intellectual performance, which it succeeded so rapidly in time, was a problem'.[14] In the second case, the woman lecturer dressed in ultra-feminine clothes, and was flippant and joking *during* her performance. Riviere analyses both cases as symptoms of the problems that arise for women who usurp 'masculine' authority: 'women who wish for masculinity may put on a mask of womanliness to avert anxiety and the retribution feared from men'.[15] The conservatism of Riviere's arguments, with their assumption of gender fixity and their equation of intellectual authority and masculinity, is undermined, however, by her ultimate refusal to distinguish between 'genuine' womanliness and the 'masquerade': 'whether radical or superficial, they are the same thing'.[16]

Riviere's arguments have been highly influential in feminist film studies, in which the concept of the masquerade has been used to explore representations of female sexuality, particularly the fetishistic representations of Hollywood cinema.[17] They have also become significant for the recent forms of 'performative' criticism with which I am concerned here. Nancy Miller closes *Getting Personal* with an essay entitled 'My Father's Penis', in which she cuts the phallus down to size. In *Thinking Through the Body* Jane Gallop repeatedly links performance (anxiety) and sexual identity and, consciously or otherwise, reworks the performances of Riviere's two intellectual women, providing a commentary on the 'intellectual' self as a sexed subject: 'those were the stakes of all my performances, to pull off being there as a body, but as a thinking body, one neither whose thought nor whose body could be dismissed'.[18] Where Riviere's first woman performs initially as the intellectual and then as the (overly) sexual woman, Gallop's 'performances', she suggests, achieved the simultaneity and consubstantiality of the intellectual and sexual, mind and body. Yet where Riviere's second woman is said to undermine her intellectual performance by her feminine clothes and frivolous behaviour, Gallop claims that the parodic nature of her own sexual style is subversive of femininity, both proper and improper: 'I was in drag . . . a poesis of the body. . . . My own sartorial style . . . was literally influenced by male homosexual fascination with a certain feminine style.'[19] Masquerade goes camp, and 'performance' comes to connote both the 'authenticity' of the embodied writing/speaking self (the performative) and the subversive parody of a stylised identity.

In her recent book *Gender Trouble*, Judith Butler asserts that 'parody' – 'the parodic repetition of gender' – is the means by and through which the constructed nature of gender identity will be revealed and opened to subversive intent: 'I describe and propose a set of parodic practices based in a performative theory of gender acts that disrupt the categories of the body, sex, gender and sexuality and occasion their subversive resignification and proliferation beyond the binary frame' – and beyond the limiting and coercive frame of compulsory heterosexuality.[20]

Substantially working in a Foucauldian framework and critiquing the 'foundationalist reasoning of identity politics',[21] Butler argues for a shift from a grammar of identity (which privileges being) to an account of 'doing gender' as a performative enactment. Here the concept of the performative appears to cover two different senses. First, it exists in Butler's account as a form of ideological mystification in which 'doing' serves to confirm or compel gender as 'being' – identity is performatively constituted. 'The notion of sex as substance', Butler writes, is achieved 'through a performative twist of language and/or discourse that conceals the fact that "being" a sex or a gender is fundamentally impossible. . . . Gender is an enactment that performatively constitutes the appearance of its own interior fixity.'[22] Second, the 'performative' and 'the performance' seem to become synonymous – or at least, closely related – terms, and are discussed as radical ways of revealing the multiple constructions of gender identity and opening up to 'the parodic proliferation and subversive play of gendered meanings'. Repeated references throughout the text to drag acts and cross-dressing reinforce the image of the theatricality of gender, of the performance aspects of the performative, and of the corporeal basis of gender acts: 'Just as bodily surfaces are enacted as the natural, so these surfaces can become the site of a dissonant and denaturalized performance that reveals the performative status of the natural itself.'[23] The radical play of the performative is pitted against the essentialism of an identity politics.

Butler's use of the concept of the 'performative' is clearly some way from formulations in linguistics and philosophy. Yet even in the more austere formulations of J.L. Austin, developing his primary distinction between 'constative' and 'performative' utterances – between using language to describe states of affairs and *doing* things with words (as, for example, in 'promising') – broader issues emerge.[24] Most prominent among these are the relation between language use and authority, noted by Austin and given greater emphasis by Émile Benveniste[25] – the authority which, for example, empowers an agent to marry people or sentence them to death – and the *commitment* embodied in the promise.

Feminist theorists have adopted two principal strategies in response to these concerns. The first involves the subversion of authority and performative commitment, brilliantly satirised in Shoshana Felman's juxtaposition of Austinian speech-act theory and Molière's *Don Juan*, where promises to ladies are made to be broken, and the spurious uniqueness of the act of promising is revealed to be just one more repetition. By repeating his promises of marriage, Don Juan also subverts the performative authority of the first person.[26] Critics such as Judith Butler have taken up this promise of the self-subversion of authority and the performative play it generates, while Jane Gallop makes seduction a woman's affair. The second strategy is to reconceptualise authority in more positive terms as a matter of (feminist) commitment. An early influential work of American feminist criticism was entitled *The Authority of Experience*, and this emphasis survives in certain texts of 'personal criticism', in which the use of the first person is assumed to authorise discourse.[27]

The ethical dimension of performative commitment is more stressed by critics who have taken up the performative promise of feminism. Tania Modleski, whose essay 'Some Functions of Feminist Criticism; Or, the Scandal of the Mute Body' addresses a number of these questions, argues against Felman's celebration of a speech of broken commitments and broken promises, and writes that 'feminist critical writing is simultaneously performative and utopian, pointing toward the freer world it is in the process of inaugurating'.[28]

I now want to move to a discussion of the second of the two related concerns in 'personal criticism' noted above – conversation, dialogue, and, more generally, 'linguistic subjectivity'. Nancy Miller writes:

> It was clear that feminist theory had arrived at a crisis in language, a crisis notably inseparable from the pronouns of subjectivity: between the indictment of the feminist universal as a white fiction brought by women of colour and the poststructuralist suspicion of a grounded subject, what are the conditions under which as feminists one (not to say 'I') can say 'we'?[29]

The defensive note struck here points to an important factor in the origins of personal criticism. Miller appears to be saying that this crisis has in part been brought about by 'women of colour' outlawing the 'we'; a more adequate analysis would be one that recognised the need for white as well as black feminists to address the problems of homogenisation and universalism.

The concern with 'the pronouns of subjectivity' described by Miller has become increasingly widespread in feminist and other theory. In a recent discussion at the Institute of Contemporary Arts in London, the American critic Mary Ann Caws, the most impassioned proponent of 'personal criticism', asked the question 'how will pronouns represent us?'; and she, unlike Miller, is unambivalent about the need to reclaim the collective pronoun: 'the saying of "we" is under siege', she asserted, adding that 'I'- and 'we'-saying allow us to alternate between the individual and the collective. In Caws's rather idealised model of reading – as in her recent book *Women of Bloomsbury* – criticism becomes a conversation:

> It is around such an experiential generosity of community that characters in and out of the text may find themselves grouped, reading together, seeing together. Such criticism is the deliberate opposite of a cool science but is not in disregard of fact; it is composed of an unshakeable belief in involvement and in coherence, in warmth and in relation.[30]

Cynically, one might suggest that Caws is establishing the community, the 'we', in a safe place, answering the problems raised by other groups about the constituents of the 'we' by proposing a dialogue between (possibly) dead authors, fictional characters, personal critics and putative readers seen as critical companions and sharers of the same values. With less scepticism, Caws's position can be allied to Tania Modleski's persuasive claim that 'feminism can only evolve through a process of dialogue . . . symbolic exchange between the critic and the women to whom she talks and writes'.[31]

While there are clearly problems in reducing issues of subjectivity and cultural identity to a linguistic analysis of subject positions, it is interesting to see that so many contributions to both fields – often following Benveniste's 'The Nature of Pronouns' (1956) and 'Subjectivity in Language' (1958) – have been concerned with the use of personal pronouns.[32] The focus on the 'pronoun-boundedness' of identity, developed by Benveniste in the late 1950s and 1960s, was taken up in the 1970s by Philippe Lejeune, who, of recent critics, has done most to theorise autobiography as a genre. Although he noted, in his influential *The Autobiographical Pact*, examples of second-person (Michel Butor, Georges Perec) and third-person autobiographies, Lejeune focused on the first person, referring to Benveniste's idea that there is no concept of 'I': 'The personal pronouns have reference only within a discourse, in the very act of utterance.'[33] Within utterance, the first person expresses the *identity* of the subject of the enunciation [*énonciation*] and the subject of the utterance [*énoncé*]. The auto-biographical contract [*pacte*] affirms the ' "identity" between the names of the author, narrator and protagonist'.[34] In a later essay, 'Autobiography in the Third Person', Lejeune notes the difficulty of Benveniste's attempt to:

> remain on a level of strictly grammatical description; any slightly advanced analysis of the play of pronouns and persons in enunciation is faced with the dizzying necessity of constructing a theory of the subject. 'Identity' is a *constant relationship* between the one and the many. . . . The first person always conceals . . . a secret third person, and in this sense all autobiography is by definition indirect.[35]

For a number of feminist critics, of course, the reverse is said to be true: the neutralities of the third person conceal the identity and situation of the first person. Luce Irigaray, whose current work includes major projects on the gendering of discourse, claims:

> It seems that, rather than becoming more human by developing the sexuate morphology of his discourse, man now wants to absent himself from language, no longer saying 'I', 'you' or 'we'. Here, the sciences, technologies and certain regressions to religiosity appear to go hand in hand. In taking over from the 'I' (here and now), from the subject and from a possible 'you', these truths seem to have the force of law.[36]

One of Irigaray's possible targets here is Jean-François Lyotard, who has expressed particular anxiety over the use of the first-person plural, in *Le différend*[37] and in 'Missive sur l'histoire universelle'.[38] If one poses the question: 'Can we continue to organise events in terms of a universal history of humanity?', the question presupposes that there is a 'we' to accept or reject that proposition. This 'we' (which may include or exclude a reference to a third party [they]) cannot itself be thought independently of the idea of a universal history of humanity, which is now no longer credible. Modernity, for Lyotard, involves the implicitly authoritarian project of speaking of, and for, others in order to incorporate them into 'our' projects so that they will become at one with 'us':

> In the tradition of modernity, the emancipatory movement means that the third party, initially outside the we of the liberating avant-garde, ends up taking part in the community of actual speakers (first person) or potential speakers (second person). There will then only be you and me. The first person position is in fact marked in this tradition as that of mastery of the word and of meaning.[39]

To 'work through' – in the Freudian sense – the question of the subject, the we, is to escape from the simple reinstatement [*reconduite*] of the subject of modernity or its parodic or cynical repetition in tyranny. This means abandoning first of all 'the structure of linguistic communication (I/you/he) which the moderns, consciously or not, have accredited as an ontological and political model'.[40]

Lyotard develops this line of argument in more detail in *Le différend*, in which the question posed could be glossed as 'How is it possible to say "we" after

Auschwitz?'. 'Personal criticism', as I have pointed out, often shares this underlying anxiety about 'speaking for others' (although usually without Lyotard's equally sceptical account of the first-person-singular author position) – in part, perhaps, because of the fear that feminist 'essentialism' might itself be figured as a form of totalitarianism. Many feminist theorists are concerned, of course, in ways which Lyotard is not, with the gendering of pronouns. Irigaray brings the question of gender into Benveniste's account of the utterance-dependent nature of the first-person pronoun when she suggests that:

> With men, the 'I' is asserted in different ways; it is significantly more important than the 'you' and 'the world'. With women, the 'I' often makes way for the 'you, the world', for the objectivity of words and things.[41]

I have not always been convinced by feminist critics discussing women's autobiography when they claim that women invariably define and write the self through its others, manifesting an essential female altruism, although Irigaray's argument that the 'I' can be differentially asserted is a significant one. It is worth noting, however, that there appears to be a general move in social theory towards the concept of 'addressivity'. Defining this concept in *Dialogism*, his account of Bakhtin's theories, Michael Holquist writes: 'My "I" must have contours that are specific enough to provide a meaningful addressee: for if existence is shared, it will manifest itself as the condition of being addressed (*obraschchennost* or *addressivnost*).'[42] The British social psychologist John Shotter refers explicitly to Bakhtin's notion of addressivity in an article which attempts to remedy the neglect of the *second* person, and argues for a shift from Cartesian privacy and possessive individualism 'to a communitarian perspective'.[43] Others' actual or possible accounts become an essential part of our identity.

Luce Irigaray's emphasis on the project of revealing 'who is speaking, to whom, about what, with what means', in order to discover the subject and its relations with the other and the world, seems to have strong links with the preoccupations of personal criticism. It may be relevant in this context to note her *anti*-autobiographical stance: 'The transformation of the autobiographical "I" into another cultural "I" seems to be necessary if we are to establish a new ethics of sexual difference.'[44] Privileging the fictional, the fabular and the imaginary, Irigaray contrasts these with the autobiographical, which for her seems to be opposed to the innovation and transformation of ethics and aesthetics. This is not the place to argue that autobiography can and does partake of – in Irigaray's terms – the structures of the imaginary. I am interested for present purposes in the concept of the non-autobiographical 'I', the subject unencumbered by her story or history, a concept which is also current in personal criticism. Mary Ann Caws, for example, while she does not share Irigaray's suspicions of the autobiographical or biographical, describes personal criticism as characterised by 'a certain intensity in the lending of oneself to the act of writing', but argues that this 'participation in the subject seen and written about doesn't necessarily require autobiographical self-representation'.[45] In other words, the critic's self-situating need not be accompanied by a confessional act.

What is the status of this 'I' which is 'personal' and 'situated', yet not 'auto-biographical'? 'Can we imagine', Nancy Miller asks, 'a self-representational practice – for feminism – that is not recontained by the preconstituted tropes of representativity?'[46] In this context, I would want to distinguish between the categories of 'speaking as a' and 'speaking for a' – given that 'speaking as a' is surely part of a model of situated knowledge which is invoked by most feminist critics. Furthermore, the distinctions Caws and others wish to make between the autobiographical, the confessional, the personal, the narrational, and so on, are not always clear-cut, nor is it always obvious where positional statement turns into autobiography.

The concept of the non-narrated but situated self was proposed in Donna Stanton's study of autobiography, *The Female Autograph*, in which she removes the life, the 'bios', from autobiography in order to resolve or evade the apparently unresolvable problem of referentiality in the autobiographical text – in her words, 'to bracket the traditional emphasis on the narration of a "life" and that notion's facile presumption of referentiality'.[47] In fact, this strategy seems closer to the current concern with the self who seeks to mark her presence, but not necessarily to recount her history.

Aspects of this discussion need to be understood in relation to the concerns of feminist epistemology, one of the major currents in contemporary feminist thought, closely tied to debates around identity politics and situated knowledge. As Liz Stanley has noted, however, 'the links between feminist auto/biography and feminist epistemology remain under-discussed'.[48] Stanley argues for a concept of 'intellectual autobiography', by which she means that the feminist researcher should record the context-dependent aspects of her approaches and understanding: 'All knowledge is autobiographically-located in a particular social context of experiencing and knowing', she states, 'while all autobiographies are theoretical formulations through and through.'[49] While I endorse Stanley's assertion of the need for 'accountable knowledge', I would want to question her claim that feminist academics should 'reject the subjective/objective dichotomy, recognizing instead that "objectivity" is a set of practices designed to deny the actual "subjective" location of all intellectual work'.[50] In other words, even if the positions from which we understand the world are necessarily 'subjective', can we not talk meaningfully about subjective perspectives on an objectively given world? The kinds of determinations which govern our knowledge are not always as readily known and available as Stanley suggests; knowledges, like identities, are complex, multiply given and – to use a well-worn phrase – 'overdetermined'. Sandra Harding has argued, in her important work on 'feminist standpoint theory', that we need more objectivity rather than less, a broader notion of objectivity grounded in but not confined to the positions of the marginalised. These are not necessarily – or, indeed, not usually – those of the theorists themselves.[51]

I now want to try out some more speculative links between 'personal criticism' and other recent movements and debates in cultural theory. I referred
above to the view in feminist theory that the 'female subject' has to be 're-
claimed' from the deconstructors of the self. The feminist argument with deconstruction is that it would seek to deny a voice to any subject, before women
have found their own: 'we have lost ourselves in the endlessly diffracted light of
Deconstruction', writes Nicole Ward Jouve.[52] Nancy Miller now generalises this
dissatisfaction with deconstructionist thought:

> It seems to me that the efflorescence of personal criticism in the United States in the
> eighties – like the study of autobiography – has in part to do with the gradual, and
> perhaps inevitable waning of enthusiasm for a mode of Theory, whose authority –
> however variously – depended finally on the theoretical evacuation of the very social
> subjects producing it (the upset and uproar surrounding the revelations about Paul
> de Man's biography figure, I think, both the limits and the costs of this fiction).[53]

Miller's (throwaway) comment about the 'de Man Affair' is, I would suggest,
worth pursuing. It would be difficult to exaggerate the crisis, the trauma, in
American academe (at least in the Humanities) that resulted from the discovery
in 1987 that the late Paul de Man, Professor of Comparative Literature at Yale
University and the most celebrated theorist and practitioner of deconstruction
in North America, had, between 1940 and 1942, written a substantial number
of articles for newspapers and a journal under the control of the Occupation
authorities in Belgium. Debates over and analysis of the anti-Semitic/pro-
Fascist content of de Man's wartime journalism have been intensive and extensive – at times taking on something of the tone of a trial for war crimes – and it is
not possible to rehearse them here.[54] A further set of debates spawned by the
discoveries are of more direct relevance to the present discussion, for they
concern questions of 'speaking out', of declaring who one is and where one has
come from, and a fear or anxiety about concealing oneself behind the 'abstrac-
tions' of theory. To put it crudely, it would seem that the anxiety is that if one
does not speak out, situate oneself or – in Mary Ann Caws's words – manifest 'a
certain intensity in the lending of oneself to the act of writing', it is because one
has something to hide. And as Lynne Higgins stated, in a review of de Man's
collected wartime journalism:

> It is the very indirect and mediated nature of the degrees of collaboration that makes
> it terrifying. The identity crisis takes the form of an urgent question: is the work I'm
> doing complicitous with something I would be horrified to be associated with? . . .
> we have to know who we are sleeping with. We want 'safe criticism'.[55]

The question of autobiography has acquired a central role in the controversies
over de Man and deconstruction – it is, indeed, 'overdetermined'. One crucial
issue – both for de Man's accusers and for his defenders – is of the break or
continuity between the de Man who wrote the wartime journalism and the de
Man of the later literary theory – in the terms of autobiographical discourse, the
relationship between past 'I' and present 'I'. Second, de Man's writings contain
very substantial reflections on the modes of autobiography – confession,

apologia, and so on – reflections which assert their generic 'impossibility' or the 'bad faith' they manifest. These elements in de Man's writings now tend to be read either as veiled and coded 'confessions' or as dissimulations – a special pleading on the part of one for whom autobiography had indeed become an impossible act.

Autobiography is, de Man suggested in his essay 'Autobiography as De-Facement', 'a figure of reading' rather than writing; it is certainly true – rightly or wrongly – that it is now difficult not to read de Man 'autobiographically'.[56] A number of commentators on de Man's history have in fact suggested that he should have cleared his name or recanted on his former self by writing a (straight) autobiography – not least, perhaps, as a way of dispelling the 'uncanny' effects of his occasional gestures towards a form of 'personal criticism'. The Foreword to the second edition of *Blindness and Insight*, for example, contains the following lines:

> I am not given to retrospective self-examination and mercifully forget what I have written with the same alacrity I forget bad movies – although, as with bad movies, certain scenes or phrases return at times to embarrass and haunt me like a guilty conscience. When one imagines to have felt the exhilaration of renewal, one is certainly the last to know whether such a change actually took place or whether one is just restating, in a slightly different mode, earlier and unresolved obsessions.[57]

The 'uncanny' elements of this narrative are, indeed, hard to dispel, for – as Neil Hertz points out – de Man's writings are replete with 'lurid figures': metaphors of defacement, disfiguration and hanging figures. Hertz (now reading de Man's theory as autobiography) traces these figures back to a version of the primal scene or originary trauma in de Man's biography: the discovery of the body of his mother, who had committed suicide by hanging. Autobiography – and to some extent writing in general – becomes defined as a telling of obsessions, in the obsessional way which is the only way in which they could be told.[58]

We might also add another lurid figure here – the trope of 'prosopopeia' which is a central figure in de Man's tropological system. De Man defines prosopopeia as 'the fiction of an apostrophe to an absent, deceased or voiceless entity, which posits the possibility of the latter's reply, and confers upon it the power of speech', and describes it as 'the trope of autobiography', 'the fiction of the voice-from-beyond-the-grave'.[59] In some sense, of course, the 'voice' is always hallucinatory in de Manian theory, for the figurative nature of language is privative, eternally depriving us of voice and condemning us not to silence but to muteness. 'Silence', de Man wrote in 'Autobiography as De-Facement', 'implies the possible manifestation of sound at our own will'; muteness, by contrast, is an affliction.[60]

Many of the agonised debates over the de Man 'revelations' centre upon the question of whether de Man himself was, in the terms just given, 'silent' or 'mute'. In one of his essays on de Man, 'The Art of *Mémoires*', written after de Man's death but before the discovery of the journalism, Jacques Derrida wrote of 'the forgetting of the pronoun, singularly of the first pronoun, the I. The effacement of the I in a kind of *a priori* and functional forgetting could be related to . . . "Autobiography as De-Facement". . . . Memory effaces remembrance (or recollection) *just as the I effaces itself.*'[61] In 'Paul de Man's War', written as a response to the wartime journalism and to the kinds of claims about the 'dangers' of deconstruction it had provoked, Derrida refers to de Man's 'silence': 'it was publicly broken on at least one occasion and thus cannot be understood in the sense of a dissimulation. . . . What could the ordeal of this mutism have been, for him?'[62]

In *Testimony: Crises of Witnessing in Literature, History and Psychoanalysis*, co-written with Dori Laub, Shoshana Felman includes her responses to the discovery of the journalism and its aftermath, in a chapter entitled 'After the Apocalypse: Paul de Man and the Fall to Silence'. Taking up the terms of 'forgetting' and 'silence', Felman also moves from the concept of 'silence' to that of 'muteness': 'it's de Man's theories', she writes, 'that inscribe the testimony of the muted witness'; and 'History as holocaust is mutely omnipresent in the theoretical endeavour of de Man's mature work.'[63] De Man's voice is now heard in or from his writings, Felman seems to suggest, as a kind of prosopopeia, as

> he addresses posthumously (or in anticipation), the question so persistently asked today both by his critics and by his admirers, of why he had not satisfied the former's sense of justice and/or cleared the latter's conscience, by giving both the satisfaction – or the reparation – of a public confession or a public declaration of remorse that would have at least proven his regret, his present repentance of past errors.[64]

Felman's deeply troubling strategy is to make de Man 'speak' posthumously in and through the words of Walter Benjamin and Primo Levi – more obviously victims of Fascism.[65]

My discussion of this difficult affair has been exploratory, and I am not seeking to draw any final conclusions. Yet for reasons that merit further investigation, a great deal of intellectual work at the moment appears to be concerned with 'speaking out' or 'remaining silent'. Shoshana Felman's essay on de Man appears in a text which contains substantial material on Holocaust testimony, and Felman writes about the ways 'in which testimony has become a crucial mode of our relation to events of our times . . . our era can precisely be defined as the age of testimony'.[66] She adds:

> In the testimony, language is in process and in trial, it does not possess itself as a conclusion, as the constatation of a verdict or the self-transparency of knowledge. Testimony is, in other words, a discursive *practice* as opposed to a pure *theory*. To testify – to *vow* to *tell* to *promise* and *produce* one's own speech as material evidence for truth – is to accomplish a *speech act* rather than to simply formulate a statement.[67]

This account of testimony as speech act – the distinction drawn between discourse and theory, the bringing together of act and discourse through the concept of the performative, the suggestion of a certain risk – links to emphases in 'personal criticism'. In opposition to her earlier account, in which the performative is marked by its duplicity and self-referentiality, Felman now shifts to an emphasis on commitment and the ethical dimensions of speaking out. The Law now appears as an ally in an essential process of historical investigation, and practice and process become formations between deconstructionist undecidability and the finalities of the legal verdict.

Felman further suggests that a crisis of truth, proceeding from contemporary trauma, 'has brought the discourse of the testimony to the fore of the contemporary cultural narrative', and that the traumas of the Second World War and the Holocaust in particular are the primary axes of disturbance. The question then becomes why these issues have recently attracted greater attention than in previous decades. One element seems to be the broadening in the range of accepted historical methodologies and a greater interest in the relation between history and memory (the title of a recently founded journal, and invoked in a number of books). A second element may be the decline of Western Marxism, which has cast doubt on progressivist histories. I am struck particularly by the current emphasis on the unsayable and on narrative impossibility, running concurrently with – as I have suggested – a demand for the utterance.[68]

One major link between the disparate forms of discourse I have examined would seem to be the concept of the performative. The shared focus on the performative suggests certain common tendencies in the cultural field: the valorisation of personal histories; a stress on the positional; a certain antitheoreticism; a sense of the importance of 'speaking out' as a way of authorising identity, while at the same time identity is said to be performatively constituted rather than pre-discursive. Yet, as we have seen, the performative is defined in a variety of ways: as experience/action opposed to theory; as de-authorising play and performance; as authenticating identity and positionality; as deceit, duplicity and self-referentiality; as an ethical discourse of commitment; as testimony. The radically different accounts of the performative invoked indicate the diversity, and perhaps the incommensurability, of the conceptual approaches and the intellectual or political contexts in which they arise. What counts (or should count) is not only that a story or a history is being recounted, nor even how it is told, but its varying content, contexts and import.

Returning to 'personal criticism', two recent feminist collections deserve mention. *Changing Subjects: The Making of Feminist Literary Criticism* sets out 'to remember and historicize' academic feminism's recent history, through the autobiographical accounts of academic feminists: 'it is a way of saying "I" that is also a way of saying "we" '.[69] Despite the inclusion of some striking accounts, the overall effect is of the transformation of C.R. into C.V. The editors of *The Intimate Critique: Autobiographical Literary Criticism* declare their intention of providing 'a politics of location, a literary criticism of personal, political and critical self-revelation' which is said to have produced a 'passionate correspondence' between contributors.[70] I want to close with a very brief assessment of these claims. First, one might question the way in which some feminist critics seek to reinvent a personal which, it could be argued, has never been forgotten. Second, there seems to be limited value in the discourse of an 'I' which declares that it speaks only for itself to an 'us' or a 'we' constituted in and by the safety of a like-minded professional group. The use of the autobiographical or personal in criticism can emerge as a defensive reaction against unwelcome political or intellectual demands rather than as the engaged writing it has the potential to be.

Notes

1 Kobena Mercer, 'Welcome to the Jungle: Identity and Diversity in Postmodern Politics', in *Identity: Community, Culture, Difference*, ed. J. Rutherford (London: Lawrence & Wishart, 1990), pp. 43–71.
2 Nancy K. Miller, *Getting Personal* (New York: Routledge, 1991).
3 *ibid.*, p. 1.
4 *ibid.*, p. 2.
5 *ibid.*, p. x.
6 *ibid.*, p. xi.
7 *ibid.*, p. 20.
8 Nicole Ward Jouve, *White Woman Speaks with Forked Tongue: Criticism as Auto-biography* (London: Routledge, 1991), pp. 7, 10.
9 Miller, *Getting Personal*, p. xiii.
10 Jane Tompkins, 'Me and My Shadow', in *Gender and Theory: Dialogues on Feminist Criticism*, ed. Linda Kauffman (Oxford: Blackwell, 1989).
11 D.A. Miller, *The Novel and the Police* (Berkeley and Los Angeles: University of California Press, 1988), pp. 193–4.
12 Hélène Cixous, 'The Laugh of the Medusa', in *New French Feminisms*, ed. Elaine Marks and Isabelle de Courtivron (Hemel Hempstead: Harvester Wheatsheaf, 1981), p. 251.
13 Joan Riviere, 'Womanliness as a Masquerade' (first published in *International Journal of Psycho-Analysis* 10 [1929]: 303–13), in *The Inner World and Joan Riviere: Collected Papers 1920–1958*, ed. Athol Hughes (London: Karnac, 1991), pp. 90–101. Riviere's essay is also reprinted in *Formations of Fantasy*, ed. Victor Burgin, James Donald and Cora Kaplan (London: Methuen, 1986), pp. 35–44, with Stephen Heath's essay 'Joan Riviere and the Masquerade', pp. 45–61.
14 Riviere, 'Womanliness', p. 92.
15 *ibid.*, p. 91.
16 *ibid.*, p. 94.
17 See, for example, essays by Mary Ann Doane in her collection *Femmes Fatales: Feminism, Film Theory, Psychoanalysis* (New York and London: Routledge, 1991); and Claire Johnston, 'Femininity and the Masquerade: Anne of the Indies', in *Jacques Tourneur*, edited by British Film Institute (London: British Film Institute, 1975), pp. 36–44.
18 Jane Gallop, *Thinking Through the Body* (New York: Columbia University Press, 1988), p. 92.
19 *ibid.*, pp. 92, 100.
20 Judith Butler, *Gender Trouble: Feminism and the Subversion of Identity* (New York and London: Routledge, 1990), p. xii.
21 *ibid.*, p. 142.
22 *ibid.*, p. 21.
23 *ibid.*, p. 146.
24 J.L. Austin, 'Performative Utterances', in *Philosophical Papers* (1st edn Oxford: Oxford University Press, 1961; 2nd edn Oxford: Oxford University Press, 1970); and *How to Do Things with Words* (Oxford: Oxford University Press, 1962).

25 Émile Benveniste, *Problèmes de linguistique générale* (Paris: Gallimard, 1966), trans. as *Problems in General Linguistics* (Florida: University of Miami Press, 1971). See pp. 233–8 of the translation for Benveniste's comments on Austin and the concept of the performative: 'A performative utterance that is not an act does not exist. It has existence only as an act of authority. Now, acts of authority are first and always utterances made by those to whom the right to utter them belongs' (p. 236).

26 Shoshana Felman, *Le scandale du corps parlant: Don Juan avec Austin ou la séduction en deux langues* (Paris: Seuil, 1980).

27 Arlyn Diamond and Lee R. Edwards (eds), *The Authority of Experience: Essays in Feminist Criticism* (Amherst: University of Massachusetts Press, 1977).

28 Tania Modleski, 'Some Functions of Feminist Criticism; Or, the Scandal of the Mute Body', in *Feminism without Women* (New York and London: Routledge, 1991), p. 48.

29 Miller, *Getting Personal*, pp. 74–5.

30 Mary Ann Caws, *Women of Bloomsbury* (New York and London: Routledge, 1990), pp. 2–3.

31 Modleski, 'Some Functions of Feminist Criticism', p. 46.

32 Benveniste, *Problems in General Linguistics*.

33 Philippe Lejeune, *Le pacte autobiographique* (Paris: Seuil, 1975), p. 19.

34 *ibid.*, p. 27.

35 Philippe Lejeune, 'Autobiography in the Third Person', from Lejeune, *Je est un autre* (Paris: Seuil, 1980), trans. in *On Autobiography*, ed. Paul John Eakin (Minneapolis: University of Minnesota Press, 1989), pp. 33–5.

36 Luce Irigaray, 'The Three Genres', in *The Irigaray Reader*, ed. Margaret Whitford (Oxford: Blackwell, 1992), pp. 140–53.

37 Jean-François Lyotard, *Le différend* (Paris: Minuit, 1983).

38 Jean-François Lyotard, *Le postmoderne expliqué aux enfants* (Paris: Gallilée, 1986).

39 *ibid.*, p. 48.

40 *ibid.*, p. 51.

41 Irigaray, 'The Three Genres', p. 146.

42 Michael Holquist, *Dialogism* (London: Routledge, 1990).

43 John Shotter, 'Social Accountability and the Social Construction of "You" ', in *Texts of Identity*, ed. J. Shotter and K.J. Gergen (London: Sage, 1989), p. 137.

44 Irigaray, 'The Three Genres', p. 148.

45 Caws, *Women of Bloomsbury*, p. 2.

46 Miller, *Getting Personal*, p. 98.

47 Donna Stanton (ed.), *The Female Autograph: Theory and Practice of Autobiography from the Tenth to the Twentieth Century* (Chicago: University of Chicago Press, 1984), p. vii.

48 Liz Stanley, 'Feminist Auto/Biography and Feminist Epistemology', in *Out of the Margins*, ed. Jane Aaron and Sylvia Walby (London: Falmer Press, 1991), p. 204.

49 *ibid.*, p. 210.

50 *ibid.*, p. 208.

51 See Sandra Harding, 'Rethinking Standpoint Epistemology: "What is Strong Objectivity"?', in *Feminist Epistemologies*, ed. Linda Alcoff and Elizabeth Potter (New York and London: Routledge, 1993), pp. 49–82; and *Whose Science? Whose Knowledge?: Thinking From Women's Lives* (Milton Keynes: Open University Press, 1991). See also Donna Haraway, 'Situated Knowledges: The Science Question in Feminism and the Privilege of Partial Perspective', in *Simians, Cyborgs and Women: The Reinvention of Nature* (London: Free Association Books, 1991), pp. 183–201.

52 Ward Jouve, *White Woman Speaks with Forked Tongue*, p. 7.

53 Miller, *Getting Personal*, p. 20.

54 De Man's early journalism has been reprinted as *Wartime Journalism, 1939–1943*, ed. Werner Hamacher, Neil Hertz and Thomas Keenan (Lincoln and London: University of Nebraska Press, 1988). A companion volume by the same editors, incorporating responses by academics to the discovery and contents of the journalism, was published as *Responses: On Paul de Man's Wartime Journalism* (Lincoln and London: University of Nebraska Press, 1989). See also David Lehman, *Signs of the Times: Deconstruction and the Fall of Paul de Man* (London: André Deutsch, 1991); and the special edition of *Diacritics* 20, 3 (1990).

55 Lynne A. Higgins, Review of *Wartime Journalism, 1939–1943*; and 'Responses: On Paul de Man's Wartime Journalism', *South Central Review* 6, 2 (1989): 110. Quoted by Deborah Esch in 'The Work to Come', Review of *Wartime Journalism, 1939–1943*; and 'Responses', *Diacritics* 20, 3 (1990): 29.

56 'Autobiography as De-Facement', *Modern Language Notes* 94, 5 (1979): 919–30. Reprinted in Paul de Man, *The Rhetoric of Romanticism* (New York: Columbia University Press, 1984), pp. 67–81.

57 Foreword to revised second edition, *Blindness and Insight* (Minneapolis: University of Minnesota Press, 1983).

58 Neil Hertz, 'More Lurid Figures', *Diacritics* 20, 3 (1990): 2–27.

59 De Man, *The Rhetoric of Romanticism*, pp. 75–7.

60 *ibid.*, p. 80.

61 Jacques Derrida, 'The Art of *Mémoires*', in *Mémoires: for Paul de Man*, revised edition (New York: Columbia University Press, 1989), pp. 55–6. The line 'Memory effaces remembrance (or recollection) *just as the I effaces itself*' (original emphasis) is a quotation from de Man's essay 'Sign and Symbol in Hegel's *Aesthetics*' (1982).

62 Derrida, 'Like the Sound of the Sea Deep Within a Shell: Paul de Man's War', in *Mémoires: for Paul de Man*, p. 227.

63 Shoshana Felman and Dori Laub, *Testimony: Crises of Witnessing in Literature, Psychoanalysis and History* (New York and London: Routledge, 1992), p. 140.

64 Felman, *Testimony*, p. 141.

65 Particularly problematic is Felman's claim that de Man could 'borrow' Levi's remarks about the suspect nature of memory: 'This very book is drenched in memory; what's more, a distant memory. Thus it draws from a suspect source and must be protected against itself' (Levi, quoted in Felman, p. 140). Levi's caution with respect to his own memories of the Holocaust and his incarceration in Auschwitz should not, I believe, be equated with de Man's reticence about his wartime collaboration; nor should de Man's 'silence' or 'muteness' be opened up to speech in and through Levi's words.

66 Felman, *Testimony*, p. 5.

67 *ibid.*

68 For recent discussion of these questions, see, for example, the essays in Saul Friedlander (ed.), *Probing the Limits of Representation: Nazism and the 'Final Solution'* (Cambridge, MA: Harvard University Press, 1992); and essays by Cathy Caruth, Vincent Pecora and others in *Literature and the Ethical Question, Yale French Studies* 79 (New Haven, CT: Yale University Press, 1991).

69 Gayle Greene and Coppélia Kahn (eds), *Changing Subjects: The Making of Feminist Literary Criticism* (New York and London: Routledge, 1993).

70 Diane P. Freedman, Olivia Frey and Frances Murphy Zauhar (eds), *The Intimate Critique: Autobiographical Literary Criticism* (Durham, NC: Duke University Press, 1993).

Chapter 2

Mixed Feelings
When my Mother's Garden is Unfamiliar
Kadiatu Kanneh

> I remember when I was about seventeen, a girl asked me if it wasn't strange that my mother was a different colour. 'She must feel like she's not quite your mother.' She asked me if I wished I looked like my mother.[1]

> Mammy why aren't you and me the same colour.[2]

Feminist theories, attempting to define the link between the personal and the political, have had to tackle or redefine the notion of feminine identity. What does it mean to be a woman? What have sexism, patriarchy and heterosexism taken away from us? How do we reconnect the 'true' histories, the forgotten 'origins'? How do we 're-mother' ourselves through rereading our mothers? Adrienne Rich's lines from nearly two decades ago sound a familiar feminist chord for the act of rewriting the feminine self:

> Birth stripped our birthright from us, tore us from a woman, from women, from ourselves so early on.[3]

The complications and difficulties of that identification – of political, national, class or racial difference – have been grappled with, denied, explained, transcended or dismissed. The absence of complicity between my story and hers, the break in the narrative thread, initiates a self-redefinition that insists on the possible overlaps, or dramatises the yearning rupture as the definitive moment of our feminist self-invention. In this essay I want to examine how Black politics and feminism have come together with a splintering set of contradictions around the imperatives of identification. Placing oneself within a historical narrative of identity, or retelling the narrative in new communal ways, has become a vital part of race, gender and class politics. Narratives of migration confusingly imagine the landscape of racial histories elsewhere, other father- or motherlands from which to ground the story's origins, or against which to place a new one, politically and culturally connected. Against some feminist urges for universal, horizontal female identification, Black feminism has

asserted cultural solidarities, national particularities, and antagonistic historical legacies. Being women is not all that we are.

The heterogeneity of Black cultures, their frequent political incommensur-
abilities, nevertheless admit of vital racial and historical narratives. For many
Black feminist and women's texts, understanding one's mother, learning her
story, becomes an act of racial and historical reassertion and self-understanding.
It becomes a personal and cultural history. Denied a recorded literary heritage of
the same recognition and visibility as that accorded to White literatures, artistic
heritages have been traced through oral memories and unwritten (as well as
written) creativities. Alice Walker's essay 'In Search of Our Mothers' Gardens'
(1984) outlines this significant act of narrative pilgrimage, where Black self-
expression begins at home:

> But this is not the end of the story, for all the young women – our mothers and
> grandmothers, ourselves – have not perished in the wilderness . . .
>   Yet so many of the stories that I write, that we all write, are my mother's stories.[4]

What are the contradictions when culture and familial heritage do not add up?
When colour and culture do not coincide? When the racial story suffers a radical
break between one's mother and oneself? Where we explore metaphors of landscape, narrative and origins, the significance and difficulties of Black and feminist
cultures of belonging reveal radical inconsistencies around the phenomenon of
mixed racial identities.

Carolyn Steedman, struggling with the insistencies of her mother's life and its
political contradictions, formed by desires and dispossessions which cut across
traditional cultural narratives, makes a telling statement. Pointing to those repressed stories which do not fit in, the barbarous threads consigned to the
wilderness outside traditional accounts of class heritage, Steedman writes:

> Personal interpretations of past time – the stories that people tell themselves in order
> to explain how they get to the place they currently inhabit – are often in deep and
> ambiguous conflict with the official interpretative devices of a culture.[5]

Identity politics has received a bad press in contemporary critical debates, where
claiming a radical identity on the basis of belonging to a specific community has
often been condemned as an unsophisticated belief in the authentic self. The
borders between culture falsely reified, or races flagrantly imagined, or sexes
socially constructed, blur or disappear under scientific or theoretical analysis.
Those living on the margins, crossing the boundaries, ambiguously placed – as
postcolonial, or second-generation migrants, or refugees and mixed race people
– are often seen as proof of the unhinging of static differences. The insistence on
hybridity as a dislocating term points not only to a critical trend, but also to an
awareness of recent (and less recent) histories of cultural change. Challenging
the dictated limits of a communal identity and its official 'interpretative devices'
is vital and necessary, precisely because those limits are not always dictated
internally, and often *prescribe* as much as they *describe*. Avoiding the danger of
coerced subscription to a rigidly coded set of behaviour, appearances, lineages,

in order to have an 'authentic' voice within or of a community, must include a keen awareness of repressions, contradictions, uncomfortable realities at the edges of identity politics.

There are, then, two types of authenticity which have been – and should be – interrogated. The first is biological or 'natural' essentialism, the idea that Black-ness, or woman-ness, or community, is simply and always born into, inherited, and metaphysically inevitable ('this is what I am'). The second is political es-sentialism – the idea that Black consciousness, or feminism, or belonging, is dependent on certain cultural criteria ('this is what I am meant to be'). The temptation, in the face of these dangers, has been to insist on the dissolution of identities – whether racial, cultural or sexual. To claim a politics or a voice based on an identity to which one has an uncritical right has been placed under the essentialist label, then denounced.

The consequences of this are at once liberating (for some) and politically disempowering. It is evident that the limits of cultures, or 'races', are not always dictated internally, but often result from discourses and practices of power; from institutional, collective victimisation. However, in order to oppose these struc-tures of exploitation, by which peoples are identified, anxiously, as discrete units, communities or cultures of resistance are and have been created, inherited and learned. Belonging may not be a simple biological fact, but may be signalled by inescapable codes of scrutiny. Having been robbed of the power of self-representation, owing to the experience of an external identification as Black and/or female, it is choking then to be robbed of the power to represent the validity of that experience and the reality of that identification. The borders between 'what I am' and 'what I am meant to be' are themselves blurred.

The difficulties arise around frozen conceptions of 'the Black woman' or, more specifically, 'the Black British woman', which may, perhaps, insist on a relationship with African-Caribbean cultures, or with being working-class, or 'loud', or other forms of stereotyping. However, there are certain kinds of experience, of politicisation, of racialisation, of mutual recognition and external hostility which enable a sense of positive belonging around the sign 'Black (British) woman' which is not endlessly movable or limitlessly able to be appro-priated. What becomes a significant exploration *within* this sign 'Black woman' is the possibility and importance of articulating it in various political ways. The term 'mixed race' makes political sense *within* the category of Blackness, and as part of Black politics, in a different way to how it might be deployed within the category of whiteness. Being a 'mix' of White English and White Scottish, for example, makes use of a different code of 'race' and its boundaries from being a 'mix' of 'White' and 'Black'.

The political consequences in terms of racial identity and racism are pro-foundly different. Black politics – in terms of organising against racism, gaining positive, collective empowerment, recognising certain aspects of experience or identification – does need to employ certain essentialist categories in order to have any kind of strategy or existence. Diana Fuss's contention that essentialism can be read or deployed in different ways, with different political effects, is a crucial one, and leads to the conclusion that the category Black is not always determined by negative racism, but can also be constructed through positive empowerment.[6] It is also a category which is variously determined by historical circumstance, geographical positioning, gender, class or sexuality. The boundaries around 'who's in' and 'who's out', and what being 'in' entails, vary according to these contingencies. In order to make political interventions or to recognise operations of power, however, these contingent boundaries often need to be employed as (temporarily but actively) valid. As Fuss states:

> There is an important distinction to be made, I would submit, between 'deploying' or 'activating' essentialism and 'falling into' or 'lapsing into' essentialism. . . . 'Deploying' or 'activating' implies that essentialism may have some strategic or interventionary value.[7]

The creation of Black women's or Black feminist cultural traditions have largely relied on notions of community and heritage; on oral communications between mother and daughter; or on mourning and imaginatively reconnecting links broken through historical violence. When those links are absent owing to a transgression of cultural, racial or geographic limits, new possibilities and interrogations emerge, often through a process of revisiting the fragile links between culture, race and family. The constant interchangeability or confusion of these categories has led to unbearable tensions within the politics of identity.

The Colour of Love: Mixed Race Relationships (1992) provides a revealing insight into racial and racist codes and taboos, and the prevalent uncertainty about where the divisions between 'races' lie. The text is a series of interviews, marketed and organised around the prevailing principle of *visible* racial difference, with the chapters arranged and titled around scopic metaphors such as 'Love is Colour-Blind' and 'Ways of Looking', while the front cover shows a benevolent white man and a smiling Black woman (Stephen Komlosy and Patti Boulaye) in *juxtaposed* profiles of marital unity. The interviewees themselves move uncomfortably and with glib unawareness between problems of 'visible' racial difference, cultural issues, religious barriers, desire and imagination. They are largely from the middle classes, which allows an explicit celebration of supposed middle-class racial tolerance, while the text constantly reveals the opposite. Patti Boulaye, for example, is quoted making what becomes a familiar claim throughout the text: 'No one has said anything to our faces, although they might say it behind our backs. . . . We don't mix with people with a low mentality, you know, fools. Class makes all the difference' (*Colour*, p. 37).[8]

The male and female narratives (the relationships are all heterosexual) are often placed side by side as gendered and racial alternatives. Patti Boulaye and Stephen Komlosy's narratives classically encode problematics of power and desire, while explicitly claiming otherwise. Patti Boulaye solves the problem of Black communities and family by positioning her white husband in the place of nurturance: 'He feels he has to protect me. I can't understand girls who want to be too independent and grown-up. . . . And just like a father or mother, Stephen is always there for me to come crying to' (*Colour*, p. 37). Stephen's story is a curious minefield of surface disavowal and hidden problematics. Repeating phrases like: 'But colour never occurs to me . . . just whether the person is attractive or not', he also claims: '[s]o my images of brown people were that they were very attractive' (p. 39). Having said about Patti: 'as a Black woman maybe she evokes some folk memories in white men: of slavery, of Black women being available . . . you could do what you liked to them', he then describes his role as anti-racist protector by telling an anecdote where his response to a white man saying about Patti 'I would really like to give her one' was '(w)ell, I frequently do!' (p. 41).

Having marketed the text around the issue of 'colour' and the problem of visibility, the interviews teeter uneasily between colour, culture, class and nationality. Difference becomes encoded in sliding ways. Richard Gifford's reflection, as a white English man, on marrying a South Asian woman has to be read through a disguised set of assumptions: 'I suppose it might have been different if I'd married someone very different – from the Caribbean, for example' (*Colour*, p. 53). What it means to be 'very different' rather than just 'different' remains obscure. Colour and culture as terms of difference are analysed at times in ways which question their commensurability. Shyama Perera, while revealing the contradictions between the terms, manages to widen the racial issues by insisting on race as a more complex set of scopic signifiers. The dialogue between mother and daughter, although they are of the same 'race', is complicated not simply by cultural difference but by a different specular interpretation of culture, of being Sri Lankan:

> I knew I was Sri Lankan, but I didn't feel that it made me different. Whereas my mother dressed in a sari, and if she walked across a group of skinheads they'd shout out 'Paki', if I walked past they would whistle at me – the opposite reaction. (*Colour*, p. 114)

What is interpreted as 'the opposite reaction' emerges, through the interviews, as one which is, in fact, barely distinguishable. Asian-ness and sexual attraction are often assessed together in ways which compress the separated reactions to sari-ed mother and sexual daughter, and expose their continuum. Mark, a 'white English man' with an Asian girlfriend, discusses her sexuality in unmitigated racial terms, replete with 'cultural' fantasies:

> sexually too she doesn't try and make me feel inadequate, or compete with me. She appreciates me. I love her wearing her sari and all that – those feelings you get when you see a beautiful Indian woman in her sensual sari, it's unbelievable. (*Colour*, p. 291)

Mark's 'liberal' contention: 'If I desire someone, why can I not have a Black or Asian or Chinese woman?' is endlessly mirrored in the statements of other white men in 'mixed race' relationships. Under the chapter heading 'Blind Prejudice', Ian Gordon claims: 'I estranged one of my first girlfriends by confessing to her that my dream for the future was to experience sex with every race in the world'

(*Colour*, pp. 85–6). This racial fantasy is sometimes explained in purely biological terms, where desire for what are perceived as other races becomes ultimately a matter of genes. Richard Gifford claims, for example:

> It seems to me that there's one basic thing that applies to mixed marriages – that it
> satisfies the instinct for what the anthropologists call exogamy, which is to cast your
> genetic net wider than the immediate circle. . . . It is as basic an instinct as the infant
> suckling on his mother's breast, it's inbuilt and has nothing to do with choice or
> decision. . . . I am very conscious of broadening the gene pool in a very wide and
> comprehensive way. (*Colour*, pp. 48–9)

The notion of some peoples being 'more different' genetically than others,
through a kind of fantasy of Blackness, is again employed here.

'Colour' and culture as popular fantasies cross over each other in implicit
ways, until the contradictions emerge in the statements of mixed race people
who experience race in radically fissured terms. Vicky Philipps, described as
'born . . . of a half Sierra Leonean, half English mother and an English father',
confronts what she calls 'that split between the self and the body', and questions
the status of 'race' in *between* visibility, culture and experience:

> So it is very complex. When I look at myself I expect people to see me as white,
> though I am Black through my experiences, my cultural background and my value
> system, and the way I function. . . . I was brought up by my Black mother in an
> African country, so my appearance is something which is rather separate from myself.
> (*Colour*, p. 276)

This gap between mother and daughter, explained as a break between 'myself'
and 'my appearance', is a matter both of perception and of national culture, or
environment. The significance of perceived physical difference, intruding in the
dialogue between mother and daughter, is described as an issue which, of itself,
transgresses the 'normal' dimensions of motherhood. Gill Danesh, a white
woman with a Black daughter, discusses 'colour' as a perceived division which
can push the social constructs of racial difference into a more valid place than
family relationships, until they appear to be 'unnatural':

> I found it rather strange having an olive-skinned child at first. You automatically
> think when you have a child it's going to be a carbon copy of you – if it's not, you
> don't love the child any the less, but it's a strange experience . . . like a duck will kick
> a strange-looking duck egg out of the nest. (*Colour*, pp. 217–18).

Love itself, as a form of 'natural' communication between mother and child,
becomes perverted by the imagined impossibility of mutual identification. The
pull to identify with one's child across racial difference seems, in some of the
text's narratives, to have profound implications for the boundaries of one's own
racial identity. Ethal, a white woman with a Black son, discusses her own sense
of alienation from him:

> I still couldn't get close to the boy, though. I didn't feel he had come from me.
> Mothers want their children to look at least a bit like them. . . . He thought I was his
> aunt or something . . . I think I was ashamed of him. (*Colour*, pp. 68, 70)

The internalised confusion leads her to a sense of racial self-mutation: 'At first I felt strange . . . I think it was like changing colour' (*Colour*, p. 68) – a statement which is echoed by Sue Norris, another white mother of Black children, who claims: '. . . it hurts. It is like that film where you wake up one day and you are Black' (p. 223).

The text itself, by insisting on the primacy of vision, seems to disallow the fact that visible difference is itself a matter of social perception. In the interviews themselves, however, exposure, voyeurism and 'biological' nightmares abound, and structure identities in powerful ways – often to such an extent that the fact of family belonging cannot transcend or compete with 'visible' racial unbelonging; one biological myth simply supersedes genetics. Sue Norris, for example, crumbles under the accusation that she is 'breeding bloody coons', and says of her own mother: 'I catch her looking at the children as if they are another species or something' (*Colour*, p. 222).

Attempting to allow another narrative thread, the possibility of nurturance and belonging across race and genes, Jackie Kay's poem for three voices, *The Adoption Papers*, explores myths of motherhood and identity without denying the power and reality of racial divisions. In this personal, poetic story of adoption, Kay writes from the imagined voices of the White birth mother, the White adoptive mother and the Black daughter, which allows her exploration of mixed race identity a confusion of narrative possibilities. Meditating on origins, the daughter confronts herself in the mirror, trying to read the secrets of her identity through her own image. The logic of genetics seems always to contradict the logic of parental love:

> I have my parents who are not of the same tree
> and you keep trying to make it matter
> the blood, the tie, the passing down
> generations.
> (*Adoption Papers*, p. 29)

If nurturance does not coincide with 'natural' motherhood, the possibilities for reading the self in reference to the mother's history become fraught with contradictions. The question '*What is in my blood?*' (*Adoption Papers*, p. 25) is further complicated by the incommensurability between mother and racialised mirror-image:

> . . . sometime when I look in the mirror
> I give myself a bit of a shock
> and say to myself *Do you really look like this?*
> as if I'm somebody else.
> (*Adoption Papers*, p. 27)

In this way, night-longing for the 'real' mother, based on body, flesh and appearance ('She's your double she really is': *Adoption Papers*, p. 32), is again crossed by whiteness, forcing another imagined thread of self-understanding through the Black father. This is a thread which becomes mediated by the physical relationship between birth mother and father, locked and conditioned by inescapable racial exposure, where Blackness threatens and fuses the boundaries between mother and father, allowing a historical narrative, spoken by the birth mother, for the daughter's face in the mirror:

> Olubayo was the colour of peat
> when we walked out heads turned
> like horses, folk stood like trees
> their eyes fixed on us – it made me
> burn, that hot glare; my hand
> would sweat down to his bone.
> (*Adoption Papers*, p. 26)

The poem allows an irresolvable tension between inherited narratives, dialogue and racial difference. Scottishness ('the land I come from/ the soil in my blood': *Adoption Papers*, p. 29) has to exist alongside a narrative of fatherland, attested in the daughter's body by a process of imaginary mirroring:

> He never saw her. I looked for him in her;
> for a second it was as if he was there
> in that glass cot looking back through her.
> (*Adoption Papers*, p. 26)

After repeated confession to the validity of inheritance beyond the mythical pressure of genetic transference ('a few genes, blood, a birth/ . . . Does it matter?': *Adoption Papers*, p. 20) the central conclusion, unnerved by instabilities, has to rely on a relentless meeting and conflict between Blackness and mothering. The despairing cry 'yet I confess to my contradiction/ I want to know my blood' (p. 29) leads to a blood-tracing of Black *cultural* inheritance, socially logical, through a Black political 'mother' of a different nationality from Black, White or adoptive parents:

> Angela Davis is the only female person
> I've seen (except for a nurse on TV)
> who looks like me. She had big hair like mine
> that grows out instead of down.
> (*Adoption Papers*, p. 27)

This identification, allowing a form of retelling of the alienation of one's own body through another image of belonging, is allowed to remain alongside the yearning for dialogue with the white birth mother, figured as a longing for a letter. The desire for written communication is a desire for a reading of her mother's identity physically, through her own inscription:

> fantasizing the colour of her paper
> whether she'll underline *First Class*
> or have a large circle over her 'i's.
> (*Adoption Papers*, p. 34)

What both *The Colour of Love*, as a set of interviews, and *The Adoption Papers*, as poetry, indicate is the compulsion towards racial narratives of belonging and inheritance, which remain potent structuring forces of identity. Black cultures of resistance as well as Black self-recognitions are not always, or ever, *simply* inherited. Black/feminist identities, in order to gain a valid political voice, have repeatedly and contextually to reinvent themselves in dialogue and conflict with racism. That tension does, however, insist on the significance of those identities which, as yet, cannot be reinvented in total, flagrant abandonment. 'Hybridity' cannot, then – except metaphorically – be merely a figure of celebration and escape.

Notes

1 Yasmin Alibhai-Brown and Anne Montague (eds), *The Colour of Love: Mixed Race Relationships* (London: Virago, 1992), p. 240. All further references will be given in parentheses in the text.
2 Jackie Kay, *The Adoption Papers* (Newcastle: Bloodaxe Books, 1991), p. 21. All further references will be given in parentheses in the text.
3 Adrienne Rich, *The Dream of a Common Language: Poems 1974–1977* (London and New York: W.W. Norton, 1978), p. 75.
4 Alice Walker, 'In Search of Our Mothers' Gardens', in *In Search of Our Mothers' Gardens* (London: The Women's Press, 1984), pp. 235, 240.
5 Carolyn Steedman, *Landscape For a Good Woman: A Story of Two Lives* (London: Virago, 1986), p. 6.
6 Diana Fuss, *Essentially Speaking: Feminism, Nature, and Difference* (London and New York: Routledge, 1989), p. 20. 'It is important not to forget that essence is a sign, and as such historically contingent and constantly subject to change and to redefinition.'
7 *ibid.*
8 See also the comment by Shyama Perara: 'Class makes a difference . . . the middle classes are educated enough to keep their prejudices to themselves, which . . . means you have a better life' (*Colour*, p. 119).

Chapter 3

Gender and Englishness in *Villette*

Terry Lovell

Feminist Criticism of Villette

> We went upstairs and I bought her *Jane Eyre*.
> She might as well start at the beginning. (Barbara Wilson, *Sisters of the Road*)

Thus the heroine of Barbara Wilson's lesbian feminist crime novel introduces a young prostitute who 'likes to read' to the feminist literary canon. Brontë's texts have been read and reread by feminist critics. *Jane Eyre* inspires the best efforts of radical feminist critics[1] and gynocriticism.[2] *Villette* lends itself to psycho-analytically informed theories of fractured subjectivity.[3] *Shirley* is perhaps the text that most insists upon a class-based historical approach.[4] All texts are grist to the deconstructionist's mill: Gayatri Chakravorty Spivak chose *Jane Eyre*.[5]

Villette has perhaps generated the greatest variety of readings: Judith Lownder Newton offers a materialist reading;[6] Nina Auerbach detects a proto-modernist text;[7] while Mary Jacobus's reading of its fissures and dislocations suggests a novel which not only lends itself to deconstruction – as all texts must, however smooth their surface – but positively invites it. Inevitably, there has been a reaction. Sally Minogue contests feminist readings, to reclaim *Villette* for an unreconstructed but revalorised realist humanism.[8]

Both gynocriticism and Marxist–feminist criticism place the literary text within a sociohistorical context, but the temporalities of class and capitalism demand closer attention to the protocols of historical narrative than does the broader historical sweep typically encompassed by the concept of 'patriarchy'. Texts read in relation to patriarchy tend to be analysed in terms of an imaginative response to forms of mental and physical confinement which are imprecisely located in class, place and time, or presented as ubiquitous and universal. Thus Gilbert and Gubar on *Jane Eyre*:

> Her story . . . a story of enclosure and escape, a distinctively female *Bildungsroman* in which the problems encountered by the protagonist as she struggles from the imprison-ment of her childhood toward an almost unthinkable goal of mature freedom are symptomatic of difficulties *Everywoman in a patriarchal society* must meet and overcome: oppression . . . starvation . . . madness . . . and coldness [emphasis added].[9]

Elaine Showalter's feminine/feminist/female progression celebrates a kind of literary/political self-unfolding in women's texts over time, which is not calibrated with any degree of precision with external historical temporalities or social determinations.[10]

Mary Jacobus's essay, one of the most sophisticated and elliptical feminist readings of *Villette*, was written at about the same time as Gilbert and Gubar's first *tour de force*, *The Madwoman in the Attic*, which contains a lengthy chapter on the novel. While the American critics draw loosely on psychoanalytic ideas from time to time, Jacobus's essay is more rigorously located within Lacanian psychoanalytic and semiotic perspectives. Yet there are common elements. The two approaches share a view of (Western) culture as functioning through the silencing of 'the feminine'. Jacobus writes: 'femininity itself . . . becomes the repressed term by which discourse is made possible',[11] while Gilbert and Gubar, from a very different organising framework, assert robustly that 'In patriarchal Western culture . . . the text's author is a father, a progenitor, an aesthetic patriarch whose pen is an instrument of generative power like his penis.'[12]

Feminine self-identification, therefore, is problematic within both perspectives, because the terms which are available within the culture for creating the self are alien, or even unavailable, to women. Thus in both approaches female authorship is particularly difficult; yet it is also potentially subversive:

> The transgression of literary boundaries – moments when structures are shaken, when language refuses to lie down meekly, or the marginal is brought into sudden focus, or intelligibility refused – reveal not only the conditions of possibility within which women's writing exists, but what it would be like to revolutionise them.[13]

Both readings of *Villette* make much of the notorious duplicity of the novel's narrator, Lucy Snowe, and its crossing of the conventions of nineteenth-century realism with Gothic Romanticism. Mary Jacobus locates the source of Lucy's oppression – about which, she argues, the text must remain silent – in Victorian sexual ideology and the institution of bourgeois marriage: 'But what the novel cannot say is eloquently inscribed in its sub-text – in the "discursive" activity of Lucy's (over)-heated imagination, and in the agitated notation and heightened language which signal it.'[14] The 'drive to female emancipation' which Jacobus locates in the Gothic Romanticism of this split text had, she argues, 'an ultimately conservative aim – successful integration into existing social structures'.[15] Feminist rage and rebellion are mapped on to the novel's Gothic elements in Jacobus's interpretation, conservative submission on to the more conventional nineteenth-century realist narrative.

Judith Lownder Newton offers a reading which is almost the inverse of that of Jacobus. She, too, highlights the deep ambivalences of the text, and of its narrator. But for Newton, the subversive 'feminist' text which is struggling to establish itself is the (realist) narrative of Lucy Snowe's struggle for independence: 'The real history of Lucy Snowe . . . begins not with the entry to the marriage mart, but onto the labour market.'[16] This history threatens to become submerged in the contradictory longings of the heroine and her author for the conventional plot of romance fiction – the longing for 'the love of a good man', and for feminine self-sacrifice: 'It is this contradiction . . . which makes of *Villette* a lesson in the virulence of the enemy within. . . .'[17] Juxtaposing these diametrically opposed feminist readings of *Villette*, Cora Kaplan remarks: 'The quotations and narrative elements cited and explored by Jacobus and Newton are so different that even a reader familiar with *Villette* may find it hard to believe that each critic is reading the same text.'[18]

Over and above these quite radical differences in feminist readings of *Villette*, there are absences and silences which are shared. Aspects of the novel which have exercised more traditional literary scholars, such as its religious and nationalist bearings, have been largely ignored or marginalised within feminist readings.[19] There are exceptions. Rosemary Clark-Beattie has written a very fine essay on the use of religious and national dualities in structuring Lucy Snowe's negotiation of her subjectivity; and Jane Miller has drawn attention to the novel's 'orientalism'.[20] More often in feminist criticism these themes are ignored, or briefly acknowledged, to be half-vindicated as no more than displaced forms of more honourably feminist motifs:

> Nothing is more irritating to some readers than the anti-Papist prejudice of *Villette*. But for Brontë, obsessively concerned with feelings of unreality and duplicity, Catholicism seems to represent the institutionalization of Lucy's internal schisms, permitting sensual indulgence by way of counterpoise to jealous spiritual restraint, and encouraging fervent zeal by means of surveillance or privation. . . . But precisely because Catholicism represents a sort of sanctioned schizophrenia, she finds herself attracted to it. . . .[21]

English and Englishness: Masculinity and Femininity

Classical Marxism has remarkably little to say about national divisions which mark off one bourgeois class from another, and the literature on the Left on nations and nationalisms remains thin, despite the recent spate of writings.[22] The view of nationalism suggested by the title of Eric Hobsbawm and Terence Ranger's edited collection of essays *The Invention of Tradition* – the sense of national belonging as an artificial and changing product forged in culture and ideology, in which the working class has no real interests at stake – probably remains the dominant one.[23] As Robert Colls and Philip Dodd put it: 'Englishness has had to be made and re-made in and through history, within available practices and relationships, and existing symbols and ideas.'[24]

Benedict Anderson's influential *Imagined Communities* takes up this position, to argue that all communities larger than face-to-face ones (and perhaps even these) have to be imagined. We who belong must imagine them in terms of a number of people whom we might – in principle – meet and come to know, and who are in some sense 'like us' – like us *because* of common belonging – and the manner of that likeness is delineated in the imaginings we trace.

Anderson believes that national imaginings have a clear (and quite short) history in the West, associated with the emergence of the nation-state from the seventeenth century onwards. Historically, nation-states may be relatively recent; but in the imagination they 'always loom out of an immemorial past and . . . glide into a limitless future'.[25] Anderson identifies several different types of nation and of nationalism. Englishness is closely bound up with British imperialism – with colonialism both internal and external, and with a long history of racism. This is why issues of nationalism and patriotism are so very difficult for the Left in Britain to confront.

In the aftermath of the Falklands/Malvinas War, in the face of a popular wave of jingoistic nationalism that swept Margaret Thatcher to two further terms of office, the Left began, somewhat uncomfortably, to re-examine these issues. The British Film Institute held a summer school in 1983 entitled 'National Fictions', which looked at British World War Two films; Raphael Samuel put together a massive History Workshop project on patriotism which resulted in three large volumes of papers. In his introduction Samuel remarks:

> I became uneasily aware that History Workshop and the causes with which it is associated – 'people's history' or 'history from below' in particular – was part of what we were attacking . . . 'people's history' is deeply attached to that spirit of place which, according to Conservative philosophy . . . is the touchstone of 'true' national feeling.[26]

In many of the papers collected in these three volumes – as also in the earlier collection edited by Colls and Dodd – an attempt was made to distinguish a tradition within which the Left might reclaim forms of patriotism which were free from the taint of jingoism and imperialist sentiment: a proper 'Englishness' from an imperialist 'Britishness'. This more acceptable face of patriotism was sought in English radicalism, and histories were assayed which traced the (mis)-appropriation of that popular radical patriotism of the 'free-born Englishman' for nationalism and imperialism. Hugh Cunningham locates 'the fall' in the middle of the nineteenth century. He argues that during the first half of that century radicals continued to use a vocabulary of patriotism 'as a constantly reforged tool of opposition, and a means of possessing the past' – tools which were later 'commandeered by conservatism'.[27] This account did not go unchallenged. Linda Colley locates the turning point of English radicalism rather earlier, in the effects of the American Civil War, and paints a very much less benign picture of mid-eighteenth-century radicalism, always liable to slide into chauvinism and xenophobia.[28] Anthony Barnett, in the same volume, draws on Tom Nairn's understanding that nationalism is 'Janus-faced'; that radical patriotism and imperialist chauvinism are simply two sides of the same coin: you can't have one without the other.[29]

The difficulty is immediately apparent once the religious affiliations of English radicalism are brought into focus. Staunchly Protestant, seventeenth- and eighteenth-century radicalism is a defence of the English revolution and the English Reformation, anti-Catholic and, by extension, all too frequently anti-French and anti-Irish. As Robert Colls asks: 'What joy could there possibly be for the Catholic Irish in a story of national identity which celebrated Parliament and the first Orangeman?'[30]

Feminism, Femininity and National Identity

There is a consensus within recent work on the development of English as a discipline that the institutionalisation of English literature and literary crit-icism within schools and colleges, and within other forums such as scholarly journals and reviews, has served a double function: defining a national litera-ture, and defining the nation – the essential, ineffable core of 'Englishness'.[31] But this task required delicate negotiations of gender and of 'race'. Although 'the nation' may be personified as a woman – as Marianne or Britannia, or as the long-suffering mother roused to defend her children, fit object for the ultimate sacrifice, to be defended against rape, pillage, captivity; and although the work of feminists such as Floya Anthias and Nira Yuval-Davis[32] and others has begun to unravel the ways in which ethnic and national identities, belong-ings and exclusions, turn crucially upon women – analysis of the active work of defining the nation has concentrated on men's texts, and on masculine imagery.

The national imaginings analysed by Anderson are exclusively male, across a wide sweep of nations of very different provenance. He accepts tacitly Woolf's dictum: 'As a woman, I have no country. As a woman I want no country. As a woman my country is the whole world.'[33]

This distancing of women from nationalism and national identity has been commonplace within feminism. Woolf's aphorism is a comforting one for femi-nists, because it fosters the illusion of (well, relatively) clean hands in relation to the less acceptable facets of radical patriotism, its racism and xenophobia. It has allowed feminists, implicitly or explicitly, to align women of imperialist nations with the *victims* of nationalism and imperialism.

Recent work has begun to address these issues within feminism. Sara Mills's study of nineteenth-century women travel writers examines the ways in which these writers negotiated the discourses of femininity on the one hand, and imperialism on the other.[34] But while she produces interesting deconstructions of these texts which challenge the tendency to treat the woman traveller as a species of eccentric proto-feminist heroine who succeeded in defying the norms of domestic femininity, she places these women and their texts in too extraneous a relationship to the discourses they negotiated. They may have worked cre-atively with them, modifying and qualifying each by the skilful deployment of the other. But these discourses are seen as discourses which do not really *belong* to women, and for which they therefore bear strictly limited responsibility.

There are distinct traces of the discourse of feminist gynocriticism in Mills's text: her women travellers tell their tales in a borrowed language not their own.

The consensus within writings on national identity and Englishness is probably well articulated in the article by Jane MacKay and Pat Thane on 'The Englishwoman'.[35] They suggest that women in the late nineteenth century – in Britain, at least – were identified with 'race' rather than nation. The attributes of Englishness for women were coextensive with those of an idealised middle-class femininity.

Alison Light endorses this view, citing MacKay and Thane, but she argues that the period between the wars saw a remarkable change:

> the 1920s and '30s saw a move away from formerly heroic and officially masculine public rhetorics of national destiny and away from a dynamic and missionary view of the Victorian and Edwardian middle classes in 'Great Britain' to an Englishness at once less imperial and more inward-looking, more domestic and more private – and, in terms of pre-war standards, more 'feminine'.[36]

Women writers made a significant contribution to this development, and Light analyses the work of middlebrow and conservative authors in this period, including Agatha Christie and Daphne Du Maurier.

Anderson recognises the importance of literature, particularly the novel, in fostering national identities, without broaching the question of gender. But because of the problematic gender identity of literature and writing generally, and the novel in particular, study of the construction of national identity in literary texts may perhaps begin to unravel these gendered differences in national imaginings. We may perhaps find in the English novel earlier examples of feminine constructions of Englishness. Charlotte Brontë's *Villette* offers fertile soil for such imaginings, for 'Englishness' and 'foreignness', Protestantism and Catholicism, provide the major terms within which she explores questions of female subjectivity and experience in her fictional world.

Englishness and Foreignness in Villette

Villette is set in England, and in 'Labassecour' (the poultry-yard) or Belgium. But we, and Lucy Snowe the narrator, encounter a range of nationalities in the course of the narrative journey: we meet a number of minor characters who are French and German, and go as far afield as Egypt and Persia in the representation of Rubens's corpulent Cleopatra on the walls of the museum, and the actress Rachel's dramatisation of the biblical proto-feminist heroine, Vashti: two oriental queens – radically Other to Lucy Snowe – on whom she may displace the sexuality and the burning, angry rebellion she disavows. Mr Home – who has another name, the Count de Bassompierre – is English, but of mixed French and Scottish extraction; and we meet one Irishwoman, stereotypically drunk and feckless, her speech a mixture of Irish brogue and 'mincing cockney'. Only Paul Emanuel is imprecisely placed. We are told that he is 'like a true Frenchman', but 'of a strain neither French nor Labassecourien'.[37] Yet his fervent patriotism commands a respect which Lucy Snowe rarely grants to the inhabitants of the poultry-yard:

> Who would have thought the flat feet and fat soil of Labassecour could yield political convictions and national feelings, such as were now strongly expressed? . . . when he looked in the face of tyranny – oh, then there opened a light in his eye worth seeing; and when he spoke of injustice, his voice gave no uncertain sound . . . (pp. 396–7)

This cast of characters offers rich opportunities for defining Englishness, as their speech, physique, dress, comportment, food, expressions of emotion, mores, manners and social institutions come under the critical eye of a narrator as skilled in techniques of surveillance as is the formidable Madame Beck – in short, through close attention to attributes to which it fell above all to domestic woman to cultivate and to monitor in middle-class society in the nineteenth century. For, as Raymond Williams always insisted, 'culture is ordinary'.[38]

Language and speech always provide a rich resource for significations of national identity and difference. In the early chapters set in Labassecour Lucy more than once laments her 'want of language', first in trying to discover the fate of her portmanteau missing from the diligence on her arrival late at night in Villette, and second during the great crisis when she faces the boisterous insubordination of sixty schoolgirls, and cries 'Could I but have spoken in my own tongue . . .' (p. 143). The language which she lacks is spoken French, and she acquires a ready competence before the novel is far advanced.

The text of *Villette* is littered with French, with no footnote translations in the original edition of 1853 to help those readers who, like Lucy, may find themselves in want of language. The use of *untranslated* French locates the reader who understands it, along with the narrator Lucy Snowe, and the author, in a common class identity, for the ability to read and to speak French is the mark of an educated middle-class Englishwoman of the mid-nineteenth century. Lucy Snowe's acquisition of French is a condition of her social advance from nursery to schoolroom.

French, then, is no simple marker of 'un-Englishness', but is used to differentiate English characters from one another, as well as Labassecourien from English. Enid Duthie[39] analyses Brontë's use of French to delineate character. For example, Paul Emanuel, who also 'wants language' – his command of English is as poor as is Lucy's of French at the start of her sojourn in the Rue Fossette – has his speech rendered by his author in English, except at those moments of irritability or emotion to which this mercurial 'little man' is prone, when the text bursts into his native French. Ginevra is English, beautiful, and middle-class. But she betrays a certain falling away from the exacting standards of a 'true' Englishness by her poor command of French, as surely as does 'Madame Svini' by her Irish/cockney inflections. Ginevra speaks in French occasionally, often where she wishes to say something that is not quite proper (p. 116). Her inner 'un-Englishness' is betrayed most fully, however, in her first encounter with Lucy, on board the *Vivid*, in relation to religion rather than language. She admits without shame that she has forgotten her religion: 'they call me a Protestant, you know, but really I am not sure whether I am one or not: I don't well know the difference between Romanism and Protestantism' (p. 115).

If language is the first marker of national identity, the second is place. Lucy's story begins in Bretton, a sleepy English backwater where her godmother of the same name lives: 'Mrs Bretton of Bretton'. Nina Auerbach comments: 'the concord between person and place . . . defines a norm which . . . Lucy Snowe is never able to achieve'.[40] But Lucy's longing for this achievement is, like most 'structures of feeling' in this complex and duplicitous novel, ambivalent. In Bretton time passes 'blandly like the gliding of a full river through a plain' (p. 62). It is an Eden which Lucy must leave, and it is true that it marks the point of reference, of home, for the sense of loss, exclusion, exile, that suffuses this novel. Yet, as Judith Lownder Newton points out, Lucy's forced removal from this backwater, and from her subsequent resting place with Miss Marchmont, gives her a surge of energy which is associated visually with the City of London, which she visits before leaving England for Labassecour.[41]

Lucy spends a day wandering alone, momentarily freezing the energetic activity of the modern commercial city in snapshot emblematic sights – St Paul's; the Thames – its bridges viewed from the dome of the cathedral; the Temple Gardens; the Strand; Cornhill; all seen 'with the sun upon them, and a glad, blue sky of early spring above; and between them and it, not too dense a cloud of haze' (p. 109). She, and we, carry these sights with us as she embarks for another country, and it is therefore a double image in which Bretton and the English countryside lie alongside the vision of a more dynamic commercial capital city.

England as place is evoked again and again in explicit and implicit contrast with what Lucy finds elsewhere, and it is these early scenes which carry its meaning in the novel: a complex meaning, in which the yearning for Bretton is qualified by a consciousness of its enervation. It is of course, in addition, a site of suffering for Lucy, since it offers her no home, no place to be. It exacts from Lucy, in the kindest fashion, the repression of anguish, the assumption of the mask of the tranquillity that is a condition of respectable femininity: the harsh lesson of feminine control that Lucy, in turn, teaches the six-year-old Polly.

There is an extraordinary scene in Chapter sixteen, just after Lucy, hysterical and in profound depression, has made her confession to a Catholic priest. On leaving the church she faints, and wakes to find herself apparently back at Bretton. England, and Bretton, are re-created in the heart of Labassecour, in all the household furnishings of La Terrasse, but above all, perhaps, in an English tea. Food, and its manner of preparation, are potent indicators of identity and difference in fiction. In Brontë's novels, food offered and accepted, food that nourishes, food that cannot be eaten, are replete with meaning.[42] The food that Lucy accepts on her arrival at the school in the Rue Fossette, out of a 'foreign kitchen', is unfamiliar, but nourishes, unlike the invalid food eaten at Miss

Marchmont's. Paul Emanuel brings less substantial fare to Lucy after her incarceration in the grenier – a 'dainty' *pâté à la crème* which is, however, exactly what she craves. Lovers and would-be lovers offer cake; the child Polly begs a slice for Graham: English 'seed-cake', which Lucy does not touch. The food in Labassecour may be strange and exotic, or dainty and frivolous, but it is consumed with relish.

Newton is surely right in her interpretation of this episode at La Terrasse as regression on Lucy's part. This Little England is again a place of (temporary) stasis. Home, where the heart is – where Lucy longs to achieve belonging – is a place where little happens as well as a place which blandly ignores her inner turmoil, taking at face value her inoffensive exterior.

Otherness carries an erotic charge. The enigmatic Lucy is pulled in contrary directions. She yearns for the tranquillity of Bretton/England, and one of the two men she is attached to – Graham Bretton – has a character that is as unimpassioned as the English landscape. He watches the great Rachel's performance of Queen Vashti's frenzied rebellion unmoved:

> he could feel, and feel vividly in his way, but his heart had no chord for enthusiasm: to bright, soft, sweet influence his eyes and lips gave bright, soft, sweet welcome, beautiful to see as dyes of rose and silver, pearl and purple, embracing summer clouds; for what belonged to storm, what was wild and intense, dangerous, sudden, and flaming, he had no sympathy. . . .Cool young Briton! The pale cliffs of his own England do not look down on the tides of the channel more calmly than he watched the Pythian inspiration of that night. (p. 341)

Paul Emanuel, by contrast, is fiery and passionate, mercurial and despotic. Associated with children and with childish treats, he has all the volatility of a passionate, loving, but imperious child:

> . . . in its . . . [his heart's] core was a place, tender beyond a man's tenderness; a place that humbled him to little children, that bound him to girls and women; to whom, rebel as he would, he could not disown his affinity, nor quite deny that, on the whole, he was better with them than with his own sex. (pp. 425–6)

Is it, perhaps, his foreignness that allows this often comic diminution of masculinity and adulthood, permitting intemperate outbursts, love of power in which he is compared to Napoleon, even religious difference, to be discounted? An absence that does not reduce but enhances his status as a lover, transforming him into 'my dear little man' (p. 490)?

Mrs Sweeny, who is summarily dispatched by Madame Beck to make way for Lucy, is a rival for work and a place in the world, not for love. Lucy has a more formidable task in centring herself vis-à-vis her rivals in love, who are both beautiful Englishwomen. The woman whose beauty masks her true nature – who, like Mrs Sweeny, is not what she seems – is, of course, a commonplace of fiction. Such antiheroines present narrative enigmas which the hero must solve in order to discover the true heroine, and Rosemary Clark-Beattie identifies just such a plot in the first half of the novel, in the Dr John/Ginevra/Lucy triangle: a plot which would, traditionally, be resolved – as it is in *Mansfield Park*, for example – by the hero's recognition of the worthlessness of the false heroine. Instead, both Ginevra and Lucy are displaced by Paulina, who matches Ginevra in beauty, Lucy in intellect and inner strength. Significantly, she speaks perfect French, holding court in that language with the savants of the Athene (p. 398). Paulina, unlike Ginevra, is a worthy heroine, but Brontë allows the rejected Lucy a certain spitefulness at her expense. Paulina as a child is a figure who feels and suffers intensely, but with more than a touch of the absurd. She is a diminutive little doll-woman, the droll, premature player of the role of angel-in-the-house. And when, as an adult, she has won the heart of Graham/Dr John, Lucy is reminded of her by Paul Emanuel's spaniel Sylvie: 'She was very tiny, and had the prettiest little innocent face, the silkiest long ears, the finest dark eyes in the world. I never saw her, but I thought of Paulina de Bassompierre: forgive the association, reader, it *would* occur' (p. 510).

But Paulina, Ginevra and Lucy share their Englishness, and all stand opposed, in their styles of beauty (in the case of the first two – Lucy, of course, is plain) and in their dress, to the bourgeois belles of Labassecour:

> Some fine forms there were here and there, models of a peculiar style of beauty; a style, I think, never seen in England: a solid, firm-set sculptural style. . . . They have such features as the Dutch painters give to their madonnas: low-country classic features, regular but round, straight but stolid. . . . Women of this order need no ornament, and they seldom wear any; the smooth hair, closely braided, supplies a sufficient contrast to the smoother cheek and brow; the dress cannot be too simple; the rounded arm and perfect neck require neither bracelet nor chain. (p. 287)

Ginevra may be a false heroine, but she is English, and may be used to detract from the beauty of the Labassecouriennes:

> the prettiest, or, at any rate, the least demure and hypocritical-looking of the lot. . . . She . . . had a slight pliant figure, not at all like the forms of the foreign damsels; her hair, too, was not close-braided, like a skull-cap of satin; it looked *like* hair, and waved from her head, long, curled, and flowing. (p. 292)

There are echoes, in the statuesque beauty of the Labassecouriennes, of French educationalists' prescriptions concerning female beauty and adornment:

> True grace does not depend on vain and affected dress . . . I would even get girls to realise the noble simplicity that one sees in statues and other figures which remind us of the women of Greece and Rome.[43]

Finally, Charlotte Brontë allows Lucy Snowe to displace her repressed and disavowed emotions – sexual passion, passionate anger and rage – on to the oriental Other – the painting of Cleopatra and the performance of Vashti: the one a figure of contempt, a sixteen-stone mountain of voluptuous flesh; the other a figure of dismayed recoil. Jane Miller links the two – one a male fantasy of woman as object of male desire; the other a female-created and enacted vision of anger and rebellion: 'a woman's vision, and a vision of a woman . . . of female power unmediated by men and beyond their judgement and understanding'.[44]

The authority of Fenelon and Rousseau is invoked in matters of more moment than dress. Père Silas, the elderly priest to whom Lucy confesses at her moment of crisis, of mental and physical breakdown, when she is left alone during the long vacation, is described as 'a benign old priest' having about him 'something of Fenelon' (p. 235). Fenelon's *The Education of Girls*, published in 1687, was translated into English in 1707, and was followed by a number of other translations, often abridged or edited with the Catholic references expunged.

Fenelon stood in much the same relationship to the convent school in Paris known as 'Nouvelle Catholiques' as Père Silas to Madame Beck's establishment: visitor/spiritual adviser. 'Nouvelles Catholiques' was a school established 'to furnish young Protestant female converts with safe retreats against the persecution of their parents and the wiles of the heretics', as was stated in the School Constitution of 1675. H.C. Barnard comments: 'There is no doubt that in some cases these girls and young women had been taken from their homes against their wish and without their parents' consent.'[45] In 1685 Fenelon was appointed to a missionary campaign as part of an intensified drive against the Huguenots at around the time of the revocation of the Edict of Nantes. Unlike many of his fellow-missionaries, Fenelon relied on persuasion and kindness, although he had no tolerance for Huguenot beliefs: 'He preferred conversion through the medium of schools and teachers and the distribution of Catholic literature to the drastic methods of force and persecution.'[46] The little tracts containing 'milk for babes; the mild effluence of a mother's love towards her tenderest and her youngest; intended wholly and solely for those whose head is to be reached through the heart . . . it sought to win the affectionate through their affections, the sympathizing through their sympathies . . .' (p. 507) which Lucy finds in her desk, inscribed with the names 'Père Silas' and with the initials of Paul Emanuel, are recalled to mind. Fenelon is a singularly apt model for Père Silas, in his attempted conversion of Lucy through her growing affection for Paul Emanuel (Chapter thirty-six).

The system followed in Madame Beck's school is modelled on a mix of Fenelon with Rousseau's plan of education for Émile's mate, Sophy. Madame Beck's regime as regards food, exercise, clothing, deportment, styles of learning, follows Fenelon's mild regime, and Lucy Snowe finds much to be admired here:

> Nothing could be better than all her arrangements for the physical well-being of her scholars. No minds were overtasked; the lessons were well distributed and made incomparably easy to the learner; there was a liberty of amusement, and a provision for exercise which kept the girls healthy; the food was abundant and good: neither pale nor puny faces were to be seen in the Rue Fossette. She never grudged a holiday; she allowed plenty of time for sleeping, dressing, washing, eating; her method in all these matters was easy, liberal, salutary and rational: many an austere English school-mistress would do vastly well to imitate it . . . (p. 136)

Madame Beck orders and controls her establishment of some 112 students with easy, exemplary authority: 'she ruled all these, together with four teachers, eight masters, six servants, and three children, managing at the same time to perfection the pupils' parents and friends; and that without apparent effort; without bustle, fatigue, fever, or any symptom of undue excitement: occupied she always was – busy rarely' (p. 135).

Madame Beck's exercise of authority, however, rests on a more sinister base: close surveillance, the linchpin of her 'mild regime'; and in this, perhaps, the model is more Rousseau than Fenelon. In a characteristic episode in which the surveyor is surveyed, Lucy describes her examination by Madame Beck while she feigns sleep. Countenance, clothing, the contents of her luggage, are all closely inspected, her money is counted, her memorandum-book perused. Finally, her keys are duplicated and returned. Lucy comments: 'All this was very un-English: truly I was in a foreign land' (p. 132). In Rousseau's educational regime, all is orchestrated by the master-tutor, Jean-Jacques, even Émile's love for Sophy, and this ability to monitor and mould the child depends on close covert surveillance.

This 'un-English' practice may be related to contemporary debates on another institution which was being reorganised in mid-nineteenth-century England: policing. Palmerston's Police Bills of 1854 and 1856 were to introduce a system of community surveillance covering the whole country, and there was much concern and debate about the form this surveillance should take. The debate focused on local accountability, and there was strong opposition to the centralised continental system founded in Napoleonic France, and widespread throughout Europe, including Belgium. This model of policing was denounced in England as a system of 'spying' and, as such, 'un-English'. Madame Beck's mode of policing her establishment clearly references this context and this debate, and her system is also roundly denounced by Lucy Snowe in the same terms as 'un-English': ' "Surveillance", "espionage", these were her watch-words'; this woman 'who in her own single person . . . could have comprised the duties of a first minister and a superintendent of police' (p. 137). In *Villette*, the strategies of generations of fictional 'educating heroines' described by Ellen Moers take a sinister cast.[47] In earlier fictions in an English context, as in Sarah Fielding's *The Governess*, Lucy Snowe would have played Jenny Peace to Madame Beck's educating heroine, Mrs Teachum.[48] But Lucy refuses this role, and the 'foreign' ends it serves, and – the better to undermine Madame Beck's 'espionage' – engages in counter-surveillance of her own: the watcher is watched, and unacceptable practices are disavowed and displaced on to others.

It has to be said that Madame Beck's school is no panopticon. In spite of all her watchfulness, the school is penetrated by a succession of intruders (Monsieur de Hamal dressed as a nun, Dr John); its grounds are sullied by a lover's billets-doux. Ginevra manages a midnight elopement, and even Lucy escapes unhindered, to wander, dreamlike, unmolested and unseen, in the transfigured parks and streets of carnivalesque Villette.

I want to close by suggesting that Brontë, in mid-nineteenth-century Britain, is writing at a time when discourses of nationality could still be used to invoke radical patriotism, but with unmistakeable overtones of xenophobic nationalism. As has been made clear, the discourse of radical patriotism is also that of Protestantism. It is anti-Catholic, and often anti-Irish: 'the Protestant construction of British identity involved the unprivileging of minorities who would not conform: the Catholic community . . . those men and women who were not allowed to be British so that others could be'.[49] The 1850s saw a resurgence of anti-Catholicism and associated anti-Irish sentiment, as Robert Colby has noted in connection with *Villette*. Brontë's own Irish extraction may have made her especially eager to disavow Irishness in the construction of a middle-class feminine Englishness.

In this narrative of identity, belonging, exile, displacement, Lucy Snowe's first action on her arrival at the Rue Fossette is to displace a false pretender, the nursery-governess Mrs Sweeny. In ill-fitting finery of dubious provenance, this Irish 'heroine of the bottle', who professes 'to speak the English tongue with the purest metropolitan accent' (p. 132), is summarily disposed of to make way for the genuine article. This is surely a most significant displacement, for while it secures for Lucy only the most precarious and lowly place in a foreign, Catholic school in a foreign, Catholic land, it establishes her also as a bona fide *Englishwoman*. She is what Mrs Sweeny pretends to be.

The discourse of radical patriotism is mobilised to legitimate Lucy's proto-feminist struggle against her oppression as a young, poor, plain woman. Brontë invokes the language of the 'freeborn (Protestant) Englishman' to claim the same freedoms for her heroine, and to challenge the system of 'foreign' surveillance to which she is subjected. Rosemary Clark-Beattie suggests that the foreign setting of *Villette* facilitates Lucy's more assertive, proto-feminist claim to independence and to emotional life. Lucy has no place in English middle-class society because she is poor and plain, without family, and without prospects of marriage. Her 'English' Protestant bona fides, argues Clark-Beattie, avail her nothing in establishing herself in England, in finding a 'place', a home.

Among the Brettons – who take her at face value, never seeking to probe beyond the calm, repressed exterior even in the face of the clearest signs of her deep distress – she is effaced. Her resentment can therefore find no legitimate expression, and must be repressed beneath the calm, unimpassioned exterior of the English lady. In England she must remain the tight-lipped narrator who observes unobserved, revealing nothing of herself. In Catholic Labassecour, in a society shaped by a religious culture that opposes the rights of the individual conscience, Lucy can resist in the name of Protestant patriotism. Yet paradoxically, it is Catholic Labassecour that reveals to the reader what little we learn of her inner self, *because* it is only in such a culture that this self comes under surveillance by others. Madame Beck, Paul Emanuel, Père Silas understand – as the Brettons do not – that the calm, frozen exterior may cover passionate desire, passionate anger, of a kind that neither culture legitimates in 'proper ladies'. Catholic Labassecour and Paul Emanuel assume that in women the wearing of a pink dress may indicate the heart of a scarlet woman, and however laughable his admonishments at Lucy's modest furbelows, the attempted exercise of control over a (presumed) rampant female nature is less painful in the end to Lucy than Protestant England, symbolised by John Graham Bretton's assumption that she has nothing to hide.

Clark-Beattie identifies the second plot of the novel as one of conspiracy. A secret junta composed of Père Silas, Madame Beck and Madame Walravens conspires to separate Lucy from Paul Emanuel. It is a deeply paranoid plot, but it presents its heroine with a force against which she may struggle in all good conscience, while 'against the threat of Protestant punishment Lucy is powerless to rebel'. It is foreignness, Otherness, that allows Lucy to assert herself, to reveal something of her rage and passion, and structures the narrative of the female self in *Villette*. In this novel subjectivity and self, identity and sexuality, class and nationality, are woven through a shifting set of oppositions which centre on gender, class, religion and nation. Charlotte Brontë draws on the Janus-faced patriotism/nationalism of her times, a moment in which the radical undertones of patriotism are still potent enough to provide the terms in which claims for female emancipation may be framed; but in so doing she helps to forge a 'grammar of national belonging' in the feminine gender in which the overtones of xenophobic paranoia are equally clear.

In the opening plenary at the Association of Cultural Studies Annual Conference in 1990, Roger Bromley[50] explored the themes of 'Culture, Meaning and Belonging' in very general terms. He might have been speaking about *Villette* and its heroine/narrator, and I want to close with some of his observations:

> Within any affiliation there is the ever-present possibility of erasure and defacement, of not belonging . . . a dialogue with loss. . . . Belonging can be converted into forms of paranoia and surveillance. . . . Not belonging can be experienced as oppressive and marginalizing, but also as liberating. . . . Not belonging begins with a sense of what we are not, which underpins an awareness of exile, outsideness, marginality. . . . So one can be in place, but out of place and differentiated, excluded from the prevailing 'we' or 'us' rhetorics – these are the grammar of belonging.

Notes

1 Adrienne Rich, 'Jane Eyre: The Temptations of a Motherless Woman', in Rich, *On Lies, Secrets, Silence: Selected Prose, 1966–1978* (London: Virago, 1980), pp. 89–106.
2 Elaine Showalter, *A Literature of Their Own: British Women Novelists From Brontë to Lessing* (London: Virago, 1978); Sandra Gilbert and Susan Gubar, *The Madwoman in the Attic: The Woman Writer and the Nineteenth-Century Literary Imagination* (New Haven, CT and London: Yale University Press, 1979).
3 Mary Jacobus, 'The Buried Letter: Feminism and Romanticism in *Villette*', in Jacobus (ed.), *Women Writing and Writing About Women* (London: Croom Helm, 1979), pp. 42–60.
4 Marxist–Feminist Literature Collective, 'Women's Writing: *Jane Eyre, Shirley, Villette, Aurora Leigh*', in Francis Barker *et al.*, *1848: The Sociology of Literature: Proceedings of*

the Essex Conference on the Sociology of Literature, July 1977 (Colchester: University of Essex, 1978), pp. 185–206; Helen Taylor, 'Class and Gender in Charlotte Brontë's *Shirley*', *Feminist Review* 1 (1978): 83–93; Terry Eagleton, *Myths of Power: A Marxist Study of the Brontës*, 2nd edn (London: Macmillan, 1988).

5 Gayatri Chakravorty Spivak, 'Three Women's Texts and a Critique of Imperialism', *Critical Inquiry* 12, 1 (1985): 243–61.

6 Judith Lownder Newton, *Women, Power and Subversion: Social Strategies in British Fiction, 1778–1860* (New York and London: Methuen, 1985).

7 Nina Auerbach, 'Charlotte Brontë: The Two Countries', *University of Toronto Quarterly*, 42, 4 (1973): 328–42.

8 Sally Minogue, 'Gender and Class in *Villette* and *North and South*', in Minogue (ed.), *Problems for Feminist Criticism* (London and New York: Routledge, 1990), pp. 70–108.

9 Gilbert and Gubar, *The Madwoman in the Attic*, p. 339.

10 Showalter, *A Literature of Their Own*.

11 Jacobus, 'The Buried Letter', p. 12.

12 Gilbert and Gubar, *The Madwoman in the Attic*, p. 6.

13 Jacobus, 'The Buried Letter', p. 16.

14 *ibid.*, p. 47.

15 *ibid.*, p. 57.

16 Newton, *Women, Power and Subversion*, p. 93.

17 *ibid.*, p. 99.

18 Cora Kaplan, 'Pandora's Box: Subjectivity, Class and Sexuality in Socialist Feminist Criticism', in *Sea Changes: Essays in Feminism and Culture* (London: Verso, 1986), p. 154.

19 See Tom Winnifrith, *The Brontës and Their Background: Romance and Reality* (London: Macmillan, 1973).

20 Rosemary Clark-Beattie, 'Fables of Rebellion: Anti-Catholicism in the Structures of *Villette*', *English Literary History*, 53, 4 (1986): 821–47; Jane Miller, *Seductions: Studies in Reading and Culture* (London: Virago, 1990).

21 Gilbert and Gubar, *The Madwoman in the Attic*, p. 415.

22 Benedict Anderson, *Imagined Communities: Reflections on the Origin and Spread of Nationalism* (London: Verso, 1983); Linda Colley, 'Radical Patriotism in Eighteenth-Century England', in Raphael Samuel (ed.), *Patriotism: The Making and Unmaking of British National Identity*, 3 vols (London: Routledge, 1989), vol. 1, pp. 169–87; Eric Hobsbawn, *Nations and Nationalism Since 1780: Programme, Myth, Reality* (Cambridge: Cambridge University Press, 1990); Tom Nairn, *The Break-Up of Britain: Crisis and Neo-Nationalism*, 2nd edn (London: New Left Books, 1981).

23 Eric Hobsbawn and Terence Ranger (eds), *The Invention of Tradition* (Cambridge: Cambridge University Press, 1983).

24 Robert Colls and Philip Dodd (eds), *Englishness: Politics and Culture 1880–1920* (London: Croom Helm, 1986), Preface.

25 Anderson, *Imagined Communities*, p. 19.

26 Samuel (ed.), *Patriotism*, p. xi.

27 Cunningham, in Samuel (ed.) *Patriotism*, p. 57.

28 Colley, in Samuel (ed.), *Patriotism*; Linda Colley, *Britons: Forging the Nation, 1707–1837* (New Haven, CT and London: Yale University Press, 1992).

29 Barnett, in Samuel (ed.), *Patriotism*, pp. 140–55.

30 Colls, in Colls and Dodd (eds), *Englishness*, p. 39.

31 See, for example, Chris Baldick, *The Social Mission of English Criticism* (Oxford: The Clarendon Press, 1983).

32 Floya Anthias and Nira Yuval-Davis, in association with Harriet Cain, *Boundaries: Race, Nation, Gender, Colour, Class, and the Anti-Racist Struggle* (London:

Routledge, 1992); Nira Yuval-Davis and Floya Anthias (eds), *Women–Nation–State* (Basingstoke: Macmillan, 1989).

33 Virginia Woolf, *Three Guineas* (London: Hogarth Press, 1943), p. 197.

34 Sara Mills, *Discourses of Difference* (London: Routledge, 1991).

35 Jane MacKay and Pat Thane, 'The Englishwoman', in Colls and Dodd (eds), *Englishness*, pp. 191–225.

36 Alison Light, *Forever England: Femininity, Literature and Conservatism Between the Wars* (London and New York: Routledge, 1991), p. 8.

37 Charlotte Brontë, *Villette* (Harmondsworth: Penguin, 1987), p. 425. All further references will be given in parentheses within the main text.

38 Raymond Williams, 'Culture is Ordinary', in Norman McKenzie (ed.), *Conviction* (London: MacGibbon and Kee, 1958), pp. 74–92.

39 Enid Duthie, *The Foreign Vision of Charlotte Brontë* (London: Macmillan, 1975), pp. 179–98.

40 Nina Auerbach, op. cit., p. 336.

41 Newton, *Women, Power and Subversion*.

42 Gill Frith, *The Intimacy Which Is Knowledge: Female Friendship in the Novels of Women Writers*, unpubl. PhD thesis, University of Warwick, 1989.

43 François de Salignac de la Motte-Fenelon, *Fenelon on Education: a translation of the 'Traité de l'Éducation des Filles' and other documents*, edited together with an introduction by H.C. Barnard (Cambridge: Cambridge University Press, 1988), p. 71.

44 Miller, *Seductions*, p. 96.

45 H.C. Barnard, Introduction to Fenelon's 'Traité de l'Éducation des Filles', p. xiii.

46 *ibid.*, p. xvii.

47 Ellen Moers, *Literary Women: The Great Writers* (New York: Anchor Books, 1977).

48 Sarah Fielding, *The Governess, Or Little Female Academy* (London and New York: Pandora, 1987).

49 Colley, *Britons: Forging the Nation*, p. 53.

50 Unpublished paper given at the annual Conference of the Association for Cultural Studies, 1990.

Chapter 4

Irigaray's Hom(m)osexuality and Gay Writing in Marlowe and Gunn

Lawrence Normand

Homosexual men present a problem to patriarchal men because they seem 'feminine' in some way, and to some feminist women because they are men. This causes many antagonisms. The cultural creations of 'woman' and 'homosexual' may have common interests arising from their subordinated relations in the dynamics of patriarchy, but are they on the same side in struggles against patriarchy, or really on opposite sides of the gender divide?[1] Some feminists find lesbianism and male homosexuality extremely problematical. Jane Gallop, for instance, is willing to 'affirm the normality of homosexuality in order to celebrate lesbianism', yet she objects to male homosexuality as being a 'highly phallocentric male sexuality [which] partakes of all the perversions of male heterosexuality: rape, pornography, child molesting, etc.'[2] The best she can say of male homosexuality is that it 'can neither be condemned nor celebrated. In the highly polarized world of feminism, male homosexuality might be *ne-uter*, neither one nor the other'. Lesbianism, too, causes conflict, according to Caroline Ramazanoglu, because '[f]eminists' problems in approaching sexual divisions remain somewhat mystified . . . [and] women remain divided rather than united by their sexual differences'.[3]

Luce Irigaray presents a particularly problematical relation to male homosexuality – which, as Jonathan Dollimore points out 'is theoretically central'[4] to her feminist project. The suspicious relations between feminism and male homosexuality come sharply into focus in several of her texts, including 'The Blind Spot of an Old Dream of Symmetry',[5] which reads deconstructively Freud's essay 'Femininity'. For Irigaray, male homosexuality is the motive of men's subjection of women. She argues that Freud's writing of femininity makes a positive representation of women impossible, for his discursive economy is dependent on what there is to be seen (in the first place, the penis); and its boundaries are set by its male-centred imaginary projections. In this scenario of one sex, the female appears not in its own representations but as a negative version of the male imaginary. Freud's phallocentric view of human sexuality casts the feminine into absence, lack and deficiency, separating women from their bodily origins, and preventing the discovery and creation of specifically female language and imagery – articulations in terms appropriate to, in the first place, women's bodily realities:

> The little girl does not submit to the 'facts' easily, she keeps waiting for 'it to grow' . . . which means that no attempt will be made by the little girl . . . to find symbols for the state of 'this nothing to be seen', to defend its goals, or to lay claim to its rewards. *Here again no economy would be possible whereby sexual reality can be represented by/for woman* [original emphasis].[6]

Irigaray does not suggest that the female (or male) body is translated directly into language or discourse; rather, she takes the sexual difference between male and female to involve different modes of experience, which in turn are mediated through different morphologies of language or imagery. Margaret Whitford, in her study of Irigaray, is careful to argue that Irigaray is 'talking about feminine specificity at the level of the symbolic, or representation . . . [and] . . . in everything she has written, she has been addressing herself to the symbolic and not to the innate'.[7] In a masculinist discourse constructed on the phallus, what passes for femininity is a projection on to the female of male castration anxiety: '[c]astration anxiety is thus palliated (but also confirmed) by the *representation* [original emphasis] of the woman as biologically lacking'.[8]

Irigaray's rereading of Freud shows him setting male heterosexuality – in effect, the penis – as the origin and norm by which all other possible sexual economies may be structured. In the Freudian schema woman is not herself but merely that which is logically necessary, given Freud's premise, to desire the phallus. The term 'castration', the 'absence' of positive sexual attributes, neatly complements the positivity of the always-to-be-desired phallus. A woman is rendered not as something positive in herself, but as the necessary bearer of a desire directed to keep the male organ in place as the only possible desirable object:

> Is it not her lot in life to sustain the penis, to prevent it from drifting into analogical substitutions, from tearing up the anchor it affords for the whole system of generalizations? Thus the woman who is a man's woman must always keep this desire. This is what man asks her to perpetuate within his 'house', as she remains unaware of the value her own sex organs might have for her.[9]

The analysis is directed to the rhetoric of Freud's text, and reveals its unconscious workings; this rhetoric, in turn, is taken to be symptomatic of the long Western tradition of negating women. Irigaray's reading practice – its detailed responsiveness, its refusal to be charmed, its production of an alternative discourse – speaks the unspoken of the text she is addressing, turns the absent into the real, and makes it possible to conceive of Freudian 'feminine lack' as, crucially, a discursive effect, and a natural fact.

Irigaray's theory of negated femininity appears to offer a way of thinking about the situation of male homosexuality, which in the history of the Christian West has been largely one of suppression and negation.[10] In discourse there has been little space for male – and even less for female – homosexuality to speak itself; from within prevailing discursive structures homosexuality has been falsely represented by alien interests, or not represented at all as and by itself.

But how does male homosexuality figure in Irigaray's discourse? A problem arises from her reading, for as it tries to account for Freud's phallocentrism, it veers into homophobia. If Freud effaces femininity by insisting that only the penis counts, and represents women as men with atrophied penises, then all human desire becomes, in Irigaray's words, 'the desire for the same, for the self-identical, the self (as) same, and again of the similar, the alter ego and, to put in a nutshell, the desire for the auto . . . the homo . . . the male, dominates the representational economy'.[11] The punning neologism 'hom(m)osexuality'[12] is created to capture the double sense of male-sexuality and homo-sexuality, and to suggest that these two are essentially one. The pun elides precisely the difference between male heterosexuality and male homosexuality; it places male homosexuality within heterosexual masculinity as its secret disguised centre.[13]

Women's exclusion from the symbolic, social, cultural realm is explained as an effect of the creation of a single (male) sex through this supposed men-only circuit of desire. Irigaray places male same-sex desire at the centre of oppressive masculinity as the motive of male effacement of the female. Such an argument conflates phallocentrism and homosexuality, thus misrepresenting male homosexuality. Femininity is the Other that Freud cannot comprehend or see as anything in itself, but whose existence is necessary to a version of masculinity which then effaces and undermines what might be a more authentic femininity. Male homosexuality is the Other that Irigaray requires within masculinity in order to account for her definition of masculinity as self-loving. Her critique of Freud is that he does not understand femininity because his phallomorphic notion of masculinity renders it inconceivable. The analogous critique of Irigaray is that she does not understand male homosexuality because her notion of singular masculinity requires male homosexuality to be subsumed within it. Freud's inability – or refusal – to see the girl's sexual organs as having a positive existence is repeated in Irigaray's inability – or refusal – to see male homosexuality as separate from male heterosexuality, with its own conditions of existence and representation.

Irigaray designates male homosexuality as the epitome of phallocentrism, as the actual male self-love which the detour of heterosexuality tries to disguise. But how does she overcome the problem that male heterosexuality is in fact extremely hostile to male homosexuality? By stating that male homosexuality is the repressed 'truth' of male heterosexuality:

> [t]he 'other' homosexual relations, masculine ones, are just as subversive [as father–son relationships], so they too are forbidden. *Because they openly interpret the law according to which society operates,* they threaten in fact to shift the horizon of that law. . . . Once the penis itself becomes merely a means to pleasure, pleasure among men, *the phallus loses its power* [original emphasis].[14]

The case is not argued, merely asserted, and the assertion is structured on metaphor, with men's socioeconomic relations taking the place in the sentence as the figurative term for the other literal term which does not appear: actual homo-sexual desire among all men. The literal meaning is tabooed, according to Irigaray – forbidden open expression, because that would be the emergence of what socioeconomic relations (involving the exchange of women) actually signify.

Irigaray's metaphorical structure of thought allows the question to be asked: why are homosexual relations designated as the (vanished) term in the meta-phor, and why may only social relations appear in the social text? The metaphor is arbitrary in its construction; one could just as easily reverse the terms and assert (probably with more accuracy) that homosexuality is the figurative rep-resentation of social and economic relations. Male homosexuality functions in Irigaray's writing as the male sexual real, which is literal, but nameable only metaphorically, not as itself. Male homosexuality is the actual stuff of the life of patriarchy, and the founding assumption which makes her thinking possible. Representing male homosexuality as the repressed centre of male heterosex-uality removes it from the realm of discourse and casts it into a pre-discursive space; it renders it as the necessary, absent, ahistorical essence of masculinity.

In an uncanny repetition of the form of discourse which she deconstructs in Freud – that '[i]n the imaginary, woman is the material substratum for men's theories, [and] their language'[15] – male homosexuality is made the material substratum in Irigaray's discourse.[16] She conflates male self-love and homosex-uality in a rhetorical move which is simple and false, and makes homosexuality appear as the secret cause of general male self-love. Irigaray states that in Freud's miswriting of the feminine, female homosexuality is also misrepresented: 'nothing of the special nature of desire *between women* [original emphasis] has been unveiled or stated'.[17] Nothing of the special nature of sexual desire be-tween men is unveiled or stated by her text; her homosexuality is merely the repressed underside of her 'one sex' notion. Irigaray's imagination does not extend to male homosexuality.

A number of objections can be made to Irigaray's specific assumption that homosexuality is love of the same. In the first place, she assumes that sexual difference is the difference that has priority over all others;[18] thus she ignores other differences of, for instance, race, nationality, class and age. Homosexuality does involve such differences; as Dollimore observes, the homosexual 'has, in historical actuality, embraced both cultural and racial difference';[19] he goes on to identify the idea that homosexuality depends on sameness as a recurrent theme of homophobia.[20] At the level of bodies, it is worth remembering that identical twins come closest to being the same; otherwise, all bodies are dif-ferent. Judith Butler makes a more general criticism of what she calls Irigaray's 'masculinist signifying economy' on the grounds that it is undercut 'by its globalizing reach'.[21] Butler details the harmful effects which this has on at-tempts to think through the particulars of oppressive situations:

> The effort to identify the enemy as singular in form is a reverse-discourse that un-critically mimics the strategy of the oppressor instead of offering a different set of

terms. That the tactic can operate in feminist and antifeminist contexts alike suggests that the colonizing gesture is not primarily or irreducibly masculinist. It can operate to effect other relations of racial, class, and heterosexist subordination, to name but a few.

The effective ways of countering Irigaray's globalising notion of hom(m)osexuality, then, would be to deconstruct it – as I have tried to do above – or to subject it to historical testing to discover if it was valid at different historical moments, or to offer 'a different set of terms' with which to describe the phenomena it attempts to enclose.

Attempting in her writing to imagine a feminine position, Irigaray imagines maleness as a single Other, but fails – or refuses – to represent the masculine as having its own splits and oppressions, margins and exclusions, and its own powerful lines of force subjecting and policing those aspiring to masculinity. Homosexual men are then condemned from two sides: by Irigaray as the true hidden centre of masculinity, and by patriarchal men as being on the border with femininity, threatening to dissolve the clear defining lines of the masculine category: in Jonathan Rutherford's words, '[a homosexual man] is the Other, a presence who simultaneously confirms the legitimacy of our own [hetero]sexual identity, yet presents it with its own relativity, that it is only one identity amongst others, disturbing and disrupting our sense of normality'.[22] For Irigaray, homosexuality is at the centre of masculinity; for patriarchy, it is at a boundary with femininity. Irigaray's text insists on a structural contradiction: of casting male homosexuality into the centre of the heterosexuality which is, in fact, virulently hostile to it. Masculinity is not single, homogeneous, or the same, but composite, constructed, split, conflicted.

Reading her text from a gay male position reveals that Irigaray's assumption of the primacy of sexual difference (the difference between male and female) both makes her critique of Freud possible, and produces an argument which misrepresents the place and function of male homosexuality within a general masculinity. Irigaray's statements on lesbianism suggest that she is willing to accept the usefulness of lesbianism for heterosexual feminists, but unwilling to countenance male homosexuality. In an interview she has considered the harm done by sharp sexual division: 'What I regret is that our society operates too much in alternatives. Either you love a man or a woman. . . . I believe that you can love the difference, but only if you're able to love those who are the same as yourself. Whatever form love takes.'[23] Loving the same sex, 'whatever form love takes', is a prerequisite for loving the other sex, but remains only a stage along the way to the heterosexual destination of love between men and women.

In that same interview Irigaray was asked about same-sex relations, and she answered that she was prepared to accept the idea of sexual relations between women as part of a strategy to discover and strengthen women's identity specifically as women, but saw it as a way of strengthening heterosexual relations: 'It's important that women discover that they also have love for other women. That doesn't *per se* have to mean that you actually make love, but you do whatever your desire inspires you to do. In fact, a woman can't love a man unless she also loves other women, and her mother.'[24] Higher value is placed on the man–woman couple, and sexual relations between men are not mentioned. In answer to the question 'When you refer to a loving couple, do you mean particularly a man and a woman?', Irigaray said: 'I think that man and woman is the most mysterious and creative couple. That isn't to say that other couples may not also have a lot in them, but man and woman is the most mysterious and creative.'[25] She went on to say that this creativity of the couple might be social: 'You could also imagine a couple who play a role in political power. Do you understand what I'm saying: people who are sexually different and who create a different relation to the world. Perhaps that could happen in the future.'[26] Only the most liberal interpretation of 'sexually different' to include lesbian and gay couples makes it possible to read Irigaray as referring to socially creative homosexualities.[27]

The challenge that Irigaray poses for gay theorists and critics comes from the assumptions she makes about the internal dynamics of masculinity, and her failure to address male homosexuality directly. Male homosexuality, positioned as a given at the base of a rhetorical structure, functions there as a quasi-natural fact, as something that cannot be questioned or examined. Her insistence on maintaining her analyses at the level of language and representation, and her insistence on the provisional nature of sexual identities, point the way, however, to a way of countering her own discourse by appropriating her own tactics. Irigaray can be challenged precisely by turning her hom(m)osexuality into what Butler calls 'a different set of terms' – that is, by turning an apparently 'natural' fact into discourse. Despite its homophobia, then, and possibly in spite of itself, Irigaray's feminist criticism does create discursive spaces for gay critique.

Even though Irigaray's notion of hom(m)osexuality is positively harmful to understanding male homosexuality, an associated strand of her critique, the problematic of representability, does offer ways of thinking about homosexuality. Like femininity in Irigaray's account of Freud, homosexuality can be thought of as a no-term, a negativity, somehow implicated in the sex-gender system but never unproblematically inscribed within it. In a system of male/female, and the derived terms masculine/feminine, there is no place for homosexuality. If hom(m)osexuality is rejected as an explanatory term, then alternative ways of articulating male homosexuality must be sought; and if adequate ones do not exist, new ones must be invented. The rest of this essay provides evidence of the different discursive formations of male homosexuality from the early modern and modern periods which, in their specificities and different functioning, are a challenge to the notion of hom(m)osexuality which, in its ahistorical, essentialising gesture, would render them invisible. What emerges is the historical contingency of the concept, and the widely different discursive formations in which it appears.

The ease with which male homosexuality may be returned to a pre-discursive confusion, and hence rendered inaccessible and incomprehensible even in the 1990s, is demonstrated by a recent incident. Alan Amos was a Conservative MP who was cautioned by the police in March 1992 after being discovered with another man one night on Hampstead Heath. Amos was reported next day as saying that he was 'not homosexual'; furthermore, he was 'innocent', because the police had not charged him with anything; and that what he had done was 'childish and stupid'.[28] Within a matter of hours, however, he had resigned as an MP, and his political career had come to an abrupt end. But what had happened, and how was it to be named? Was it the committing of what he called a childish act, something everyone is surely liable to do at times? Was it the caution by the police, even though they did not charge him with 'committing an act of gross indecency', as the law calls sexual contact between men? Did his action on Hampstead Heath suddenly reveal his real identity – a homosexual – or was it the fact that it happened outdoors that doomed him?

What this incident generated was a discursive incoherence, like that of the early modern period, which makes it impossible to name or speak or think of what it is we might be referring to: we have a 'nothing-to-be-seen'. In *The Observer*, Simon Hoggart casually referred to Amos as 'gay'.[29] A set of conflicted terms circulates round an unidentified happening on Hampstead Heath: 'gay' – a social identity; 'a homosexual' – an identity based on sexual desire; 'childish act' – a primitive form of behaviour returning to the adult; 'innocent' – not guilty in terms of law or morality. Sex has been turned into discourse, but only in the incoherence of what Foucault calls 'that utterly confused category'.[30] This incident presents, in miniature, the difficulty of writing male homosexuality: there are no agreed terms for an obscure something that is only conjecturally there. The putative sexual act that started it all – an encounter of bodies, and what that meant to the actors – has simply disappeared. Some undefined act, however, released a storm of social forces that were powerful enough to destroy Amos's social existence.

This discursive incoherence had a particular name in the early modern period: it was called 'sodomy'. Sodomy combined discursive indefinition with a terrible social power, and within it homosexuality was invisible. The historian Alan Bray has described how the crime of sodomy was conceived purely negatively, as something that could not be represented: it was 'not . . . part of the created order at all; it was part of its dissolution'.[31] Sex between men was generally not considered significant, or indeed registered at all, and certainly not recognised as sexual activity in its own right. Certain sexual acts between men, however, did appear in ideology – and occasionally in the courts – as sodomy, which was not defined exclusively as a sexual act, but as a theological offence associated with sacrilege and heresy, witchcraft and the Devil – acts dedicated to the subversion of the God-given natural order.

But sixteenth-century England presented a different discursive economy from a late-twentieth-century one for representing sexual acts between men. A mental gulf, Bray argues, separated the heinous crime of sodomy from the generally unremarked homosexual acts which occurred 'between neighbours and friends'.[32] In sixteenth-century England homosexual acts did not carry the same power to destroy social identity as Amos suffered; only those understood as sodomy were accorded power to subvert the entire social order. When Christopher Marlowe wrote *Edward II* in 1592, it was in the context of general indifference to homosexuality. In early modern writing homosexuality hardly appears in discourse at all, for it was not yet invented. In thinking about early modern 'homosexuality', a name is given to something which did not then exist as such. The signifier is necessary to indicate something whose problematical existence and meaning are precisely what is being sought.

This is like Irigaray's naming a 'femininity' which has not yet been accorded its own representation; and the femininity she names is not one that pre-exists its realisation in the symbolic, any more than the 'homosexuality' pursued by writers can be assumed to exist. It needs more than the name 'homosexuality' for same-sex desire to appear as it is. Homosexuality shares a feature of Irigaray's femininity: it is still producing its own positive self-representations in order to counter the systematic negation and misrepresentations that are imposed on it. From Irigaray the idea may be inferred that homosexuality is like femininity, a 'nothing-to-be-seen', something that has been cast into a negative, devalued mode of misrepresentation, is unknown to itself, and requires positive realisation in the symbolic if it is to discover its ontological potential.

Marlowe's *Edward II* is one of the first cultural productions which attempts to fashion something like homosexuality. Where that formation appears in the play it turns out not to be monolithically constructed in the way that Irigaray implies; it is variously constructed. And it is in direct opposition to and subversive of patriarchal power, not a part of it. *Edward II* fashions something we can recognise as homosexuality as a form of relationship, not merely same-sex acts which are insignificant, nor sodomy as a subversive social act. The play can be read as an attempt on Marlowe's part to refashion existing discourses of same-sex feeling to represent a homosexual relationship, even a proto-identity politics, on the English stage – that men who share emotional and sexual affinities also share a distinct self-consciousness that we might call homosexual. It is this early modern representation of homosexuality that allows Derek Jarman to use, in his film, aspects of the play's sexual politics which anticipate the modern idea of a homosexual identity.

Marlowe deploys a range of existing early modern discourses – sodomy, Neoplatonism, friendship, patronage – as he portrays his characters trying out various ways of adequately representing the Edward–Gaveston relationship, so doing what Irigaray recommends women should do: producing forms of words and images for what has been unexpressed.[33]

It is evident from Marlowe's play that homosexuality is not a transhistorical constant but a historically variable cultural construct. Not until the late seventeenth or early eighteenth century – at the same time as witchcraft was disappearing as a distinct social construction – did homosexuality gradually appear as one, as fragments of behaviour, certain differences of sexuality, and biases of affectivity were clustered together to construct a social fiction which was (and is) taken to be a part of reality. There is no concept of homosexuality in Marlowe's play, and it is therefore important not to interpret male same-sex behaviour in terms of our prevailing twentieth-century notions of homosexuality. Same-sex object choice does not define Edward as a homosexual, since this concept was unavailable; sodomy is not mentioned; effeminisation of the lovers is not automatically produced, for the male–female division remains intact; and homosexuality does not involve essential disablement for being king. Homosexuality in 1592 is not so powerful as to dominate all other aspects of identity, so in the play Marlowe can show several social systems operating simultaneously: kinship, friendship and patronage. Homosexuality is inscribed in the midst of these bonds. Jarman cut Gaveston's marriage, presumably because it would have blurred the 1990s gender difference of straight/gay that the film maintains, and confused the audience's responses.

Ideology demands that as king, Edward should embody the principle of phallocentric power. Homosexuality disrupts the prevailing oedipal economy in Edward's realignment of gender positions. His homosexual desire appears not so much in sex but in the different gender positions homosexuality affords within the oedipal economy, for Edward holds the archetypical masculine positions of king, husband, father, but also the feminine position of object of male desire. Asked why he persists in his relation with Gaveston, he replies: '[b]ecause he loves me more than all the world' (I.iv.77).[34] He refuses to occupy a single position, and thus disorders established social hierarchies. Intimacy and power are bound together but, crucially, homosexual love overturns the hierarchical relations which social position imposes, and creates an alternative social space where relations of equality can appear: 'Thy worth, sweet friend, is far above my gifts,/ Therefore to equal it, receive my heart' (I.i.160–61). The barons cannot tolerate the relation of equality that the lovers establish.

But male same-sex desire appears in several divergent discourses. It may be the unnameable, as when Edward appears grieving for his banished lover, and Lancaster cries '*Diablo!* What passions call you these?' (I.iv.318) – having no name for what he is seeing, and reaching for a language other than English. Edward himself uses Neoplatonic ideas to represent his love for Gaveston. When Gaveston first returns from France, Edward asks: 'Know'st thou not who I am?/ Thy friend, thy self, another Gaveston' (I.i.141–2). In this version of male friendship, two men are so similar that they effectively share a common soul and body. As elaborated by Ficino in fifteenth-century Italy, this was a way of sublimating the eroticism of same-sex attachments into high-minded chaste love.[35] But there is no attempt in the play to make this ideal of love the mainspring of the action, as it is, for example, in Sir Philip Sidney's 1582 sonnet sequence *Astrophil and Stella*. The fragments of Neoplatonic friendship theory are articulated only in the brief moments of Edward and Gaveston's secluded intimacy; but it is inadequate as a way of giving expression to homosexuality as part of a whole social scene.

Marlowe runs the gamut of possible ways of thinking about male homosexuality in 1592, some of which have now become familiar. When Mortimer Senior advises his nephew to let Edward have his lover, since 'riper years will wean him from such toys' (I.iv.400) – a version of the familiar 'It's a stage you're going through' argument – he cites rulers, heroes and statesmen who had male lovers:[36]

> The mightiest kings have had their minions:
> Great Alexander lov'd Hephaestion;
> The conquering Hercules for Hylas wept;
> And for Patroclus stern Achilles droop'd':
> And not kings only, but the wisest men.
> The Roman Tully lov'd Octavius.
> (I.iv.390–95)

Here Marlowe constructs a specific idea of homosexual passion. He places male homosexuality in a classical frame where it acquires a positive value as an attribute of 'mightiest kings' and 'wisest men'. This may be the first appearance in English literature of what has become a cliché of revaluing homosexuality by citing famous homosexuals. In Armistead Maupin's 1980 novel *More Tales of the City*, the hero resolves for the new year to give up citing a list of famous queers: 'I will make friends with a straight man. . . . I will not make fun of the way he walks. . . . I will not tell him about Alexander the Great, Walt Whitman or Leonardo da Vinci.'[37] Marlowe, however, uses Mortimer's list to create a previously unimaginable category from among men who recognise shared desires, and he seems to be making a recognisably modern move towards constructing a subjectivity which includes constitutive sexual desire. The gesture makes little impression, though, on Mortimer, who understands Edward's love as 'wanton humour' (I.iv.401) – that is, a perturbation of the body producing a psychic effect.

Homosexuality also appears in relations of patronage, as Edward dispenses gifts and offices to first Gaveston and then Spencer.[38] Patronage from the king is exactly what the nobles seek as much as Gaveston, and it is only the displacement of patronage from the nobility which traditionally received it to the upstart newcomers that enrages them. They do not see a homosexual relationship; rather, a changed political relationship. Marlowe shows homosexuality appearing in the particular social relation of patronage, and consequently drawing part of its cultural meaning from that relation. The barons object to Edward's favourites because they receive political favour and material rewards at their expense. Their political opposition to Edward is on the grounds that benefits are flowing to foreigners and social inferiors; they do not recognise sexual feeling as the motive for the king's redefined favouritism. It is easier for a modern reader to grasp the underlying notion of homosexuality (because it is so powerful) than of patronage relations which are the vehicles and form in which same-sex desires appear. It is out of the prevailing social relations of patronage that homosexuality begins to be constructed as an other kind of motive that might inhabit and find expression in that system. The barons do not see homosexuality in Edward's redirected patronage; rather, they see their political disadvantage.

Edward's gender, his masculinity, is not compromised by homosexuality until he is imprisoned in the castle dungeon. Lightborn (whose name translates

Lucifer) brings sodomy into the play for the first time, when he kills Edward by thrusting a heated poker into his body through the anus. This metaphorical action elides sex and death, displacing homosexuality with sodomy, with all its associations of the anus, evil, the Devil, and negative, disordering, disintegrating action. It is the barons who impose the familiar interpretation of sodomy on Edward. Significantly, Jarman avoids this tragic ending, transforming Marlowe's (and Holinshed's) accounts of Edward's death from a fact into a nightmare from which Edward awakes to turn Lightborn from murderer into lover. Instead of Marlowe's dramatisation of a sexualised death, Jarman has sex prevent the death which has been ordered. The film invents a scene in which sexual loyalties subvert state power, and invites the viewer to identify with the political effect of that sexual desire.

These different ways of writing homosexuality in *Edward II* appear at that historical moment when male homosexuality begins to be conceivable; and in the play the first signs of that concept are beginning to form.[39] Historicising homosexuality in *Edward II* produces a critique of Irigaray's hom(m)osexuality by showing it not to be present in male heterosexuality in an unproblematical way but, rather, to be in conflict with dominant masculinities. The play shows homosexuality to be barely conceivable or recognisable as such, for same-sex desire is represented in an unsettled way in a range of discourses; and if it does appear it is a sketchy, primitive version of what it would become. It was in the 1590s that the word 'sex' was first used in its modern sense of physical desire by John Donne:[40] in 'The Extasie' he writes: 'This Extasie doth unperplex/ (We said) and tell us what we love,/ Wee see by this, it was not sexe,/ Wee see, we saw not what did move.'[41]

In 1592 Marlowe writes without a developed concept of homosexuality; in the 1990s writers have concepts of homosexuality that are so developed as to constitute not just relationships but individual identities, and also developed subcultures. The situation in the late twentieth century is very different from that in 1592, for there is a plethora of competing accounts of homosexuality: sociological, religious, psychoanalytic, biological, juridical. The problem of writing homosexuality now is dealing with these vociferous, presumptuous explanations, aetiologies and judgements in which homosexuality is represented according to the presuppositions, prejudices and hostilities of others' discourses. Homosexuals are willy-nilly caught up in these cacophonous discourses which presume to present, explain and judge; and those very explanations may function as reverse discourses which form the grounds for diverse homosexual behaviours. They are, nevertheless, the very discourses in which selves are fashioned and lives pursued.

Homosexuality is now subject to at least two apparently contradictory cultural forces: one maintains it as a thing and imposes on it false representations (this is the work of the tabloids, the law, the churches); the other works to silence and erase it (Irigaray is an example). What constitutes homosexuality today is a diverse, changing bundle of affects, acts and lifestyles. Writers' responses to either of these forces will produce different kinds of writing. Jarman attacks the social forces which misrepresent homosexuality; he draws from the stock of contemporary gay male images, confronts his audience with images which emphasise homosexual difference, and asserts the right to enjoy them.[42] Alternatively, writers may counter the force of silencing and misrepresentation by presenting gay life as enmeshed with the ordinary. In the work of David Leavitt and Thom Gunn, homosexuality appears in complex subjectivities, entwined with aspects of ordinary life. In Allan Hollinghurst's *The Swimming-Pool Library*, Edmund White's *A Boy's Own Story* and *The Beautiful Room Is Empty*, Thom Gunn's *The Man with Night Sweats*, and Oscar Moore's *A Matter of Life and Sex* we read the *phenomena* of male homosexuality as the dictionary defines 'phenomenon': 'A thing that appears, or is perceived or observed . . . applied chiefly to a fact or occurrence, the cause or explanation of which is in question.'[43]

But nothing can appear or be perceived without a pre-existing cultural text which gives those appearances or perceptions meaning. Phenomenology is already infused with ideology, and writing homosexuality is therefore always political. Nevertheless, as a political tactic writing the phenomena of homosexuality can help to counter the effects of pre-emptive or hostile theorisation. Since in different times and places homosexuality may be positively valued, or considered insignificant or invisible, or regarded with loathing and hostility, it has no fixed cultural meaning. Irigaray's globalising hom(m)osexuality is opposed by writing which is attentive and detailed, and which for a moment ignores its enemies. While same-sex desire or acts may be universal, homosexuality is a social construction whose meaning varies widely.

Gunn's *The Man with Night Sweats* is political in Irigaray's sense of creating 'a different relation to the world'.[44] The first poem, 'The Hug', is about going to bed with his partner of many years in a friend's house after a birthday dinner party.[45] Immediate perception seems more prominent than *post facto* theorising, but the poem creates an idea of what two men sleeping together might mean:

> I dozed, I slept. My sleep broke on a hug,
>   Suddenly from behind,
> In which the full lengths of our bodies pressed:
>   Your instep to my heel,
> My shoulder-blades against your chest.
> It was not sex, but I could feel
> The whole strength of your body set,
>   Or braced, to mine,
> And locking me to you
> As if we were still twenty-two
> When our grand passion had not yet
>   Become familial.
> My quick sleep had deleted all
> Of intervening time and place.
>   I only knew
> The stay of your secure firm dry embrace.

'It was not sex' repeats the phrase from Donne's 'The Extasie', a poem which imagines what meanings a woman and man having sex might embody. Donne projects his meanings beyond sex into the spiritual, and Gunn does the same, transforming sex from 'grand passion' into the 'familial'. The poem is itself, of course, its own testimony to the spiritual creativity of homosexual love. The 'familial' is banal only if one forgets that it has been decreed that lesbian and gay lives cannot be familial, for in the malevolent words of the Local Government Act, homosexuals can have only 'pretended family relationships'.[46] Although the poem is not explicitly political, Gunn writes politically when he reinscribes the word 'familial' as producing what Irigaray calls 'a different relation to the world'. Sex in 'The Hug' is not phallocentric; it is 'Your instep to my heel,/ My shoulder-blades against your chest'; and it is through the hug that the writer becomes the subject of gay knowledge, opening up an articulable history from the single action which also encloses past and present.

The last poem in the book presents another version of gay writing which creates a 'different relation to the world'. The writer sees a man who has become the adoptive father of a young boy, having put into effect a plan he had voiced to the writer two years before in a bedroom where they had met to have sex: 'He said "I chose to do this with my life."/ Casually met he said it of the plan/ He undertook without a friend or wife.'[47] Sexual feeling between men has been refashioned into paternal feeling between new father and son: 'he transposed/ The expectations he took out at dark/ – Of Eros playing, features undisclosed – / Into another pitch, where he might work/ With the same melody . . . .'. This is the last poem in the volume, and it seems to be placed to leave the reader with a sense of possibilities of becoming gay (though such an adoption is impossible at the present time in the United Kingdom). The poem's title, 'The Blank', indicates how the previously unimaginable is given symbolic, social form in the lives of the man and the boy, and in its language. Irigaray's injunction to women to discover themselves in the symbolic, to write themselves in the optative mood as what they might become, describes precisely the workings of Gunn's poem.

Irigaray writes how femininity is not represented as itself under a Freudian regime. Homosexuality, too, is not represented as itself under the discursive regimes under which it falls, including Irigaray's own philosophico-psychoanalytic one. In present conditions, however, the immediate problem lies in gay representation. And here it is not how we might deconstruct ourselves that is the problem, but rather how we avoid becoming subject to misrepresentations, or to simple deletion. The publicity for a showing of *Edward II* at the Edinburgh Filmhouse included this blurb:

This adaptation of Marlowe's tragedy becomes one of Derek Jarman's most perfect and more personal films. The play, written around 1592, was at once a thriller of love, jealousy, murder and the killing of a king; and a series of reflections on universal themes – the corruption *of* power and *through* power, and the notion of social responsibility. Jarman retains the thriller elements, and enlarges the scope of Marlowe's wider reflections by demonstrating graphically their relevance to the present.

> The performances are intense and wonderful, with Steven Waddington as Edward and Tilda Swinton as his chill vampire queen.[48]

It would hardly seem possible, but this manages not to mention homosexuality. In a familiar gesture of avoidance, the mainspring of the action is deleted in a blur of platitudes.

If homosexuality is problematic because dominant discourses misrepresent, avoid and silence it, then the two approaches I have touched on here may be used to counter this: the investigation of homosexuality in history (with all its problems of naming something that is differently there with words which may be anachronistic and distorting); and the creation of cultural images that give us the detail of our lives with which, if we wished, we could then name ourselves.

Notes

I would like to thank Diana Collecott, Derek Duncan and especially Gareth Roberts for their help.

1 On the relations between feminism and male homosexuality, see Gisela T. Kaplan and Lesley J. Rogers, 'The Definition of Male and Female: Biological Reductionism and the Sanctions of Normality', in *Feminist Knowledge: Critique and Construct*, ed. Sneja Gunew (London and New York: Routledge, 1990), pp. 205–28; and Jonathan Dollimore, *Sexual Dissidence: Augustine to Wilde, Freud to Foucault* (Oxford: Clarendon Press, 1991).
2 Jane Gallop, *Thinking Through the Body* (New York: Columbia University Press, 1988), p. 110.
3 Caroline Ramazanoglu, *Feminism and the Contradictions of Oppression* (London and New York: Routledge, 1989), p. 165.
4 Dollimore, *Sexual Dissidence*, p. 30.
5 In Luce Irigaray, *Speculum of the Other Woman*, trans. Gillian C. Gill (Ithaca, NY: Cornell University Press, 1985; first publ. in French 1974), pp. 13–129.
6 *ibid.*, p. 49.
7 Margaret Whitford, *Luce Irigaray: Philosophy in the Feminine* (London and New York: Routledge, 1991), p. 85.
8 *ibid.*, p. 84.
9 Irigaray, *Speculum*, p. 79.
10 Recent surveys of gay history include *The Gay Past: A Collection of Historical Essays*, ed. S.J. Licata and R.P. Petersen (New York: Harrington Park Press, 1985); *Hidden from History: Reclaiming the Gay and Lesbian Past*, ed. Martin Duberman, Martha Vicinus and George Chauncey Jnr (Harmondsworth: Penguin, 1991); David F. Greenberg, *The Construction of Homosexuality* (Chicago: University of Chicago Press, 1988).
11 Irigaray, *Speculum*, p. 26.
12 The term appears in the essay 'Women on the market', in *This Sex Which Is Not One*, trans. Catherine Porter (Ithaca, NY: Cornell University Press, 1985; first publ. in French 1977), p. 171.
13 Irigaray, *This Sex*, p. 172: 'Reigning everywhere, although prohibited in practice, hom(m)osexuality is played out through the bodies of women, matter, or sign, and heterosexuality has been up to now just an alibi for the smooth workings of man's relations with himself, of relations among men.'

14 *ibid.*, p. 193.

15 Whitford, *Luce Irigaray*, p. 104.

16 Femininity and male homosexuality do not have analagous positions and functions in Irigaray's discourse. The relationship between femininity and masculinity is one of Otherness, in which two different modes of experience face each other as different, and her critique is that the masculine term dominates and deletes the feminine. Her ideal is for women to recognise and articulate their side of sexual difference, then for an exchange between the sexes to take place on equal terms. Male homosexuality is accorded no place on the same level as male heterosexuality and femininity. For Irigaray it is the repressed content of male heterosexuality, and becomes its unconscious. It could therefore have no direct expression as itself, and ideally would presumably have to disappear into a new, different configuration of (heterosexual) masculinity. One problem in Irigaray's thinking, then, is that she suggests on the one hand the provisional nature of sexual identities, and on the other the essential homosexual nature of masculinity.

17 Irigaray, *Speculum*, p. 101.

18 Mandy Merck, 'Difference and its Discontents', *Screen* 28, 1 (1987): 2–9, observes that for sexual difference theorists 'homosexuality can only be thought as a disavowal of difference. No non-genital differences (of race, class, age, etc.) can signify such total Otherness, no genitally similar object can be legitimately eroticized' (pp. 5–6). For an account of how the male–female gender system might have come into being, see Salvatore Cucchiari, 'The Gender Revolution and the Transition from Bisexual Horde to Patrilocal Band: The Origins of Gender Hierarchy', in *Sexual Meanings: The Cultural Construction of Gender and Sexuality*, ed. S.B. Ortner and H. Whitehead (Cambridge: Cambridge University Press, 1981), pp. 31–79.

19 Dollimore, *Sexual Dissidence*, p. 250.

20 *ibid.*, ch. 17, 'Homophobia (2): Theories of Sexual Difference'.

21 Judith Butler, *Gender Trouble: Feminism and the Subversion of Identity* (New York and London: Routledge, 1990), p. 13.

22 Jonathan Rutherford, 'Who's That Man', in *Male Order: Unwrapping Masculinity*, ed. Rowena Chapman and Jonathan Rutherford (London: Lawrence & Wishart, 1988), pp. 21–67 (p. 59).

23 Kiki Amsberg and Aafke Steenhuis, 'An Interview with Luce Irigaray', *Hecate* 9, 1–2 (1983): 192–202 (201).

24 *ibid.*, p. 197.

25 *ibid.*, p. 199.

26 *ibid.*, p. 199.

27 Whitford, *Luce Irigaray*, makes the strongest case she can for Irigaray's acceptance of lesbian relationships: 'one should keep in mind as a horizon that the sexual difference has to be rearticulated within the symbolic for any radical change to take place; this would be true whether one is homosexual or heterosexual' (p. 154); and she interprets Irigaray as not implying that 'heterosexuality is superior to homosexuality as a practice, since the fertility Irigaray is describing is symbolic, "of the spirit"; women or men together could merge in this creative way' (p. 167; see also p. 104). It seems, though, that Irigaray has nothing positive to say directly about male homosexuality.

28 Quoted by James Parks in *The Observer*, 15 March 1992; he attributes blame for the incident neither to 'the public's muddled moral attitudes . . . [nor] . . . policemen . . . the law . . . the tabloids . . . [but] [j]ust the emotional ignorance bred into Englishmen over many generations'.

29 Simon Hoggart, *The Observer*, 15 March 1992:24.

30 Michel Foucault, *The History of Sexuality, Volume One: An Introduction*, trans. Robert Hurley (Harmondsworth: Penguin, 1981), p. 101.

31 Alan Bray, *Homosexuality in Renaissance England* (London: Gay Men's Press, 1982), p. 25.

32 *ibid.*, p. 43.

33 According to Kathleen Martindale, Irigaray, in her utopian writing, 'seems to be speaking "as if"'. She writes in the optative mood, about a world that is not yet in existence': 'On the Ethics of "Voice" in Feminist Literary Criticism', *Documentation sur la recherche féministe/Resources for feminist research* 16, 3 (1987): 16–19 (18). Irigaray writes her versions of what a discursive economy with a female morphology might be. This is not a discourse of literal truth but, rather, a projection into language of one possible way of *imagining differently* women's experience, to be read by women (and men too?) to effect a change in the ways in which they can imagine themselves. It is poetic writing, using language in ways which are beyond prevailing linguistic codes and common understanding, and projecting imaginary states in which the reader may recognise something which does not yet exist, but might.

34 Christopher Marlowe, *Complete Plays and Poems*, ed. E.D. Pendry and J.C. Maxwell (London, Melbourne and Toronto: Dent, 1976). All further quotations appear parenthetically in the text.

35 See Giovanni Dall'Orto, ' "Socratic Love" as a Disguise for Same-Sex Love in the Italian Renaissance', in *The Pursuit of Sodomy: Male Homosexuality in Renaissance and Enlightenment Europe*, ed. K. Gerard and G. Hekma (New York and London: Harrington Park Press, 1989), pp. 33–65.

36 Jonathan Goldberg, in *Sodometries: Renaissance Texts, Modern Sexualities* (Stanford, CA: Stanford University Press, 1992), discusses what he calls this 'extraordinary moment in the play' (pp. 117–19).

37 Armistead Maupin, *More Tales of the City* (London: Corgi, 1984; 1st publ. 1980), pp. 7–8.

38 Alan Bray discusses the play in terms of friendship in 'Homosexuality and the Signs of Male Friendship in Elizabethan England', *History Workshop* 29 (1990): 1–19.

39 Bray argues that it was only in the last quarter of the seventeenth century that male homosexuality first appeared 'as the distinguishing characteristic of a separate, sexually nonconformist culture': *Homosexuality in Renaissance England*, p. 112. For other discussions of male homosexuality's emergence into culture, see *The Pursuit of Sodomy*, ed. Gerard and Hekma; and Bruce R. Smith, *Homosexual Desire in Shakespeare's England: A Cultural Poetics* (Chicago and London: University of Chicago Press, 1991).

40 *Oxford English Dictionary*, 2nd edn (Oxford: Clarendon Press, 1989), 'sex', sb.3a.

41 John Donne, *The Elegies, and the Songs and Sonnets*, ed. Helen Gardner (Oxford: Clarendon Press, 1965), pp. 59–61.

42 Derek Jarman gives an account of his film in *Queer Edward II* (London: BFI Publishing, 1991).

43 *Oxford English Dictionary*, 'phenomenon', sb.1a.

44 Amsberg and Steenhuis, 'An Interview', p. 199.

45 Thom Gunn, *The Man with Night Sweats* (London and Boston, MA: Faber & Faber, 1992), p. 3, 'The Hug'.

46 The words of the Local Government (Amendment) Act 1988, Section 28, quoted and discussed by Simon Watney, are '(1) A local authority shall not (a) intentionally promote homosexuality or publish material with the intent of promoting homosexuality; (b) promote the teaching in any maintained school of the acceptability of homosexuality as a pretended family relationship': Watney, 'School's Out', in *Inside/Out: Lesbian Theories, Gay Theories*, ed. Diana Fuss (New York and London: Routledge, 1991), pp. 387–401 (p. 388).

47 Gunn, *The Man with Night Sweats*, pp. 84–5.

48 'Edinburgh Filmfest Notes', in *Edinburgh Filmhouse Programme*, January 1992.

Part II

Epistemologies

Chapter 5

Unseating the Philosopher-Knight

Jane Moore

In its maneuvers distance strips the lady of her identity and unseats the philosopher-knight.[1]

What is the relationship between knowledge, style and sexual difference? I wish to address this question in the light of the return by some feminists to an essentialist theory of sexual difference, which can be seen as an explicit attempt to counter the anti-essentialism of much male French theory that has brought about a vast questioning and overturning of the privileged concepts of Western philosophy: 'Man, the Subject, Truth, History, Meaning'.[2] These feminists have argued that the problematisation of truth, the subject, or any other of the essentialising concepts that underline the history of patriarchal thought, has had the paradoxical effect of reproducing the impossibility of a female knowing subject. In this respect, it has been suggested that the de-essentialising drift of continental philosophy has led to the production of a new masculinist discourse, in which women continue to be invisible, and in which the feminist project to specify the truth of sexual inequality is discounted as an impossibility because it rests on those empiricist and rationalist modes of knowing which French theory consistently undermines.

Jacques Derrida's short work *Spurs: Nietzsche's Styles* has been targeted as an exemplary instance of the dangerous effects of French theory on feminism's health. Focusing in particular on the text's inscription of the signifier, woman, as a metaphor for undecidability in writing, a symbol of non-truth, it has been argued that the effect is to produce a theory of knowledge that declares itself gender-neutral but actually allows the male philosopher to use woman as an instrument of his self-assertion. *Spurs* will also be the focal text of this essay. However, I wish to argue, against the general insistence on its antifeminist message, that the text is not inimical to feminism. As part of this argument, in the final section I place alongside *Spurs* the interpretation given by the contemporary critic Gary Kelly of Mary Wollstonecraft's key Enlightenment feminist text *Vindication of the Rights of Woman* (1792).[3] Admittedly, Wollstonecraft and Derrida are poles apart, and I bring their texts together here not with the intention of eliding the differences which separate them, but in the hope that the coupling will enable me to give a reading of *Spurs* which releases it from the charge of antifeminism, and also to produce an interpretation of *Vindication* that allows a rethinking of Enlightenment feminism as something other than the description given in *Spurs*, where it is alleged that 'Feminism is nothing but the operation of a woman who aspires to be like a man' (*Spurs*, p. 65).

Such a blatantly anachronistic coupling of texts undoubtedly calls for further qualification. I do suggest that *Spurs* and *Vindication* share a way of reading which pushes the internal logic of sexist philosophies to the limit, to the point of collapse, and that the result is the unseating of so many philosopher-knights. Nevertheless, the argument is not that Mary Wollstonecraft somehow anticipated a deconstructive reading practice – an argument that would lead straight back to the author and ground meaning within a humanist frame of reference; rather, it is that by reading *Vindication* in the shadow of *Spurs*'s own textual practice, it is possible to recognise, in Wollstonecraft's readings of male-biased philosophy, a mode of Enlightenment feminism that is very different from the description of feminism given in *Spurs*.

Of course, this is not to claim that *Spurs* and *Vindication* declare a common project. On the contrary, *Spurs* renounces truth in the name of style, while *Vindication* denounces style in the name of truth. Before turning to Wollstonecraft's writing, however, I wish to expand on the readings of *Spurs* as an antifeminist text, and then proceed to discuss at some length the relationship of the text to the contemporary debate on essentialism, and the implications of this debate for the separate but related questions of style and knowledge.

The Feminist Spur

The most sceptical readers of *Spurs* have tended to be those theorists (mainly North American, but also some British) who heard something friendly to feminism in poststructuralism's proposition that meanings are produced in culture, not rooted in nature, but remained troubled by the dominance within poststructuralism of male, antifeminist voices.[4] Jane Gallop, Mary Jacobus and Stephen Heath, whose skilled interpretations of French theory did much to explain and popularise its difficult concepts for British and American readers, have none the less consistently criticised Derrida for what is taken as 'his' blind rejection of feminism.[5] Jane Gallop, for example, has argued that 'In *Spurs*, Jacques Derrida celebrates Nietzsche's "femininity" while attacking the feminists' "masculinity." This male champion of the attack on the phallus is still too busy attacking feminists for being phallic. Being anti-phallic becomes the new phallus, which women come up lacking once again.'[6]

In recent years, the feminist suspicion towards *Spurs* has increased in intensity. In her book *Gynesis*, published in 1985, Alice Jardine takes Gallop's criticism to the point where it becomes the basis for charging Derrida with all but reproducing the misogynist assumptions of traditional philosophy. Referring at one point to the 'Derridean pornosophical wink',[7] Jardine argues that Derrida's inscription of the 'hymen' and 'invagination' as privileged metaphors for undecidability in writing reproduces some 'very traditional, recognizable images and destinies of women', and she concludes her discussion of Derridean theory with the suggestion, phrased as a question, that his 'genderization' of the reading and writing processes is just another example of the male appropriation of the female body:

> Is this merely a question of a new ruse of reason, a kind of 'seducing' of feminist discourse; an attempt to render feminist discourse seductive (to men)? Might there be a new kind of desire on the part of (Modern) Man to occupy all positions at once (among women, among texts?) Are we here only brushing up against a new version of an old male fantasy: that of escaping the laws of the fathers through the independent and at the same time dependent female? Are men projecting their own 'divisions' onto their primordial interlocutors – women? Do they hope to find a way of depersonalizing sexual identity while maintaining the amorous relationship through women?[8]

While Jardine phrases her criticisms precisely as questions, one of Derrida's most recent antagonists, Rosi Braidotti, is not nearly so tentative. On the contrary, she boldly declares: 'Derrida's anti-feminism is so well expressed and so explicitly admitted that it does not warrant long discussion; he has explained his position at length in several interventions, particularly in the United States.'[9] Braidotti does not, however, leave matters here. She goes on to substantiate her charge against Derrida within a wider analysis of the relationship between feminist theory and French thought that features the same male names as Jardine's *Gynesis* – Descartes, Derrida, Deleuze, Foucault, Lacan, Lyotard – but offers a far more negative evaluation.

Jardine does argue strongly in *Gynesis* that (North American) feminism, with its humanist concentration on the essential sexuality of the female person, author or fictional character, and its Enlightenment belief in the grand narrative of emancipation, is precisely an impossibility of a postmodern condition. But while she regrets this, she also suggests that the notion in male French theory of woman as a signifier of all that is unintelligible within the limits of Western philosophy opens out a potential space for resisting patriarchal truth. She coins the neologism 'gynesis' to designate that space, 'coded as *feminine*, as *woman*' (original emphasis), over which the male master-narratives are losing control.[10]

Braidotti, however, firmly insists on the incompatibility of French theory and feminism. Her argument is that far from opening up the options for resistance to patriarchy, there is a very real danger that gynesis, the transformation of woman into a de-sexualised textual space, is contributing to the renewal of a philosophical discourse from which women continue paradoxically to be excluded. On the basis of this reservation, she proposes a new feminist project that would anchor discussions of sexual difference in the material reality of the sexed body – would take as its starting point 'the refusal to disembody sexual difference into a new allegedly postmodern anti-essentialist subject, and the will to re-connect the whole debate on difference to the bodily existence and experience of women.'[11]

To the extent that Braidotti urges us to *begin* thinking about sexual difference from the body, not from an analysis of the positions it has historically occupied in the symbolic order of language and culture, her thesis implies the possibility of an originary, pre-cultural, essential sexuality. However, she goes on to stress that the feminist project to redefine the subject as essentially sexed is *not* a return to the old, patriarchal insistence on the irreducibility of sexual difference, nor is it a straightforward rejection of poststructuralism's insistence on the discursive construction of subjectivity. Rather, the challenge that Braidotti asks feminism to confront consists in retaining a concept of sexual identity as the precarious, changing, and radically contradictory effect of the subject's entry into the symbolic order, while also 'defending the specificity of the female subject as a theoretical, libidinal and ethical political agent'.[12]

Braidotti's rethinking of essentialism as a concept that feminism needs to take seriously, not pejoratively, is confusing. Certainly the sexed body signifies, and of course it is a material being that is both acted upon and acts out meaning, often apparently autonomously of the conscious mind. It is not clear to me, though, why Braidotti urges that it is necessary to retain a concept of essence in order to define and defend the specificity of real women's speech and actions. Moreover, if feminism is committed to changing social and sexual relations, as well as theories of knowledge, then it is surely at the level of culture – understood, that is, not so much as nature's binary opposite but as the place where nature's ultimately unpresentable essences are represented, and thus acquire meaning – that feminists must intervene. Moreover, there is a danger that the revindication of essence in the name of a new feminist materialism risks sacrificing the enigma of sexuality, reducing the sexual self to a purely material category whose opaque but transcendent truth is there to be discovered under the multiple overlapping layers of culture, language, history.

It is these questions and doubts about Braidotti's work that lead me to return to *Spurs*, a text that displaces all forms of essentialism without discarding the body as a signifier of sexual difference, and rehearse the feminist objections to it: for what is at issue in the feminists' disagreement with *Spurs* is not just a quarrel over one man's alleged rejection of the project of Enlightenment feminism but, rather, a philosophical and political debate over the concept of the author; over the status and definition of truth, especially in its relation to Enlightenment forms of feminism; over the relationship between style, knowledge and sexual difference; over the concept of essence itself.

The Question of Style

Spurs is not clear about the meaning of the 'feminism' it invokes: it speaks vaguely of an Enlightenment commitment to discovering the truth of woman.

Equally troubling, however, is the way in which feminist commentators – even arch-poststructuralists such as Jane Gallop – have muddied distinctions between Derrida and Nietzsche, and persistently blamed Derrida for references to feminism made in *Spurs*, when the attribution of these remarks is in fact uncertain. I wish to propose that the treatment of the author, Derrida, in feminist readings of *Spurs* is centrally linked both to Braidotti's defence of essentialism and to Jardine's and Gallop's suspicion that the textualisation of the concept, woman, in *Spurs* is a straightforward repetition of man's constant desire to appropriate woman's body for his own philosophical and sexual ends.

From its beginning, in its styles, which are at least double (Nietzsche's and Derrida's), *Spurs* brings forward the concept of the author as an issue. As numerous readers of the text have observed, it is virtually impossible to demarcate 'Derrida's' commentary from 'Nietzsche's' text. The commentary so closely follows the Nietzschean narrative – miming and mimicking its style; pursuing and repeating its propositions; sometimes within quotation marks, thus signalling an ironic distance, sometimes not – that it is impossible to attribute a single signature to the text. In instances when antifeminist statements are made, this question of authorship has been seen by feminist readers as a problem to be solved.

Alice Jardine, for example, begins her reading of *Spurs* with the statement: 'Any attempt to summarize the Derridean "positions" as to "woman" in *Spurs* and Nietzsche would be doomed to failure.'[13] Yet she goes on to argue that since it is precisely the question of *Derrida's* inscription of 'woman' as a textual effect in *Spurs* that interests the feminist reader, she will attempt to 'follow, very metonymically, a certain string of attributes predicating "woman", that is writing, in *Spurs*'.[14] What happens in the process, however, is that these attributes of 'woman', of writing, are in turn attributed directly to Derrida. The result is to reclaim the author as the single essence or source of textual meaning. An example is Jardine's reading of the following passage from *Spurs*:

> On the other side of the passage is found Nietzsche's indictment of feminism, of the 'eternal womanly,' of the 'woman in itself.' Condemned here in all their 'bad taste' are Mme. Roland, Mme. de Staël and M. George Sand. (*Spurs*, p. 103)

> [et le réquisitoire contre le féminisme, l'"éternel féminin', la 'femme en soi', Mme Roland, Mme de Staël, M. George Sand, leur 'mauvais goût'. (*Spurs*, p. 103)]

This passage is typical of the style of *Spurs* in so far as it exemplifies the difficulty the reader has in defining the status of Derrida's commentary on Nietzsche's text. Is it a straightforward report on Nietzsche's condemnation of feminists, or is Derrida actively participating in and condoning Nietzsche's antifeminism? The syntax of the passage withholds the possibility of giving a straightforward answer to this question. In the French version the difficulty is even greater. Because of the interminably long sentences, which defy all prescriptions for 'good style', the English translation is forced to fabricate sentences which do not exist in the French text. Where the English text names Nietzsche, though not Derrida, the French version names neither.

Yet when Jardine reads these passages, she gives a version of the text which firmly situates both Nietzsche and Derrida as the authors of antifeminism:

> Derrida adds that all 'feminists' – 'Mme. Roland, Mme. de Staël, M. [Monsieur] George Sand [Nietzsche adds George Eliot]' – are 'rightfully chastised' by Nietzsche for their 'bad taste.' (*Spurs*, p. 103)[15]

The page number that Jardine gives is to the bilingual edition of *Spurs*, translated by Barbara Harlow. Yet there is no reference in either the French or the English version to support Jardine's statement, which looks like a quotation, that 'Derrida adds that all "feminists" . . . are "rightfully chastised" by Nietzsche'.

I wish to suggest that Jardine's attribution of Nietzsche's antifeminist statements to Derrida goes against the grain of the text's anti-essentialist styles, and effectively recuperates it within a humanist reading. In other words, Jardine's interpretation of this passage as a piece of unmitigated antifeminism is silently but firmly influenced by recourse to the 'truth' of Derrida's male sex. It would be crude to accuse Jardine of reading the author, not the text. Nevertheless, this is what seems to be happening here.

However – and this may seem paradoxical – I do not want to suggest that Derrida's sexual identity is irrelevant to a reading of *Spurs*. Nor would I want to maintain that the style of *Spurs* is unsexed, or that Derrida writes like a woman. On the contrary, the images that *Spurs* uses to describe the philosophical project are unremittingly sexual; they are sexed from a male perspective, and appear sexist from the feminist one – a point to which I shall return in a moment. But there is a distinction to be to drawn between seizing on Derrida's sex as evidence of antifeminism (which is what I think Jardine does in the example given above) and acknowledging – to paraphrase a point made by Gayatri Spivak – that because writing is caught within the metaphysical or phallogocentric limit, a male author can problematise, but not fully disown, his status as subject.[16]

On the question of the sexual imagery of *Spurs*, the distinction drawn above becomes crucial and has quite specific implications for the debate on essentialism. There are two sets of sexed images running throughout *Spurs*. One set connotes masculine attributes of aggression, self-assertion, arrogance – and anxiety. These images are generally invoked to describe the project of the philosopher-knight, who is introduced in the text as a caricature of the Enlightenment philosopher's commitment to getting at Truth. And, in so far as Enlightenment feminism is seen to share in the truth-seeking project, the knight's qualities are also extended to women. Hence the sentences to which contemporary feminist critics have consistently objected:

> And in truth, they too are men, those women feminists so derided by Nietzsche. Feminism is nothing but the operation of a woman who aspires to be like a man. And in order to resemble the masculine dogmatic philosopher, this woman lays claim – just as much claim as he – to truth, science and objectivity in all their castrated delusions of virility. Feminism too seeks to castrate. It wants a castrated woman. Gone the style. (*Spurs*, p. 65)

The other set of images connote attributes that are associated with woman: with metaphors of the feminine, and with a sexed female body. In picking up on bodily images, such as the 'hymen' – or, more precisely, the 'hymen's graphic' – *Spurs* alludes to the lasting purchase that the female sexed body has on determining men's understanding of woman: 'in so far as woman has meant in patriarchal writing the unknown, the dark continent, all that is unintelligible within the limits of Western philosophy'.[17] The 'hymen' is thus invoked in *Spurs* in recognition of the strength of the body's hold on shaping and maintaining the meaning of woman in the history of Western philosophy. Yet crucially, while on the one hand the inscription of the 'hymen' in *Spurs* acknowledges patriarchal history's general insistence on the existence of essentially sexed subjects, on the other hand it testifies to the impossibility of tracing back to the body the truth of sexual difference. In this respect it is notable that *Spurs* invokes not the 'hymen' itself, but the 'hymen's graphic'. This image works well, because it simultaneously acknowledges the existence of the 'hymen' and hints at the impossibility of knowing its essence in representation. In so far as it is invisible to the naked eye, the hymen as an internal sexual organ is unpresentable in its essence in representation; and this, I think, is why *Spurs* proposes that 'the hymen's graphic [is] that of the pharmakon, without itself being reduced to it'; thus it is inscribed in Nietzsche's text as a signifier of non-truth which 'describes a margin where the control over meaning or code is without recourse, [which] poses the limit to the relevance of the hermeneutic or systematic question' (*Spurs*, p. 99).

The question of truth in *Spurs* is never far from the question of woman. *Spurs* introduces the figure of the philosopher-knight to show how, in the history of Western philosophy, the drive for knowledge, and for truth, cannot be divorced from the desire to master the truth of woman. The question that continually haunts the knight is the unanswerable one: 'what is woman?' (*Spurs*, p. 71). *Spurs* mocks the knight's attempts to find the truth of woman:

> the credulous and dogmatic philosopher who *believes* in the truth that is woman, who believes in truth just as he believes in woman, this philosopher has understood nothing. He has understood nothing of truth, nor anything of woman. Because, indeed, if woman *is* truth, *she* at least knows that there is no truth, that truth has no place here and that no one has a place for truth. And she is woman precisely because she herself does not believe in truth itself, because she does not believe in what she is, in what she is believed to be, in what she thus is not.
>
> In its maneuvers distance strips the lady of her identity and unseats the philosopher-knight. (*Spurs*, p. 53, original emphasis)

Feminist readers of this passage have responded with the accusation that the placing of woman as 'non-truth' does not so much unseat the knight as reaffirm his position of authority. Referring directly to this moment in the text, Rosi Braidotti argues:

> in this instance, the feminine is used by the (male) thinker so as to avoid confronting the problem of the reality of women and their relation to truth, both of which have

been declared fluid and indefinable. What is more, this inexpressibility is raised to the status of absolute truth: not only is woman indefinable, but she becomes besides the sign of unrepresentability itself; definitively other than the system of truth. Derrida can therefore make the enunciation of truth a typically masculine 'habit': it is man who believes in woman as in truth.[18]

Braidotti suggests, then, that if Derrida knocks one knight (the Enlightenment philosopher) off his horse, he quickly replaces him with another (the deconstructionist philosopher). The philosopher of deconstruction, no less than the 'credulous dogmatic' man, is obsessed with the question 'what is woman?' And it is his answer, 'There is no such thing as the essence of woman' (*Spurs*, p. 51), that leads Braidotti to propose that if women are to retain a political and sexual identity in the face of the Derridean onslaught, it is necessary to revindicate essentialism as an indispensable feminist strategy in the 1990s.

Braidotti's criticism of *Spurs* raises two issues: the issue of style and the issue of truth. To take the question of style first. The use of the 'hymen' by a male writer is clearly not without sexual connotations, implying the inevitability of acts of appropriation, penetration, mastery. It is important, however, to remember that *Spurs* does not repeat the old move of locating the truth of woman in her essence, in her essential organs. On the contrary, as Derrida insists in the interview 'Choreographies': 'Anything constituting the value of existence is foreign to the "hymen."'[19] Moreover, ' "hymen" and "invagination" . . . no longer simply designate figures for the feminine body. They no longer do so, that is, assuming that one knows for certain what a feminine or masculine body is, and assuming that anatomy is in this instance the final recourse.'[20]

On the basis of these remarks – and recalling Derrida's countless reminders that he does not believe in the possibility of simply escaping metaphysics[21] – I want to propose that the 'hymen' is inscribed in *Spurs* precisely in order to call into question the metaphysics of presence and of essence, and also to draw attention to the extent to which it is impossible to think about sexual difference without recourse to notions of sexual essence. I suggest, then, that the use of the 'hymen' is at once a reminder of Derrida's male subject status as one who has inherited a history of metaphysical assumptions about sexual identity, and a problematisation of man's and woman's faith (*pace* Braidotti) in the truth of an essential sexual difference. I would add that to use heavily sexualised images and turn them against the discourse that produced them is a project that should not be confused with aiming to transcend the phallogocentric tradition, and to find a new truth of woman.

Braidotti's point, however, is focused precisely on a demand for truth. She notes – and is unhappy about – the sexual connotations implied by a male philosopher's use of the 'hymen', but the crux of her disagreement is that the 'hymen' does constitute or stand in for a sexual truth, and Derrida can thus be said to be offering a deconstructive trope that appears sexually to neutralise the language of knowledge, but effectively keeps the masculine principle intact. She writes: 'The most striking contemporary example of metaphorization of the feminine with a view better to assimilate it to a falsely neutral mode of thinking is the Derridean idea of the becoming-woman of philosophy.'[22]

Braidotti's objection draws the debate on essentialism to our attention again. Her defence of essentialism is based on the premise that 'in order to make sexual difference operative as a political option, feminist theoreticians should re-connect the feminine to the bodily sexed reality, refusing the separation of the empirical from the symbolic, or of the material from the discursive, or of sex from gender'.[23] It strikes me that Braidotti's insistence on not separating the empirical from the symbolic is shared by Derrida – nowhere more so than in the refusal to separate the physical connotations of the 'hymen' which, I would suggest, are too redolent of sex to be forgotten by the majority of readers, even while Derrida declares that 'Anything constituting the value of existence is foreign to the "hymen";[24] hence the constant enclosure of 'hymen' within quotation marks. In other words, I find in Derrida's use of 'hymen' evidence of a double strategy, which acknowledges the strong empiricist sway on contemporary thought and simultaneously questions empiricism's recourse to essentialist truths which would permanently fix the meaning of the body and sexual difference.

I am suggesting, then, that to some degree – and at least in so far as an acknowledgement of the material existence of the body is required – *Spurs* performs what Braidotti asks feminists to do, *but does so without needing a concept of essence*. Additionally, I would argue that the feminist project to attain female equality and women's rights does not need a concept of essence. On the contrary, to ground sexual difference in essence is surely to block change – it is to fix the meaning of woman and man in a transcultural and transhistorical truth. Moreover, the histories feminism tells are of changes in the definition of woman, and in the *representation* of sexuality which have brought about political changes, however limited they be. Mary Wollstonecraft's *Vindication of the Rights of Woman*, for example, seems to me to be a text that recognises that representations or styles of sexual difference cannot be divorced from political claims for sexual equality, and from claims to truth, and it is to this text that I now want to turn. I do not do so innocently: if I have a criticism of *Spurs*, it is not that the text is antifeminist but, rather, that it closes off the Enlightenment as a single project and, in consequence, passes over what – from the perspective of *Spurs* – is the remarkably heightened awareness of the question of style that Enlightenment feminist texts display.

Unseating the Philosopher-Knight

Published towards the end of a century in which the various Enlightenment movements of social and cultural criticism based on rationalism and materialism had culminated in the French and American declarations of the universal 'rights of man', Mary Wollstonecraft's *Vindication of the Rights of Woman* is a text firmly based in the English Enlightenment tradition of social critique. It is also, of course, one that derives its claims to female equality and women's rights from an Enlightenment faith in reason and truth.

But what is striking about Wollstonecraft's text from the perspective of the contemporary debate over the relationship between style and truth is how, in the process of seizing rights for women out of their point of origin in a discourse that privileged Man, the text brings back the relationship between gender and language as a central concern. Moreover, while the text seeks a place for women within the symbolic order of reason and rights, it does not achieve this aim at the expense of negating sexual difference, which is inscribed in it as a difference of style. Gary Kelly makes this argument at length in *Revolutionary Feminism*, which offers a convincing case for reading Wollstonecraft's *Vindication* as a transformative Enlightenment text and an experiment in feminist writing. He observes how Wollstonecraft

> avoids an objective, detached, learned, syllogistic or sarcastic and sharply polemical style that could be considered as that which a man would use. That could 'unsex' her, undermining her rhetorical authority. But she also avoids what would be con-sidered as a woman's belletristic, domestic, personal style and relative lack of formal argument. That could undermine her claim that women given the same education, culture and rights as men would be able to take an equal if different role in culture and society with men.[25]

Kelly goes on to list the qualities that make up Wollstonecraft's experimental style and indicate its difference from conventional philosophical treatises of the day. He singles out for attention the way the text's numerous personal modes of address, used to indicate immediacy, expressivity and intensity, are imbricated with a rational, general, abstract and philosophical method.[26] Of particular interest is his suggestion that this combination of styles, which can be seen as 'the only resources available to a woman in a society that systematically denies her intellectual equality, and therefore moral, professional and civic equality',[27] gives rise to a rhetorical strategy that uses patriarchal definitions of feminine writing to turn on and question the patriarchal order that produced them. As Kelly puts it: 'By arguing against women's oppression with discursive materials that betoken that oppression she [Wollstonecraft] indicates how the discursive order reproducing oppression can be broken.'[28]

This reading strategy, used by Wollstonecraft to transform or dethrone the reasoning of her male contemporaries without thereby destroying the privileged concepts of reason and truth, is, ironically, very close to the 'double gesture' that defines the style with which Derrida unhinges philosophical verities. Asked to describe his style in *Positions*, Derrida replies:

> I try to keep myself at the *limit* of philosophical discourse. I say limit and not death, for I do not at all believe in what today is so easily called the death of philosophy (nor, moreover, in the simple death of whatever – the book, man, or god, especially since, as we all know, what is dead wields a very specific power).[29]

In the light of Derrida's description of a deconstructive textual practice and Kelly's observations about Wollstonecraft's styles, I would like to propose a reading of Enlightenment feminism which would try to replace the interpretation of its project as a single drive towards discovering the truth with another reading, one whose possibilities have been opened up precisely by a Derridean style of reading, but one which is occluded in *Spurs*. Such a reading would thus attempt not so much to situate styles in opposition to truth, theory in opposition to practice, essence in opposition to representation. Nor would it – however paradoxical this may seem – attempt to conflate an Enlightenment faith in truth with the sceptical attitude towards truth that defines a postmodern condition. Rather, the project would be to work with and between truth and styles, to treat neither as closed concepts that are fixed within separate historical moments, but to acknowledge the extent to which certain aspects of the Enlightenment (democracy, rights, emancipation) are released into the present as political interventions in time, in culture and language, not given by God or his surrogates: truth, reason, nature.[30]

This, at least, might be one way of addressing the specific feminist problematic given in both Wollstonecraft's work and in Braidotti's – how to reconcile the claim for equal rights with the acknowledgement of sexual difference (with the stress falling on difference, not opposition). And it would, perhaps, make possible the continuation of the political feminist struggle without needing to secure the demand for various forms of emancipation in the name of essentialist notions of femininity or, indeed, by the appeal to the absolute truth. It would involve, therefore, releasing truths as constantly contested and changing consequences of language, of history and styles.

Indeed, a remarkable feature of *Vindication* is its challenging engagement with contemporary cultural myths of true femininity. Focusing on culture's most revered texts, including the Bible and Shakespeare, Wollstonecraft denaturalises gender stereotypes and unseats a range of would-be knights, in particular the conduct-book writers James Fordyce and Dr Gregory, and the philosopher and novelist Jean-Jacques Rousseau. The debunking of Fordyce and Gregory is especially well done. Fordyce encouraged women to present themselves as 'gentle trusting creatures', capable of little independent action.[31] Gregory persuaded them to be mistresses of dissimulation, pretending to be of inferior intelligence among men so as to keep men's vanity intact: be ever cautious in displaying your good sense in mixed company, is Dr Gregory's advice to his daughters.[32] The work of both writers is quoted extensively in *Vindication* in a rather witty way (bringing to mind Kate Millett's treatment of D.H. Lawrence's fiction) – long extracts, quoted out of context, collapse under the weight of their own absurdity.[33]

When it comes to Rousseau, however, the critique takes on a different style. References are made throughout *Vindication* to Rousseau's novel *Émile*, published in 1762. *Émile* is a fictional treatise on education; it is the story of the ideal schooling of a young man, which includes the fantasy of a young woman's education entirely for her future husband's benefit. The text argues that women are born with an excess of sensibility, or sexuality, which makes them simultaneously vulnerable to corruption by men as well as a threat to men's hold on the social and sexual order. Here is Rousseau hypothesising on the dangers which female sexuality poses to patriarchy:

> Women so easily stir a man's senses and fan the ashes of a dying passion, that if philosophy ever succeeded in introducing this custom [sexual equality] into any unlucky country, especially if it were a warm country where more women are born than men, the men, tyrannised over by the women, would at last become their victims, and would be dragged to their death without the least chance of escape.[34]

Placing geography and climate within a libidinised, gendered economy, Rousseau reaffirms the myth of an originary rampant female sexuality which simultaneously attracts and repulses men. Moreover, this idea of woman is collapsed into the founding moment of femininity. 'Dissipation, levity, and inconstancy', Rousseau asserts, 'are faults that readily spring up from [women's] first propensities, when corrupted or perverted by too much indulgence.'[35]

But Rousseau's claim that 'female nature' is corrupted by society makes no sense when the sexual characteristics that signify women's degraded state are acquired at birth. Wollstonecraft's reading of Rousseau recognises the contradiction, and she uses it to discredit one of the consequences of his argument: to make women culpable for an unchanging, because apparently natural, inferiority. Wollstonecraft ridicules the logic of this argument, and suggests instead that the excessive sexuality attributed to women is acquired at the level of culture, not nature. In this way she makes the male-dominated culture which constructs and confines women culpable for their subordination, rather than women's actual bodies.

As a consequence, it is possible to glimpse in *Vindication* the suggestion that woman is not where man thinks she is, and does not necessarily believe in what man says she is. And to the extent that *Vindication* identifies a *distance* between man's idea of woman and woman's lived reality, it endorses Derrida's suggestion in *Spurs*: 'In its maneuvers distance strips the lady of her identity and unseats the philosopher-knight.'[36]

Notes

I am particularly grateful to Elaine Jordan at the University of Essex, whose comments on an earlier draft of this essay considerably revised my views on Enlightenment feminism. I should also like to thank the editors of this volume for their helpful comments.

1 Jacques Derrida, *Spurs: Nietzsche's Styles/Éperons: Les Styles de Nietzsche*, intro. Stefano Agosti, trans. Barbara Harlow (Chicago and London: University of Chicago Press, 1979), p. 53. All further references will be included in parentheses in the text.

2 Alice Jardine, *Gynesis: Configurations of Woman and Modernity* (Ithaca, NY and London: Cornell University Press, 1985), p. 25.

3 See Gary Kelly, *Revolutionary Feminism: The Mind and Career of Mary Wollstonecraft* (London: Macmillan, 1992).

4 Gayatri Spivak's work is a notable exception. Although they are not uncritical, her essays 'Displacement and the Discourse of Woman', in *Displacement: Derrida and After*, ed. Mark Krupnick (Bloomington: Indiana University Press, 1983), pp. 169–95; and 'Love Me, Love My Ombre Elle', *Diacritics* 14, 4 (1984): 19–36, do not accuse Derrida of antifeminism.

5 For a representative sample of criticisms of Derrida's antifeminism by poststructuralist theorists, see Alice Jardine and Paul Smith (eds), *Men in Feminism* (New York and London: Methuen, 1987), in particular Stephen Heath, 'Male Feminism' and 'Men in Feminism: Men and Feminist Theory', pp. 1–32, 41–6; and Jane Gallop, 'French Theory and the Seduction of Feminism', pp. 111–15. See also Mary Jacobus, *Reading Woman: Essays in Feminist Criticism* (London: Methuen, 1986), pp. 278–92.

6 Jane Gallop, *Thinking Through the Body* (New York: Columbia University Press, 1988), p. 100.

7 Jardine, *Gynesis*, p. 180.

8 *ibid.*, p. 207.

9 Rosi Braidotti, *Patterns of Dissonance: A Study of Women in Contemporary Philosophy*, trans. Elizabeth Guild (Oxford: Polity Press, 1991), p. 105. The allusion is to the interview with Christie V. McDonald, 'Choreographies', *Diacritics* 12 (1982): 66–76, and 'Women in the Beehive: A Seminar with Jacques Derrida', in Jardine and Smith (eds), *Men in Feminism*, pp. 189–203. Both pieces respond to feminist readings of *Spurs*. I do not read either of them as a straightforward rejection of feminism.

10 Jardine, *Gynesis*, p. 25.

11 Braidotti, 'The Politics of Ontological Difference', in Teresa Brennan (ed.), *Between Feminism and Psychoanalysis* (London: Routledge, 1989), pp. 89–105 (p. 91).

12 Braidotti, *Patterns of Dissonance*, p. 282.

13 Jardine, *Gynesis*, p. 192.

14 *ibid.*, p. 192.

15 *ibid.*, p. 197.

16 Spivak, 'Displacement and the Discourse of Woman', p. 173.

17 Catherine Belsey, 'Critical Approaches', in *Bloomsbury Guide to Women's Literature*, ed. Claire Buck (London: Bloomsbury, 1992), pp. 237–43 (p. 242).

18 Braidotti, *Patterns of Dissonance*, p. 103.

19 Derrida and McDonald, 'Choreographies', p. 75.

20 *ibid.*

21 See, for example, Jacques Derrida, *Positions*, trans. Alan Bass (London: Athlone Press, 1987), p. 17.

22 Braidotti, *Patterns of Dissonance*, p. 98.

23 Braidotti, 'The Politics of Ontological Difference', p. 93.

24 Derrida and McDonald, 'Choreographies', p. 75.

25 Kelly, *Revolutionary Feminism*, p. 108.

26 *ibid.*, p. 110.

27 *ibid.*

28 *ibid.*

29 Derrida, *Positions*, p. 6.

30 I owe this last point to a dialogue with Elaine Jordan.

31 James Fordyce, *Sermons to Young Women* (1765), cited in Wollstonecraft, *Vindication of the Rights of Woman*, in *The Works of Mary Wollstonecraft*, ed. Janet Todd and Marilyn Butler, 7 vols (London: Pickering, 1989), vol. 5, pp. 162–6.

32 John Gregory, *A Father's Legacy to his Daughters* (1774), cited in Wollstonecraft, *Vindication of the Rights of Woman*, pp. 166–70.
33 Kate Millett, *Sexual Politics* (London: Virago, 1977). For a superbly styled and quite irreverent reading of *Lady Chatterley's Lover*, see pp. 237–45.
34 Jean-Jacques Rousseau, *Émile* (1762), trans. Barbara Foxley (London: J.M. Dent, 1974), p. 322.
35 Cited in Wollstonecraft, *Vindication of the Rights of Woman*, p. 151.
36 Derrida, *Spurs*, p. 53.

Chapter 6

'Who Fancies Pakis?'

Pamella Bordes and the Problems of Exoticism in Multiracial Britain

Gargi Bhattacharyya

Cultural studies is an academic endeavour which relies upon a conception of reading as a privileged mode of understanding the world.[1] Although it is, among other things, a critique and an extension of more strictly literary education, British cultural studies has retained a large part of the method of literary criticism. The notion of reading has been extended to include non-written representation, and a variety of texts may be studied side by side, but still the activity of cultural studies remains a version of expert interpretation. Reading is how you find out about the world.

This can lead to some difficulty when the reader is implicated in the structures being read. What sort of relation to a text is demanded if you are to read yourself into the story? What if your text is, in part, a version of some section of your life? What if the project of cultural studies calls upon you to read your own autobiography? Or when the act of reading becomes indistinguishable from a telling of life story?

This is a story about being racialised and educated, and about trying to use my education to understand what it means to be racialised. It is a story about being 'black' (in the old 1980s sense of being part of a range of dark-skinned peoples who find that their social identities are constructed through a language of 'race') and 'British', and a woman, and trying to read the cultural meanings of skin and genitals at a particular time in Britain. In Britain (where I live) black people who engage in the cultural study of 'race' are often *read* anecdotally. Our authority to speak about such subjects is seen to be connected to our experience or cultural background or social positioning – the black academic is supposed to give voice to those knowledges which have been excluded and silenced. This can be exciting – suddenly just reading a few books becomes a crucial part of the fight for justice for your people – but it also has its drawbacks. If your speech is authorised by who you are, rather than by the work you have done, then insights are seen to stem from autobiography rather than from study. Unfortunately, for the black academic this can mean that no one cares how many books you have read, because your job is to talk about yourself. In this scenario, the scholarship of the black speaker is mistaken for anecdote. This means that non-racialised people can never understand the contemporary meanings of 'race' for themselves, because understanding comes from living it, not studying it. It also means that black academics who work on 'race' are never studying (even when they are), only talking about themselves. Their role is both to embody and to articulate a realm of exotic darkness for a white audience filled with desire and fear. In the manner of the reader's-wife story of men's magazines, this speech is made authoritative and pornographic in the same stroke.

In this essay I discuss this situation in which black people are seen both as the embodiment of a sexualised difference and as bearers of the incontrovertible truth of 'race'. My discussion takes place through a series of anecdotes, as a way of both staging and critiquing this practice. I am using the anecdote as a way of being explicit about the place of autobiography in contemporary criticism, particularly feminist, particularly by black women. I don't much like this tendency to resort to telling stories about yourself (or your family and friends) as a way of conducting an argument – I think that the 'see, it happened to me' genre can make dialogue impossible, freezing people into the positions of authentic voice or deferential listener without much possibility of constructive interaction. I take the recent work of Nancy K. Miller and Michele Wallace to be examples of the kind of valorising of autobiographical insight which makes me uncomfortable, because both seem to imply that understanding can stem from previously marginalised speakers coming clean and telling the truth about themselves.[2] At the same time, though, it is hard for a black person to talk about 'race' and not be read as saying, in however veiled a manner, 'see, it happened to me'. I have yet to see a mode of presentation which will protect the author from the possibility of this reading. And I know, too, that the choice of studying 'race' is somewhat overdetermined for the racialised student, so the 'see, it happened to me' must be in there somewhere. Perhaps my point is no more than to suggest that although this autobiographical input seems unavoidable, this is a problem, not something to be celebrated without examination.

However tempting it is to believe otherwise, anecdote is not experience. Anecdote, here, is a means of creating self-contained narratives out of things which happen. It is a reading and rewriting of the messiness of events, a way of selecting key components for the formation of a neat story. The point here is that I choose what to tell; access to the meaning of 'race' in this set of scenarios depends upon my proficiency as reader/narrator. The white reader cannot bypass the mediation of my 'see, it happened to me' and still get the point.

In some ways this might seem like a necessary validation of black experience – black people get to speak, and white people learn a little humility. The payoff, however, is that the construction of 'race' cannot be a subject of general analysis – people who are not themselves racialised can only listen to those who are. This means that the meanings of 'race' can be grasped only through the process of reading the autobiographical accounts of black people – this social phenomonen must be analysed through either confession or literary criticism, and a very particular and deferential literary criticism at that. This essay is a staging of this problem, an example of just how difficult it is to escape this trap.

I wanted to write this as a means of working through various suspicions I have been harbouring about the nature of cultural study and the status of reading as a method of enquiry. That said, it is also interesting to me as a version of auto-biography, and part of what I would like to discuss is how 'autobiographical' input can be negotiated in cultural understanding.

This essay is also related to a larger problem which I have been trying to work through – something like 'how useful is the category of "Otherness" to contemporary discussions of "race" in Britain?' In this I am thinking of theories of racism which are loosely based around psychoanalysis, and posit the racially disadvantaged as the necessary supplement to subject formation for the racially privileged.[3] What the introduction of a notion of the 'Other' appears to do in this situation is to extend the almost unquestionable premiss that the identity of the powerful can be constituted only in relation to those in thrall to power, so that this social manoeuvre is seen to derive from the same pre-social structures which organise the physical into the social and sensation into sexuality. The racial 'Other' which supplements white subjectivity thus takes on the status of the unspeakable upon which articulation depends, and with this racism becomes explainable in terms of the fear and fascination which accompany the dependency of the powerful. While I have some sympathies with this portrayal of racist fantasies as stemming from white anxiety, so that much of what is going on in racism is at this level of neurotic fantasy, it seems to be only a partial explanation of an element of a wider structure. Many versions of British racism would seem to stem not from a fear of the unknown but, instead, from pragmatic utilitarianism. If we are to view racism not as an unfortunate pathology, but instead as an at least semi-rational structure of power which privileges some people at the expense of others, sexual fascination need not necessarily be a part of racial dynamics. Black might mean 'disadvantaged' without being 'exotic'.

At various points, from the late 1980s onwards, I have suspected that some changes have been occurring in popular conceptions of Asian women. Having grown up in a largely white area of a notably 'multiracial' city in the Midlands, it seemed to me that in the 1970s at least, the conception of Asian women in this country was largely that of a trampled passivity. Newspapers and schools showed obvious concern about young Asian women only as victims of the apparent barbarism of the arranged marriage. Immigrants were always potentially 'illegal', and the uncertainty of this status seemed to be exemplified in state-sponsored sexual assaults on Asian women in British airports.[4] In the whole virginity-testing debacle, what became apparent was that nationality was intimately connected to a notion of proper 'Asian' sexual behaviour, as this was formulated by the British state's understanding of 'Asian' culture. Although this was some acknowledgement of the interrelation of race and sexuality in the lives of Asian women in Britain, here minority ethnicity was seen primarily as a sexual handicap. An accommodation of the identity 'Asian' was seen as an acceptance of a pre-sexual identity for women, with Westernisation offering escape into the freedom of romance and sexual activity. In this scenario 'Asianness' figures as a kind of pathological virginity for women – attractive only in its gaucheness. When I was growing up, although ethnic identity was clearly sexualised in some manner, you were not supposed to fancy pakis. Asian was not a sexy identity.

At some point in the late 1980s I began to suspect that this was no longer straightforwardly true. As the Asian community in this country became more established, 'Asian' no longer seemed to be an identity of complete alienness to the wider British public. This is not to say that racism subsided, only that the languages through which racial diversity could be understood perhaps grew more complex. This seems to be borne out in the more recent media representation of Asians in Britain – although of course, a lot has changed since the Rushdie affair and the Gulf War. It is also borne out through a series of conversations.

This is a random series of anecdotes, all in some sense autobiographical in that they stem from conversations, rather than from any reading of a written text.

The first concerns a conversation which took place in either 1988 or 1989, in which a woman I know in Leicester spoke about her workplace. The woman is white, and she worked at that time for the council housing department – as a branch of the city council, her workplace is subject to the council code of equal opportunities. In practice this seems to entail watching what you say. The incident which she recounted to me went like this: during a break my friend interrupts two colleagues talking. What they are discussing is the huge sexual appetite of Asians. (Remember that this is in a city with a population which is more than 25 per cent Asian.) As a good liberal and responsible member of the city council, my friend reminds them that this sort of talk can constitute a disciplinary offence in their workplace. 'No, it's true,' her workmates counter, 'they're all oversexed. It's the spicy food.'

My friend recounted this story as an example of how unthinking day-to-day racism is, even among those who should know better. But while I agreed with her that the remarks were shaped by racism, part of me took – and takes – pleasure in the tone of envy – particularly as this seems to be a new experience of the identity 'Asian' in Britain.

This story could be read as part of some wider trend towards the sexualisation of Asian identity, if only we had the information to chart this kind of cultural shift.

My next anecdote concerns an event which took place in summer 1989, in a pub near the Mile End Road in London. In March of that year the tabloid press had been full of the Pamella Bordes 'scandal' – which turned out to be little more than a rumour of prostitution in the House of Commons, with the added scare value of a possible Libyan connection. The affair had centred around the figure of Bordes, a young and good-looking House of Commons researcher, and the allegation that she had been sexually involved with a number of eminent men – perhaps for money, and perhaps endangering state security. Bordes's Indian origin did not seem to be particularly stressed in coverage of the story, or in its reception. That summer was very warm. People in Britain were wearing less, and talking more – there was even talk of a new British street culture, facilitated by the unfamiliar weather. The group of friends I was with were young white men and women. We all looked like students. The pub we went into was, apart from the bar staff, exclusively male and white – almost no one was sitting down. My friends and I were slightly uncomfortable in that middle-class-kids-in-a-working-class-bar sort of a way, but the only thing I actually heard any of the regulars say about our group was 'Pamella Bordes'. In this situation the invocation of some exotic sexual prowess did not seem so agreeably tinged with envy.

There was a certain oddness about this event. In the months following the fatwa against Salman Rushdie, 'Asian in Britain' had become a heightened sort of identity. This, however, was the first time I had witnessed any explicit link being made between the 'exotic beauty' Bordes and the identity of British Asian. The Rushdie affair caused a resurgence of portrayals of Asians as culturally backward and barbarically 'fundamentalist' – if anything, sex for Asians seemed even further from the agenda than it had been previously. The familiarly British sex scandal whipped up around Bordes appeared to have little connection with this newly and frighteningly vocal section of the British population. Asian seemed more the stuff of monstrousness than of titillation – or so I had thought. But 'Bordes' is a different kind of public insult from 'paki'.

I remembered both these stories recently in the course of a conversation between a group of young British Asian women, of whom I was one. The majority of the women involved were Pakistani Muslims, born and raised in this country. In the course of the conversation, one woman remarked that Asian women were now being publicly accosted by white men, which in her experience was a new and recent development – 'Even us salwar-kameez types', so that a public staging of ethnicity could no longer be relied upon as a defence against sexual advances. 'That Pamella Bordes has a lot to answer for,' she said.

At this point I started to think that it might be possible to read personal events as more than 'just' autobiography – and also that some (maybe all) types of academic endeavour contained a large autobiographical input which could not be dealt with simply through the adoption of an objective tone.

A different sort of anecdote. Some indication of my academic 'autobiography', the languages which link me to my chosen 'ethnicity' of bookreaders.

I wanted to try to make sense of the recent history of 'race' and sexuality in this country. I was particularly interested in the iconic significance of Pamella Bordes. Like a good student of contemporary culture, I went in search of documentation. This took the form of contemporary tabloid newspapers. I was not fazed by this because I felt that I knew something about popular culture,

and that it was just like reading literature really. Documentation here had little
to do with 'Truth', and far more to do with tracing what appeared to be
culturally significant. Understanding the world was both about finding and
having access to relevant artefacts and knowing how to interpret them, how to
read them in the right register. Clearly I had to inhabit the world which I was
attempting to chart if I was to know what the tabloids meant. Fortunately my
attitude towards the popular press was already shaped by a Left cultural studies
knowingness – I was familiar with the genre, and the mixture of attentiveness
and scorn which it was seen to require.[5] This is how critique works – through
this tension between involvement and distance. But we should remember that
this is a very particular type of understanding.

The Bordes story first hit the British press on Monday 13 March 1989. *Today*
carried a front-page story and colour photograph. The paper also misspelt her
name, calling her Pamella Bardes. At this point the story is a simple sex scandal –
the British public was being informed of the outrageous 'fact' that a House of
Commons researcher might also have been an expensive prostitute. *Today*
writes:

> Bardes had full security clearance at the Commons . . . and had access to sensitive
> areas.
>   No one ever checked on how she could afford to live in the flat, wear £3000
> Chanel dresses and Cartier jewellery. Even her background was a mystery. She
> claimed to have been born in India and lived in New York and Spain. That was never
> checked either. (*Today*, 13 March 1989)

Sex-workers are seen to be of an untrustworthy nature – and therefore completely incompatible with the business of government. Also there is the implication that the nation's leaders spend their time getting off with exotic women,
and that they have to pay for the privilege. What was seen as both scandalous
and laughable was that a series of influential men had required a massaging of
their egos by a beautiful young woman who was only in it for the money. The
men concerned were thus portrayed as at once sexually profligate and painfully
unattractive. Bordes, on the other hand, had the glamour of a smooth operator.
She lived the life of the jet set, moving about the world. In that her background
is described as mysterious, Bordes is not seen to be subject to the limitations of
ethnic identity. She is not part of that placed and disadvantaged community
'black in Britain'. Instead, in a more familiar model of exoticism, Bordes's
attraction is linked to her mystery.

In the early reporting of the story, much was made of the apparent obscurity
of Bordes's origins. On 13 March, the day the story broke, *Today* ran an inside
headline: 'Fooled by the Beauty from Nowhere'. On 14 March *Today* quoted
her flatmate 'and top lawyer' Carlo Colombotti:

> I met Pamella at a party about 2 years ago. I do not really know where she came
> from. . . .
>   The only thing she told me about her background was that she was a former Miss
> India and a former model.

In a country in which many white residents still seem to feel that black Britons should go back to where they came from, it is significant that Bordes's country of birth is seen to be nowhere at all. Her 'ethnic' identity is described as deriving from her experience as a model and beauty queen – 'background' becomes past employment rather than racial origin.

This erasure of a different ethnic identity, replacing it with no ethnicity at all, was taking place at a time when the repercussions of *The Satanic Verses* were making 'Asian' into a very British preoccupation with foreignness. In the *Daily Mirror* of 20 March 1989, opposite the Page Three headline 'Sexy Commons Girl Could Be a Movie Star', there is a story headed 'Rushdie Riot – Backlash as Gang Strikes at Moslems'. This recounts the violent attack on a Sheffield mosque, during which the building was daubed with the apparently disparate slogans 'Leave Rushdie in Peace' and 'Pakis Die'. Although the Rushdie affair rendered a great deal of very crude racism speakable, it also allowed public attention to be focused on questions of ethnic identity and allegiance. The religious affiliations of Britain's Asians became the crucial determinant of their suitability as British citizens – in popular representation, at least. It is presumably in relation to these concerns that *Today* reported on 16 March that when David Sullivan, editor of the *Sunday Sport* and purportedly a friend of Bordes, was asked 'if Indian-born Pamella is a Hindu, a Muslim or a Sikh, he added: "It would be fair to say she is not very religious" '. The public identity of Pamella Bordes was not seen to be articulable within the contemporary discourses of ethnicity. Pamella may have been 'Indian-born', but she seemed very definitely not to be 'British Asian'. Throughout her period of publicity Bordes was conspicuously not associated with the immigrant community which had recently become both more politicised and more openly vilified. At a time when the term 'fundamentalist' often appeared to stand in as a reference to skin tone, this is particularly remarkable – or predictable, given the difficulty in reconciling sexual titillation with denouncements of cultural backwardness.

In many ways, the press portrayal of Bordes was that of a fairly standard exoticism. She was beautiful and mysterious, desirable and manipulative. In the classic manner of exotic foreign pieces, she was dangerously unpredictable. The *Mirror* of 15 March quotes a former boyfriend:

> One minute, he said, she was a sweet young thing and her escort the envy of all other men.
> THE NEXT, SHE WAS TRANSFORMED INTO A RAGING, VINDICTIVE WOMAN – 'LIKE A LOOSE CANNON ON A DECK'.
>   He said: 'She can turn suddenly from a sweet, vivacious beauty to a vicious and vindictive woman, unable to separate fact from fantasy'.

Bordes's sexual attraction is linked to her unreadability. In the dynamics of sexual exoticism, what is desirably 'Other' is this element of the unknown, and the threat which accompanies it. The point I want to make is that this has not normally been the position occupied by Asian women in Britain. The stereotype of Asian women in this country has not consisted of this sort of fantasy, and this is as good as acknowledged in the press fiction of Pamella Bordes.

On 22 March *Today* featured a front-page 'story' of a large colour photograph of Bordes with the caption 'Pamella's Eastern Promise'. The photograph had Bordes pictured in a version of Indian show costume – neither the sari nor the salwar-kameez which are the familiar everyday clothes of many British Asian women, but still an instantly recognisable mark of staged ethnicity. This was Bordes wearing her roots as 'Other' – the 'Indianness' being displayed was Merchant–Ivory, not everyday Leicester or Bradford, and the picture called up the mythology of bejewelled village girls and pre-industrial innocence, rather than the dullness of an immigrant working class. The twist was that Bordes had pushed aside her skirt to reveal her bare legs to thigh level. The newspaper comments:

> Any other Indian girl in beautiful traditional peasant dress would show only shyness. But in this exclusive picture, Commons hooker Pamella Bordes could not resist showing off her legs. It is a calender style-shot that would have horrified her family back home in Bombay.

Pamella Bordes is seen to assume her position as sexual fetish at the expense of her Indianness. She is 'exotic' not so much because of her ethnicity as despite it. In the Britain of the late 1980s, 'Asian' was not an exciting foreignness – rather, it was all too familiar a mark of cultural difference. This difference is too knowable to be titillating – of the nature of a political dispute rather than a psychoanalytic 'Other'. Conflicting interest groups do not constitute an object of desire. Exoticism relies upon identities which are not those of any day-to-day political arena. In her media portrayal, Bordes could become fetishised in relation to her foreignness – but foreignness had to become a mark of the unfamiliar, rather than any strict reference to nationality or country of origin. The status of Asian in Britain is too everyday to serve as the exciting Other of exoticism. Some foreigners are too close to home to be fancyable.

Bordes could be made desirable because her origin was uncertainly foreign. Later her scandalousness was linked to her non-typicality as an Asian woman. 'Any other Indian girl' could not fill the role of exotic beauty in Britain at this time.

More anecdotal evidence. At the time of Bordes's fame, most people I spoke to were surprised to find out that she was Asian. Although this quickly became apparent through the references to the 'Indian-born beauty' and 'former Miss India', this seemed incongruous material for a British sex scandal. Both white and black people I knew found this unexpected. Before we slide into the familiar explanation of a colonised or racialised Other who assumes an increased sexual potency in relation to their material disappropriation, so that the exotic becomes the move through which we come to fancy those we simultaneously dispossess and fear, this surprise is worth noting. As far as I can tell, Asian women have not been associated with the category 'whore' recently in Britain. If they are fetishised, it is in their status as 'virgin' – this signalling not only sexual inexperience but also a wider awkwardness, an inability to enjoy the pleasures of Western civilisation without help.

This is the belief to which my reading of the world had led me. It is in relation to these assumptions that I first made sense of the Bordes phenomenon. Now it seems that despite my excessive education, my reading failed to register what was significant about this set of stories. It is only because of minor events in my life, the textual detail of my autobiography, that I reformulated my reading to include the possibility that some stories may alter the way in which many people make sense of the world. Read 'straight', the Bordes story tells us little about the situation of British Asians. However, in a context of change – which, let's face it, is the only context there is – Bordes seems to have assumed a certain iconic significance in relation to the shifting identity of 'Asian'. What is unclear is what sort of reading skills would be required to chart this.

Autobiography.

I am unwilling to grant my anecdotes the status of textual evidence. Things that happen to you are not the same as books you read. If I make sense of the category 'race' in this country by recounting my own life, I seem dangerously close to forgoing the authority of academic discourse, and instead rendering myself the object of study. This is the dangerous possibility of any study in which the identity examined is also an identity inhabited by the speaker. Who needs to increase this sense of risk? I feel disempowered enough. But the sense I make of the Pamella Bordes story is possible only through the introduction of autobiography. It is the everyday events which allow me to read change – the more strictly textual reading relied upon pre-existing assumptions which were necessarily fixed, if only momentarily. 'Asian' was a complex identity, but it was not adapted in the process of reading. These changes are in the realm of event.

Put this way, the use of anecdote appears politically astute – a means by which study can place itself in the world as simultaneously social process and social explanation. But I am not happy with this. If the significance of the identity 'Asian' is comprehensible only by living the identity 'Asian', where is the place of study? Can I understand the terms of 'white' only by listening to what white people say about themselves?[6] This may be true to some extent, but how do we develop the reading skills required to make sense of these multiple autobiographies? If social significance can be recognised only through the individual account, what sort of metanarrative should we employ in order to read at all? For a cultural studies tradition which takes 'culture' or 'the social' generally as the frame in which meaning is made, there would seem to be a difficulty in distinguishing individual accounts from this fiction of the whole. Autobiography, either our own or someone else's, may be all there is. If reading is how to find out about the world, then we need to understand more about how this activity is positioned.

I still feel that theories of exoticism fail to appreciate the closeness of racial difference and friction in Britain. What is needed is a reading which can somehow link racist fantasy to racist pragmatism in a dynamic model. Unfortunately, I have no idea what this would be – only that the detail of disgust and desire cannot be understood broadly, because it is not static. And that understanding relies upon 'broad' concepts, because that is how sense is made.

A last anecdote.

I had a dream in which I wanted to speak privately to a white friend while we were in a crowd of white people. I was convinced that we had a special understanding, and spoke to him in fluent Bengali (far more effortlessly than I can manage when I am awake), all the while gesticulating wildly to aid his comprehension. Because this was an anxiety dream, everyone stared at me with open surprise. Later I asked my friend whether he understood what I had told him. 'No, of course I didn't,' he replied. 'You know I don't speak Bengali.'

I would like to think that failure of translation is not inevitable, but I am not sure how any of us can stop being stuck in this sort of miscommunication.

It seems to me that the racial embarrassments of Left academia in Britain can lead to scenarios which seem governed by the logic of sadomasochism. The white audience greets the introduction of any discussion of 'race' as a deserved and longed-for punishment, so that the only interchange becomes a version of the bottom's pleas to stop to a top who is in fact constrained and determined by this contract of enclosed discipline. The black academic must continually pander to her white colleagues' desire to be scolded – 'Tell us again how bad we are . . . oh stop . . . no, go on. . . .' This is fine if we are concerned only with the immediate pleasures of correctness and correction, but it might not help us to learn anything, let alone deploy any gains in knowledge in places beyond this academic contract.

The notion that the black academic is an intrepid border-crosser who can show us truth by recounting this journey is a seductive one, but it might not be an accurate depiction of the intersections of blackness and education. Border-crossing assumes discrete entities with the translation of scholarship coming from the border-crosser – here being a border-crosser is like being bilingual, and knowledge arises from occupying the privileged point of doubleness. If, instead of this, the black British academic, say, is viewed as being structured by 'race' and 'education' in ways which do not necessarily render her personal testimony typical – in the sense that the social meaning of 'race' in Britain can be extrapolated from this narrative of experience – then the cultural study of 'race' has access only to the peculiar autobiographies of black academics, which may not square with each other anyway. Any further confessions from the border-crosser can only replicate this impasse. The argument I am making here is not that there is, somewhere outside the contamination of the academy, an authentic black voice where the real meanings of 'race' reside (although I know some people will read it like this, among them a section of the white masochists who cannot forgive black breakers of the contract). Instead I am trying to make a plea for a reassessment of how we think about study which wants to be on the side of justice. It is, perhaps, right and proper that there are attempts to listen politely to what the previously silenced have to say. Now we have to find ways of understanding the things that are said, instead of assuming that the speech of the disadvantaged (any one of them) will in itself render our knowledge whole.

There is a section from one of the original anecdotes which I forgot to include, but it now seems as fitting an ending as any. The woman who first suggested to me that Asian women had recently become the recipients of street-corner come-ons from white men had asked her mother's advice about this difficulty. Her mother had scolded her and said that she should say 'No speak English', and walk away quickly. The suggestion is that she should reclaim an impassable difference as a defensive strategy – in many ways a very astute analysis of how ethnics might be able to ride popular understandings of multiculturalism for their own benefit. But the problem, as the young woman pointed out, is that the white men know that we speak English now. The come-ons stem, presumably, from the perception that dark girls are not necessarily *so* foreign.

I take the unhelpfulness of this mother's advice as an indication of how to start to understand 'race' in contemporary Britain. There are no discrete communities of difference – there are some things which we all understand. The project is to work out how the terms of 'race' can still operate within this shared arena, not to fall back upon a theory of 'race' which assumes that being racialised is a property which black people bring from home, what the black body just is – theories which grant authority to the authentic voice of black experience are a version of this. Somehow we have to relinquish this if we are to learn anything. And I know that I am back where I started, but I only promised to stage a problem. . . .

Notes

1   The most recognizable and possibly the most important theoretical strategy cultural studies has developed is that of 'reading' cultural products, social practices, even institutions, as 'texts'. Initially borrowed from literary studies, its subsequent wide deployment owing significant debts to the semiotics of Barthes and Eco, textual analysis has become an extremely sophisticated set of methods – particularly for reading the products of the mass media.

   Graeme Turner, in *British Cultural Studies, An Introduction* (London: Unwin Hyman, 1990), p. 87.
2 Nancy K. Miller, *Getting Personal* (New York: Routledge, 1991); Michele Wallace, *Invisibility Blues* (London: Verso, 1990). The work of Patricia J. Williams (*The Alchemy of Race and Rights*: Cambridge, MA: Harvard University Press, 1991) is more illuminating to me, perhaps because she examines the proof status of the first-person narrative as a problematic, rather than as an established authority.
3 For some indication of the influence of the term 'Other' in thinking about 'race', see Antony Easthope, *Literary into Cultural Studies* (London: Routledge, 1991), in which the author schematises the theoretical debates leading to divisions within English and cultural studies under the six terms 'sign system', 'ideology', 'gender', 'psychoanalysis', 'institution', and 'the Other' (this latter incorporating discussions of 'race'). While Easthope's attempt to make a variety of complex debates intelligible in relation to each other is admirable, his choice of terms would seem to back up my argument that it is

the model of the Other which has determined much of how 'race' can be thought about in recent British cultural studies.

4 In 1979 the Labour Home Secretary, Merlyn Rees, sanctioned the compulsory medical testing, in cubicles at Heathrow Airport, of young Asian brides for 'proof' of their virginity. The assumption was that the sexual codes of Asian culture were so constraining that a woman could not be both a non-virgin and a bride-to-be.

5 This might be seen as part of a wider – and unresolved – difficulty in cultural studies whereby privileging the text, in the manner of literary criticism, facilitates a neat analysis but cuts out a lot of what is going on. In his overview, *British Cultural Studies*, Graeme Turner suggests that it is this sort of difficulty which leads to interest in audiences and the more contextual meanings of artefacts.

6 Joan W. Scott writes about this difficulty in an essay entitled 'Experience', collected in *Feminists Theorize the Political* (ed. Judith Butler and Joan W. Scott [New York and London: Routledge, 1992]):

> When experience is taken as the origin of knowledge, the vision of the individual subject (the person who had the experience or the historian who recounts it) becomes the bedrock of evidence upon which explanation is built. Questions about the constructed nature of experience, about how subjects are constituted as different in the first place, about how one's vision is structured – about language (or discourse) and history – are left aside. The evidence of experience then becomes evidence for the fact of difference, rather than a way of exploring how difference is established, how it operates, how and in what ways it constitutes subjects who see and act in the world. (p. 25)

Chapter 7

Sex and Secrets in Central Australia

Walter Baldwin Spencer and Gendered Ethnography

Lynnette Turner

A short time ago I read through Miss Kingsley [*Travels in West Africa*] – it was just as much as I could do to get through it – & after expecting much was greatly disappointed. . . . There are secret customs amongst the women just as amongst the men but whilst (white) men can find out 'sub rosa' from the women, women cannot find out anything from the men. . . . A man may, if he knows the savage mind well enough, find out some of the women's secrets but a woman will never find out mens' [sic], wherefor from this point of view Miss Kingsley might as well stay at home.[1]

In the written account of the 1895 Horn Expedition into the Central Australian desert, the delegated 'anthropologist' within the team, Dr E.C. Stirling, makes the comment 'To no country is the remark of a distinguished traveller more appropriate than to Australia – that "as a rule the men who know don't write, and the men who write don't know" '.[2] The following year, word was 'about' in anthropological circles that two members of the expedition, the biologist Walter Baldwin Spencer and the 'intermediary' and photographer Frank Gillen, were collaborating on a ground-breaking piece of ethnological fieldwork, accompanying the Arunta for three months of sustained research and witnessing a restaged version of the 'great periodic initiation ceremony'.[3] Baldwin Spencer was avidly telegraphing colleagues with the news that the Arunta 'allowed me to come in and see everything & we are now seeing things which no white men have ever seen before or are likely to again for some time . . . they [take] no more notice of me than if I were one of themselves which in fact I am now'.[4] As George Stocking Jnr has pointed out: 'When the ceremonies ended, Spencer and Gillen had a wealth of ethnographic detail about native ritual life of a sort that armchair anthropologists had never previously experienced.'[5] Following the publication of their monograph *The Native Tribes of Central Australia* (1899),[6] Spencer and Gillen were promoted in English and American anthropological circles as men who *wrote* and men who *knew*.

This essay forms a necessarily partial reading of the Walter Baldwin Spencer corpus.[7] It will explore the semantics of anthropological knowing and writing at the end of the nineteenth century, and particularly the dependency of these activities on gendered images and topoi. These gendered terms lend discursive stability at a crucial turning point in the methods and principles of British anthropology.[8] The period from the late 1880s to around 1910 is often seen as the 'twilight' stage of anthropological enquiry, and the writings of Spencer and Gillen are crucially positioned within the history of the transformation of the 'fieldworker' from the Victorian 'investigator' or 'inquirer' (who was not re-quired to witness events)[9] to the modern (participant) 'observer'. It is therefore necessary to acknowledge that consideration of *Native Tribes* as an early eth-nography goes against current disciplinary tracking of an origin for modern ethnography, which sees Malinowski's statement of 'intensive' study (1921) or W.H. River's 1913 declaration of the need for 'intensive work' as a recognisable beginning.[10] Yet the text was conceived and received within the new discipline of Anthropology and, according to Stocking, was 'recognizably "modern" in its ethnographic style'.[11]

In late-nineteenth-century ethnographies, 'knowing' and 'writing' are both highly gendered activities, and in *Native Tribes* the epistemological and rep-resentational crisis indicative of such a transitional text is frequently given a gendered treatment. In a similar way to the crisis of representation enunciated in a contemporaneous text such as *Heart of Darkness* (1899), *Native Tribes* im-plicitly questions the modes of cross-cultural analysis and comprehension avail-able to it. Yet *Native Tribes* smooths over its own disciplinary anxieties about the limits of its epistemology by displacing these anxieties on to femininity – or, indeed, on to 'Aboriginal woman'. The text offers geographical and metaphori-cal sites in which the failure of knowledge and the limits of translation become encoded as feminine. But in a fascinating move which perhaps reflects an early attempt at intercultural identification, this codification then leaves open a provi-sional or tentative statement of masculine plurality or differentiation, one which goes against the dominant Victorian rhetoric of evolutionary anthropology.

What follows, then, is an exploration of the ways in which gender binaries and racial taxonomies intersect with questions of knowledge and authority at a crucial moment in the history and development of fieldwork in British anthropology. But to begin this analysis, I want first to look at the current use of the category of the Other within anthropological writings in order to demon-strate why the use of this term is frequently unhelpful when attempting to tease out the nuances of sexual difference in late-nineteenth-century ethnographic accounts.

It is a commonplace worth reiterating that anthropology is predicated on 'the fact of otherness and difference'.[12] As Claude Lévi-Strauss has put it, 'Anthro-pology is the study of culture from the outside'.[13] Current debates within Anglo-American anthropology and cultural theory are using the notions of 'Insiders' and 'Outsiders' and of the insider–outsider relationship to facilitate a renewed discussion of cross-cultural understanding.[14] Although a powerful element within these discussions is the indeterminacy of the 'self' in the textual production of the 'insider' anthropologist, the history of anthropology is structured on relationships of foreignness and non-equivalence. This relationship of non-equivalence between observer and native informant, or between the Western Academy and non-industrial, non-literate society, is generally – and certainly was at the end of the nineteenth century – inscribed in similar terms as the base or fundamental power asymmetry which underwrites the colonial project.

In his Inaugural Lecture at the Collège de France in 1960, Lévi-Strauss was keen to address the fact that anthropological investigations have frequently been described as ' "Sequels to Colonialism" ',[15] and criticism of the imbrication of the two projects has been taken up more recently both inside and outside the discipline of Anthropology.[16] Many of these critiques of anthropology utilise the category of the Other to stand as a signifier of the subordinated counterpart within a series of conceptual and actual binaries. Such criticism has borrowed and reworked the notion of Other/Otherness from other disciplines and traditions which foreground the fact that 'Western thought has always thematized the other as a threat to be reduced, as a potential same-to-be, a yet-not-same',[17] a pattern of thinking that underlies colonialism. In feminist scholarship the term Other or the use of 'otherness' generally operates within a binary model of hegemony and subordination, and signifies the denial of the representation and of the signifying practices of women as social subjects.[18] Throughout a variety of discourses (feminism, cultural politics, etc.) which have appropriated the term from traditions such as philosophy and psychoanalysis, the Other conveys inauthentic presence (non-equivalence is reconstituted within the economy of the Same) or signifies a textual gap or absence.

Social and cultural anthropology have been forced to confront these challenges to the assumption of authority in their representations of other cultures. The emergent 'reflexive' tradition in Anglo-American anthropology has produced theoretical accounts and ethnographies which attempt to be 'more self-conscious about the production of its texts'[19] and attuned to the impact of the anthropologist's presence on the people with whom she or he is working.[20] An important development within these anthropological commentaries on textual production is an active engagement with the question of the category of the Other – an engagement which acknowledges critiques produced by feminism and cultural criticism. Yet all too frequently the Other is simply rendered as the 'other', and the ethnographic process is transcribed within a benign self–other dialectic which does not sufficiently (re-)address the division of power that is inevitable in the fieldwork situation. The 'other' of reflexive anthropology tends to be synonymous with the 'not-us'.[21] It is used in a sense often devoid of both a power problematic and any reference to the other important dynamic between the representable and the non-representable.

For instance, Kirsten Hastrup's essay 'Writing Ethnography: State of the Art' (1992)[22] summarises and develops many of the recent arguments about 'how to write ethnography – and why' (p. 116). It proposes a self-conscious ethnography which 'realise[s] that "othering" is part of the anthropological practice' (p. 121), and Hastrup attempts to move ethnography out of a 'Modernist rationality' which 'introduced an absolute distinction between subject and object' (p. 129). She begins by making the important observation that 'self and other . . . are categories of thought, not discrete entities'; that 'there are selves and others, but no absolute and exclusive categories of *ego* and *alter*' (pp. 117, 129). Yet where Hastrup's essay is aware of gender implications in the fieldwork situation (p. 120), she does not develop this aspect, and this oversight becomes a significant part of the way in which her argument tends to lend the term 'other' a – paradoxical – semantic stability.

In fact, while Hastrup carefully works through the potential violence and invasiveness of ethnography, her version of postmodern ethnography is one in which the 'ethnographic text is of a peculiar and paradoxical nature which defies the simple logic of the western power game' (p. 124). Furthermore, Hastrup consistently talks about ethnography as the product of a '*dialectical* process' (p. 117; emphasis added), in which 'Difference is continually transcended' (p. 129). The idea of a dialectical process has inevitable Hegelian resonances. As such it is a pattern of argument which connotes transcendence of difference into the law of One.[23] And such an account of the self–other dialectic shows a certain blindness to questions of language, and to the sites of resistance within linguistic practice to the totalising implications of the dialectic. At the very least, Hastrup's belief in an intersubjective synthesis is a utopian gesture that runs the risk of pulling cultural difference back into a stable discourse which forecloses on those instances of the intransmissible and heterogeneous.

R.S. Khare has recently advanced anthropological debates which see the Other as synonymous with the ' "not-us" ' by recognising that the Other, in all its 'polyvocal vitality . . . continually leaves ever new traces of difference for anthropology to deal with'.[24] 'Such Other', Khare argues, 'can be neither totally subsumed nor dissolved but only recognized for what it is by itself' (p. 21). Pertinent though Khare's argument is, the Other nevertheless stands in for *cultural* alterity. This prioritising of the wholly cultural over and above the simultaneity of sexual and cultural difference in the semantics of the Other is dominant in anthropological discourse as well as cultural theory. To acknowledge that the Other is a class or series of Others frequently neglects the fact that while alterity might be written in the terms of an irreducible other-cultural difference, *absolute* alterity is often marked as feminine and figured as 'native' woman.

Thus if the history of anthropology shows a reluctance to cope with sexual difference, the more recent theorisation of 'Self' and 'Other' does not help matters, ignoring the important significations of sexual difference in the ethnographic monograph and the reconstitution of the category of the Other in *specific* ethnographies. As I will go on to argue, *Native Tribes* inevitably posits Aboriginal man as a paradigmatic instance of 'primitive' man: the opposite of European identity and rationalism. Yet Aboriginal woman is precisely that Other which is figured in the text as the limit case of representation, an *untranslatable* abyss of alterity. It is this gendered structuring of cultural difference that facilitates a characterisation of Aboriginal man as 'diverse' in his Otherness – which in turn is suggestive of a gendered apprehension of the unfamiliar or Other.

The Native Tribes of Central Australia sits uneasily on the cusp of two competing theoretical frameworks. The evolutionary comparative schema had held sway as the methodological norm for anthropological inquiry throughout the mid-nineteenth century, and continued to dominate the system-building anthropology written by the metropolitan scholar-scientists in the early years of institutionalised anthropology. Yet in the 1880s and 1890s a transition was occurring in the 'field' whereby research and investigation were becoming far more 'specialist' activities. Researchers such as Lorimer Fison, Alfred Howitt and, later, Walter Baldwin Spencer and Francis Gillen were working with a body of data that frequently challenged the cultural expectations of evolutionism. In addition, their constant communication with each other and knowledge of each other's work meant that individual research activities could be used to corroborate each other's field findings rather than operating only to confirm and validate the occurrence of similar cultural phenomena found in other areas of the world. In short, if the announcement in the Preface to *Native Tribes* that 'The result of our work is undoubtedly to corroborate that of Messrs. Howitt and Fison in regard to these matters' (p. viii) is a declaration of a more geographically specific form of inquiry, then it also proposes a distance from the authority of 'metropolitan' comparative theory. The difference between the form of the Horn Expedition (a general scientific expedition into the Central Australian desert which acknowledged that 'ethnological investigations have been too little considered as part of the functions of an exploring party in Australia'[25]) and the type of research that led to the production of *Native Tribes* is indicative of the rapid increase in anthropological interest in such a short period.

'Abstract' anthropology demanded little more from its geographically remote data-collectors than that they would 'supply the information which is wanted for the scientific study of anthropology',[26] answering a list of preconceived questions 'without prejudice arising from his individual bias' (p. v). As Morrell and Thackray have argued, most 'new' sciences emerging in the mid-nineteenth century were under great pressure to establish themselves along the lines of the physical sciences,[27] and the very idea of the ethnographic questionnaire (a method maintained throughout the nineteenth century) upheld the belief that the written accounts supplied by travellers and others could function in the same way as archaeological or geological specimens. Anthropology set a premium on accounts which provided objective, stable, transportable 'realities'; and in a similar way to the early scientific faith in photographic mimesis, these completed questionnaires became the image of perfectly self-present meaning. Indeed, after James Frazer had read the manuscript of *Native Tribes* he commented to Spencer that while anthropological theory might change, 'books like yours, containing records of observation, will never be superseded'.[28]

Edward Tylor, generally regarded as the 'founding father' of British anthropology, argued in his important *Primitive Culture* (1871) that the phenomena of culture should be 'classified and arranged, stage by stage, in a probable order of evolution',[29] and for this reason each aspect of culture was to be considered as a discrete typological category. Although *Native Tribes* shows strong links to descriptive, questionnaire-based accounts of 'primitive' culture, utilising their categories and suggestions, the text is given focus, as George Stocking points out, by a 'totalizing cultural performance'[30] whereby the 'Engwura' ceremony is granted a metonymic function, emblematising the entirety of Arunta cultural and social life. Thus Spencer's involvement with Tylorean anthropological theory (Spencer had helped in the installation of the Pitt Rivers collection of material culture in a special annex to the University Museum) is written into *Native Tribes* at momentary points of instability. The text shows an interest in Tylor's idea of 'survivals', and Frazer's ideas of Totemism are used to verify or demystify the scattered and complex information on totemic systems. But throughout, the study is based on local particularities and the text constantly restates its resistance to interpretations of 'origins'.

Native Tribes not only declares its non-continuity with its Victorian forebears in methodological terms, but also revises the version of the 'economy of Manichean allegory' that dominates early-Victorian anthropological thinking. According to Abdul R. JanMohamed, 'the Manichean allegory – a field of diverse yet interchangeable oppositions' is the 'central feature of the colonialist cognitive framework and colonialist literary representation'.[31] Social evolutionism, with its *a priori* emphasis on the spiritual and material inferiority of non-European cultures, takes this opposition as its starting point. As a form of colonialist discourse, nineteenth-century evolutionary theory commodifies the native subject into a stereotyped or fetishised object which is utilised for its explanatory comments on the European past, or to provide a commentary on its own potential for self-annihilation.[32]

The break with the evolutionary comparative method evident in geographically specific ethnographies, such as *Native Tribes* and the writings of Mary Kingsley,[33] is generally written in the rhetoric of a liberalist cultural relativism which, in producing diversity rather than difference, is a cross-cultural mode of comprehension that questions the precise (gendered) terms of the earlier binary, but nevertheless retains its organising *potential*.[34] Spencer was not averse to describing the indigenous Australians as 'crude and quaint' examples of 'creatures . . . that have elsewhere passed away and given place to higher forms'.[35] Yet the manner in which the late-nineteenth-century fieldwork encounter produces reworkings and realignments of the coherent ordering binaries of an earlier anthropological moment demands a critical analysis of the potential multiplicity in which the categories of 'observer' and 'observed', and of the observer–observed relations, are produced. The proto-syncreticism of *Native Tribes* offers evidence of a modification of the observer's position and a treatment of 'primitive culture' which is frequently inconclusive. Thus, I note here Gayatri Spivak's important criticism of the constitution of the 'colonial subject as Other' that obliterates 'the trace of the Other in its precarious Subject-ivity',[36] and especially her dissolution of the knower/known binary within the 'subaltern problematic', a commentary on colonial sexual politics to which I will return.

Spencer is among the few Victorian 'fieldworkers' whose declared 'intimacy' with his native informants did not compromise the status of his work. At crucial points in the history of anthropology, the disciplinary requirement of the observer's distance and impartiality is reiterated.[37] Spencer's commitment to scientific neutrality was endorsed by his academic standing in the Chair of Biology at Melbourne University. Francis Gillen's position as 'sub-protector' of the local Aborigines for twenty years before he met Spencer similarly conferred objectivity, discipline and 'impartiality'. Yet Gillen was also a forthright Irish republican ('You thank God that you are an Englishman. I thank God that I am not. I have no ambition to belong to such a race of Hippocrites'[38]) whose racial identity and difference are also reaffirmed through his assumed position within the Spencer–Gillen relationship as the 'native' informant.

Gillen is presented as knowing the Arunta 'language deeply enough to understand most of what they say', and Spencer was also convinced that 'the blacks have implicit faith in Gillen & trust him'.[39] Gillen's role of 'sub-protector' and his familiarity with the Arunta had enabled him to be adopted as a member of the Witchety Grub totem. During the restaged 'Fire Ceremony' ('Engwura') Gillen had managed to convince the Arunta elders that Spencer was his younger classificatory brother, and Spencer was 'adopted as a member of the tribe and allowed to see everything'.[40] Yet Gillen, as his 'informant' role would suggest, took only a minor part in the writing of the monograph, articulating a backstage role that bestowed upon Spencer the dual ability of *knowing* and *writing*; in short, Gillen was helping to construct Spencer as an *ethnographer*. Thus Spencer was not only granted the privilege of 'insider's' knowledge; he also benefited from the 'gift' of translation:

> You know the blackfellow as well as I do, perhaps better, for with the intuitiveness of genius you are able to project yourself into his mind, to think and feel and reason as he does. . . . You can give expression to your thoughts and ideas and experience in suitable language, which I can't.[41]

Gillen's articulation of Spencer's capacity for transcultural identification and appropriate translation is upheld also by James Frazer, Lorimer Fison ('You are a born anthropologist'[42]), Edward Tylor and Spencer's biographers.[43] It is also confirmed by Spencer himself as a methodological principle: 'A man may be really honest and well meaning, but unless he can put himself into the position of a native, and think as he does, he will in all good faith write, as some of them do, the veriest nonsense.'[44]

Yet this assumption of transcultural identification is predicated on a *gendered* point of entry into Arunta 'life' as a *male* ethnographer. Spencer's participation in the 'Engwura' – 'a long series of ceremonies concerned with totems' (p. 271) – between September 1896 and January 1897 is as a man permitted entry into an exclusively male event. In a similar manner to Clifford Geertz's well-known analysis of the Balinese cockfight,[45] the significance given to this all-male ceremony as a totalising cultural performance, and as a scene in which tradition, law and knowledge are handed on, relegates the feminine, and woman as a participant in social law, to the geographical and textual perimeter. Although it is frequently difficult to distinguish between Spencer's textual exclusions, Spencer's phantasm of Aboriginal patriarchy, and Arunta forms of patriarchy, Spencer is nevertheless keen to reproduce indigenous women as having no social significance, and therefore no anthropological 'value'. More interestingly, he produces the category 'Aboriginal woman' as undifferentiated.

Spencer's extensive discussion of the initiatory 'Engwura' ceremonies pays scant attention to female initiation rites: 'certain' initiation ceremonies of women 'are evidently the equivalents of the initiation ceremonies concerned with men . . . [but] there being amongst the women no equivalents of the *Lartna* (circumcision) or Engwura ceremonies of the men' (p.269). Significantly, '*There is no special name given to a female after any initiation rite*' (p. 269; emphasis added) – a point to which I will return. And where the restaged 'Engwura' places the women's camp across the river ('The men are separated from the women and live on the Engwura ground, where sacred ceremonies are performed day and night' [p. 271]), the narrative point of view stays firmly within the confines of the men's camp. *Native Tribes* consistently draws Aboriginal woman as without 'knowledge', without tradition, and without access to the 'most' sacred. The function of the 'Engwura', Spencer writes, is 'to show the younger men who have arrived at mature age, the sacred secrets of the tribe which are concerned with the Churinga and the totems with which they are associated' (p. 271). As Spencer detailed to Henry Balfour: 'It is only the most sacred ceremonies which they will allow a white man whom they have known for long and thoroughly trust to see which are of real value.'[46]

Even if Spencer's blindness to the female ceremonies, or to the social significance of Arunta women, is an unwittingly accurate reproduction of indigenous patriarchal culture, an important methodological issue remains here. The social and textual centrality accorded the (male) 'Initiation Ceremonies' which systematically dislocate Aboriginal women from a performative role neatly parallels the methodological issue posed by Spencer's emergence as an ethnographer, a position which casts *participant* observation as a masculine preserve. Spencer's comments on Mary Kingsley foreground a (paradoxical) gendering of the observer's scientific credentials as cultural and sexual neuter: the white male ethnographer 'invisibly' passes 'in and out amongst them', seemingly at will, and is privy to the totality of other-cultural knowledge, whereas white femininity connotes visibility and a gendered identity which imposes limits on ethnographic knowledge: 'the information of a woman like Miss Kingsley is only of value in regard to the secret or sacred ceremonies of the women'. If Spencer wanted the women's secrets, he could, he believes, 'find out "sub rosa" from the women'.[47]

And women remain a homogeneous category in Spencer's discourse. *Native Tribes* is a text that visibly fractures under the failure of dominant nineteenth-century anthropological theory. The evolutionary comparative paradigm, with its concomitant emphasis on Australian Aborigines as – in Frazer's words – 'approximating most closely to the *type* of absolutely primitive humanity',[48] demanded that primitive humanity be a fixed, demonstrable, self-identical opposite to European modernity. *Native Tribes* generally refuses to make comparisons; readers, of course, would take for granted the meaning of 'primitive' or 'savage' man, but Spencer and Gillen refused to 'date' the 'Central Tribes' in the manner of, say, Mary Kingsley, who describes contemporaneous West African culture as 'thirteenth century'.[49]

Yet the points of textual and epistemological instability in *Native Tribes* not only recognise the knower–known relationship as a problematic but amount to the emergent attempt to articulate intra-tribal differentiation, which itself disturbs the closure of 'primitive man' and the stability of British anthropological interpretations of the social and mythic value of the totem. Where E.C. Stirling's anthropological section of the *Report on the Work of the Horn Scientific Expedition* foregrounded similarity and standardisation ('their homogeneous physical characters, the general similarity of their habits, customs, handicrafts and mental attributes . . . all suggest a common origin for the whole race'[50]), Spencer's introduction to *Native Tribes* is keen to emphasise that though it is not uncommon to find in 'many works of anthropology' reference to ' "the Australian native" . . . as regards social organisation and customs . . . there is great diversity' (p.34).

Contemporary reviews of *Native Tribes* confirm this attention to detail and particularity. The *Popular Science Monthly* commented that the 'authors insist upon the differences between the groups of tribes',[51] and the unsigned review reiterates the authors' own claim that 'groups of tribes differ from one another to a great extent, and the customs of no one tribe or group can be taken as typical of Australia generally' (Preface, p. vii). James Frazer commended Spencer's ability to write as if 'unaware of the existence of any race but the one he is describing'.[52] Much of the 'data' supplied by the text goes against contemporaneous anthropological theory, as the subsequent debate between Frazer and Andrew Lang on totemism illustrates.[53] Yet the manner in which this diversity and specificity are written allows for masculine particularity, but no inscription of feminine plurality. In *Native Tribes*, 'diversity' is a gendered term.

Spencer's 'Narrative' of the Horn Expedition includes accounts of discussions with informants that record these (male) informants' names, each name carefully transcribed from the 'original' language. *Native Tribes* does not carry through this use of the informants' personal names, but kinship terms and 'status names' (p. 260) – that is, the names attributed to a ceremonial role or duty – are again carefully transcribed and translated. The text clearly attempts to acknowledge specificity and particularity, and the ethnographers' 'first-hand' account of Arunta 'life' enables the diversity of masculine role-calls to be 'faithfully' transcribed. Yet this privileging of masculinity as the vehicle for attention to local credentials confines femininity to a fixed and stable transcultural anonymity, reducing 'Aboriginal' woman to the status of a sexed, not a social, subject.

In the short description of the 'operation called *Atna-ariltha-kuma* (*atna*, vulva; *kuma*, cut)' (p. 92) in the discussion of 'Ceremonies concerned with marriage' (Chapter 3), the male 'actors' are all positioned and named in relation to the woman undergoing the operation. But where the men's relational and 'status' names are transcribed in/from Arunta, the female subject remains 'closed' within the unspecific and generic/biological category 'girl' (pp. 92–3). Indeed, this is a common characteristic of the text. At another point, Spencer describes a scene in a male initiation ceremony in which certain women become involved in the 'presentation of the fire-stick'. The Aboriginal terms for the women all correspond with their relational position to the male subject in the context of marriage classes: *Mia, Uwinna, Mura tualcha* (p. 222).[54] The men involved are described in both senses: marriage classes and status names – *Wurtja, Urinthantima, Okilia, Kurdaitcha* (p. 222)[55] – and Spencer also details the status names 'indicating the different grades of initiation . . . applied to the boy, youth and man at the times [in the ceremony] indicated' (p. 260). It is worth repeating again: 'There is no special name given to a female after any initiation rite' (p. 269).

In a text so concerned with precision and nomenclature, an absolute resistance to female individuality is signalled by the use of the term 'lubra' ('a lubra with nothing on except an ancient straw hat and an old pair of boots is perfectly happy' [p. 17]), a word used by *white* settlers and travellers to denote a 'native woman'. Although the term 'lubra' appears in the 'Glossary' with the additional comment that the 'native term in the Arunta tribe is *Arakutja*' (p. 652), the Arunta term is displaced in favour of the white Australian slang. The use of 'lubra' as a transcultural signifier of disreputable or amoral femininity reiterates the textual privileging of 'native woman' as (only) a sexual subject. But it is also important to read this homogenising strategy in relation to the question of epistemology. The insistence on 'local' knowledge throws up a series of anomalies that undermine the cultural expectations of 'abstract' metropolitan anthropology. Yet the text manages cultural diversity by drawing a line between men and women, and between masculine and feminine, which posits 'woman' as its exegetical horizon.

The wealth of detail about male activities is a strategy which suggests that the nuances of (male) ceremonial activity are knowable and transmissible. The silencing of feminine 'diversity' which represents 'woman' as transculturally (always-already) knowable, because she is a non-participant in the difference of Arunta social law and custom, is also suggestive of the way in which Australian femininity negates anthropological conceptualisation. The use of generic asocial categories foregrounded in the textual recourse to the definition of Aboriginal woman as 'lubra' is also indicative of the limits of Victorian ethnographic knowledge. Slipping in and out of Spencer's text, 'native woman' connotes the (displaced) failure of representation, ultimately demonstrable but homogeneously indeterminate. In another telling parallel with methodological issues, as 'diversity' and 'specificity' become gendered masculine, femininity similarly becomes positioned beyond a textual threshold which allows activity, diversity, tradition, writing, authority and knowledge to reiterate and confirm one another. Most ceremonies within the 'Engwura' are 'matter[s] of the deepest mystery to women' (p. 369), while women's expression – as in the 'woman's dance' which, Spencer suggests, closes the 'Engwura' – is 'of the most *monotonous* description possible' (p. 381; emphasis added).

The centrality of the semantic nexus 'knowledge–authority–masculinity' in the texts supports the crude formulation of the sign 'native woman' as constitutive of the denial of access both to knowledge and to writing. It is a sign that 'soaks up' these displaced points of potential textual crisis. Like many late-nineteenth-century ethnologists, Spencer was especially interested in myth and custom which foreground the contaminating and disruptive potential of women. In his reading of Aboriginal tradition, women's malevolent potential is highlighted in a traditional topography that limits women's access to the sacred and to writing. The engraved 'Churingas', sacred objects which 'are never allowed to be seen by women or uninitiated men' (p. 128), and the 'sacred' rock paintings associated with the totems – and thus, in Spencer's formulation, with modes of being – are 'tabu' to the women, who carefully avoid the spot, for once it is subjected to the female gaze, the 'peculiar sacredness of the spot was lost' (p. 196).

This is not to deny the 'reality' of indigenous cultural forms and practices which are highly gendered; my point, rather, is to highlight the fact that in Spencer's discourse, Aboriginal women are not 'different', but they are benighted: 'there comes a time when each man is allowed to see and handle his [churinga], the women not only may never see them but . . . they are unaware of the existence of such objects' (p. 134). If, once again, Spencer is accurately detailing an indigenous prohibition, the various scenes in the text which re-enact the exclusion of the feminine from traditional knowledge consistently affirm the masculinisation of both tribal and ethnographic knowledge. Spencer's account of the fully initiated Arunta man, who 'must have shown himself capable of self-restraint and of being worthy by his general demeanour to be admitted to the secrets of the tribe' (p. 138), is a statement of 'maturity' that reflects the principles of competence and reliability which form the basis of 'approved' ethnographic observation.

Spencer's assumption of authority in *Native Tribes* is displayed through his awareness of the 'meaning' of specific cultural practices and his ability to elucidate each stage of the complex male ceremonies. He may well be stating an ethnographic 'truth' when he comments that the 'white man stands outside the laws which govern the native tribe' (p. 102), but his narrative position, despite himself, is far from that of cultural and sexual neuter. Throughout the letters written during the research and writing up of *Native Tribes*, Spencer reiterates his fundamental ethnographic principles: first, that it is the 'most sacred' which is of 'real value'; second, that only white *men* can find out both men's and women's 'secret customs'.[56] Spencer's identity as ethnographer positions him, in fact, as potentially privy to the totality of other-cultural knowledge, a position of superior knowledge to that held by indigenous women. Indeed, Spencer's authority seems to gain its momentum and status from a transference of not-knowing, a transference of the uncertainty or bewilderment of confronting phenomena that strike us as Other on to the women of the Central Tribes. The reader is witness to a drama in which this feminised aporia – the site where understanding and knowledge are blocked – is forced back on to Aboriginal woman, becoming both a feminised problematic and a feminine problem.

Spencer's reluctance to work the 'deep mine'[57] of Aboriginal femininity repeats a version of feminine activity as 'meaningless' and 'monotonous', a strategy that then allows the diversity of Arunta masculinity momentarily to break through or disturb the transcultural closure of 'primitive man'. Within the textual promotion of specificity and particularity can, perhaps, be determined a 'trace' of commonality of gender suggestive of the masculinised observer's role. The crudely mistranslated 'lubra' as the site of inaccessibility, but also the limit case of representation, indicates the failure of the most minimal commonality. It is here also, in the assertion of native woman as homogeneous, stable and ahistorical, that a feminisation of the primitive occurs.[58]

As Gayatri Spivak has argued, 'Within the effaced itinerary of the subaltern subject, the track of sexual difference is doubly effaced. . . . If, in the context of colonial production, the subaltern has no history and cannot speak, the subaltern female is even more deeply in shadow.'[59] In *Native Tribes*, a text which consistently substitutes undifferentiated 'native woman' for the perplexities of sexual/ social difference, Arunta femininity forestalls recuperation into Spencer's scientific discourse. Unlike the nineteenth-century text which cannot enunciate the difference of feminine secrets, current anthropological debates which systemise the question of the Other run the risk of repeating a form of dualistic logic at best ambivalent to, but frequently repudiating, the demands of sexual difference.

Notes

1 Walter Baldwin Spencer to Henry Balfour (20 September 1897). All MS. letters cited are in the Walter Baldwin Spencer Papers, Balfour Library, Pitt Rivers Museum, Oxford. I wish here to express my thanks to Elizabeth Edwards, archives curator at the Pitt Rivers Museum, for permission to consult this material; and also to Richard Hanson, librarian at the Balfour Library, for supplying additional information.

2 Dr E.C. Stirling, 'Anthropology', in *Report on the Work of the Horn Scientific Expedition to Central Australia*, ed. W.B. Spencer, 4 vols (Melbourne: Melville, Mullen & Slade, 1896), vol. IV, p. 3.

3 George W. Stocking Jnr, 'The Ethnographer's Magic: Fieldwork in British Anthropology from Tylor to Malinowski', in *Observers Observed: Essays on Ethnographic Fieldwork*, ed. G.W. Stocking Jnr (Madison: University of Wisconsin Press, 1985), p. 78.

4 Baldwin Spencer to Lorimer Fison (21 November 1896), W.B. Spencer Papers.
   In order critically to assess Spencer's nomenclature within the context of late-nineteenth-century anthropology, I have followed the Spencer and Gillen spelling of Aboriginal words. The correct term for 'Arunta' is 'Aranda', and 'churinga' is more commonly spelled 'tjuringa'. 'Engwura' has been corrected by T.G.H. Strehlow to 'Inkura'.

5 Stocking, 'The Ethnographer's Magic', p. 79.

6 Baldwin Spencer and Francis James Gillen, *The Native Tribes of Central Australia* (London and New York: Macmillan, 1899). All further page references will be given in parentheses in the text.

7 Baldwin Spencer, in collaboration with Francis Gillen, produced a number of monographs on the Australian Aborigines: *The Northern Tribes of Central Australia* (London: Macmillan, 1904), *The Native Tribes of the Northern Territory of Australia* (London: Macmillan, 1914), *Across Australia* (London: Macmillan, 1912), and *The Arunta: Study of a Stone Age People* (London: Macmillan, 1927). Spencer's own autobiographical *Wanderings in Wild Australia* was published in 1928 (London: Macmillan). As I will discuss below, Francis Gillen did not take an active role in the drafting of *Native Tribes*, and he comments in a letter to Baldwin Spencer: 'I shall hold it an honour to have my name associated with yours' (25 April 1896), W.B. Spencer Papers.

8 I will use the term 'anthropology' to identify both 'theory' and the system-building and synthesis recognised in the late nineteenth century as 'anthropology' proper. I use 'ethnography' to describe the written account of 'first-hand' observation and inquiry.

9 Stocking, 'The Ethnographer's Magic', p. 91.

10 *ibid.*, pp. 92–3.

11 *ibid.*, p. 79

12 Edward Said, 'Representing the Colonized: Anthropology's Interlocutors', *Critical Inquiry* 15, 2 (1989): 213.

13 Claude Lévi-Strauss, 'Anthropology: Its Achievement and Future', *Current Anthropology* 5 (1966): 126. For a more comprehensive understanding of Lévi-Strauss's definition of the ethnographic 'self', see his *Introduction to the Work of Marcel Mauss* (London: Routledge & Kegan Paul, 1987).

14 See, for instance, Trinh T. Minh-ha, *Woman, Native, Other: Writing Postcoloniality and Feminism* (Bloomington and Indianapolis: Indiana University Press, 1989).

15 Claude Lévi-Strauss, *The Scope of Anthropology* (London: Jonathan Cape, 1967), p. 51.

16 In a powerful extension to his argument in *Orientalism*, Edward Said has once again invoked the category of the Other to question whether anthropology is still caught in the (colonial) power problematic of its founding moment (see Said, 'Representing the Colonized'). See also Johannes Fabian, *Time and the Other: How Anthropology Makes Its Object* (New York: Columbia University Press, 1983); J. Clifford and G.E. Marcus, *Writing Culture: The Poetics and Politics of Ethnography* (Berkeley: University of California Press, 1986); more recently, J. Okely and H. Callaway (eds), *Anthropology and Autobiography* (London and New York: Routledge, 1992); D. Bell, P. Caplan and W. Jahan Karim (eds), *Gendered Fields: Women, Men and Ethnography* (London and New York: Routledge, 1993).

17 Wlad Godzich, 'The Further Possibility of Knowledge': 'Foreword' to Michel de Certeau, *Heterologies: Discourse on the Other* (Manchester: Manchester University Press, 1986), p. xiii.

18 Lisa Lowe, *Critical Terrains: French and British Orientalisms* (Ithaca, NY and London: Cornell University Press, 1991), p. 23.

19 Judith Okely, 'Participatory Experience and Embodied Knowledge', in Okely and Callaway (eds), *Anthropology and Autobiography*, p. 13.

20 Diane Bell, 'Introduction 1', in Bell *et al.* (eds), *Gendered Fields*, p. 4.

21 R.S. Khare, 'The Other's Double – The Anthropologist's Bracketed Self: Notes on Cultural Representation and Privileged Discourse', *New Literary History* 23 (1992): 1.

22 Kirsten Hastrup, 'Writing Ethnography: State of the Art', in Okely and Callaway (eds), *Anthropology and Autobiography*. All page references are given in parentheses in the text.

23 For an alternative reading of the Hegelian dialectic, see Richard Terdiman, 'The Response of the Other', *Diacritics* 22, 2: 2–10.

24 Khare, 'The Other's Double', p. 21, n.31. All further page references are given in parentheses in the text.

25 Stirling, 'Anthropology', p. 3.

26 BAAS: British Association for the Advancement of Science, *Notes and Queries on Anthropology: For the Use of Travellers and Residents in Uncivilized Lands* (London: Edward Stanford, 1874), p. iv. All further page references are given in parentheses in the text.

27 Jack Morrell and Arnold Thackray, *Gentlemen of Science: Early Years of the British Association for the Advancement of Science* (Oxford: Clarendon Press, 1982), pp. 28–9, 343–5.

28 James Frazer to Baldwin Spencer (26 August 1898), in R.R. Marett and T.K. Penniman, *Spencer's Scientific Correspondence with Sir J.G. Frazer and Others* (Oxford: Clarendon Press, 1932), p. 23.

29 Edward Burnett Tylor, *Primitive Culture: Researches into the Development of Mythology, Philosophy, Religion, Language, Art, and Custom*, 2nd edn, 2 vols (London: John Murray, 1871), vol. I, pp. 5–6.

30 Stocking, 'The Ethnographer's Magic', p. 79.

31 Abdul R. JanMohamed, 'The Economy of Manichean Allegory: The Function of Racial Difference in Colonialist Literature', in *'Race', Writing, and Difference*, ed. Henry Louis Gates Jnr (Chicago and London: University of Chicago Press, 1986), p. 82.

32 Gillian Beer, 'Speaking for the Others: Relativism and Authority in Victorian Anthropological Literature', in *Sir James Frazer and the Literary Imagination: Essays in Affinity and Influence*, ed. Robert Fraser (Basingstoke: Macmillan, 1990), pp. 38–60. Beer's approach is more cautious:

> Edward Tylor, despite his insistence on a developmental pattern to the emergence of human culture, always emphasised the congruities between primitive and advanced culture: indeed, the title *Primitive Culture* (1871) emphasises, as it were against the odds, that no human society, past or present, lacks a complex culture of its own. (p. 49)

What I wish to stress here is the almost unanimous belief within British anthropology that the Aborigines were 'fast dying out' (W.A. Horn, 'Introduction', *Report on the Work of the Horn Expedition*, vol. I, p. viii).

33 Mary Kingsley, *Travels in West Africa* (1897; London: Virago, 1986); and *West African Studies* (London: Macmillan, 1899).

34 JanMohamed, 'The Economy of Manichean Allegory': 'The power relations underlying this model set in motion such strong currents that even a writer who is reluctant to acknowledge it and who may indeed be highly critical of imperialist exploitation is drawn into its vortex' (p. 82). The political distinction between 'diversity' and 'difference' is drawn by Homi K. Bhabha in a version of his essay 'The Commitment to Theory', published in *Questions of Third Cinema*, ed. Jim Pines and Paul Willeman (London: BFI Publications, 1989). Bhabha argues that his own theorisation of

'difference' as the 'split-space of enunciation may open the way to conceptualising an *inter*national culture, based not on the exoticism or multi-culturalism of the *diversity* of cultures, but on the inscription and articulation of culture's *hybridity*' (p. 131; original emphasis).

35 Baldwin Spencer, *The Arunta, a Study of a Stone Age People* (1927), quoted by John Mulvaney in *The Aboriginal Photographs of Baldwin Spencer*, ed. Ron Vanderwal (Victoria: National Museum of Victoria Council, 1982), p. x.

36 Gayatri Chakravorty Spivak, 'Can the Subaltern Speak?', in *Marxism and the Interpretation of Culture*, eds Cary Nelson and Lawrence Grossberg (London: Macmillan, 1988), p. 280.

37 The vexed predicament of 'going native' haunts anthropological inquiry. James Clifford records the case of Frank Hamilton Cushing, who lived among the Zūni Indians, and argues that Cushing's 'excessively personal understanding of the Zūni could not confer scientific authority': 'On Ethnographic Authority', *Representations* 1, 2 (1983): 123. Hastrup is also concerned to point out that her discussion of the 'blurred self' should not be construed as identifying a 'weak personality . . . [who] simply "goes native" ': 'Writing Ethnography', p. 120.

38 Francis Gillen to Baldwin Spencer (31 January 1896), W.B. Spencer Papers.

39 Baldwin Spencer to Lorimer Fison (21 November 1896), W.B. Spencer Papers.

40 Baldwin Spencer to James Frazer (12 July 1897), in Marett and Penniman, *Spencer's Scientific Correspondence*, p. 4. See also Baldwin Spencer to Lorimer Fison (21 November 1896), W.B. Spencer Papers; Stocking, 'The Ethnographer's Magic', p. 79.

41 Francis Gillen to Baldwin Spencer (28 September 1899), in Marett and Penniman, *Spencer's Scientific Correspondence*, p. ix.

42 Lorimer Fison to Baldwin Spencer (4 December 1896), W.B. Spencer Papers.

43 See especially Marett and Penniman, *Spencer's Scientific Correspondence*, p. viii.

44 Baldwin Spencer to Henry Balfour (28 January 1898), in Marett and Penniman, *Spencer's Scientific Correspondence*, pp.138–9.

45 Clifford Geertz, 'Deep Play: Notes on the Balinese Cockfight', in *The Interpretation of Cultures* (New York: Basic Books, 1973).

46 Baldwin Spencer to Henry Balfour (20 September 1897), W.B. Spencer Papers.

47 Baldwin Spencer to Henry Balfour (20 September 1897), W.B. Spencer Papers.

48 James Frazer, 'Preface', *Native Tribes of Central Australia*, 3rd edn (London: Macmillan, 1938).

49 Kingsley, *West African Studies*, p. 330.

50 Stirling, 'Anthropology', p. 32.

51 Review of 'Scientific Literature', *Popular Science Monthly* 55 (1899): 417–18.

52 James Frazer to Baldwin Spencer (13 July 1898), in Marett and Penniman, *Spencer's Scientific Correspondence*, p. 23.

53 James Frazer, 'The Origin of Totemism', *Fortnightly Review* 71 (1899): 647–65; Andrew Lang, 'Mr. Frazer's Theory of Totemism', *Fortnightly Review* 71 (1899): 1012–25.

54 Spencer's translations from the 'Glossary of Native Terms Used': *Mia*: stands for all women whom his father could have married (p. 653); *Uwinna*: 'the sisters of the boy's father' (p. 222); *Mura tualcha*: 'the woman whose eldest daughter, born or unborn, has been assigned to the *Wurtja* [see n.55 below] as his future wife, so that she is potentially his mother-in-law' (p. 222).

55 Spencer's translations: *Wurtja*: 'Name given to the novice during the ceremonies attendant upon that of circumcision after he has been painted and before the actual operation' (p. 657); *Urinthantima*: 'Name given to the man on whose lap the novice sits during the ceremony of circumcision when the fire stick is handed to him by his *mia* or mother' (p. 656); *Okilia*: 'blood and tribal elder brothers' (p. 222);

Kurdaitcha: 'Name applied to a man who has been either formally selected or goes out on his own initiative, wearing emu-feather shoes, to kill some individual accused of having injured some one by magic' (p. 651).

56 Baldwin Spencer to Henry Balfour (20 September 1897), W.B. Spencer Papers.

57 This is James Frazer's metaphor in his perpetuation of archaeological analogies:

> You have opened up, in my opinion, a deeper mine into the past of human institutions than any one else has ever done; the rest seem by comparison to be scratching the surface. I have worked at the products you have brought up from the mine, as hundreds of people are doing and will do for generations to come.

(Frazer to Baldwin Spencer [undated], in Marett and Penniman, *Spencer's Scientific Correspondence*, p.126)

58 My thanks to Steven Connor for drawing my attention to the way in which both *Heart of Darkness* and *Native Tribes* feed into a more general theoretical and conceptual shift during this period in which the 'Primitive' becomes feminised.

59 Spivak, 'Can the Subaltern Speak?', p. 287.

Chapter 8

From Omphalos to Phallus
Cultural Representations of Femininity and Death

Elisabeth Bronfen

Representations of death articulate both an anxiety about and a desire for death. In so doing, they function like a symptom, which psychoanalytic discourse defines as a repression that fails. In the same displaced manner in which art enacts the reality of death we wish to disavow, any symptom articulates something that is so dangerous to the health of the psyche that it must be repressed. At the same time, it is so strong in its desire for articulation that it cannot be repressed. In a gesture of compromise, the psychic apparatus represents this dangerous and fascinating thing by virtue of a substitution, just as the aesthetic enactment represents death, but at the body of another person and at another site: namely, in the realm of art. A symptom hides the dangerous thing even as it points precisely to it. Fundamentally duplicitous by nature, a symptom tries to maintain a balance of sorts. Yet it does so by obliquely pointing to that which threatens to disturb the order. In respect to death, one could say, it names one thing ('I am the spectator/survivor of someone else's death, therefore I can tell myself there is no death for me'). Yet it means something else ('Someone else is dead, therefore I know there is death'). In short, representations as well as symptoms articulate unconscious knowledge and unconscious desires in a displaced, recoded and translated manner. At stake in the following discussion is precisely this strategy of double articulation in respect to representations of feminine death, and its implications for our culture's attitude towards death.

The central thesis of my book on cultural representations of feminine death can be formulated in the following way.[1] Narrative and visual representations of death, specifically those of dead women, drawing their material from a repertoire of common cultural images, can be read as symptoms of our culture. Through representations of the dead feminine body, culture can both repress and articulate its unconscious knowledge of death, which it fails to occlude yet cannot express directly. If symptoms are failed repressions, representations are symptoms that visualise even as they conceal that which is too dangerous to articulate openly, but too fascinating to repress successfully. They repress by localising death away from the self, situating it at the body of a beautiful woman. At the same time these representations let the repressed return, albeit in a disguised manner.

In this essay I will present some of the theoretical implications that emerged from my work on the aesthetic use of femininity coupled with death. My choice of title indicates a theoretical divergence from and a debt to Freud's discussion of castration, for which the Oedipus complex is the linchpin. For in this theoretical model, the issue of having or not having the phallus is the pivotal indication for the position one can take within culture, regardless of whether one follows classical patriarchy's privileging of the phallus, or a feminist critique of phallocentrism. My title suggests that one should add a second somatic sign, the omphalos, Greek for navel, to a discussion of the subject's position within culture. For the crux of my argument is that beyond the issue of having or not having a culturally privileged sexual organ, what is at stake in representations of feminine death is the failed repression of the unencompassable body of materiality–maternity–mortality, whose anatomical sign is the navel. In fact, I realised as I was writing that I could equally well have called this essay 'From Phallus to Omphalos', because it is a shift through issues of gender designation towards a discussion of death's presence in our psychic and aesthetic representations that I will want to advocate as a possible ethos for feminist critique. But before I can explain what I mean by the navel, and why I suggest a return to the ancient Greek cult object – the omphalos, found at Delphi – a lengthy digression will be necessary – a return to Freud's formulation of the castration complex and a rereading of Sophocles' *Oedipus Rex*, so as to shed light on a moment in this play Freud chose not to read.

In his book on the interpretations of dreams, Freud isolates this play as the illustration for the distressing disturbance in the child's relationship with his parents owing to the first stirrings of sexuality, because the Oedipus legend, according to him, springs from some primeval dream-material which corresponds to two universally persistent dreams – that men dream of having sexual relations with their mothers not only as the 'key to the tragedy' of Oedipus but also as the 'complement to the dream of the dreamer's father being dead'.[2] He calls *Oedipus Rex* a 'tragedy of destiny', whose lesson for the spectator is the 'submission to the divine will and realization of his own impotence'. The compelling force of destiny moves us even today because Oedipus' destiny, he suggests, 'might have been ours – because the oracle laid the same curse upon us before our birth as upon him. It is the fate of all of us, perhaps, to direct our first sexual impulse towards our mother and our first hatred and our first murderous wish against our father. *Our* dreams convince us that is so.' The cultured subject, according to Freud, is one who can abandon these childhood wishes articulated by the Sophocles' tragedy – who can detach his sexual impulses from his mother and forget his jealousy of his father.

Given that incest and patricide are the essence Freud draws from the play, it is interesting to look carefully at his summary of it. The action of the play, he suggests:

> consists in nothing other than the process of revealing with cunning delays and ever-mounting excitement – a process that can be likened to the work of a psycho-analysis – that Oedipus himself is the murderer of Laïus, but further that he is the son of the murdered man and of Jocasta. Appalled at the abomination which he has unwittingly perpetrated, Oedipus blinds himself and forsakes his home. The oracle has been fulfilled. (p. 262)

Yet if we turn to Sophocles' play, we can see that the feminine body is eliminated in a far more dramatic sense than is implied by the standard psychoanalytic formulation 'renunciation of the maternal body'. Freud suggests that this is a story about how it is the destiny of man to recognise his fundamental impotence. Furthermore, he reads it as an allegory about the subject's move from a drive-orientated 'natural' existence to a renunciation of his 'drives', as this renunciation is concomitant with his becoming a cultured being. In so doing, however, he elides a significant moment: the death of Jocasta.

In Sophocles' rendition, Jocasta, after she has warned Oedipus: 'God keep you from the knowledge of who you are', returns to her house and goes straight to her marriage bed, tearing her hair, calling upon her first dead husband Laïus, groaning and cursing her bed, in which – in the words of the messenger – 'she brought forth husband by her husband, children by her own child, an infamous double bond'.[3] Significantly, her actual death is elided by the play, for the rest of the messenger's report renders it only obliquely, concentrating instead on Oedipus' rage and distress. The messenger explains:

> how after that she died I do not know – for Oedipus distracted us from seeing. He burst upon us shouting and we looked to him as he paced frantically around, begging us always: Give me a sword, I say, to find this wife no wife, this mother's womb, this field of double sowing whence I sprang and where I sowed my children! . . . Bellowing terribly and led by some invisible guide he rushed on the two doors – wrenching the hollow bolts out of their sockets, he charged inside.[4]

What this suggests is that there is a dream articulated by Sophocles' play other than the one about our incestual desires for the mother and our patricidal hatred and murderous wishes directed against the father – namely, a dream of matricide. For directly before Oedipus becomes appalled by his unwitting crimes – indeed, just after he has found out that he is the murderer of his father – his response is not atonement but, rather, the desire to commit another murder. Sword in hand, he rushes into the bedroom of his mother/wife, hoping that by killing her he might discharge the guilt he is suddenly burdened with, and thus assert his potency against the curse of facticity which Jocasta brought upon him in the double gesture of giving birth to him and bearing his children.

However, Jocasta thwarts his efforts. As he and his servants enter the room, they find his wife:

hanging, the twisted rope around her neck. When he saw her, he cried out fearfully and cut the dangling noose. Then, as she lay, poor woman, on the ground, what happened after was terrible to see. He tore the brooches – the gold chased brooches fastening her robe – away from her and lifting them up high dashed them on his own eyeballs, shrieking out such things as: they will never see the crime I have committed or had done upon me![5]

Now, if we ask: What would Oedipus have done if Jocasta hadn't committed suicide?, I would venture a speculation. He would have deflected his aggressive instincts from himself on to her, as his initial response indicates he wanted to, and killed her. And – to continue with the question – if he had been successful in this initial matricidal urge, would he have had to blind himself? I would speculate further by answering 'no'. If he could have destroyed 'this mother's womb, this field of double sowing whence I sprang', he would have destroyed the site of his origin, and by extension the so-called curse laid upon him before birth. He could have given birth to himself anew and, in this self-engendered refashioning, cleansed himself from the historical responsibility with which he was born. Killing the mother would have reinstalled his imaginary fiction of omnipotence. One could then read his matricidal impulse as rendering a universal desire other than the one isolated by Freud – the desire to obliterate the guilt and facticity of our historical situation, to establish the illusion that we can become, or remain, innocent, not complicitous and not responsible.[6] It is precisely because Oedipus cannot sever himself from history, cannot move beyond the mortality which the maternal body, the 'field of double sowing', so tragically inscribed in his life, that he must resort to blinding himself.

One might speculate that he becomes appalled at his own abomination (to return to Freud's formulations) precisely because he cannot kill Jocasta. The sight of her dead body lets him realise his own impotence before fate – not only because it becomes a sign for the death and the guilt which any notion of potency would require that he repress, but also, and maybe above all, because his impotence lies precisely in the fact that he himself could not kill this site of his origin. I would add that the fate from which he wishes to escape is not just the crimes of patricide and incest, as Freud would have it. Indeed, Freud has chosen to read the gesture of self-blinding as a symbol for sexual castration and, as such, a gesture of disavowal in response to guilt about incestual and patricidal instincts. Yet it can also be read as a disavowal of a different guilt: the matricidal desire with which he responded when the oracle told him he was not omnipotent. Because over and above incest and patricide there is another fate common to all of us, or perhaps common to men and women alike, in a way the Oedipus complex is not – the curse the oracle laid upon us before our birth: our mortality, and our position within a fateful family line from which we cannot escape; much as Oedipus cannot escape the relation between his own death and his guilt for crimes against his parents and community.

Any fundamental realisation of impotence, I want to argue, involves a recognition of this lack grounding our being. The imaginary reversal of this recognition, the dream of omnipotence, is thus directed towards two moments which Freud's discussion of castration elides. First, the desire for immortality in the face of our recognition that we are fated to be mortal; second, the desire for mythic innocence, for a sacrificial cleansing, against our recognition that we must accept the responsibility of history that comes with birth. The desire to refashion ourselves mythically, so to speak, outside and beyond such historical facticity, is related to, and as illusory as, any myth about immortality. These, I would argue, are two equally fundamental dreams which we not only carry with us from childhood on, but which are also articulated in Sophocles' play – in the representation of the death of Jocasta.

By shifting my reading of the Oedipus story from incest and patricide to failed matricide, and by interpreting the ensuing self-castration as the metonymic substitute for a desire to eradicate the site of one's origin – the mother's womb and the child's remnant of this connection, the navel – I want to move away from the sexual nature of castration to suggest that at the epicentre or navel of all human trauma – what Freud calls the 'recognition of human impotence' – lies a recognition of mortality. This awareness of death, of an *Unheimlichkeit*, a not being fully at home in the world, is handled by displacement; aggression either directed outside or displaced among other body organs – turning into fantasies or realisations of partial dismemberment. Oedipus, unable to kill Jocasta, blinds himself – and this shifts the fear of death into an issue of seeing. Freud's psychoanalysis in turn transforms eyes into a metaphor for the male sexual organ, in a hermeneutic gesture which the existential therapist Irving Yalom calls a 'press for translation' engendered by a recognition of death. Indeed, as Yalom explicates, Freud came to view the nature of trauma as explicitly and exclusively sexual, emphasising abandonment and castration as primary and privileged sources of anxiety in an effort to avoid or exclude a discussion of death.[7]

This inattention to death is particularly striking, given that in the case studies on which Freud initially based his theories about anxiety, trauma, castration and, for that matter, femininity – *Studies in Hysteria* – death pervades the clinical histories of his patients. Each of the three main patients, Anna O, Emmy von N and Elisabeth von R, describes her hysterical symptoms with reference to death, as a fundamentally fateful lack in being. For example, Anna O's hysterical symptoms first developed when her father fell ill, and it is while nursing him that she has her hallucinations and her paralysis – she sees her father with a death's head; sees a snake attack him; sees her own fingers turning into snakes, and her fingernails becoming tiny skulls. Emmy von N's hypnosis reveals that all anxiety-inducing episodes in her life were death-related – having her siblings throw dead animals at her; seeing her sister in a coffin; being frightened by her brother dressed as a ghost; seeing her aunt in a coffin; nursing her tubercular brother, followed by hallucinations at his deathbed; finding her mother unconscious from a stroke and, four years later, finding her dead; and finally, the sudden death of her husband, which triggered the hysterical attacks that brought her to Freud. Finally, Elisabeth von R's illness also began while she was nursing her

118   Elisabeth Bronfen

dying father, and erupted in full force when the disintegration of her family culminated in the death of her much-loved elder sister. Yet Freud, in his final interpretation of each case, either overlooks this connection between hysterical trauma and death, or translates it into issues of sexual loss – castration (as the loss of the phallus) or abandonment (as the loss of the loved object).

What is repressed in Freud's phallic reading, as Yalom emphasises, is that the common denominator of abandonment, separation and castration is the loss and annihilation connected to death. In his very late writings on the death drive, Freud returned to the issue of mortality, which he had chosen to efface at the turn of the century in his *Interpretation of Dreams* and *Studies on Hysteria*. However, he never abandoned the primacy of sexual castration as an explanatory model for psychic organisation and disturbances. As a result of Freud's work on hysteria – where he chooses not to read hysterical symptoms as representations of death anxiety but, rather, insists on these symptoms as articulations of sexual trauma – the so-called 'riddle of femininity' is born. Phallic monism posits Woman as an enigma, so as to elide the other story Freud's hysteric patients were telling him: a story about real death anxiety – just as the insistence on incest and patricide and the non-reading of the desire for matricide in *Oedipus Rex* served to translate issues of mortality and facticity into sexuality, and in so doing served also to repress the knowledge that death lies at the navel of all feelings of impotence.

Phallic monism, I want to argue, translates femininity into an enigma for the masculine subject by devising a twofold symptom-representation – the castrated and the demonic Woman. This Woman becomes the site on to which the patriarchal self can project the recognition of death he is anxious about and, in the double strategy of the symptom, repress this even as he articulates it, because it has been transferred to a different – that is, sexually Other – body. For a feminist hermeneutics, to solve the riddle of femininity means, then, to de-construct such strategies of repression and denial, and to give back to the masculine subject those aspects of the self he has projected on to femininity – such as loss, drives, facticity, vulnerability – all of which emerge as transforma-tions of the concept of mortality.

To be precise, what the phallus, as the privileged signifier for patriarchal notions of potency, ultimately screens out is a recognition of death. Under the aegis of the phallus, culture can insist on concepts of immortality by deflecting notions of mortality, in a 'press for translation', on to the feminine body, sex-ualising them in the image of the castrated or demonic Woman who, as the feminine equivalent of the phallic masculine subject, harbours the denied recog-nition of death. Resolving the 'enigma Woman' in the way I am suggesting, by turning from phallus back to omphalos, means confronting this denied, repress-ed, deflected aspect of human existence – the facticity of being, a recognition of our impotence before death – not as a symptom or a fetish, but as the navel of our being; and I mean navel both literally and metaphorically. The divided subject poststructuralism has advocated does, after all, have a centre – the fact that the presence of death irrevocably produces a split in the subject, from which sexual desire, cultural images of potency and immortality, and neurotic symptoms may emerge. In other words, at its centre the subject is split, because – as the navel, our anatomical sign for the cut from the umbilical cord, indicates – with birth, death inscribes itself into the existence of each child. But this split is also the centre, or navel, of human existence.

Mythopoesis has always seen the navel as a symbol for the connection between child and mother, between human and earth, and as such for ideas about being centred, about a site of origin and termination of being. One speaks of the navel of the world, or the navel of life. Concomitant with this idea of a centred existence is the notion that all life departs from and returns to a sacred centre. Christian mythology sees the altar as an *umbilicus terrae*. Mythopoesis has also drawn on the connection between notions of the navel and the grave.[8] At the same time, the navel, as the centre of existence, always marks the division of the human from the divine, standing as a sign for mortality, for the sin with which all human life is tainted from birth. To give one example: in Plato's *Symposium*, Aristophanes, describing the birth of sexuality, claims that because the initially androgynous humans tried to reach up and set upon the gods, they were punished by being cut in half. The sight of the gash was meant to frighten them into keeping quiet, and although Apollo tied the skin together over the one opening, 'smoothing most of the creases away', Aristophanes suggests: 'he left a few puckers round the navel, to remind us of what we suffered long ago'.[9] As a mythopoeic symbol, the navel represents a truth of origins, the division from

Figure 8.1 The omphalos at Apollo's temple in Delphi

Figure 8.2 Greek omphalos stone

divine immortality, the emergence from and return to the grave. It stands as a sign for the centre, but at the centre there is a void.

This image of the truth of human existence emerging from a centre that is split recalls the priestess at Delphi in a cave-like shrine, chanting the oracle's truth over a cleft in the earth, inspired by mephitic vapours that rose from the earth; and allows me to return to and specify the second concept in my title: the omphalos. In Greek mythology, the omphalos signifies the navel, and refers to a mound-shaped stone cult object, a supremely sacred fetish-thing, to which the suppliant clings, and whose most famous example is found in Apollo's temple in Delphi (see Figures 8.1 and 8.2). Jane Ellen Harrison suggests that this religious fetish was a crucial stake in the conflict between the old matrilinear order of the daimones of Earth and the Olympian Apollo, representative of the new patriarchal order.[10] For the omphalos was initially the sanctuary of Gaia – herself transparent, representing Earth as a maternal divinity. In her power to nourish and protect, she represented a cyclical divinity, giving forth and reclaiming mortal existence. The cult of Gaia acknowledged human mortality and its debt to Earth, and in this religious order, the omphalos as maternal emblem relates both aspects (nourishment and mortality) to the realm of a feminine originary divinity.

In Harrison's reading, the sequence of cults from Gaia to Apollo, during which the progenitrix of all generations of gods was transformed into an antagonistic demonic nature force, was seen as the conflict between the dream-oracle of Earth and Night and the truth of heaven's light and sun. This conflict crystallised precisely in the myth of Apollo's slaying of the snake Python – Gaia's child and guardian of the omphalos, maternal emblem and oracle. There is a

Figure 8.3 A Pompeiian fresco

Pompeiian fresco showing the Python, still coiled around the omphalos, with the high pillar behind it giving it a grave-like look (see Figure 8.3).[11]

Significantly, however, after the displacement of Gaia by Apollo through this sacrificial murder, the general apparatus of her cult, the mephitic cleft in the earth and the omphalos are maintained. The fetish-stone and maternal emblem is transformed into a different signum of the earth's centre upon which Apollo's monistic faith in a paternal God is based – the story that Zeus, seeking the centre of the earth, released two eagles from the eastern and western edges of the world, and they met over Delphi. In his cult, too, the omphalos is the site of prophecy, only now the Delphic navel-stone transforms into a grave-mound, commemorating the sacred snake Python. One could say that this new religious realm was constructed at the site of the grave of the sacred snake, and indeed navel stones are often seen in conjunction with gravestones.

I would like to add a further aspect to this interpretation of the Apollonic omphalos, by suggesting that it is also a fetish or symptom of negation that disavows even as it articulates what it seeks to displace. For we can see the omphalos as displacing Gaia, and with her an acknowledgement of death's presence in life, of our debt to Earth, by commemorating the killing of the snake, our manifest connection to her, our mythopoeic umbilical cord. In other words, even as it displaces the snake, now no longer encircling the omphalos but buried beneath it, it reminds us of the visible connection to the source of life which is also the source of death. The sequence from Gaia's to Apollo's omphalos could then be read in the following way. First, the omphalos signifies the maternal emblem, and serves as a manifest worship of the chasm at the centre of existence – Earth's cleft – with a visible connection to the transparent maternal force given shape in the figure of Python. In the second, Apollonic phase, the omphalos is used as an apotropaic emblem, shielding us from any direct acknowledgement of death as our debt to the maternal Earth. With this shift engendered by virtue of a form of matricide, the omphalos now serves as site of purification and prophecy, but at the same time it commemorates the now invisible umbilical cord – so that (albeit in a displaced manner) Apollo's omphalos, as centre of the world and site of truth, is a gravestone, a latent acknowledgement of death.

I am not advocating the abolishing of a patriarchal, Apollonic world in favour of a return to a matrilinear system. Rather, I want to suggest that it may be useful to see those values which are connected with the cult of Gaia – the earth, the night, the maternal power speaking out of a chasm, explicitly connecting birth with death – as a world-view at the ground and vanishing point of any paternal system, occulted by it, but not absent. My interest in the omphalos is precisely its value as a symbol of loss and commemoration: not so much the omphalos of Gaia's altar, but that of Python's grave-mound. I suggest that we can use this mythopoetic representation to describe an aspect of the destiny of our anatomy other than Freud's story of the phallus – namely, to see the navel as precisely such a gravestone commemorating the death of our Python, the umbilical cord we have lost, which once connected us to the maternal body, site of the renunciation of the maternal body, and recalling what we renounce. With this we enter into the paternal symbolic order, reminiscent of Apollonic laws of clarity, whose reason and order are meant as an apotropaic gesture against the anxiety an acknowledgement of death induces. I would add: it is here that the dream of potency and immortality begins. Yet this navel-grave also admonishes us to remember it as the maternal signature we carry with us into the paternal cultural order, and the sign of the legacy of our debt to death.

The omphalos not only marks the interface between the cult of Gaia and Apollo, the connection between the underworld and heaven, the maternal and the paternal, but in so doing also links the navel as symbol of a ritually marked central source of life and fertility, with its function as a sacred site of sacrifice and commemoration, as a gravestone monument. The shift from omphalos to phallus describes the acceptance of paternal castration – language, culture, law. By turning from the omphalos – the maternal emblem which signifies that life is inscribed by facticity – to the phallus, the human subject can refashion itself beyond facticity (it can imagine its immortality), and beyond its position in a biological generation (it can invent a new family order), even if such self-fashioning involves accepting the fictions of imaginary unity and a community based on placing faith in a self-preserving reality principle.

My redefinition of the omphalos follows Lacan's discussion of sublimation as an ethical category. He sees our psychic histories structured by a fundamental loss of the maternal body – a loss we never possess or represent but, rather, repeat: 'It isn't the lack of this or that, but lack of being whereby the being exists' – one could say an originary and primary cleft.[12] Sublimation works against fictions of potency and immortality by 're-creating' the void left by this loss. Rather than assuaging, sublimation points to what is fundamentally *unheimlich* in our ethos, our way of inhabiting the world; it is omphalic in its re-creation of the cleft that deconstructs imaginary unities, and points to an excess beyond the pleasure principle. Indeed, in 'Direction of Treatment and Principles of its Power', Lacan suggests that when Freud questions the meaning of life, he wishes 'to say that it has only one meaning, that in which desire is borne by death'.[13] In 'The Function and Field of Speech and Language', Lacan adds: 'so when we wish to attain in the subject . . . what is primordial to the birth of symbols, we find it is in death, from which his existence takes on all the meaning it has'.[14]

For Lacan, castration involves coming to terms with what one is not, with what one does not have, with what one cannot be, with a recognition of finitude – that something crucial is always-already lost, and irretrievably so. As Richard Boothby suggests, Lacan's notion of castration 'is only incidentally related to a paternal threat of violence', to the threat of sexual dismemberment; he adds: 'acceptance of castration means [instead] abandoning the narcissistic dream of absolute self-adequacy and submitting to an original being at-a-loss'.[15] It is precisely because the paternal threat and its privileged signifier, the phallus, is only incidental to this death-related notion, castration, while the maternal loss is endemic to it, that I suggest (reformulating Lacan) that the site of castration be relocated – at the navel – and that we read the navel in the sense of Lacan's *objet a* – as a remainder or residue, 'which harkens back to the primordial object of satisfaction, that original object in relation to which every subsequent attempt at satisfaction must be deemed a refinding of the object: the mother'.[16] Precisely because, as Boothby explicates, castration is the detachment of desire from the imaginary Other, and as such part of sublimation; and the *objet a* is 'cut free from the maternal relation' so as to 'circulate in the signifying chain', it is the omphalos which is as much a 'key signifier in the unconscious' as Lacan's phallus. While, in the symbolic order, the phallus points the way to ever-ongoing signification and deferral of desire, the omphalos points to the real, to death, excluded from the imaginary organisation of identity. As an emblem of what I have called the unencompassable body of 'materiality–maternity–mortality', the omphalos can be seen as a crucial site engendering moral law, for in Lacan's formulation, 'the presence of the moral agency is that by which in our activity, in so far as it is structured by the symbolic, the real presents itself'.[17]

The crux of representations of feminine death lies in the way they allow the phallic subject to imagine itself beyond facticity, beyond its omphalos. But – as we found in our discussion of the symptom – they do so by turning precisely to a body encoded with values deriving from this realm to be repressed, namely death and femininity. In the most self-conscious – one could say deconstructive – examples, the real of death ultimately returns to implode imaginary fantasies of omnipotence. I want to end, therefore, with a brief look at a modern rewriting of Oedipus – Hitchcock's *Psycho*, with Norman Bates succeeding at the matricide his mythic forefather was unable to fulfil and displacing his unappeased matricidal impulses among other body-parts in the sense that he turns into an auto-matricidal fetish, by harbouring his dead mother within himself, speaking in her voice, dressing in her clothes, whenever he repeats the first matricidal impulse to kill potential wives/mothers. Like Oedipus, he enters into the privacy of a feminine realm, sword in hand, to stab Marion Crane in her shower at the navel of the film, and visually speaking, the first time we see the knife touch her body, it is pointed just beneath her navel.[18] With the same gesture, Norman enters the basement of his house, ready to kill Marion's sister Lila with a knife as she faces the fetish of his dead mother. In this scene, since Lila and the mother are virtually in the same position, it is unclear who is to be the object of Norman's thrust. While Sam overpowers Norman, the light bulb begins to swing and the mother-fetish seems reanimated, as her image dissolves into that of the courthouse.

If the omphalos as gravestone buries and recalls the absent Python, and with it our connection to the maternal body, it finds two articulations in *Psycho*, correlatives to Oedipus' castrative self-blinding: (1) in the serial murder of women, recalling and potentially replacing the dead, psychically preserved mother; feminine corpses that can be buried in the swamp without leaving traces; (2) in Norman's artistic effort at creating a twofold dead-mother-fetish – the stuffed corpse and his own impersonation of her – by virtue of which he overcomes death even as he preserves death. Indeed, he seems to become a figure of feminine death – killing other women, and himself embodying a dead woman. The body in this case is imperfectly buried because the fetish disavows and acknowledges his crime. This, then, is a story about how matricide grounds a self-fashioning, where the subject disavows death by translating it into a fetish that articulates even as it displaces death.

Yet the reason I want to end with *Psycho* is that while its structural navel lies with the murder of a woman, which is used to articulate/deny the murder of the mother, it ends with birth, and thus with the image of a second navel. After Bates has been brought to the courthouse and the impersonation of the dead mother has been fulfilled, the film closes with three images dissolving into each other. First, Bates smiles, then the face of the mother-fetish is superimposed over his face, merging the two. The next and final shot shows an iron chain pulling the car which contains Marion's corpse out of the swamp. Fundamentally disquieting, however, is the fact that for a split second the iron chain as umbilical cord is superimposed over the throat of Norman/the dead mother, as if it were this fetish, not the car and, with it, Marion's corpse, which is reborn. Then this superimposed image is exchanged for the car, Norman/the dead-fetish-mother's eyes and grinning mouth fade into the swamp as the car is borne out of the black water, the cleft of departure and return, connecting murderer and victim, man and woman (see Figure 8.4).

These three last images are all images of fatal births: Norman giving birth to himself as his dead mother; the mother-fetish as the artificial body he has given birth to, to surpass himself as his mother's natural-born son and the maternal function of natural birthgiving; and the police giving birth to all that is repressed – Marion's corpse and the stolen money. Marion, who was killed in the shower so that she could not be reborn, cleansed of her crime, is here reborn out of the muddy water, but returns already dead. She displaces but also recalls the super-

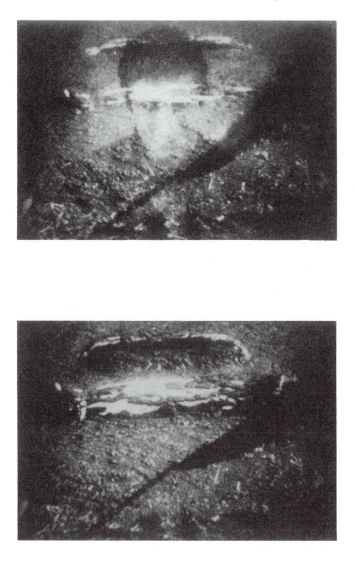

Figure 8.4 Alfred Hitchcock, *Psycho* (1960)

imposed images of No(r)man/the dead mother which, visually speaking, are the progenitors of this still-born-epitome of the unencompassable body of materiality–mortality–maternity, real beyond paternal symbols. In this conglomerate of three feminine death figures, it is as though the phallic is imploded by the omphalos as a chain Python re-emerges, to force upon us, in an image of triple horror, what we would otherwise prefer to deny: the legacy of our mortality.

Notes

1 Elisabeth Bronfen, *Over Her Dead Body: Death, Femininity and the Aesthetic* (Manchester: Manchester University Press, 1992).

2 Sigmund Freud, *The Interpretation of Dreams, Standard Edition*, vol. 4 (London: Hogarth Press, 1955), pp. 261–4.

3 Sophocles, *Oedipus the King*, in *The Complete Tragedies I*, ed. David Grene and Richmond Lattimore (Chicago: University of Chicago Press, 1954), lines 1250–51.

4 *ibid.*, lines 1252–63. I would suggest that, psychoanalytically speaking, the 'invisible guide' leading him to rush so violently upon her bedroom can be interpreted as his destructive drives.

5 *ibid.*, lines 1263–72.

6 Although her conclusions are different from those I am proposing here, Luce Irigaray also places matricide at the centre of her discussion of masculine subjectivity and culture. See *Le corps-à-corps avec la mère* (Montreal: Les éditions de la pleine lune, 1981), pp. 11–33.

7 Irving Yalom, *Existential Psychotherapy* (New York: Basic Books, 1980), pp. 59–74.

8 For a summary of artistic and religious representations of the omphalos, see Bruno Kauhsen, *Omphalos. Zum Mittelpunktsgedanken in Architektur und Städtebau dargestellt an ausgewählten Beispielen* (Munich: Scaneg, 1990).

9 Plato, *Symposium*, in *The Collected Dialogues*, eds Edith Hamilton and Huntington Cairns (Princeton, NJ: Princeton University Press, 1961), p. 543.

10 Jane Ellen Harrison, *Epilegomena to the Study of Greek Religion and Themis: A Study of the Social Origins of Greek Religion* (New York: University Books, 1962), pp. 386–429.

11 Harrison offers one version of this myth where the guardian snake of Gaia is feminine at first and becomes a male serpent only when it has to be killed by Apollo, for only as a masculine being is it a 'foeman worthy of Apollo's steel'. *Epilegomena*, p. 429.

12 Jacques Lacan, *The Seminar of Jacques Lacan. Book II: The Ego in Freud's Theory and in the Technique of Psychoanalysis, 1954–1955*, ed. Jacques-Alain Miller, trans. Sylvana Tomaselli (New York: Norton, 1988), p. 223.

13 Jacques Lacan, *Écrits: A Selection*, trans. Alan Sheridan (New York: Norton, 1977), p. 277.

14 *ibid.*, p. 105.

15 Richard Boothby, *Death and Desire: Psychoanalytic Theory in Lacan's Return to Freud* (London and New York: Routledge, 1991), p. 149.

16 *ibid.*, pp. 165 ff.

17 Lacan, *Le Séminaire de Jacques Lacan. Livre VII, L'Étique de la Psychanalyse*, ed. Jacques-Alain Miller (Paris: Seuil, 1986), p. 28. My translation: 'ma thèse est que la loi morale, le commandement moral, la présence de l'instance morale, est ce par quoi, dans notre activité en tant que structurée par le symbolique, se présentifie le réel'.

18 For a frame-by-frame analysis of this film, see William Rothman, *Hitchcock: The Murderous Gaze* (Cambridge, MA: Harvard University Press, 1982). As an aside, one can note that this scene significantly represents how a cleansing of guilt is not possible. Marion, who has just stolen $40,000, showers to indicate that she has decided to return the money, thus hoping proleptically to wash away the guilt of her crime. Yet it is in this gesture that she is interrupted and stabbed by Norman Bates, refashioned as a feminine death figure, his impersonation of his dead mother.

Part III

Aesthetics

Chapter 9

Unblocking the Oedipal
Karoline von Günderode and the Female Sublime

Christine Battersby

The creation of the aesthetic category of the sublime as a counterpart to the beautiful was integrally bound up with the profound changes in subjectivity that accompanied the agricultural and industrial revolutions of early modernity. Thus although Longinus' *Peri Hypsos* was written sometime before the third century AD, it was only after the appearance of Boileau's famous French translation of 1674 that 'the sublime' became a general – indeed, much overworked – category of aesthetic praise. Retranslations of Longinus followed in scores: not only into English, but also into most other European languages. Boileau had touched on a chord of contemporary taste. It was English-language theorists and critics writing in the eighteenth century, however, who were most influential in setting the parameters for the Romantic sublime: an imaginative and sensory encounter with overwhelming power, magnitude or infinity which was theorised as enabling certain privileged individuals to transcend self for a few, fleeting moments. It was also this English tradition that fed into the aesthetic orthodoxy which restricted to *male* subjects the ability to use the semi-mystical experience of the sublime to create – or often even to appreciate – great works of art.

The choice of the word 'sublime' to translate *hypsos* (by no means an exact equivalent) played an important part in gendering the notion of aesthetic transcendence. From the start, the English word 'sublime' connoted masculinity. Thus, for example, A. Day, in his *English Secretorie* (1586), had described the sublime as a lofty style 'expressing the heroical and mighty actions of kings, etc.'. And in the Preface to Edward Benlowes's *Theophilia* (1652), we can find an even more explicit linking of 'Sublime poets' with 'the masculine and refined pleasures of the understanding', which 'transcend the feminine and sensual of the eye'. These links with masculinity remained embedded in later usage. The gendering of the notion of a self capable of transcendence reaches back to the originary stages of modernity; but not directly to Longinus or to ancient Greece.

Notions of transcendence of the ego remain important within contemporary literary and art criticism, and have been theorised psychoanalytically in ways which, in effect, carry on the traditions of the Romantic sublime. What seem at first sight to be universal and gender-free accounts of the moment of sublimity turn out, on closer inspection, to offer only historically specific and gendered analyses of the dynamics of the modern male self. Thus although Neil Hertz appeals to Longinus as grounding for his model of the dynamics of the sublime in 'A Reading of Longinus' (1973), he also represents the sublime in terms of oedipal power struggles within – and between – male selves. This puzzling and paradoxical move succeeds only by both simultaneously registering and refusing to see that, for Longinus, it was an ode by Sappho addressed to her female beloved that exemplified the sublime: 'Do you not marvel how she seeks to make her mind, body, ears, tongue, eyes, and complexion, as if they were scattered elements strange to her, join together in the same moment of experience?'[1] For Longinus, it was a woman who reconstituted the self, 'Lost in the love trance', from a collection of trembling, sweating, faltering elements. Hertz analyses the sublime in terms of an agonistic competition between self-unity, on the one hand, and that which would overwhelm the self and fragment it.[2] But for Hertz – though not for Longinus – it is the psychic dramas of the male ego that act as both ideal and norm.

Hertz's blindness to the role of women in the Longinian scheme even stretches to describing another of Longinus' paradigm examples of the sublime – Euripides' treatment of Orestes – as the treatment of a 'parricide'.[3] Technically, this might be defensible, given the *OED* definition of parricide: 'One who murders his father or either parent or other near relative'. However, the refusal of the exact term – 'matricide' – which could capture the specificity of Orestes' act is striking. Hertz provides us with a model of psychic relations which, on the surface, is gender-neutral but which, in reality, takes the son's antagonistic relationship with his father as the paradigm for all tensions, oppositions and bondings that exist between the child and others. A hidden matricide is the underpinning for Hertz's account of the sublime: Clytemnestra disappears. And what vanishes even more completely are mother–daughter relationships, and other female–female authorial bondings allowed within the Longinian, but not the Romantic, sublime.

Hertz's essay was an originary contribution to a sequence of writings by American psychoanalytic critics who use Freudian and Lacanian analysis to provide a rationale for Romantic understandings of the sublime experience. Thomas Weiskel extended the psychoanalytic implications of Hertz's argument in his influential volume *The Romantic Sublime* (1976). Weiskel argued that in the negative sublime of the Romantics the self registers excess and the infinite, and forms itself against that moment of recognition of that which is transcendent. Using Kant's analysis in the *Critique of Judgment* (1790) as his model, Weiskel detects two sets of defensive gesture against excess:

To put it sequentially: the excessive object excites a wish to be inundated, which yields an anxiety of incorporation; this anxiety is met by a reaction formation against the wish which precipitates a recapitulation of the oedipus complex; this in turn yields a feeling of guilt (superego anxiety) and is resolved through identification (introjection).[4]

For Weiskel, then, the mother/woman has a role in the story; but only as the underlying threat to the ego, and 'still only [as] a tributary of the Oedipal system into which it invariably flows'.[5]

This last phrase is taken from an important later essay by Hertz, 'The Notion of Blockage in the Literature of the Sublime' (1978). Here Hertz opens up his earlier position in the face of Weiskel's insights, accepting a kind of primary matricide at the root of the sublime. Like Weiskel, Hertz now suggests that it is only against the threat of feminine gaps, excess, formlessness and inundation that the boundaries of the male self are constructed. The sublime reveals the author confronting the blockages – the difficulties – in exerting his self: producing anxieties that are transformed into guilt as they manifest themselves at the secondary (mature) level of the adult self, locked into oedipal struggles of son against father. In this drama of confrontation there is once again no place for mother/daughter bondings, nor for an ego that is not sent into defensive anxiety by confrontation with excess.

Hertz will extend his argument on gender and the sublime one more time: in the afterword to his collected essays, *The End of the Line* (1985). By now, Hertz has confronted feminist criticism; knows his Kristeva; and also discusses a female author (George Eliot) *en route* to an understanding of how femininity figures in the dynamics of the Wordsworthian sublime. In *Daniel Deronda*, he claims, the Princess represents a 'double darkness' – that of the mother, and that of preoedipal chaos – which is cast out as the female author stabilises her identity and places herself within the symbolic contract that exists between author and reader (Hertz, *The End of the Line*, p. 229). Hertz's model has as its underpinning the anxieties of an ego that can become a self only by expelling the other/the mother to whom she/he is bonded. Like males, Hertz's females are also thrown into crisis by unclear boundaries, by excess, by emptiness, by the formless. Female authors now have a place in the scheme; but only – to use Luce Irigaray's terminology – within a 'ho(m)mosexual' economy of the same. Hertz's female authors mimetically reproduce the patterns of male authors, and differ only at the secondary (oedipal) stage. On Hertz's model, if a female author were to be sublime, she could be so only by making herself a Promethean figure who both rebels and identifies with her father/God, and cuts herself off from her mother/chaos/blackness/Nature. She would have to make herself masculine; and her pre-oedipal relationship with her mother would have to resolve itself into oedipal patterns of anxiety and competition.

In 'Toward a Female Sublime' (1989), Patricia Yaeger exploits the pre-oedipal space left in Hertz's later model to argue that three new modes of the female sublime have come into existence in recent decades. The most interesting of these is the one she dubs the 'feminine' or 'pre-oedipal' sublime – renamed the 'lesbian' sublime by Lee Edelman in his response to her paper, because of the daughter's homosexual object choice at the pre-oedipal stage.[6] In the oedipal model that Yaeger inherits from Hertz and Weiskel, we all live within an oedipalised reality in which the self–other relationship is oppositional, and the power of the mother is subordinate to that of the father. In Yaeger's 'feminine' sublime, however,

> the agon typical of the Romantic sublime is retained as part of a narrative or poetic structure, but this oedipal conflict is rewritten so that the pre-oedipal desire for closeness and nearness with the other that the conventional sublime tries to repress, remains visible and viable; it hums pre-oedipal songs from the ruins of an agonistic and oppositional poetics.

Her female author thus 'revels, for a brief poetic moment, in a pre-oedipal longing for otherness and ecstasy'.[7]

Other recent critics have tried to offer alternative analyses of the female sublime. Thus, for example, Timothy Gould has returned to Kant's analysis of the sublime in order to make his 'feminist' turn. Like Yaeger, however, Gould does not stray far from the psychoanalytic model. A revealing footnote expresses his debt to Hertz, and also makes a crucial admission: Gould is convinced 'that the sublime occurs in the shapes first of all not of masculine power as such but of paternal power'.[8] All humans in our culture, on this model, conceive power first and foremost in terms of a father's relationship with his offspring; not in connection with the all-powerful, nurturing mother whom she/he will confront as a baby in the pre-oedipal stage. Perhaps because of this deeply masculinist assumption, Gould also retains another premise of the Kantian/Romantic/psychoanalytic framework: he asks us to 'assume that the experience of the sublime was initially the province of male writers' (Gould, 'Intensity', p. 307).

Patricia Yaeger adopts a similar starting point, remarking in her first sentence: 'In recent decades women have begun to write in the sublime mode – a mode which has, conventionally, been the domain of masculine writers and poets' (Yaeger, 'Toward a Female Sublime', p. 191). Such assertions place an unnecessary divide between a present – in which the female sublime is possible – and a female past, in which it was not. While she stresses mother–daughter relationships at some primary unconscious level, Yaeger thus makes it impossible for contemporary female writers to find and identify with their literary foremothers. It seems to me that this happens because Yaeger adopts the oedipal model of psychic relationships – which treats the antagonistic model of father–son relationships as the norm – before going on to write of the new, female and 'feminine', forms of the sublime, in which there is a less oppositional self–other relationship. Although in the latter the pre-oedipal desire to bond with the (m)other's body is not repressed, and breaks instead 'into consciousness, and [is] welcomed as a primary, healthful part of the writer's experience, as part of the motive for metaphor' (p. 205), Yaeger is still only *modifying* the Hertz model. But within that frame, the epitome of sublime power remains the oedipal father.

I want to put these psychoanalytic starting points into question by looking at one of the ways in which the experience of the sublime was handled subversively by a female writer before the twentieth century. If we fail to see the literary foremothers of the present-day 'feminist' sublime, it is because we are viewing the sublime from a perspective that treats male psyches, experiential histories and dynamic interrelations as norm and/or ideal. From this point of view, past female writers have to be understood as mimetically doubling – or, rather, as failing perfectly to match – the psychic dramas recorded by the males. Thus, for example, Gould suggests that the genre of female 'Gothic' results from women's failure to replicate exactly the social and authorial positions that made the sublime possible for past generations of males (Gould, 'Intensity', pp. 309–10). There are, however, other ways of analysing women writers' relations to the sublime in the early modern period, during which the category was being shaped and marked by gender distinctions.

I have argued elsewhere that Mary Wollstonecraft's *A Short Residence in Sweden, Norway and Denmark* (1796) is an early prose appropriation of the sublime for women, and similar comments apply to her daughter's *Frankenstein* (1818) and *The Last Man* (1826).[9] Such examples might be dismissed on the grounds that the women wrote minor prose, rather than poetry. Here I argue against such dismissals by offering an analysis of a long poem by Karoline von Günderode (1780–1806), '*Einstens lebt ich süsses Leben*'. Since Günderode is little known in England (despite her importance to the contemporary novelist Christa Wolf), my own version, 'Once I Lived a Sweet Life', can be found in the Appendix to this essay.[10]

One of the interesting things about Günderode from a feminist point of view is that she is a theorist herself. Deeply immersed in the systems of Kant and the early Schelling, she develops a female sublime which refuses many of the oppositional categories of Kantian aesthetics that were so central to the Romantic sublime.[11] In particular, she collapses the Kantian distinctions between mind and body; self and other; individuality and infinity. She does not abandon all notion of self, but she wants an individuality that is in harmony with, and permeated by, the opposing forces that together constitute Nature and the All. She rejects Kant's subject/object binarism, and suggests that the ego is an illusion produced by Western culture. Her longing to rejoin the earth and simultaneously dissolve her identity into fluidity resonates throughout her poetry and prose, but cannot be equated with the masculine sublime of her contemporaries, in which ego is transcended and then recuperated. Instead, Günderode reworks the self–other relationship as a way of voicing female poetic transcendence.

In terms of bodily and literary survival, hers is a precarious position. Born in 1780, Günderode ended her poetic career with her suicide on the banks of the Rhine, at the age of 26: a silver dagger stabbed through her heart. She had tied stones in a cloth, clearly intending that her corpse should float free; but she remained on land, only her hair floating in the water. Günderode's suicide was not a transitory whim but the fulfilment of a long-considered objective of dying (gaily) at the right time. Deprived of the possibility of living with the (married) man she loved, she left the house laughing, calling her goodbyes, going back for the cloth in which to wrap the stones. She attempted to merge with the earth and the waters of the Rhine in ways that were consistent with her mystical/ poetic writings.

Although two small volumes of that poetry appeared during Karoline von Günderode's lifetime, and some also appeared in the epistolary novel *Die Günderode* (1840) by her friend Bettina von Arnim, most of her work – including her drama and prose works – remained unpublished for around a hundred years. Much of it seems to have been completely destroyed, including material that her lover, Professor Friedrich Creuzer – perhaps *the* most important German Romantic mythographer – committed himself to publish, and then withdrew at the last moment, for fear of compromising his reputation and his marriage. The poem 'Once I Lived a Sweet Life' comes from her literary remains.

In male Romantic writers of the sublime, there is a narrative 'I' – entrapped in a mortal body – and an imaginative experience in which the finitude of the body is left behind in the confrontation with infinity. Sometimes the transcendent moment is framed as an imaginative tour of the heavens or the deep: technically, Kant's mathematical sublime. Sometimes transcendence comes via a confrontation with the power of nature – storms, gaunt mountains, waterfalls, heroes, wars – technically, Kant's dynamical sublime. In every case, however, there is a move from body to transcendence, and then back to an (ennobled) self. The logic of Günderode's poem could not be more different. We start up in the heavens. And although there is an 'I' flitting like a cloud through the 'deep, holy/ unnameable space of the heavens', this 'I' is bodiless and ephemeral. The repeated word *gaukeln* positions her both as moving like an insect, and as enjoying a state of deceptive illusion. Any sense of solidity in this narrative 'I' is produced only fleetingly, by pain and by loss. The first playfellows – no more substantial than coloured lights – are scared away by 'the great/ hurrying shadow/ who followed them,/ to snatch them up'. Their replacements – the children playing with poisonous snakes – are more substantial, but remain tantalisingly distant.

Indeed, it is the desire of the ephemeral 'I' to position herself among these embodied children, and kiss the feet of their protectress, which sets up the 'deep longing' that will lead to the ejection of the 'I', alone in the immensity of space 'like a child gone astray'. Günderode could hardly be more explicit about the role of the mother in this primary separation: 'And it was as if once I had/ torn myself away from a sweet body,/ and now for the first time/ the wounds of this ancient agony bled.' The 'I' is temporarily presented as a Jesus crucified into selfhood: expelled from glory by God the Mother. No sooner is the separation secured by the processes of loss and rejection, however, than the 'I' turns back towards a state in which self and other interpenetrate.

The 'I' permeates backwards 'through the flowers,/ deeper and deeper'. The way forwards is the way back into childhood, and then further back to a place that grounds life itself. Günderode's desire to rejoin the mother's lap/the earth's shoots/the womb – the German word *Schosse* at the end of the poem collapses all three – is a desire for melting her identity into that of otherness. She wills permeation/fluidity/to flow like tears. She has permeated/penetrated [*durchdrang*: the connotations are sexual] back through all the calyxes/chalices [*Kelche*] to the earth/the spring/source/fountain [*Quelle*] of life: she becomes both self and (m)other. Although for a brief poetic moment this disembodied 'I' had longed for a body – the body of the other – by the end of the narrative all sense of embodiment, or of stability to the ego, is once again lost.

Günderode's sublime involves inversions of space, of time – and of identity itself. It involves no anxiety in the face of the other/the mother, but a double position of reverence for and identification with the mother. There is no struggle for domination here, and no confrontations between an 'I' and an 'it'. Thus, the 'I' nowhere exalts itself by a process of overcoming matter, body or the earth. The 'I' flits 'first here and then there,/ enjoying the lightness of life' – drifting through space, time and identity itself – without abrupt movements of perpendicular transcendence. Neither does this 'I' plummet back down to the earth in an ecstasy of domination. 'I had to cry/ *ich musste weinen*'. Active and passive combine as the 'I' responds to the draw of the earth; overspills in tears; sinks down; is permeated; and also penetrates. Since bodies and identities are not fixed, there is no master.

Indeed, the ultimate power in this poem does not rest with the male. Neither the bridegroom (the heavens) who rocks the earth, nor the sun (a feminine noun in German), nor the 'blissful and laughing' gods exert the power of a patriarchal ruler. Rather, it is the virgin 'Radiant with grace' (Mary? Isis?) who controls [*beherrschend*] the 'fierceness', the 'warring heroes' and the 'powerful beasts'. Günderode evokes a force that is not terrorising: a power that protects children at play, and keeps snakes and threatening shadows at bay.

Günderode is subverting the model of the sublime that she found in Kant and the Romantic poets and philosophers whose work she read so avidly. For Kant, the sublime requires both an appreciation of the terribleness of the object surveyed and a (simultaneous) transcendence of terror in awe for that which could overwhelm the ego. He claims that such pleasures are closed off to all except the 'moral man' who has been educated into confidence in the power of his own ego *over nature*. And Kant is quite explicit about denying women this capacity for negative pleasure: Kantian women are confined to the gentle realm of the beautiful.[12] For him, the pleasures of the beautiful are those which come from recognising the harmony between nature and man's limited senses, needs, appetites and capacity for understanding. The sublime, by contrast, involves a tension between imagination, reason and excess. It involves registering nature as a noumenal, superhuman, non-constructed infinity.

Kant's sublime involves a mastery *over* nature; but it also involves a respect *for* nature, considered as infinity that can never be grasped as a unity. Kant can conceive nothing more sublime than 'the famous inscription on the Temple of

Isis (Mother Nature): "I am all that is and that was and that shall be, and no mortal hath lifted my veil" '.[13] Thus, in a late essay, Kant mocks those who claim to see through the veil and penetrate the secrets of the whole. This is misplaced boasting. Emasculation of reason [*Entmannung*] comes via this polluting contact with matter.[14] Thus, the truly mighty men acknowledge and kneel before 'The veiled goddess . . . that is the moral law in us in its invulnerable majesty'. They 'hear her voice' and 'understand her commandments', but they recognise the impossibility of discovering 'whether she comes from man and originates in the all-powerfulness of his own reason, or if she emanates from some other powerful being whose nature is unknown to him'.[15] According to Kant, the sublime must remain as inexhaustible labour, and not be allied with that which is given as determinate (beauty).

For Kant, nature is constructed in such a way as to be consistent with its invention by man, the lawgiver; but it is also consistent with the laws of a supersensible (and unknowable) God who brought it into existence. We are caught within a dynamic of the (male) transcendental self who probes infinity with his reason, and constructs phenomenal nature – and morality – by the play of his imagination and reason searching after the ungraspable. The 'I am'/ consciousness is powerful enough to bring knowable reality into existence, but will lose its potency (be castrated) if that reality is constructed in such a way as to be exhaustible by reason. Nature and infinity (otherness) have to remain elusive; excess (the sublime) is the object *against* which the fictions of the (male) transcendental self and phenomenal reality are formed.

The early Schelling – and Günderode, who knew her Schelling well – read this infinity of uncompletable nature in a more positive way than Kant had intended. For Günderode, what nature is becomes a non-graspable play of contradictions in which the 'I am' is merely a transitory, fleeting moment expelled from the whole. In the 'Letters between Two Friends' from her posthumous *Melete*, she writes to her friend 'Eusebio' (in reality, Friedrich Creuzer):

> I have stood at the dividing point between life and death . . . I am happy every night and prefer unconsciousness and dark dreams to bright living, why then should I be afraid of the long night and the deep sleep? . . . That you could be lost to me is for me the most painful thought. I said your I and mine would become dissolved in the old, original material of the world. But then I comforted myself again that our elements are so allied that they would respond to the laws of attraction and seek each other out in infinite space and join together with each other again.[16]

Günderode goes on to speculate that it is possible to posit a perfected form of earthly existence when 'all appearances melt into a communal, organic whole; when spirit and body are so interpenetrated that all bodies, all forms are simultaneously thoughts and soul, and all thoughts have at the same time form and body'. Thus, Günderode does not want transcendence of body, but a transformation of the form/matter, self/other, spirit/body dualisms. She wants an attitude to flesh that makes it possible for bodies to be perfect, in a way 'that is very different from what we call form and body'.[17] From her lover, she wants an interpenetration (and completeness) of bodies that involves refusing separation into an 'I' – or, rather, valuing each 'I' as a unique element in the greater organic whole.[18] She wants *him* as a substitute for the *her* which is her lost Mother.

Günderode's male contemporaries understood her as writing the sublime, and their responses mixed admiration with attempts to dissuade. Thus, for example, Clemens Bretano's enthusiasm for her poetry is excessive, but also poisonous. Encouraging her to develop further her gift for creating 'lyrics that are nothing but profound, truth-telling turtle-doves', he complains of her first book:

> you must take care to replace the grey thoughts with bright, lively images. . . . The only thing that can be an objection to your entire collection is that you shift between the masculine and feminine . . . where, for example, words like 'adept', 'apocalyptic' etc are in the titles.[19]

Friedrich Creuzer, by contrast, can accept her mysticism, as long as it is allied to the childlike or to intuitions into nature. He refers approvingly to her ability to position herself as a child 'lying in the lap of the great Mother' – evidently a reference to 'Once I Lived a Sweet Life'. However, he lectures her at some length against tackling 'systematic-heroic dramas' which have come to represent the sublime. Creuzer dissents from this traditional view; nevertheless, he comes out with some very conventional advice in trying to deflect his beloved from writing tragedies. Myths, romances, lyrics and oriental subjects, it seems, are suitable for women; but not *Julius Caesar* or other heroes of Western culture. Awkward enough for a male (unless he is Plutarch or Shakespeare), such histories are 'doubly awkward for a woman'.[20]

When recent psychoanalytic critics represent the sublime as an exclusively masculine genre, they are, therefore, echoing the responses of the male Romantics who worked hard to maintain the gender boundaries around the sublime. The purpose of this essay is not simply to celebrate a literary foremother. It is, rather, to show the continuities between Romantic fathers and their psychoanalytic sons and daughters, and to indicate the consequent limitations on the current options for a feminist, female or feminine sublime. Being a woman is not merely a matter of having a particular biology or set of experiences; it is instead, to be allocated to a non-privileged position in a social and conceptual nexus of power on the basis of the way one's biology is perceived. In terms of Romantic and Kantian aesthetics, 'woman' is part of the excess *against* which the male self is constructed. As such, she is granted neither a fully developed ego, nor the capacity to move 'beyond' ego.

In order to recognise what might be specifically female in aesthetic strategies of the sublime that take us 'beyond self', we must first recognise the blind spots in our current conceptual frame that come from treating the dynamics of the modern male ego as norm and/or ideal. Only by so doing can we see, understand and evaluate the diversity of women's response to their conceptual predicament. The aesthetics of the sublime refuses women an ego firm and secure enough to allow transcendence. But this does not mean that women in our cultural past have not devised their own alternative strategies for charting another form of otherness – for moving beyond their own precarious, female selves.

When Patricia Yaeger and Timothy Gould attempt to develop a feminist perspective on the sublime, they find their backward gaze into literary history blinkered by psychoanalytic assumptions. Not only are female authors erased from that history; but also, the radicality of the female sublime is diluted into that of the far less challenging 'feminine' sublime. Thus by comparing 'Once I Lived a Sweet Life' with Yaeger's essay 'Toward a Female Sublime', we see that Günderode matches – but also exceeds – the pattern of the female sublime depicted there. Günderode fits Yaeger's model in that the pre-oedipal desire to bond with a mother's body is not repressed; the 'subject is infiltrated with the world', and 'otherness is carried to the very heart of selfhood' (Yaeger, 'Toward a Female Sublime', p. 205). In Yaeger's account, however, 'the agon typical of the Romantic sublime is retained as part of a narrative or poetic structure' (p. 204). Thus, Yaeger's poet only 'revels, for a brief poetic moment, in a pre-oedipal longing for otherness and ecstasy' (p. 209). Günderode, by contrast, situates herself in the pre-oedipal; eschews Yaeger's 'agonistic and oppositional poetics' (p. 204); and makes selfhood itself seem transitory. Furthermore, we misunderstand the dynamics of loss and longing in Günderode's work if we read them as simply opening a space for the oedipal triangulations based on father.

In the oedipal model that Yaeger inherits from Hertz and Weiskel, we are all trapped within the father's reality, and the power of the mother can be understood only in terms of that of the father. Yaeger opens a space within that model for a fragile – if compelling – pre-oedipal sublime. For Günderode, however, the fundamental power is that of the mother, and it is a power very dissimilar to that exercised by the father. Yaeger links her feminine sublime with that of two contemporary theorists of *écriture féminine*, Hélène Cixous and Luce Irigaray. But I read these two French writers as in many ways opposed; and Yaeger as closer to Cixous than to Irigaray. The latter raises much more fundamental questions about the presuppositions of psychoanalysis than does Cixous.[21] Indeed, Irigaray denies that mother–daughter relationships can simply be conceptualised by opening a gap within the economy of the male. Nor is she interested merely in a 'feminine' writing that is open equally to males and females. For Irigaray there is no gender-free pre-oedipal moment. Rather, she aims at a female economy based on a mechanics of fluids rather than solids.[22] This cannot resolve itself into agonistic or oedipal power struggles, because it involves an ontology in which boundaries are unclear. Identity does not disappear, but is maintained only by flowing excess.

Like Irigaray, Günderode privileges fluidity over matter, and becoming over being. Both would also agree that what is necessary is to rework the fundamentals of the Kantian scheme: space, time, the 'I am', God, and the relationship between the sensible and the transcendental. It is a shame, therefore, that Irigaray seems unaware of her as a foremother; indeed, that she seems to think it is not worth looking for female precursors within post-Platonic history. For Irigaray treats history as a monolithic unity in which only the male symbolic could find expression. Because she is working to deconstruct and oppose a psychoanalytic model, she finds herself oppositionally confined within a conceptual space in which the structures of the psyche are fixed in the manner of a grammar or language. What I am suggesting, by contrast, is that the maleness of the ego and notions of transcendence are the historical products of modernity, not of ancient Greece or of all patriarchal thought. Furthermore, within modernity there never was a time in which women artists, writers and thinkers did not develop oppositional models for thinking self and transcendence.

This essay should not be read as essentialising a female self or a female sublime. Nor should it be supposed that I am blind to the dangers inherent in Günderode's fate. Instead, I have used Günderode – a historical impossibility in terms of many recent theorists of the feminine – to show how differently positioned are male and female writers with regard to the constructions of self and other during the early modern period. In Freudian and Lacanian theory, the dialectical processes that have erased female authors and artists from history are given a spurious, timeless necessity. If we want to rethink aesthetics from a feminist perspective, we need to open ourselves up to this impossible past and examine the tactics employed by previous generations of creative women. We need a woman-centred history that judges women's achievements in their own terms, not simply as those of 'deviant males'. We need a history turned inside out and upside down: a history that moves 'through the flowers', following the patterns of movement towards the future (via our female origins) that Günderode's poem itself evokes.[23] In this way, we can free ourselves from the oedipal blockages in notions of aesthetic transcendence of the self, and devise strategies for conceptual change. We can also register traps – as well as advances – in the current search for a female sublime. The future for feminist theory lies not in the type of postmodernism that gives up on history but in a thoroughly radicalised and feminised approach to the past.

Appendix

'Once I Lived a Sweet Life', by Karoline von Günderode

Once I lived a sweet life
for it was as if I had suddenly become
but an airy cloud.
Above me I could observe nothing
except a deep blue sea
and I navigated easily around
on the waves of this sea.
Merrily I fluttered in the breezes
of heaven the whole day long,
then lay down happy and fluttering

at the edge of the earth
as, steaming and blazing,
she tore herself from the arms of the sun,
to bathe in the cool of the night,
to refresh herself in the evening wind.
Gripped by the sadness of parting,
the sun's arms went round me then,
and the beautiful, bright rays
loved all and kissed me.
Coloured lights
came spilling down,
skipping and playing,
airy partners
waving in the breezes.
Their garments
purple and golden,
like the deepest blaze
of fire itself.
But they became
fainter and fainter,
paler the cheeks,
extinguished the eyes.
Suddenly my playfellows
completely disappeared,
and as I looked
sadly after them,
I saw the great
hurrying shadow
who followed them,
to snatch them up.
Deep in the west
I still saw the golden
hem of their garments.
Then, flapping slightly, I rose upwards,
flitting first here and then there,
enjoying the lightness of life,
resting in the clear aether.
And in the deep, holy
unnameable space of the heavens
I saw strange and wondrous shapes
and figures that moved.
Eternal gods
sat on thrones
of glittering stars,
looked one at another,
blissful and laughing.
Ringing shields,
clanging spears
were borne by
powerful, warring heroes;
and running before them
were powerful beasts,

others moved
round earth and heaven
in broad bands,
following each other
in eternal circles.
Radiant with grace
a virgin stood
amongst this fierceness,
controlling all.
Lovable children
played amidst
poisonous snakes. –
I wanted to flit over
to the children,
to play with them
and then kiss
the virgin's feet.
And I was caught up in
a deep longing within myself.
And it was as if once I had
torn myself away from a sweet body,
and now for the first time
the wounds of this ancient agony bled.
And I turned towards the earth
as, sweet in drunken sleep,
she rocked in the arm of heaven.
The stars were tinkling softly
so as not to wake the beautiful bride,
and the breezes of heaven played
softly over her tender breast.
Then it was as if I had sprung out
of the innermost life of the mother,
and had reeled forth
into the aetherial spaces
like a child gone astray.
I had to cry,
dripping with tears
I sank down
into the lap of the mother.
Coloured calyxes
fragrant flowers
caught the tears,
and I permeated them,
all the calyxes,
trickled backwards
through the flowers,
deeper and deeper,
right down to the shoots,
to the hidden place
from which life springs.

(Translated by Christine Battersby)

142 Christine Battersby

Notes

1 Longinus, *On Great Writing (On the Sublime)* (Indianapolis: Bobbs-Merrill, Library of Liberal Arts, 1957), pp. 17–18.
2 Neil Hertz, 'A Reading of Longinus' (French 1973; English 1983), reprinted in *The End of the Line: Essays on Psychoanalysis and the Sublime* (New York: Columbia University Press, 1985), pp. 1–20.
3 *ibid.*, p. 9.
4 Thomas Weiskel, *The Romantic Sublime: Studies in the Structure and Psychology of Transcendence* (Baltimore, MD: Johns Hopkins University Press, 1976), p. 105.
5 Neil Hertz, 'The Notion of Blockage in the Literature of the Sublime' (1978), reprinted in *The End of the Line*, p. 53.
6 Patricia Yaeger, 'Toward a Female Sublime', in *Gender and Theory : Dialogues on Feminist Criticism*, ed. Linda Kauffman (Oxford: Blackwell, 1989), esp. pp. 204 ff.; Lee Edelman, 'At Risk in the Sublime', in Kauffman (ed.), *Gender and Theory*, p. 220.
7 Yaeger, 'Toward a Female Sublime', pp. 204, 209.
8 Timothy Gould, 'Intensity and its Audiences: Notes Towards a Feminist Perspective on the Kantian Sublime', *The Journal of Aesthetics and Art Criticism* 48 (1990): 314 note 8; see also note 3.
9 Christine Battersby, *Gender and Genius: Towards a Feminist Aesthetics* (London: The Women's Press, 1989/Bloomington: Indiana University Press, 1990), pp. 92, 100–02.
10 For the German text, see Karoline von Günderrode [*sic*], *Der Schatten eines Traumes*, ed. Christa Wolf (Frankfurt am Main: Sammlung Luchterhand, 1981), pp. 73–6.
11 For Günderode's interest in philosophy, see Bettine [*sic*] von Arnim, *Die Günderode* (1839), ed. Christa Wolf (Leipzig: Insel Verlag, 1983), pp. 21, 132.
12 Immanuel Kant denies women the sublime most explicitly in *Observations on the Feeling of the Beautiful and the Sublime* (1764); but it remains implicit in his analysis in the *Critique of Judgement* (1790), trans. J.H. Bernard (New York: Hafner, 1972), sections 28–9, pp. 99 ff.
13 Kant, *Critique of Judgement*, section 49n, p. 160n.
14 Kant, 'On a Newly Arisen Superior Tone in Philosophy' (1796), in *Raising the Tone of Philosophy*, trans. and ed. Peter Fenves (1796; Baltimore, MD:John Hopkins University Press, 1993), pp. 51 ff. Fenves' translation of 'Von einem neuerdings erhobenen vornehmen Ton in der Philosophie' has only recently appeared, and I am, therefore, deeply grateful to my colleague, Tony Phelan, for allowing me access to the first draft of his own translation. For the passage on the emasculation of reason see pp. 64–6.
15 *ibid.*, p. 71 (amended translation). I have discussed this passage and the role of gender in Kant's system in much greater detail in 'Stages on Kant's Way: Aesthetics, Morality and the Gendered Sublime', in *Feminism and Tradition in Aesthetics*, ed. Peg Brand and Carolyn Korsmeyer (Pennsylvania: Penn State University Press, 1994). This article also includes a brief discussion of Schelling and of Günderode herself. As such, it complements the analysis offered here.
16 Günderode, *Schatten*, p. 115 (my own translation).
17 *ibid.*, p. 117.
18 *ibid.*, p. 124.
19 Brentano's letter of 2 June 1804, *Schatten*, p. 190.
20 Creuzer's letter of 20 February 1806, in *Die Liebe der Günderode: Ein Roman in Briefen*, ed. Franz Josef Görtz (Munich: R. Piper GmbH, 1991), pp. 161–2 (my own translation).
21 See, for example, Luce Irigaray, *Speculum of the Other Woman* (1974), trans. Gillian C. Gill (Ithaca, NY: Cornell University Press, 1985); also *This Sex Which Is Not One* (1977), trans. Catherine Porter and Carolyn Burke (Ithaca, NY: Cornell University Press, 1985).

22 Irigaray, *Speculum*, pp. 106–18.

23 By coincidence, 'Through the Flower' was the title of Judy Chicago's 1974 auto-biography, and of the company which staged her feminist art exhibition 'The Dinner Party'. Chicago adopts a biologistic view of the relationship between female art and the female body (with the flower/calyx directly symbolising female sex organs). By contrast, I see no unmediated relationship between a woman and her body. Since our experience as women is socially, historically and culturally conditioned, it is variable and often conflicting. Female experience is, however, given overall patterning by the social, cultural and symbolic codes that position women as both excess and lacking in regard to the patterns of male development which serve as ideal and/or norm.

Chapter 10

The Gender of Modernity

Rita Felski

In Marshall Berman's influential book *All That Is Solid Melts Into Air: The Experience of Modernity*, the author hails Goethe's Faust as the exemplary hero of the modern age. In the character of Faust, Berman argues, the contradictions of modernity are portrayed with penetrating clarity: on the one hand, an exhilarating sense of liberation resulting from the challenge to tradition and established forms of hierarchical authority; on the other, a nascent bourgeois individualism which asserts itself in the desire for uncontrollable growth and domination over nature. Thus Faust comes to stand for the adventures and horrors, the ambiguities and ironies, of modern life, as exemplified in the creative destruction and constant transformation unleashed by the logic of capitalist development.

And what, one might ask, of Gretchen, the young village girl who is seduced and abandoned by Faust in the course of his striving for new experiences and unlimited self-development? Berman notes that Faust is at first 'enthralled with her childlike innocence, her small-town simplicity, her Christian humility', but gradually finds that 'her ardour dissolves into hysteria, and it is more than he can handle'.[1] 'Drawn impatiently towards new realms of experience and action', Berman explains, 'he has come to feel her needs and fears as more and more of a drag.'[2] While he is aware of some of the complexities of Gretchen's position, Berman's sympathy clearly remains on the side of Faust and his inevitable rejection of the closed, narrow world that Gretchen represents; woman is aligned with the dead weight of tradition, conservatism and an outmoded past which the active, newly autonomous and self-defining subject must seek to transcend. Thus she functions as a sacrificial victim, exemplifying the losses which underpin the ambiguous, but ultimately exhilarating and seductive logic of the modern.

Berman's book had a significant impact on cultural theory in helping to disrupt a recurring equation of modernity with modernism within an Anglo-American tradition of literary and art criticism. Against a purely formal definition of modernism as an array of self-consciously experimental techniques associated with early-twentieth-century high art, Berman drew on a European tradition of theorising modernity as the contradictory ensemble of social, cultural and aesthetic phenomena endemic to capitalist, urbanised, industrialised Western societies. Within such an expanded framework, high modernism was only one of a series of complex cultural responses to the rapid transformations of social relations brought about by modern development. Thus, as Berman eloquently shows, textual expressions of ambiguity, fragmentation and rupture were by no means the exclusive property of the twentieth-century avant-garde, but could be discovered in many nineteenth-century texts which were not overtly experimental in form but nevertheless revealed a profound awareness of the conflicts and crises engendered by processes of modernisation.

Such an expanded and socially embedded conception of the modern text might appear to be highly relevant to feminist critics concerned with rethinking issues of periodisation within literary and cultural history. While efforts have been made in recent years to include more female writers within the modernist canon, a more sustained questioning of existing premises of textual classification leads to an inevitable sense of the inadequacy of classic theories of modernism for understanding women's modernity.[3] Yet in this respect, as my opening paragraph suggests, Berman's richly textured argument remains remarkably monologic; the gender of modernity is unambiguously male.

The exemplary heroes of Berman's text – Faust, Marx, Baudelaire – are, of course, symbols not just of modernity, but also of masculinity, historical markers of the emergence of new forms of bourgeois and working-class male subjectivity. Both in Berman's account of Faust and in his later evocation of Baudelaire's *flâneur*, the stroller who goes 'botanizing on the asphalt' of the streets of Paris,[4] the modern subject is assumed to be an autonomous individual free of familial and communal ties. More generally, established histories of both modernity and modernism have typically relied upon narratives of oedipal revolt against the tyranny of authority, couching their view of the modern as a culture of negation through metaphors of contestation and struggle grounded in an ideal of competitive masculinity.[5] In recent years feminism has developed an extensive critique of such idealised representations of the autonomous male subject, arguing that this ideal of freedom carries within it the seeds of domination in its desire to subjugate the other and its fear of a dependency aligned with the feminine.[6] From such a perspective, Berman's fascination with the ideal of 'restless, endless, self-expansion' embodied in the figure of Faust appears more problematic than he may have intended.

The equation of modernity with masculinity is not, of course, an invention of contemporary criticism. Many of the key symbols and figures of the modern in the nineteenth century – the public sphere, the man in the crowd, the stranger, the dandy, the *flâneur* – were, indeed, explicitly gendered; there could, for example, be no female equivalent of the *flâneur*, given that any woman who loitered in the streets of the nineteenth-century city was likely to be taken for a prostitute.[7] Thus, as Janet Wolff notes, a recurring identification of the modern with the public was largely responsible for the belief that women were situated outside processes of history and social change.[8] In the texts of early Romanticism one finds some of the most explicitly nostalgic representations of femininity as a redemptive refuge from the constraints of civilisation, symbolising a pre-lapsarian condition before the fall into self-consciousness and subject–object relations with nature. Seen to be less specialised and differentiated than man, located within the household and an intimate web of familial relations, more closely linked to nature through her reproductive capacity, woman embodied a sphere of authenticity seemingly untouched by the alienation and fragmentation of modern urban society.

This Romantic view of woman was to retain a significant purchase throughout the nineteenth century, reiterated not just in literature but in a growing range of scientific, historical and anthropological texts which sought to demonstrate women's greater continuity with organic processes and the natural rhythms of pre-industrial society. The establishment of sociology as an academic discipline, for example, both drew upon and reinforced a nostalgic paradigm that defined modernity in terms of the pervasiveness of instrumental rationality and the domination of the cash nexus, while simultaneously revealing a yearning for a purportedly more authentic identity that had been lost.[9]

Here the work of Georg Simmel, one of the few *fin-de-siècle* sociologists to have written extensively about women, provides an illuminating rendering of the gendered subtext underlying much sociological thought. For Simmel, modernity is unambiguously a product of male activity; man is a transgressor of limits, exemplifying becoming rather than being, objectifying himself through a constant dialectic of creativity and production. Woman, by contrast, remains outside of and prior to the subject–object dualism, embodying a condition of archaic, non-differentiated unity. The fragmentation and objectification which define modern culture remain antithetical to a feminine identity that is unmediated, intuitive, directed towards process rather than production. Simmel's debt to a Hegelian paradigm is evident in his assumption that women lack the negativity caused by an alienation from nature which is necessary for reflective self-consciousness. As a result, for Simmel, a feminisation of culture would inevitably require a de-modernisation.[10]

The belief that an authentic female culture would reverse the dehumanising effects of modern urban industrial society remains an influential one in present-day thought. Women's purported affinity with a non-alienated nature has been evoked both by conservatives nostalgic for an idealised pre-modern past and by a tradition of Marxist and feminist critical theorists for whom such a feminine principle embodies a utopian alternative to the domination of instrumental reason and the tyranny of Enlightenment thought. I wish to suggest, however, that such a view of the quintessential maleness of modernity is not a transparent rendition of a pre-existing historical logic, but an interpretative construct shaped by pre-existing ideological premises and narrative tropes. The fantasy ideal of a redemptive organic femininity is itself a product of modern thought, a part of rather than an alternative to the history it claims to transcend. As such, it constitutes only one of several differing and conflicting perspectives on women's relation to modernity.

In the late nineteenth century, for example, this nostalgic vision of woman coexists uneasily with a competing set of representations which define the feminine as emblematic of rather than opposed to the modern. As prevailing attitudes reveal a sharpened sense of the erotic, aesthetic and non-rational dimensions of social life, so the figure of woman is mobilised by artists and intellectuals as a symbol of the contemporary crisis in Enlightenment norms of rationality and progress. Thus a number of critics have noted the significance of the prostitute in the nineteenth-century social imaginary, and her emblematic status in the literature and art of the period.[11] Both seller and commodity in one, the prostitute offered the ultimate instance of the commodification of eros, a disturbing example of the ambiguous boundaries separating economics and sexuality, the rational and irrational, the instrumental and the aesthetic. Like the prostitute, the actress could also be seen as a 'figure of public pleasure',[12] whose deployment of cosmetics and costume bore witness to the artificial and commodified forms of contemporary female sexuality. This motif of the female performer easily lent itself to appropriation as a symptom of the pervasiveness of illusion and spectacle in the generation of modern forms of desire. Positioned on the margins of respectable society, yet graphically embodying its structuring logic of commodity aesthetics, the prostitute and the actress fascinated nineteenth-century cultural critics preoccupied with the decadent and artificial nature of modern life.

The changing status of women under conditions of urbanisation and industrialisation further expressed itself in a metaphorical linking of women with technology and mass production. No longer positioned in simple opposition to the rationalising logic of the modern, women were now also seen to be constructed through it. The mechanical woman is another recurring symbol of modernity, exemplified in such texts as Villiers de l'Isle Adam's story of a female android, *Tomorrow's Eve*.[13] This image of the woman-as-machine comes to crystallise a range of ambivalent responses to the modern. On the one hand, contemporary anxieties about the pervasive effects of industry and technology are evident in the image of the mechanised woman, which explicitly subverts and demystifies the Romantic nostalgia for femininity as a last remaining site of redemptive nature. Yet this figure of the female automaton can also be read as the reaffirmation of a patriarchal desire for technological mastery over woman, expressing a dream of creation without the mother in its vision of artificial reproduction.[14]

The prostitute, the actress, the mechanical woman – it is such *female* figures that crystallise ambivalent responses to capitalism and technology which permeated late-nineteenth-century culture. The list can easily be extended. Baudelaire, for example, draws on an existing cult of lesbian exoticism in depicting the lesbian as a 'heroine of modernity' who defies traditional gender roles by subverting the identification of femininity with natural processes of biological reproduction. The representation of woman as an insatiable consumer is another recurring focal point for anxieties and fantasies about modernity arising out of an ideological shift from traditional values of scarcity and moral restraint to an increasing emphasis on female desire and the pleasures of consumption.[15] Émile Zola's *Nana* is an illuminating text in this regard, bringing together these various notions of femininity with particular clarity.

In his description of Nana's rise from the Parisian slums to the status of celebrated courtesan and woman of fashion, Zola explores the complicated intersections of femininity and modernity. Nana is above all a product of the city; her class mobility is a function of changing social conditions which allow her to make use of the new erotic and aesthetic possibilities of modern urban culture for her own advancement. Rather than existing outside modernity, Nana is clearly revealed to be constructed through it; prostitute, actress, insatiable consumer, she is situated at the very heart of the cash nexus, her social and sexual identity shaped by fashion, image and advertising, her 'perverse' erotic desires linked to modern urban decadence. Nana first appears in the novel as an unknown actress, yet her name is already on everyone's lips, a titillating enigma created through skilful publicity techniques. In the words of Peter Brooks, Nana is revealed as 'a representation *of* a representation, a consciously created and self-creating sex object'.[16] The same will hold true for her later career as high-class courtesan, where her sexual allure remains indissolubly linked to the circulation of her public image. Nana exists in a symbiotic relationship with her audience, her erotic identity a product of the desire of the crowd.

Significantly, public space is also associated in Zola's text with a fear of contamination, confusion and disorder. At the theatre, at the races, at the balls and soirées depicted in the novel, the anonymity and promiscuity of the crowd subvert established social divisions; class hierarchies are undermined in the public domain as disparate individuals rub shoulders in the common pursuit of pleasure. At one point, the text states that Nana's bedroom had also 'become a veritable public place, so many boots were wiped on its threshold'.[17] The metonymic relationship of the bedroom and its inhabitant is quite overt; Nana herself exemplifies the ultimate threat to class distinctions, her body a private site of public intimacy within which the seminal fluids of workers, bourgeois and aristocrats indiscriminately commingle. In Zola's novel, fantasies about the female body merge indistinguishably into anxieties about the modern city, as twin zones of social instability which exemplify the risk of contamination, corruption and the subversion of the law by the tyranny of desire. Indeed, the metropolis will increasingly come to be depicted as a woman in modernist culture, a demonic *femme fatale* whose seductive cruelty exemplifies the delights and horrors of urban life.[18] This identification of femininity with artificiality is further underlined by Nana's perverse desires, her aggressive pleasure in lesbian and sadomasochistic practices overtly at odds with ideals of chaste, domestic womanhood. Thus while female sexuality is demonised in Zola's novel as a source of cultural disorder, this sexuality is itself historicised as a product of the modern social conditions that it simultaneously threatens to undermine.

As eros becomes commodified in the figure of the prostitute, so too the commodity is eroticised within an emerging consumer culture targeted towards female desires. With the introduction of the department store in the mid-nineteenth century, and the expansion of advertising, conspicuous consumption was to become increasingly aligned with middle-class femininity. Women were hence to be identified as the archetypal consumers, bedazzled by the seductive dream-worlds of a nascent mass culture. As Rosalind Williams notes: 'to a large extent the pejorative nature of the concept of consumption itself derives from its association with female submission to organic needs'.[19] In the works of both radical and conservative cultural critics, the idea of modernity was to become inseparable from a pessimistic vision of an irrational femininity seduced by the false allures and glittering promises of capitalist consumerism.

Significantly, to consume also carries negative connotations of to use up, to waste, to exhaust[20] – associations that are clearly in evidence in Zola's representation of Nana's endless and insatiable spending. The text refers to her 'open contempt for money which made her openly squander fortunes . . . men were swallowed up – their possessions, their bodies, their very names – without even leaving a trace of dust behind'.[21] In the novel to consume is indeed literally to destroy, as Nana's voracious passion for commodities brings about the financial ruin, and even the death, of her lovers. The culture of consumerism reaches into and disrupts the sanctity of the private sphere, encouraging women to indulge their appetites in defiance of male authority, and traditional moral and religious prohibitions. Such representations of the insatiable greed of woman in turn suggest displaced anxieties about female sexuality in their depiction of Nana's destructive orality; she is literally a man-eater, consuming her lovers one after another, cannibalistically devouring and destroying the men who desire her. Fears of the 'carnivorous vagina'[22] and of an uncontrolled female desire come together with a pessimistic view of the hedonism and materialism engendered by capitalist expansion to create a dystopian vision of the monstrous consuming woman.

My discussion so far has uncovered two very different visions of gender and modernity circulating within nineteenth-century culture. Whereas the first equates the modern with a male-directed logic of rationalisation, objectification and developmental progress, the second emphasises the centrality of 'feminine' qualities of artificiality and decadence, irrationality and desire. And here one must qualify Janet Wolff's claim that writing about modernity has historically centred upon the experiences of men in the public domain. While this is an accurate description of the sociological texts she discusses, it is much less true of the domain of literature. As art becomes increasingly self-conscious about its own status as representation, and simultaneously turns its gaze towards the enigmatic zone of desire and the unconscious, so the figure of woman emerges as a key symbol of the crisis of the age.

While for Zola this feminisation of culture was linked to a pessimistic vision of degeneration and social decline, for other writers of the period it offered the hope of a radical challenge to the forces of positivism, progress ideology and the sovereignty of the reality principle. Among many of the late-nineteenth-century European avant-garde, for example, an imaginary identification with the feminine provided a strategy for subverting dominant sexual and textual norms. Repudiating realist and naturalist techniques associated with bourgeois masculinity, male aesthetes and early modernists turned towards a decadent aesthetic of surface, style and parody that was explicitly identified as both 'feminine' and 'modern'.[23] Femininity, in other words, emerged as a central motif in the *fin-de-siècle* crisis of literary representation, linked to an aesthetic definition of modernity that emphasised, with Nietzsche, the opacity and ambiguity of language, and the omnipresence of desire.

Of course, the metaphorical centrality of the feminine to nineteenth-century images of modernity remains a not unproblematic phenomenon, given the misogynistic sensibility with which these images were frequently imbued. How, then, do the contrasting visions of male writers compare to women's own representations of the problems and promises of the modern age? Such representations, one may assume, were as diverse and conflictual as those of men, even as they were also framed by the prevailing ideologies of gender within the period. One of the most visible – if not necessarily the most typical – of women's responses to the modern was expressed in the various texts of *fin-de-siècle* feminism which succeeded – in England, at least – in gaining a certain prominence in the public domain. While the New Woman novel has been analysed in some detail in recent years, much less attention has been paid to the various other texts and genres which helped to shape a feminist vision of modernity. Whereas the realist novels of the period remained largely bound by the constraints of the marriage-or-death plot, other forms of writing, such as the political essay and the utopian novel, explicitly invited the imaginative projection of alternative futures. They were thus increasingly appropriated by feminist activists and intellectuals, who were often interested in the modern less as an existing reality than as a promise whose benefits for women had yet to be realised. Feminist writing here acquired a rhetorically performative and prophetic function, seeking to bring into existence, through its own writing practice, that future politicised community to which it aspired.

In other words, rather than comprising purely factual or scientific documents, the feminist essays of the *fin de siècle* created alternative myths of modernity that were powerfully imbued with metaphor, narrative, allegory and a range of other rhetorical devices. In reading Olive Schreiner's *Woman and Labour*, for example, one is immediately struck by the frequency of its appeals to the future, the modern, the new. If a dominant metanarrative shaping the perspective of the male intelligentsia at the turn of the century was one of decline and exhaustion, a sense of having reached the end of an epoch, then one finds in feminist discourse a contrasting narrative of history as progress in which women appear as harbingers of a new age of social change. They are presented as the embodiment of a new spirit, refusing the dead weight of the past and the tyranny of the present in a quest for a more liberating and emancipated future. Thus Schreiner's text ends with these words:

> It is because so wide and gracious to us are the possibilities of the future; so imposs-
> ible is a return to the past, so deadly is a passive acquiescence in the present, that
> today we are found everywhere raising our strange new cry: 'Labour and the training
> that fits us for labour!'[24]

The emancipation of women is presented as inseparably linked to their movement into the workplace and the public sphere. Only under such conditions will
they be freed from 'sex parasitism' – Schreiner's term for the debilitating in-
activity to which middle-class women of the period were condemned. While
Schreiner assumes that this parasitism is an inevitable outcome of modern development, as industry and technology take the place of traditional feminine
skills, she also paradoxically sees history as exemplifying an inexorable movement towards ever greater equality between modern men and women. Thus two
competing metanarratives are at work in Schreiner's text. Her views on female
enervation and debilitation are clearly shaped by prevailing *fin-de-siècle* images of
modernity as an era of decadence and decline – and here Schreiner is not unlike
Zola in describing the 'parasitism' of women (epitomised in the pervasiveness of
prostitution) through recurring metaphors of corruption and disease. Yet at the
same time, she also evokes a competing metanarrative of progress which identifies the New Woman as an inspiratory symbol of modernity at the forefront of
history and social change. Strongly influenced by the evolutionary models of
Darwin and Spencer, while simultaneously contesting their relegation of women
to the margins of temporality and history, Schreiner's text gestures outwards
boldly and restlessly to a distant and dimly envisioned feminist future.

Clearly Schreiner's text, which was seen by many at the time as the 'bible of
the Women's Movement',[25] cannot be read as the unproblematic articulation of
an oppositional feminine voice. It is striking, for example, that her vision of the
emancipated woman describes her as 'active, virile and laborious' – a telling
phrase in its assumption of the necessarily masculine nature of any striving for
autonomy and independence. Schreiner's appeals to a quasi-scientific model of
evolutionary change also locate her firmly within a period which legitimated its
imperialist politics through elaborate justifications of the cultural inferiority of
primitive societies – the assumed inevitability of such a hierarchical ranking of
cultures underpinned even the more progressive feminist texts of the period.
Nevertheless, *Woman and Labour* and other similar works openly challenged
established evolutionary doxa by disrupting a traditionally masculine lineage of
teleological history. Through an appropriation and refashioning of the categories of both evolution and revolution, first-wave feminists articulated their own
growing sense of historical agency as subjects of modernity and liberatory agents
of the new.[26] Many of these texts blurred the distinction between literature and
politics, melodrama and manifesto, as writers drew on a variety of genres to
articulate their sense of the transformative – even revolutionary – promise of

feminism. Women's positioning at the margins of the social and public world meant that their appropriation of existing ideals of progress and equality had potentially threatening implications in challenging the authority of traditional sex roles; hence the widespread condemnation of the New Woman in both popular and high culture texts of the period.

In this context the relationship between feminists and the literary avant-garde of the *fin de siècle* was an ambiguous one: while in certain cases a strategic alliance developed between the two camps, as in the case of Oscar Wilde, more commonly the avant-garde's disdain for political ideals as irrevocably bourgeois was overtly at odds with women's struggle to enter the public sphere. In other words, a non-synchrony of interests emerged between the male intelligentsia's fascination with a transgressive aestheticised femininity arising out of their disenchantment with the Enlightenment project and the feminist interest in appropriating a historically masculine political discourse of progress and citizenship for the benefit of women. The 'modernity' to which each of these groups appealed as a means of legitimating its own enterprise was clearly of a very different order.

In this brief account of some prevalent views of the modern circulating within late-nineteenth-century Europe, I have attempted to explore both the semantic instability of the term and its intimate interconnections with questions of gender. As the idea of the modern reveals different facets and dimensions in its deployment across diverse textual fields, so too representations of woman accrue shifting meanings and metaphorical associations within the various discourses of the *fin de siècle*. 'Modernity' here reveals its inescapably hermeneutic dimension; rather than designating an objectively given referent, it emerges as a contested concept open to appropriation and redefinition in struggles over meaning and interpretation. As a category it is not simply descriptive but constitutive and evaluative, tied to distinctive political and aesthetic agendas which help to define the very reality they claim to describe. What is striking here is the simultaneous imprecision of any invocation of the modern and its discursive power to structure and control new realities[27] – a power of which both men and women availed themselves in the nineteenth century, though often to very different ends.

While the ambiguities of postmodernism have been extensively discussed in recent years, many writers continue, however, to refer to the modern as if it possessed a single and universally acknowledged meaning. As I have already noted, most contemporary theorists have taken male experience as paradigmatic, and failed to consider the question of women's distinctive and complicated relationship to varying aspects of modernisation. Here critics reveal a blindness to gender questions that is strangely at odds with many of the nineteenth-century writers they discuss, for whom the Woman Question was clearly *the* central problem posed by the upheavals of the modern age. Yet some feminists have also tacitly endorsed this view in equating modernity with the monolithic will to power of an Enlightenment rationality.[28] In doing so, however, they deny the contradictory and self-critical dimensions of modern development, which have undeniably engendered new forms of domination, rationalisation and control, but have also made possible expressions of resistance and critique arising out of social transformations within women's experience. One can cite in this context the close interconnections between industrialisation and urbanisation and the emergence of feminist movements in late-nineteenth-century Europe. More generally, such modern phenomena as fashion, consumerism and mass culture have generated new possibilities as well as new constraints for women – a point that is often lost in the context of a powerful Romantic current within feminist thought that remains deeply suspicious of the seductive pleasures of city life.[29]

By contrast, one can point to an alternative – primarily French – intellectual tradition which conceives of modernity in very different terms. In the work of certain poststructuralist theorists, femininity becomes a privileged metaphor for a modernity of aesthetic indeterminacy and libidinal excess linked to the subversion rather than the promotion of Enlightenment ideals. I have explored the origins of this tradition in nineteenth-century representations of woman as an emblematic figure of performance, artifice and desire. Yet this second definition remains equally limiting in its exclusive location of the modern within an aesthetics of rupture and ambiguity at the expense of any consideration of such other – quintessentially modern – phenomena as capitalism, bureaucracy and the private/public distinction. From a feminist standpoint, there are obvious problems with claims for the subversive effects of a feminine textuality which float free of any anchoring in specific analyses of the social positioning and material constraints shaping the lives of men and women.

To read the category of the modern through the perspective sketched out in this essay therefore, is to question the grand theoretical schemata of contemporary critics who proclaim themselves to be 'for' or 'against' modernity. It is to acknowledge that the term is an ambiguous and contested one, its meanings shaped not only by conflicting gender ideologies but by the intellectual traditions of specific national cultures as well as the frameworks of particular disciplinary knowledges. As a multifaceted phenomenon, modernity cannot be summarily designated as either emancipatory or repressive, masculine or feminine; it contains not one logic, but many. As Peter Stallybrass notes: 'It is impossible to define the "modern" as if it had a single referent. Rather, one needs to look at the particular classifications, practices and institutions which the term is used to initiate and support.'[30]

On the one hand, I have argued in this context that the various conceptions and formulations of the modern were – and remain – intimately interconnected with the symbolic politics of gender. In this sense, to write about modernity is always to be already implicated – whether unwittingly or self-consciously – in discourses of sexual hierarchy. Yet I have also questioned the belief that 'modernity' can be reduced to a particular array of institutional or cultural logics which invariably support either patriarchal or feminist interests. Admittedly, a long-standing tradition invites us to identify masculinity with the realm of reason and public discourse, and femininity with the libidinal and the aesthetic. Yet the late nineteenth century saw an unsettling as well as a reinforcement of such dualisms; male artists developed a fascination with a feminised aesthetic sphere at the same time as feminist intellectuals and activists appropriated aspects of a supposedly masculinist discourse of progress. Such instances of cultural 'cross-dressing' indicate the need for careful contextualisation of the changing meanings and political valencies of masculinity and femininity as shaped by the contingencies of sociohistorical context. If gender politics played a central role in shaping processes of modernisation, these same processes in turn helped to initiate an ongoing reconstruction and reimagining of gender.[31]

Notes

1 Marshall Berman, *All That Is Solid Melts Into Air: The Experience of Modernity* (London: Verso, 1983), pp. 53–4.
2 *ibid.*, p. 57.
3 See Meaghan Morris, 'Things to do with Shopping Centres', in Susan Sheridan (ed.), *Grafts: Feminist Cultural Criticism* (London: Verso, 1988), p. 202.
4 Walter Benjamin, 'The Paris of the Second Empire in Baudelaire', in *Charles Baudelaire: A Lyric Poet in the Era of High Capitalism*, trans. Harry Zohn (London: New Left Books, 1973), p. 36.
5 See, for example, Carl Schorske, *Fin-de-Siècle Vienna: Politics and Culture* (Cambridge: Cambridge University Press, 1981), p. xxvi.
6 Jessica Benjamin, *The Bonds of Love: Psychoanalysis, Feminism and the Problem of Domination* (New York: Pantheon, 1988), p. 221.
7 Susan Buck-Morss, 'The Flâneur, the Sandwichman and the Whore: The Politics of Loitering', *New German Critique* 39 (1986): 119.
8 Janet Wolff, 'The Invisible Flâneuse: Women and the Literature of Modernity', *Theory, Culture and Society* 2, 3 (1985): 37–46.
9 See Georg Stauth and Bryan S. Turner, 'The Moral Sociology of Nostalgia', in *Nietzsche's Dance: Ressentiment, Reciprocity and Resistance in Social Life* (Oxford: Blackwell, 1988); Bruce Mazlish, *A New Science: The Breakdown of Connections and the Birth of Sociology* (New York: Oxford University Press, 1989).
10 Guy Oakes, 'Translator's Introduction', in *Georg Simmel: On Women, Sexuality and Love* (New Haven, CT: Yale University Press, 1984), p. 54. See also Suzanne Vromen, 'Georg Simmel and the Cultural Dilemma of Women', *History of European Ideas* 8, 4/5 (1987): 563–79.
11 Recent articles which draw on the work of Walter Benjamin include Buck-Morss, 'The Flâneur, the Sandwichman and the Whore'; and Angelika Rauch, 'The *Trauerspiel* of the Prostituted Body or Woman as Allegory of Modernity', *Cultural Critique* 10 (1989): 77–88. See also Charles Bernheimer, *Figures of Ill-Repute: Representing Prostitution in Nineteenth-Century France* (Cambridge, MA: Harvard University Press, 1989); Alain Corbin, *Women for Hire: Prostitution and Sexuality in France after 1850* (Cambridge, MA: Harvard University Press, 1990); and Lynda Nead, *Myths of Sexuality: Representations of Women in Victorian Britain* (Oxford: Blackwell, 1988).
12 Charles Baudelaire, *The Painter of Modern Life and Other Essays* (London: Phaidon Press, 1984), p. 36.

13 See, for example, Mary Ann Doane, 'Technophilia: Technology, Representation and the Feminine', in Mary Jacobus, Evelyn Fox and Sally Shuttleworth (eds), *Body/Politics: Women and the Discourse of Science* (New York and London: Routledge, 1990).

14 Andreas Huyssen, 'The Vamp and the Machine: Fritz Lang's *Metropolis*', in *After the Great Divide: Modernism, Mass Culture and Postmodernism* (Bloomington: Indiana University Press, 1986), pp. 65–81.

15 For discussions of the lesbian as symbol of modernity, see Benjamin, *Charles Baudelaire*, pp. 90–94; and Lillian Faderman, *Surpassing the Love of Men: Romantic Friendship and Love Between Women from the Renaissance to the Present* (London: Junction Books, 1981), pp. 254–76; for the woman as consumer, see Rachel Bowlby, *Just Looking: Consumer Culture in Dreiser, Gissing and Zola* (New York: Methuen, 1985).

16 Peter Brooks, 'Storied Bodies, or Nana at Last Unveil'd', *Critical Inquiry* 16, 1 (1989): 8.

17 Émile Zola, *Nana* (Harmondsworth: Penguin, 1972), p. 439.

18 See Patrice Petro, 'Modernity and Mass Culture in Weimar: Contours of a Discourse on Sexuality in Early Theories of Perception and Representation', *New German Critique* 40 (1987): 115–46.

19 Rosalind Williams, *Dream Worlds: Mass Consumption in Late Nineteenth-Century France* (Berkeley: University of California Press, 1982), p. 308.

20 Raymond Williams, *Keywords: A Vocabulary of Culture and Society* (London: Fontana, 1983), pp. 78–9.

21 Zola, *Nana*, p. 409.

22 Bernheimer, *Figures of Ill-Repute*, p. 201.

23 Rita Felski, 'The Counter-Discourse of the Feminine in Three Texts by Huysmans, Wilde and Sacher-Masoch', *Publications of the Modern Language Association of America* 106, 5 (1991): 1094–05.

24 Olive Schreiner, *Woman and Labour* (London: Virago, 1978), p. 283.

25 Ruth First and Ann Scott, *Olive Schreiner* (London: André Deutsch, 1980), p. 265.

26 See, *inter alia*, Ann Ardis, *New Women, New Novels: Feminism and Early Modernism* (New Brunswick, NJ: Rutgers University Press, 1990); Sandra M. Gilbert and Susan Gubar, *No Man's Land: The Place of the Woman Writer in the Twentieth Century*, vol. 1, *The War of the Worlds* (New Haven, CT: Yale University Press, 1988), and vol. 2, *Sexchanges* (New Haven, CT: Yale University Press, 1989); Wim Neetens, *Writing and Democracy: Literature, Politics and Culture in Transition* (New York: Harvester, 1991), ch. 5; Elaine Showalter, *Sexual Anarchy: Gender and Culture at the Fin de Siècle* (New York: Viking, 1990).

27 Peter Stallybrass, 'Modern', unpublished Ms.

28 See, for example, Juliet McCannell, *The Regime of the Brother: After the Patriarchy* (New York: Routledge, 1991).

29 For a recent feminist re-evaluation of the city, see Elizabeth Wilson, *Adorned in Dreams: Fashion and Modernity* (Berkeley: University of California Press, 1987); and *The Sphinx in the City: Urban Life, the Control of Disorder and Women* (London: Virago, 1991).

30 Stallybrass, 'Modern'.

31 I would like to express my appreciation to the Commonwealth Center for Literary and Cultural Change at the University of Virginia for institutional and financial support during the writing of this essay.

Chapter 11

AIDS to Narration
Writing Beyond Gender
Derek Duncan

The attribution of the acronym GRID (Gay Related Immune Deficiency Syndrome) to the first presenting cases of what would later be recategorised as AIDS (Acquired Immune Deficiency Syndrome) restored the virulent and only partially outmoded connotations of deviancy and disease to affirmative models of same-sex desire. This pathologised account of the AIDS syndrome has been inexorably linked to the alleged sexual practices and lifestyles of gay men; other cases of HIV infection or AIDS deploy their deviancy precisely in that they stray from the accepted, perverse path of contagion. In terms of this construction, lesbians are stigmatised by contingency, and IV drug users – in many Western countries the other major group affected – remain largely invisible, their public representation being conducted through the channels of the medical establishment. This enforced invisibility derives its energy from the wish to see straight society as impervious to this 'sexually transmitted' virus, and leads to the necessity of conflating acts and essence, as if the presence of AIDS represented nothing other than the truth of its own being. The violence which brands gay men as the rightful bearers of contagion brutally disavows the existence of other PWA (People With AIDS) – women, Blacks, Hispanics, the urban poor, haemophiliacs – unless it is to reassert claims of national or masculine inviolability in displacing the malevolent source of infection on to the dark continents of Africa or of female sex-workers.[1]

In consequence, the gay community has borne a double burden throughout the epidemic – both as a community grievously stricken by HIV and AIDS, and as the community most often perceived to be the source of infection, polluted and polluting in its essence and practices. The gay response to this upsurge in orchestrated homophobia has – as one might expect – been contradictory and complex. The gay community has visibly mobilised and become politicised; first in mainly liberal, reformist activities such as fund-raising and health education, but more recently in direct action and public non-violent assault on institutional neglect. Other responses have been to repudiate the gay identity constructed in the 1970s grounded in specific patterns of sexual behaviour and consumption, and to advocate a 'return' to the values of monogamy or celibacy as a means of staving off the risk of infection and keeping the gay body intact.[2]

What unites these varying responses from the gay community, however, is the notion that since the advent of AIDS, being gay is not what it was. A vast chasm separates the sexual exuberance of the 1970s from the moral austerity of the next decade. This in many ways spurious divide indicates the impermanence of sexual identities, and reveals that 'being gay' is somehow inseparable from 'doing gay': that gay identity is something created and re-created in its performance.[3]

In this essay I will begin an exploration of the ways in which gay identity has become a performance inflected by AIDS by examining some of the cultural forms through which this identity is articulated. I will focus initially on constructions of gay identity in written narrative fiction, a medium which has traditionally foregrounded the negotiating process between subjectivity and the social.[4] Recent feminist criticism has provided the framework for engaging in such analysis particularly with reference to fictions of gender. Eve Sedgwick's comment that 'the difficult questions of generic and thematic embodiment resonate so piercingly with another set of difficult questions, those precisely of sexual definition and embodiment' concisely sets out the challenge to explore the relationship between gender and genre as the space where an aesthetics of identity is enacted and – to reiterate her metaphor – 'embodied'.[5] My purpose here is to begin an examination of how AIDS has affected constructions of gender and of genre, and – no less crucially – how their pre-existing forms have affected the reception of AIDS.

David Leavitt and Edmund White, two of America's most prominent contemporary gay novelists, have written on the entry of AIDS into fiction. In his essay 'The Way I Live Now', Leavitt recalls the prophecy made in 1982 by Richard Howard, another gay writer, that AIDS would change gay literature 'utterly, inexorably'.[6] In the nurturing isolation of Yale, Leavitt affected disbelief, interestingly displacing the prospect of 'gay cancer' on to a group of older and more sleazily promiscuous homosexuals. In time Leavitt would come to concur with Howard's prediction, and he tells of how his cathartic encounter with Susan Sontag's short story 'The Way We Live Now' propelled him to participate in the radical New York ACT UP movement. Leavitt records the inspirational effect of Sontag's work, but omits to explain how AIDS has in fact altered gay literature, even to the point of eliding the questions posed by Susan Sontag's putative presence within that classification. For Leavitt, writing about AIDS is redemptive of unjust suffering and a spur to collective action.

Alternatively, however, Edmund White's analysis of the effects of AIDS on gay cultural production is more solipsistic, albeit less thematic. AIDS, he argues, underlines the artist's precarious mortality. Its spectre induces the abandonment of frivolous pleasure-seeking, and – unlike the popular, essentially corporeal expressions of gay cultural life characteristic of the 1970s — concentrates the mind on the exigencies of high art. The return to an elitist, modernist aesthetic is – apparently unconsciously – linked by White to a sterile, onanistic preoccupation with and imprisonment in an unloved body. Since AIDS, White laments,

> I feel repatriated to my lonely adolescence, the time when I was alone with my writing and I felt weird about being a queer. Art was a consolation then – a consolation for a life not much worth living, a site for the staging of fantasies reality couldn't fulfill, a peopling of solitude – and art has become a consolation again.[7]

AIDS thus invites a regression on both an artistic and an experiential level. Like Leavitt, White concludes his essay, 'The Artist and AIDS', with a plea for political militancy lodged in anger, yet it is an anger constructed nostalgically in redemptive self-oppression.

To view the impact of AIDS on writing in terms of redemption and consolation at best can be said to purge 'gay literature' of any contestatory value, stifling its challenge to heterosexist hegemony, locating it securely within the liberal humanist tradition which has striven to silence it. Less optimistically, it speaks of the impossibility of 'gay literature' articulating an aesthetic which can do anything other than reinscribe its own oppression in terms of regressive and nostalgic formal practices and fantasies.

A correlation between social practices and aesthetic practice in the era of AIDS is also perceived by Susan Sontag:

> The behaviour AIDS is stimulating is part of a larger grateful return to what is perceived as 'conventions', like the return to figure and landscape, tonality and melody, plot and character, other much vaunted repudiations of difficult modernism in the arts.[8]

In contrast to White, Sontag espouses a return to the aesthetic of common sense, of realist transparency, and evinces a longing for the time before AIDS and non-representational art had muddied the artistic agenda. While neither critic embraces a simple reflectionist view of art, both take comfort in the idea that the form of the past can guarantee consolation for aberrant conduct, for an identity misconstructed. In this context AIDS is the death knell of gay literature.

But what had gay literature become, in any case? After the Stonewall riots which led to the birth of the Gay Liberation Movement in the USA, and the partial decriminalisation of homosexuality in England, the gay novel developed strategies for coping with the rigours of the 'gay' plot. Perhaps the earliest and most persistent of these was the 'coming out' novel in which the quest for self-discovery and public recognition provided a narrative trajectory implicitly capable of both 'euphoric' and 'dysphoric' endings.[9] Self-discovery and self-revelation were rewarded by integration into the social body, but their denial resulted in alienation, loss of self, and banishment. The narrative trajectory of this affirmative plot, however, is at odds with its resolution. In the 'coming out' novel, the traditionally masculine quest for self-determination can be said to resolve itself by means of a feminine ending.

Nancy Miller argues that typically, in the eighteenth-century novel, the heroine's plot could end only in marriage or in death. These figures symbolised her success or failure in obtaining social approval and integration. Unlike the libertine, whose sexual adventures nurtured the myth of a conquering masculine ego, the heroine's sense of self depended on her recognition by the world. Caught between the contradictory demands of plot and resolution, the contemporary gay hero, whose act of masculine self-affirmation requires public acknowledgement, finds his quest impossibly engendered. His struggle to accede to masculine entitlement becomes an accession to the double-bind of femininity. The form of the 'coming out' novel challenges – but in the end capitulates to – the binary structure of compulsory heterosexuality, and responds to the demand that gender ambiguity be resolved. The very nature of the 'coming out' narrative reinscribes the notion of the gay man as a feminised subject.

The question of the gay plot as a strategy of resistance to oppressive configurations of gender is crucial to the development of a gay writing practice. For women writers, one way of contesting the oppressive ends of femininity was to write beyond marriage, and to interrogate what happened next. In the context of gay writing and experience, the challenge was to chart what happened after coming out.

Andrew Holleran's novel *Dancer from the Dance* (1978) is an obsessive meditation on plot. It is set for the most part in the clubs of Manhattan and on Fire Island, the archetypal spaces of post-Stonewall mythology; the main section of the text focuses on the gorgeous Malone, 'the emblem of so many demented hearts', the most desired and most enigmatic of all those captured in the vertiginous quest for love.[10] Yet the quest and the novel are premissed on the very impossibility of gay love, grounded as they are in the imitative priority of the heterosexual romance. They are ironic evocations of impossible longings. The novel begins and ends with Malone's mysterious disappearance, and the text is an anxious reworking of the past in an attempt to glean clues as to what became of him. Malone's commitment to love had been enacted in the frantic repetition of his search, and the impossibility of writing his end rehearses precisely the impossibility of this search.

The dysphoric ending of Malone's 'death' is also reflected in the exchange of letters between the narrator and another of the 'doomed' New York circuit queens which frames the narrative. Like Malone, both have missed out on the utopian resolution. The narrator abandons bourgeois respectability to become a hustler, while his correspondent has 'married' and retired over the rainbow to the Deep South, and to a parody of bucolic bliss. The camply ironic correspondence humorously and irrevocably underlines the fact that once you have come out, going back to Kansas is no longer an option. The novel betrays the lie of the feminine ending, but is unable to plot a gay trajectory as anything other than gender pastiche. The novel's narrator ends up by making love pay in an ironic conflation of masculine and feminine ends. Miller's pithy remark about the plight of the heroine finds an echo in the dilemma of the gay hero: their 'Bildung tends to get stuck in the bedroom'.[11]

The post-Bildung gay man moved out of the bedroom and into the bath-house, yet his new location represents an uncomfortable re-creation of domestic space in a quasi-public setting. His gender still consists in his performance as a sexy subject. The novel is unable to inscribe gay masculinity without recourse to already gendered fictions, and narrative's need for resolution invariably leaves the gay subject a 'marked' man. Masculine and feminine coalesce in a fiction of gender which appeals to the heterosexist binary by inverting the purportedly masculine into the truly feminine, and reminds us that one is never both.

But by all accounts, AIDS has altered gay literature. If so, how has it altered the fictions of gender and genre? The AIDS activist and critic Douglas Crimp states: 'AIDS does not exist apart from the practices that conceptualize it, represent it, and respond to it. We know AIDS only in and through those practices.'[12] Crimp's words are an admonishment. AIDS in the novel will become an effect of the novel. The generic conventions in which the novel is embedded will produce an AIDS respondent to the discursive strategies inherent in the genre. Just as the novel is a gendered practice, it follows that AIDS, too, will become implicated in its engendering fiction.

Indeed, if Sontag's account of the syndrome is accurate, AIDS should prove ideal fodder for narrative. She views AIDS as 'progressive, a disease of time' (*AIDS*, p. 21) and, as such, amenable to the developmental pattern of the novel. She particularly notes the slow-moving nature of its progression – a feature which, no doubt, would render it conducive to the realist aesthetic she champions. It is said to possess the virtue of historicising sex, as sex becomes 'a chain of transmission from the past' (pp. 72–3). AIDS can, in addition, supplement the hermeneutic tension of the text: 'the illness flushes out an identity that might have remained hidden' (p. 25). Whodunits easily become whohasits. This ties up with her contention that 'the marks on the face of a leper, a syphilitic, someone with AIDS are the signs of a progressive mutation, decomposition, something organic' (p. 41), indicating the availability of AIDS to semiotic analysis. It is the perfect tool for revealing the truth (of identity). Finally, it is the vehicle for prelapsarian nostalgia: 'sexual behaviour pre-1981 now seems for the middle classes part of a lost age of innocence – innocence in the guise of licentiousness of course' (p. 76). Of course. AIDS is also a morality tale.

These features say nothing about the experience of PWA, but feed uncritically into the ways in which AIDS has been discursively produced. They are precisely the kinds of features which structure Randy Shilts's epic of the AIDS crisis, *And the Band Played On*.[13] Shilts's text is a massive fictionalised account of AIDS up until Rock Hudson's death in 1985, itself a significant endpoint, at least in American perceptions of the syndrome. Promoted as a piece of investigative journalism, Shilts's transcontinental reporting knows no bounds as he unveils the secrets of government inaction and underfunding, the paralysis of health agencies, rivalry between those competing for scarce research resources and kudos, and, in good measure, the lurid practices of sexually active gay men. Shilts's work can be seen as admirable in its intentions but, as Crimp notes, his adoption of an omniscient, universal and consequently heterosexist point of view 'erased his own social condition, that of being a gay man in a homophobic society'.[14] Omniscience, however, comes in many guises, and the effects of Shilts's strategy are most revealing in the light of his appropriation of the already gendered conventions of the thriller and of the mini-series – the ways in which he makes a drama out of a crisis.

The thriller can be said to personify good and evil. The hero engages in a quest or chase to capture the villain, who is always a projection of himself. Having adopted this genre, Shilts is unable to pursue the complexities of the institutional indifference which have magnified the epidemic, and is forced to locate the source of evil/contagion in the figure of an imaginary but identifiable Other. This source he locates in the body of Gaeton Dugas, a French-Canadian airline steward, also known as Patient Zero, whom Shilts regards as responsible for having brought the virus to North America.

The author is indefatigable in his quest to apportion blame, yet the stability of his narrative construction (which necessitates the identification of a single, stable body) can operate only on condition that Gaeton's guilt is perpetually renewed. Gaeton's apparent coherence as the unitary source of contagion functions only as a condition of the renewability of his desire. Thus Shilts's analysis that 'sex wasn't just sex to Gaeton; sex was who Gaeton was – it was the basis of his identity'[15] represents the performative nature of both gay subjectivity and the narrative construct.

Gaeton Dugas is, however, more than this. Hopelessly beautiful, 'Gaeton was the man everyone wanted, the ideal for this community, at this time and in this place'.[16] Gaeton embodies gay desire; he is both its subject and its object. In Shilts's projection it is this desire itself rather than the virus which is fatal: '[Gaeton] was the type of man everyone wanted. What everyone had wanted was bringing them death.'[17] The alleged circularity of same-sex desire instigates a cycle of polluted polluting as Gaeton continues to have sex and, it is implied, to infect others. Peculiarly, those with whom Gaeton has sex (surrogate Shilts) bear no blame, and figure (like Shilts) as the positive term in the narrative dynamic.

Shilts's thriller rewrites what Eve Sedgwick has called the 'paranoid Gothic', that most homophobic of genres, which she defines as 'Romantic novels in which a male hero is in a close usually murderous relation to another male figure, in some respects his "double," to whom he seems to be mentally transparent'.[18] As a result, Shilts writes himself as a victim of the homosexual panic from which gay men ought to have become exempt.

The regressive turn of Shilts's aesthetic practice is also inscribed as he adopts the conventions of the mini-series. This, like soap opera, domesticates issues by bringing them back into the family and allowing them to be explicable solely in its terms. As a result, perverse sexual desire can be only temporarily accommodated. Shilts charts the spread of the virus in the form of an extended family tree; and Gaeton, too, is obsessed by the source of his own infection. More curious, however, is the fact that this obsession parallels an obsession to discover his true family origins. In a bizarre subplot it is revealed that the exquisite Gaeton is not what he seems. Adopted, abused and then disabused of his fantasies of familial grandeur once his real mother is found, Gaeton is both absolved of guilt and robbed of his identity, as the cause of the infection is displaced on to his birth mother. Sadistic and misogynistic, this narrative trajectory serves to bring AIDS back into the family. AIDS, by implication, is inconceivable outside domestic confinement.[19]

The shifting parameters within which gay identity is constructed here obtain a tainted coherence through a pernicious attachment to AIDS essentialism. From the beginning of the novel, Gaeton is affected by 'those embarrassing purple spots'[20] which the reader knows to be the mark of Kaposi's Sarcoma. In Sontag's terms, it is Kaposi's Sarcoma, not AIDS, 'which flushes out an identity that may have remained hidden' (*AIDS*, p. 25). Like the misnamed AIDS test, Kaposi's Sarcoma allows the reader to foreclose the question of identity through the acquisition of a knowledge which exceeds the idea of identity as a social construct. Its lesions are the necessary signs revealing the depth to which homosexuality can descend. As Paula Treichler writes: 'Whatever else it may be, AIDS is a story or multiple stories, read to a surprising extent from a text that does not exist: the body of the male homosexual. It is a text people so want – need – to read that they have gone so far as to write it themselves.'[21] The question of identity will find its resolution through the textualisation of the body: the semiotics of essence and of behaviour.

The visibility of Kaposi's Sarcoma allows the homosexual body to be viewed as an ornamented body, an indelibly mutilated and castrated body. The ornamented/infected homosexual body reveals itself to be a feminised text. Kaposi's Sarcoma betrays the deep truth of an unreliably gendered subject. Similarly, in the generic cross-fertilisation of thriller and mini-series, Shilts attempts to oppose this unreliability with a hermeneutic of gender which would resolve itself in either masculine or feminine terms. The fact that Shilts's narrative ends with the death of Rock Hudson is not accidental, for Hudson's death provided the American media with the spectacle of gendered ambivalence being resolved in the morbid revolt of the masculine body, entrapped and duped by a feminine fiction of the self.[22]

If the presence of Kaposi's Sarcoma allows the spectator to feel secure in the difference of his body, the HIV antibody test intensifies anxiety, advancing the proposition that identity is not a case of visible difference, that one might even be the same – an infected homosexual.

In *People in Trouble*, Sarah Schulman explores the homosexual panic induced by the heterosexual's uncertain proximity to undisclosed deviancy and disease. Peter, the novel's straight male protagonist, wanders by chance into a Catholic church where the Mass is suddenly interrupted by a group of AIDS activists:

> These forty men turned their backs to the pulpit while the service was in progress. Peter's eyes happened to focus on the face of one who seemed somewhat familiar.

Perhaps he lived in the same neighbourhood. The man was thin and unsure of what he was doing. He was lanky and older with a gray mustache and bushy gray hair. He was uncomfortable. The man wore a black T-shirt with a pink triangle and the word Justice across his chest. It did not make him look like Superman. . . .

The men stood with their backs to the priest who continued his service as though nothing had happened. . . .

These are men with AIDS, Peter realized. *Forty of them. But that one doesn't look like he has it. He looks like he works out. The thin one has definitely got it.* . . .

That black man, thought Peter, *I wonder if he's gay or if he got it from drugs.*

Then the black man spoke. . . . Peter noted that the man's voice and gestures were campy.

They shouldn't have let him be the spokesman, Peter thought. *They should have picked somebody more masculine, so people would be more sympathetic.*

Then the mass was over and the men filed out. . . . The ones who were used to being sick always carried sweaters, which they put on over their T-shirts. . . . Once those shirts were covered, they stopped looking like gay men with AIDS. They looked just like everyone else.

That, thought Peter, *is their most effective trick.*[23]

Peter tries to construct a coherent text from these male bodies, but discovers that deviancy and disease are undecidable signs. Is the black man gay or a (straight) drug user? The response is given by the black man's campy body. Thus engendered, the spokesman loses authority, castrated through ornamentation and excess. Peter's categories are subsequently thrown into disarray as the 'men' don their sweaters and – horrifyingly – become the embodiment of everyone else. Their mundanity is duplicitous: it is 'their most effective trick'.

This illicit donning of sweaters is a particularly insidious form of sexual anarchy. As Michael Tolliver in Maupin's *Babycakes* almost remarks to an incredulous acquaintance whose idea of safe sex is to abandon the meat racks in favour of the more respectable genre of the sweater bar: 'disease is no respecter of cashmere'.[24] The notion of gay men in sweaters is one of the central sexual paradoxes of our time, for it tricks the spectator as to the relative significance of the essence of behaviour.

It is the determination to write the homosexual body as a feminised body which characterises discourses of AIDS, and new versions of scientific medical and popular prescriptions have emerged to read punitively the signs of an inherent internal corruption. Once again Sontag presents the case: 'Besides the commonest "presenting" illnesses . . . a plethora of disabling, disfiguring, and humiliating symptoms make the AIDS patient steadily more infirm, helpless, and unable to control, or take care of basic functions and needs' (*AIDS*, p. 21). In the move from disabling to humiliating, physical symptoms swiftly become moral stigmata. Her further contention that while cancer is a disease of the body's geography, AIDS is a temporal affliction, and thus subject to change, demonstrates that for Sontag, AIDS has character. AIDS reconstitutes the self at the very moment when it dissolves corporeal confines.

For Sontag, it is this notion of AIDS as a marker of time that renders it narratively effective: 'The fear of AIDS imposes on an act whose ideal is an experience of pure presentness (and a creation of the future) a relation to the past to be ignored at one's peril. Sex no longer withdraws its partners, if only for a moment from the social' (*AIDS*, p. 72). The fear of infection robs those who assume that they are uninfected of the transcendent joys of sex, yet awards them a personal sense of continuity with the past. For those writing from inside the experience of AIDS, however, the comfort of even such a precarious sense of temporal self-identification breaks down.

In *A l'ami qui ne m'a pas sauvé la vie*, Hervé Guibert rehearses the possible narrative of his infection until he is forced to admit the fatal illusion of his story: 'c'est cette chronologie-là qui devient mon schéma, sauf quand je découvre que la progression naît du désordre' ('it is that chronology which becomes my form, except when I discover that it is born of disorder').[25] Barely in possession of his present, Guibert is dispossessed of his future: 'le plus douloureux dans les phases de conscience de la maladie mortelle est sans doute la privation du lointain, de tous les lointains possibles, comme une cécité inéluctable dans la progression et le rétrécissement simultanés du temps' ('the most painful thing in the phases of consciousness of the fatal illness is, without doubt, being deprived of a sense of distance, of all possible distances, like an inescapable blindness in the simultaneous progression and contraction of time').[26] Similarly, in Maupin's *Sure of You*, Michael remarks: 'Most people thought you got this thing and died. In truth you got this thing and waited.'[27] The future experienced as a perpetual present ill accommodates the exigencies of narrative. If the story of AIDS is to be told – if the self caught up in the syndrome, its effects, and its representations is to find its measure – other means are required.

Paul Monette, himself HIV positive, admits at the beginning of *Borrowed Time*, his memoir of his lover's experience of the progression of AIDS, that the AIDS prognosis causes time to fracture: 'I don't know if I will live to finish this. Doubtless there's a streak of self-importance in such an assertion, but who's counting? . . . All I know is this. The virus ticks in me.'[28]

Monette does live to complete the text, but the terrifying swiftness of his lover's death in the final pages affirms the gallant nature of the attempt. Yet as one reviewer remarked, *Borrowed Time* is an 'elegiac memoir'. The enthusiastic reception which Monette enjoyed in the straight press owed much to his finely worked prose, and the consolatory and dignified manner in which personal suffering is invoked and redeemed through its transformation into art. Monette's writing of AIDS in terms of private grief and fragmented time restores the syndrome to a depoliticised and already gendered context. Unlike Shilts, whose male, heterosexist omniscience seeks to elide gendered difference, Monette writes within the feminine gendered tradition of the first person, the perspective of those excluded from masculine entitlement.

To write AIDS in a manner which contests indiscriminate homophobia is to write from the margins in genres which themselves belong to marginal traditions, and in which protest can be voiced only indirectly. Armistead Maupin's exquisitely written and brilliantly constructed series of novels *Tales of the City* is a soap in which the disparate characters occupy the reconstituted space of an imaginary family. The conventions of the genre impede the articulation of a politics of AIDS in the public sphere, and such comment is only uneasily voiced in the final volume through Thack, Michael's lover, newly arrived from South Carolina for the purpose. His most radical gesture, the building of a spectacular triangular trellis over which he hopes to train a display of pink roses or clematis, remains poignantly domestic. This is symptomatic of the way in which Maupin's novels themselves ineffectually link the personal and the political, despite the weight of the telling commentary on the lived dimension of the AIDS crisis.

Hervé Guibert's two novels about AIDS are written almost in diary form, as past and present overlap in mutual exploration. The temporality of the texts eschews the heroic retrospective of narratives such as Monette's. Guibert writes 'dans cette frange d'incertitude, qui est commune à tous les malades du monde' ('in that margin of uncertainty, which is common to all the sick in the world').[29] Yet the optimistic familiarity of the genre distances him from his experience, for he recognises that the forms of his illnesses dictate the form of the book. He can write only in periods of respite: fatigue determines his capacity for work, the duration of his book's chapters, and seals the organic link between the termination of the narrative and the fatality of his condition. Guibert is neither redeemed nor consoled by his text: 'la mise en abîme de mon livre se referme sur moi. Je suis dans la merde' ('the *mise en abîme* of my book swallows me up. I'm in the shit').[30]

This last expression is more than an exasperated exclamation of disgust and despair. Guibert is in the shit. Confines of body and self have disbanded as he discovers an abjected self whose corporeal anarchy performs itself in spectacle and revelation.[31] His art is born of the body in a way unimagined by White.

Times change, and one of the most marked effects of AIDS is its disruption of projected narratives which narrative, in turn, seeks to contain. But as Guibert demonstrates, AIDS cannot be contained, and narrative becomes an impossible medium for AIDS activism and gay literature. Vibrant and moving as much of this writing has been, established conventions of genre have instituted discursive modes incompatible with politically aggressive reformulations of gender identity and strategies of resistance. If the only plot on offer ends in death, do we really need it?

Perhaps it is because narrative can express gay sexuality only through regressive and oppressive constructs that the most significant cultural productions to come out of the AIDS crisis have emerged in non-narrative artistic practices. Elaine Showalter refers to one of these, the AIDS Memorial Quilt or Names Project, in an essay on the female arts of piecing and quilting. This domestic tradition combines ingenuity, thrift and creativity, and is said to be characteristic of the 'fragmentation of women's time, the scrappiness and uncertainty of women's creative or solitary moments'.[32] Showalter posits a strong link between the formal aspects of quilting and women's lived experience before going on to extend the analogy to female writing practices. She wonders if the AIDS Quilt can be part of this feminine and highly prized tradition, but her response is indirect:

> Folklorists have debated whether the AIDS Quilt belongs to the authentic tradition of women's quilt making or whether it reflects the immensity and distance more characteristic of masculine monuments. The AIDS Quilt cannot be treasured, stroked, held, used to solace sleep. It is not an intimate object. Its attendant metaphors of football, sales conventions and cargo planes evoke a normative, American masculinity perhaps in a deliberate effort to counter the stigma of homosexuality associated with AIDS.[33]

Showalter feels that the public enormity of the Quilt is indicative of a masculinity at odds with the private, domestic female tradition. Astonishingly, she argues that its size represents an affectation of masculinity (mediated through the spaces where the Quilt is shown, and the means of transport required in order to carry it) and a ploy to offset the risk of femininity of which homosexuality is an inexorable effect.[34] Gender and genre are resolved through the knotting and unknotting of compulsory heterosexuality.

Showalter further declines to allow the Quilt a place in the female inheritance, contrasting the monumental time evoked by the durative activity through which burial quilts complete the work of grieving with the haste with which the crudely designed pieces of the AIDS Quilt are assembled. 'Its pieces', she writes, 'are a solace for grief not because they are made privately in a slow process but because they link individual mourning to a national loss.'[35]

In the end Showalter is correct to locate the AIDS Quilt outside the tradition. Unlike the burial quilts which ensured that grief and loss remained family affairs, the AIDS Quilt explodes the boundaries of genre and of gendered space, refusing to allow anger and sorrow to turn inward and pollute the hearth, demanding instead that rage and mourning be turned out into the public domain.

The size of the Quilt is such that it can no longer be shown in its entirety; its dimensions far exceed those masculine arenas which, according to Showalter, metonymically engender it. Like the Quilt, the experience of those living with AIDS exceeds gender. The Quilt mourns and celebrates the lives of all those who have died on account of AIDS, in difference and without indifference.[36]

The transgression of gendered notions of space achieved by the AIDS Quilt is comparable to the effect of the graphics of the New York ACT UP movement.[37] These collectively produced graphics challenge in their modes of representation and their content, yet it is at the site of their consumption that they have their most telling resonance. Exploiting the techniques of advertising and of Pop Art, the posters of ACT UP occupy sites designated precisely for images of mass public consumption. Information regarding safe sex and governmental inaction in the AIDS crisis is no longer restricted to isolated coteries of gay activists, but impertinently disrupts the urban vision and the bland omniscience of the advertising billboard. AIDS activism challenges notices of gendered time and space. Similarly, groups such as Outrage, ACT UP and Queer Nation have abandoned reformist political tactics in favour of terrorist-type, non-violent acts of civil disobedience in response to the death-dealing silence imposed on diversity in gender by the grand democratic narrative.

The timeless graphics of ACT UP are active and reactive. They set political agendas and respond to past acts of malevolence. No elegies, no plots – their meaning is contingent and mobile. Subject to change, their changing subjects become neither encrusted nor entombed in narratives already foreclosed. These acts of resistance produce gay identities in the flux beneath the only apparent stasis of compulsory heterosexuality, relocating the margins and refusing proscriptions of gender already tainted by the heterosexist agenda.

The feminisation of the male, homosexual body is not new; nor is the fatal association of femininity, disease and death. What must be resisted is the too-easy conflation of these ideas which cohere in the fiction of gay subjectivity as its own nemesis. Conversely, what can be embraced by gay men is the feminine as a position on the margins from which to speak desires and identities other than those allowed by the punitive hegemony of heterosexuality. AIDS has become an apparently indelible part of gay men's identities. Identities, however, are fictions of uncertain value, and susceptible to rewriting. As Crimp insists, AIDS as we know it is an effect of discourse: it is thus an effect of gendered discourse. Constructions of gender are notoriously unreliable. The task of gay literature must be to abandon narratives which underwrite the fictitious stability of gender, celebrating instead its treachery – without consolation, without redemption.

Notes

1 Cindy Patton, in *Inventing AIDS* (London and New York: Routledge, 1990), offers the most wide-ranging analysis of the politics and representations of AIDS in relation to different identity groups.

2 David Bergman, in 'Larry Kramer and the Rhetoric of AIDS', in *Gaiety Transfigured: Gay Self Representation in American Literature* (Madison: University of Wisconsin Press, 1991), pp. 122–38, deals with the manner in which this moralistic discourse fed into pre-existing prescriptions of sexual conduct.

3 Diana Fuss writes:

> [i]n both lesbian and gay literature, a familiar tension emerges between a view of identity as that which is always there (but has been buried under layers of cultural oppression) and that which has never been socially permitted (but remains to be formed, created, or achieved). (*Essentially Speaking: Feminism, Nature, and Difference* [London and New York: Routledge, 1989], p. 106)

As Fuss notes, in discussions of lesbian and gay gender formation, emphasis between these poles varies. It is a question of strategy rather than truth.

4 Both Bergman and Thomas Piontek have insisted on the importance of literature in providing a framework of identification for gay subject formation. Piontek also sets this in context by offering a definition of 'gay literature' with which I would largely concur:

> What sets gay literature apart from all other historical forms of homosexual writing . . . is the fact that, for the first time, openly homosexual material was specifically written, produced for, and marketed to a gay audience. . . . What the development of gay literature highlights, then,

is the intimate connection between social formations (for example, the 'gay community') and cultural production. ('Unsafe Representations: Cultural Criticisms in the Age of AIDS', *Discourse* 15, 1 [1992]: 128–53 [137])

In addition, I would want to include material with a homosexual content, relatively explicit or highly encoded, written before this period and subsequently remarketed as 'gay'. Forster's *Maurice* would be an example.

5 Eve Kosofsky Sedgwick, 'The Beast in the Closet: James and the Writing of Homosexual Panic', in *Speaking of Gender*, ed. Elaine Showalter (New York and London: Routledge, 1989), pp. 243–68 (p. 244).

6 David Leavitt, 'The Way I Live Now', *New York Times Magazine*, 9 July 1989, p. 29.

7 Edmund White, 'The Artist and AIDS', *Harper's Magazine*, May 1987, p. 22.

8 Susan Sontag, *AIDS and its Metaphors* (Harmondsworth: Penguin, 1988), p. 78. (All further references are given parenthetically in the text.) Sontag's book is extremely problematic. Her intention to strip AIDS of its metaphors is admirable, if misplaced, implying that there is a true version of AIDS beneath the rhetoric. Ultimately what she writes is a confused and confusing compendium of liberal myths on homosexuality in which it is difficult to isolate an authorial voice amidst the plethora of received ideas. I refer extensively to Sontag because of the attention she pays to the narrative of AIDS and to its literature, but remain distant from the views expressed. D.A. Miller has written the most substantial critique of her project: 'Sontag's Urbanity', *October* 49 (1989): 91–101.

9 These terms are taken from Nancy K. Miller's study of female plotting in the eighteenth-century novel, *The Heroine's Text: Readings in the French and English Novel, 1722–1782* (New York: Columbia University Press, 1980). Miller's work offers a useful perspective from which to consider the development of the gay novel. In the eighteenth century, both the genre and its fictions of gender were just being mapped out and, as in the contemporary gay novel, there was an emphasis on youth as the founding period in identity formation. Her concluding remarks on female identity and the novel might also usefully be applied to gay men:

> Because the form of the novel, more than any other form of art, is forced by the contract of the genre to negotiate with social realities in order to remain legible, its plots are over-determined by the commonplaces of the culture. Until the culture invents new plots for women, we will continue to read the heroine's text. Or we could stop reading novels. (pp. 157–8)

The serviceable nature of the 'coming out' structure is indicated in its adoption by Edmund White to convey both the story of individual sexual development in *A Boy's Own Story* (London: Picador, 1983) and later, in *The Beautiful Room is Empty* (London: Picador, 1988), that of acceding to an understanding of sexual politics in the wake of Stonewall.

10 Andrew Holleran, *Dancer from the Dance* (New York: Bantam, 1978), p. 236.

11 *ibid.*, p. 157.

12 Douglas Crimp, 'AIDS: Cultural Analysis/Cultural Activism', *October* 43 (1987), Special Issue on AIDS, ed. Douglas Crimp: 3–16 (3).

13 Randy Shilts, *And the Band Played On: Politics, People, and the AIDS Epidemic* (New York: St Martin's Press, 1987). The problematic structure of this book has attracted much critical comment. See Douglas Crimp, 'How to Have Promiscuity in an Epidemic', *October* 43: 237–71, in particular 238–46; Thomas Yingling, 'AIDS in America: Postmodern Governance, Identity, and Experience', in *Inside/Out: Lesbian Theories, Gay Theories*, ed. Diana Fuss (New York and London: Routledge, 1991), pp. 291–310; Jeff Nunokawa, ' "All the Sad Young Men": AIDS and the Work of Mourning', in *Inside/Out*, pp. 311–23, in particular pp. 312–14; Ellis Hanson, 'Undead', in *Inside/Out*, pp. 324–40, in particular pp. 331–3; and James Miller, 'AIDS in the Novel: Getting it Straight', in *Fluid Exchanges: Artists and Critics in the AIDS*

Crisis, ed. James Miller (Toronto, Buffalo and London: University of Toronto Press, 1992), pp. 257–71, in particular pp. 257–65. Unlike the above critics, my focus is on the inscription of gender in Shilts's text.

14 Crimp, 'How to Have Promiscuity', p. 245.

15 Shilts, *And the Band Played On*, p. 251.

16 *ibid.*, p. 21.

17 *ibid.*, p. 156.

18 Sedgwick, 'The Beast in the Closet', p. 266.

19 As Lawrence Normand notes above, however (p. 65), there can be subversive political effects of relocating gay relationships within a familial context.

20 Shilts, *And the Band Played On*, p. 79.

21 Paula A. Treichler, 'AIDS, Homophobia, and Biomedical Discourse: an Epidemic of Signification', *October* 43: 31–70 (42).

22 Richard Meyer analyses the ambiguously gendered nature of representations of Rock Hudson's body: 'Rock Hudson's Body', in Fuss (ed.), *Inside/Out*, pp. 259–88.

23 Sarah Schulman, *People in Trouble* (London: Sheba, 1990), pp. 58–9.

24 Armistead Maupin, *Babycakes* (London: Black Swan, 1988), p. 29.

25 Hervé Guibert, *A l'ami qui ne m'a pas sauvé la vie* (Paris: Gallimard, 1990), p. 59.

26 *ibid.*, p. 194.

27 Maupin, *Sure of You* (London: Black Swan, 1991), p. 192.

28 Paul Monette, *Borrowed Time* (London: Flamingo, 1990), p. 1.

29 Guibert, *A l'ami*, p. 11.

30 *ibid.*, p. 267.

31 The political possibilities offered by the dissolving of identities by AIDS are discussed by Leo Bersani in 'Is the Rectum a Grave?', *October* 43: 197–222; and by Thomas Yingling in 'AIDS in America'; they interpret differently the figural and literal valences of the 'death' of the gay subject.

32 Elaine Showalter, *Sister's Choice: Tradition and Change in American Women's Writing* (Oxford: Clarendon Press, 1991), p. 149.

33 *ibid.*, p. 172.

34 Bergman also draws a parallel between the dimensions of the Quilt and masculinity: *Gaiety Transfigured*, p. 138.

35 Showalter, *Sister's Choice*, p. 172.

36 Yingling argues that the effect of the Quilt is so powerful because it communicates 'experience' rather than 'information' through foregrounding the labour which has gone into its making. As a result: 'it allows . . . an affirmation of identity not fated to succumb to the traps of affirmative, bourgeois culture in the determination to seal [gay] identity and those meanings in a world of alienation and death': 'Aids in America', p. 307.

37 For an account of the movement and its graphics, see Douglas Crimp, *AIDS DEMO GRAPHICS* (Seattle, WA: Bay Press, 1990). Catherine Saalfield and Ray Navarro discuss the issues raised by the unrepresentative nature of the movement in terms of gender, racial and class difference, but retain – as I would like to – the strategic value of its political interventions: 'Shocking Pink Praxis: Race and Gender on the ACT UP Frontlines', in Fuss (ed.), *Inside/Out*, pp. 341–69.

Part IV

Repressions

Chapter 12

'The Tyranny of the Passions'

Feminism and Heterosexuality in the Fiction of Wollstonecraft and Hays

Vivien Jones

I

Two hundred years on, one of the central challenges for modern feminism is still – as it was for Mary Wollstonecraft and her contemporaries – to rewrite dominant heterosexual narratives, to tell different stories. The project is a crucial part of any commitment to social and sexual transformation. If we can change the fantasy scenarios through which sexuality and pleasure are structured, we can begin to redefine both 'pleasure' and 'danger', those 'ambivalent and contradictory extremes women experience in negotiating sexuality'.[1] Heterosexuality as romantic love; heterosexuality as violence and violation: by exploring, and celebrating, the complexity and multiplicity of difference, feminism works to resist and redirect the power of these collusive narrative alternatives.

Under what has come to be known as 'second-wave' feminism, that resistance has taken a variety of forms. At one end of a theoretical spectrum the radical lesbian analysis, and some anti-pornography arguments, have confronted heterosexual practice and its representation in particularly uncompromising terms: heterosexual (penetrative, objectifying) sex always, inevitably, enacts and eroticises unequal power relations; 'sleeping with the enemy' is thus beyond political redemption; and feminists are offered a clear choice between heterosexual desire and 'freedom'. From a very different theoretical position – associated again with issues of pornography and representation, as well as with an almost exclusive focus on liberating female sexuality – feminists have joined with gay activists in endorsing a much more libertarian stance, taking up Foucault's appeal to 'bodies and pleasures' as 'the rallying point for the counterattack against the deployment of sexuality'.[2] But old forms remain difficult to displace. At the most recalcitrant level, they stubbornly inform our identities and fantasies. As Kate Soper has recently commented, utopian visions of a society 'freed

from the forms of possessiveness or limits on the possibilities of intimacy between the sexes' can also have a dystopian effect:

> I think we have to accept that even as we welcome these de-gendering develop-
> ments, we are also pulled by our existing identities, and not simply in the sense of
> feeling them to be an obstacle to modes of being which we think are more desirable;
> but also in the sense that a great deal of our excitement and erotic interest is
> dependent upon them.[3]

This, perhaps, is why the editors of a recent collection of essays on heterosexuality can claim that, in spite of everything, it remains 'largely untheorized'
within feminism (Wilkinson and Kitzinger, *Heterosexuality*, p. 1). Heterosexuality, it seems, is still feminism's 'guilty secret': our desires and pleasures cannot
be transformed at will to fit our political analysis.[4]

   This is not to suggest that we should not believe in and struggle for transformations of perhaps a more gradual kind. 'Flesh', as Angela Carter points out,
'comes to us out of history.'[5] And as Freud recognised, one of the most powerful ways in which history writes itself into 'flesh', into 'bodies and pleasures', is
through narratives of desire, the content and objects of which – as Freud more
grudgingly and crucially acknowledged – are unfixed, culturally and historically
specific, and thus subject to change: 'It has been brought to our notice that we
have been in the habit of regarding the connection between the sexual instinct
and the sexual object as more intimate than it in fact is.'[6]

   For women, one of the most pervasive forms of sexual narrative has been
romantic fiction, a genre which – from eighteenth-century novels about resisting
the rake to Mills and Boon – eroticises female passivity. In recent years, as part of
a growing general interest in popular culture and the politics of pleasure, feminists have begun to come out as romance readers – or, at least, as still subject to
the fantasies romance embodies and engenders.[7] Perhaps, as Angela Carter's
postmodern recuperation of romance in her own fictions suggests, one of the
most effective ways of changing heterosexual politics and pleasures is through a
creative rewriting of popular narrative paradigms.[8] In Tania Modleski's words:
'Feminist artists don't have to start from nothing; rather, they can look for clues
to women's pleasure which are already present in existing forms.'[9]

   In this essay I shall be looking at two novels written by radical women in the
revolutionary decade of the 1790s: *Memoirs of Emma Courtney* (1796) by
Mary Hays; and Mary Wollstonecraft's unfinished and posthumously published work, *The Wrongs of Woman* (1798). The focus in both novels is on the
heroine's sexual subjectivity, and their project is precisely to interrogate and
alter dominant narrative, and thus psychic, structures. When women radicals
of this period wrote the history of the French Revolution, they wrote it as
romance or Gothic narrative, seeking to redeem and redirect revolutionary
violence through established 'feminine' plots of sentiment and sexuality. In
their fiction, Mary Hays and Mary Wollstonecraft are concerned to write
revolution and rewrite history by refashioning the inherited form of
eighteenth-century sentimental romance – and with it, female subjectivity.[10]

Very differently situated in relation to discourses of pleasure, and subject to different narratives, 1790s feminism throws our own preoccupations into relief. My hope is that a focus on Wollstonecraft's and Hays's struggles with recalcitrant forms of desire can also be a way of contributing to the history of present sexual subjectivities.

II

For Wollstonecraft and Hays, writing new sexual narratives means bringing the 'rational creatures' imagined in Wollstonecraft's *Vindication of the Rights of Woman* (1792) into confrontation with the power – and attraction – of libertine masculinity. Those 'rational creatures' are the women of the new revolutionary world whom Wollstonecraft brings into being, addressing them as her implied audience, in *Vindication*:

> My own sex, I hope, will excuse me, if I treat them like rational creatures, instead of flattering their fascinating graces, and viewing them as if they were in a state of perpetual childhood, unable to stand alone.[11]

The libertines, responsible here for that alternative, infantilising gaze, represent for Wollstonecraft the old political/sexual order. According to *Vindication*, women become 'rational creatures' precisely by rejecting their 'attachment to rakes' (p. 223), by forging an identity outside libertine constructions and transforming female subjectivity into the '*active* sensibility, and *positive* virtue' described in *The Wrongs of Woman*.[12] 'Sensibility' and 'virtue', when associated with women, had primarily passive and sexual connotations. Wollstonecraft's emphasis on 'active' and 'positive' thus constitutes a redefinition of women's moral and mental capabilities: it gives women the capacity for and the right to social and political intervention.

Wollstonecraft's understanding of the power of the libertine gaze in a fictional context is evident in a review, written in 1791, of Elizabeth Inchbald's novel, *A Simple Story*. In her review, Wollstonecraft complains that 'all female writers, even when they display their abilities, always give a sanction to the libertine reveries of men'. Those 'reveries', she suggests, dictate fictional conventions, producing female fiction as male fantasy: heroines who 'boast of a delicate constitution', and the melodrama of popular sentimental novels, 'the ridiculous and deleterious custom of spinning the most picturesque scenes out of fevers, swoons, and tears' (Todd and Butler [eds], *Works of Mary Wollstonecraft*, vol. 7, p. 370). As Wollstonecraft saw, the 'libertine imagination'[13] dominates eighteenth-century fiction: its structuring gaze denies the possibility of anything other than sexualised heroism, constructing femininity as – in our terms – the passive condition of '*to-be-looked-at-ness*';[14] more insidiously, it motivates plot as the illicit object of desire in popular – particularly women's – fiction through the myth of the reformable rake. In those popular fictions, in which the middle-class heroine attempts to resist premature seduction by the attractive, untrustworthy, aristocratic rake, class aspirations are played out through sexual narrative. Their success as bourgeois myths depends, as Samuel Richardson's *Pamela* (1740) classically demonstrates, on the possibility of taming, and so controlling, the social and economic power represented by the morally reprehensible, but sexually and aesthetically fascinating, libertine figure. Upward social mobility is thus legitimated through female sexual fantasy.

Wollstonecraft's polemical writings offer one of the most incisive analyses we have of the ways in which women internalise the libertine gaze. Yet her writings are themselves still haunted by the fictional paradigm they are concerned to deconstruct. Before turning to the novels, then, I want to look briefly at Wollstonecraft's engagement with the 'libertine imagination' as embodied by her major intellectual adversaries, Burke and Rousseau.

'Libertine reveries' had an urgent political referent for Wollstonecraft in 1791. The previous year, her *Vindication of the Rights of Men* was one of the first radical defences of revolutionary ideals to be written in response to Edmund Burke's *Reflections on the Revolution in France*. In it, she exposes the constitutional implications of Burke's 'debauched' imagination, and makes clear how thoroughly she understood the collusion between sexual ideologies and more general modes of power:

> your politics and morals, when simplified, would undermine religion and virtue to set up a spurious, sensual beauty, that has long debauched your imagination, under the specious form of natural feelings. (Todd and Butler [eds], *Works of Mary Wollstonecraft*, vol. 5, p. 48)

In his *Philosophical Inquiry into the Origin of our Ideas of the Sublime and the Beautiful* (1757), Burke had associated the (feminine) category of Beauty with 'the softer virtues', those 'of less immediate and momentous concern to society'. He had also asserted that 'Beauty in distress is much the most affecting beauty'.[15] In this passage from *Rights of Men*, Wollstonecraft reads Burke against himself to demonstrate the political effects of gendered binary oppositions. In one of the most famous passages in the *Reflections*, Burke laments the end of the 'age of chivalry', evident when 'a nation of gallant men, of men of honour' failed to defend Marie Antoinette: 'I thought ten thousand swords must have leaped from their scabbards to avenge even a look that threatened her with insult.'[16] Behind Burke's own gallant defence of the distressed queen of France, Wollstonecraft detects static essentialist categories which exclude women from historical process by denying them the possibility of rational and spiritual improvement:

> If beautiful weakness was interwoven in a woman's frame, if the chief business of her life is to inspire love, and Nature has made an eternal distinction between the qualities that dignify a rational being and this animal perfection, her duty and happiness in this life must clash with any preparation for a more exalted state. So that Plato and Milton were grossly mistaken in asserting that human love led to heavenly . . . (Todd and Butler [eds], *Works of Mary Wollstonecraft*, vol. 5, p. 46)

'Rational beings' and 'animal perfection'; 'beautiful weakness' and 'a more exalted state': Wollstonecraft reduces the familiar, gendered, eighteenth-century binaries of reason and feeling, beauty and sublimity, to the conditional tense, and so refuses the political, spiritual and sexual stasis ('an eternal distinction') which they underwrite. In its place, she offers a progressivist vision of continuity and transformation, a utopian narrative movement which governs all her writing.

This denial of the objectifying effect of the libertine gaze by telling a story of female (and human) perfectibility is, of course, also central to the *Vindication of the Rights of Woman*:

> if [women] be moral beings, let them have a chance to become intelligent; and let love to man be only a part of that glowing flame of universal love, which, after encircling humanity, mounts in grateful incense to God. (Wollstonecraft, *Vindication*, p. 160)

Here again, gendered binaries are (re)fused as intelligence and love are brought together: 'intelligence' makes women's 'love to man' continuous with a wider social responsibility ('universal love') and, beyond that, the possibility of salvation.

From a modern point of view, passages like this can look disturbingly sublimatory. In reaction against the sexualised femininity produced by 'libertine reveries', *Vindication* famously stresses the conduct-book heroism of rational motherhood as an immediate social programme: 'She no longer thinks of pleasing . . . . Her children have her love, and her brightest hopes are beyond the grave' (p. 139). Some modern feminist commentators have felt that the cost ('in the bloom of life [she] forgets her sex') is too high. Cora Kaplan, for example, in what is still some of the best recent work on Wollstonecraft, argues that in *Vindication*:

> by tampering with the site of degraded sexuality, without challenging the moralising description of sexuality itself, Wollstonecraft sets up heartbreaking conditions for women's liberation – a little death, the death of desire, the death of female pleasure. (Kaplan, *Sea Changes*, p. 39)

In the novels, on the other hand, 'women's feelings and desires, as well as the importance of expressing them, are valorized' (Kaplan, *Sea Changes*, p. 35). In Kaplan's reading, then, sexuality, openly acknowledged in the fiction, becomes the Gothic unconscious disrupting (and thereby, by implication, redeeming for twentieth-century readers) the *Vindication*'s repressive puritan rationalism. And the whole process – the conflict between a bourgeois Enlightenment ethic of moral health and a politics of the body – is seen as symptomatic for the history of feminism itself:

> It is Mary Wollstonecraft who first offered women th[e] fateful choice between the opposed and moralized bastions of reason and feeling, which continues to determine much feminist thinking. (Kaplan, *Sea Changes*, p. 155)

In an attempt to contribute further to that history of the present, I want to raise questions about the implications of reducing 'desire' and 'pleasure' to the narrowly sexualised definitions implicit in this repressive model – definitions which serve only to perpetuate the reason/feeling, reason/sensibility binary which, as I have just suggested, Wollstonecraft herself was trying to break.[17]

The corrective emotional investment of Kaplan's own text ('heartbreaking conditions') is in the liberation of pleasures – though she is properly sceptical about the difficulty and plurality of that project. Already central to the feminist agenda of the 1970s, the valorisation of 'feelings and desires' must also be read in terms of that very specific moment in the early to mid-1980s when the combined pressures of political demoralisation, Thatcherite consumerism and postmodern theory produced on the Left an accommodation of market discourses. For good as well as bad political reasons, 'bodies and pleasures' were – and possibly still are – much more likely to be celebrated than deferred rational utopias. The danger comes in treating forms of sexual liberation and rationalist projects for long-term change as a kind of binary opposition. At that point, 'bodies and pleasures' – whether valorised, as in liberationist models, or rejected, as in some anti-pornography arguments – become de-historicised, fragmented in the perpetual present of postmodernism, or condemned to an endless repetition of the same story.[18] Through their own struggle to break out of imprisoning binaries, Wollstonecraft's texts invite us to address the difficult dialectical relationship between present, deferred and transformed pleasures, between desire and possible narratives for change.

Desire, as a structure of feeling, is actually far from dead in *Vindication*, even if, given different ideological pressures and the importance of a religious frame of reference, it is expressed in terms very different from our own. 'The delusions of passion', Wollstonecraft writes, 'are a strong proof of the immortality of the soul' (p. 169). The comment comes at the end of a symptomatically tortuous passage in which Wollstonecraft confronts the fatal attraction of Rousseau's idealising libertinism. In 1794, in a letter which I shall come back to, she confessed to having 'always been half in love with him' (Wardle (ed.), *Collected Letters*, p. 263).[19] Here, she describes his mind:

> condemned in a world like this, to prove its noble origin by panting after unattainable perfection. . . . An imagination of this vigorous cast can give existence to insubstantial forms, and stability to the shadowy reveries which the mind naturally falls into when realities are found vapid. It can then depict love with celestial charms, and dote on the grand ideal object – it can imagine a degree of mutual affection that shall refine the soul . . . (*Vindication*, p. 168)

Surprisingly, perhaps, given the tone of breathless celebration, this is officially offered as critique, not model. In context, this intellectual love is compared negatively with 'the eager pursuit of the good, which everyone shapes to his own fancy' (p. 169), a more moralised, perfectibilist – and comparatively biddable – version of the Rousseauian mind. Wollstonecraft's text struggles desperately to contain her vision of transcendent romantic (Romantic?) love, deflating the masculine sublime with a discourse of moral improvement. Lying behind Wollstonecraft's attempt to reject Rousseau's romantic ideal is, of course, her recognition of it as exclusively male, a manifestation of his 'voluptuous reveries' (p. 107). But the 'vigorous' libertine imagination proves too seductive, as her next paragraph acknowledges: 'it is not against strong, persevering passions, but romantic wavering feelings, that I wish to guard the female heart' (p. 169). It is difficult to tell whether women are subject or object of the 'passions' and 'feelings' here. And the confusion, like the emotional valorisation of romantic love, betrays the persistence of dominant sexual narratives: allowing women to think of themselves as the objects of 'strong, persevering passions' is, after all, a version of reforming the rake.

But the libidinised subject/object confusion also suggests Wollstonecraft's struggle to become the object of desire, to transform what could be a passive sexual attraction for Rousseau into active identification. As *subjects* of 'strong, persevering passions', women are invited to take on an intellectual identity which refuses static categories and fuses sexual, moral and political desires: they are offered transgressive access to a psychic economy seen as exclusively mas-culine in contemporary ideologies of gender, and with the power to envisage change, to 'give existence to insubstantial forms'.[20]

Later in *Vindication*, Wollstonecraft addresses these issues again, in a tantalis-ing passage which imagines change as having happened. I want to look at that briefly now, before turning to explore questions of desire and progress in the fiction. Wollstonecraft has been discussing women's present 'attachment to rakes' or even 'being rakes at heart' as 'the inevitable consequence of their education':

> Supposing, however, for a moment, that women were, in some future revolution of time, to become, what I sincerely wish them to be, even love would acquire more serious dignity, and be purified in its own fires; and virtue giving true delicacy to their affections, they would turn with disgust from a rake. Reasoning then, as well as feeling, the only province of woman, at present, they might easily guard against exterior graces . . . . They would recollect that the flame, one must use appropriated expressions, which they wished to light up, had been exhausted by lust, and that the sated appetite, losing all relish for pure and simple pleasures, could only be roused by licentious arts or variety. (*Vindication*, p. 223)

'Attachment to rakes' is what must be exorcised in the new order. Wollstone-craft envisages rational, feeling women well able to resist the temptation to try to reform the libertine whose improvable 'flame' has been 'exhausted by lust'. But the imagery of fire complicates the moral message, since it is clearly both spir-itual ecstasy and physical passion. Love 'purified in its own fires' is another version of the transformed and transforming romantic love produced by the 'vigorous imagination' – or, as Wollstonecraft puts it just before the passage quoted, 'the sympathy that unites hearts, and invites to confidence . . . take[s] fire, and thus mount[s] to passion' (p. 223).

This can be usefully glossed by a passage from the letter, to her lover Gilbert Imlay, in which Wollstonecraft confessed to being 'half in love' with Rousseau. Here, 'fire' becomes explicitly the Promethean fire of the imagination.

Wollstonecraft writes from revolutionary Paris. Imlay is on a business trip to London (a trip during which, it later became apparent, he was unfaithful to her):

> There is nothing picturesque in your present pursuits; my imagination then rather chuses to ramble back to the barrier with you . . . [the site of their meetings in Paris].
>
> Believe me, sage sir, you have not sufficient respect for the imagination – I could prove to you in a trice that it is the mother of sentiment, the great distinction of our nature, the only purifier of the passions . . . . The impulse of the senses, passions, if you will, and the conclusions of reason, draw men together; but the imagination is the true fire, stolen from heaven, to animate this cold creature of clay, producing all those fine sympathies that lead to rapture, rendering men social by expanding their hearts, instead of leaving them leisure to calculate how many comforts society affords.
>
> If you call these observations romantic . . . I shall be apt to retort, that you are embruted by trade and the vulgar enjoyments of life . . . (Wardle [ed.], *Collected Letters*, p. 263)[21]

The sexual imagination transmutes seamlessly into a (feminine) version of the Romantic imagination and a revolutionary social vision. Imaginative fire, 'producing all those fine sympathies that lead to rapture', is explicitly opposed to Imlay's bourgeois masculinity, 'embruted by trade'. But Wollstonecraft teases Imlay not just with an alternative feminine discourse, but with a rival lover: her aesthetic and epistemological ideal inevitably invokes Rousseau, with whom she had just admitted to being 'half in love'. In Wollstonecraft's intellectual romance, this affair of the heart and mind, the upward social mobility of sentimental fiction is replaced by a visionary ideal of community. Her task in writing fiction, then, is to realise this radicalised heterosexual romance within a popular genre – and to produce a new masculinity as the object of (imaginative) desire.

III

Wollstonecraft's *Wrongs of Woman* and Mary Hays's *Memoirs of Emma Courtney* are 'experiments'[22] in writing that alternative romance in extended form and for a wider audience in order to bring about a 'future revolution of time'. As Wollstonecraft saw, 'one must use appropriated expressions'. But in trying to reinterpret terms like 'feeling', 'sensibility' and 'passion', both writers – and their heroines – inevitably come up against the power of existing romance paradigms which those vocabularies carry with them – along with recalcitrant structures of desire and, crucially, of masculinity. Their struggle with those structures is a measure of their radicalism: of their consistent engagement with Wollstonecraft's critique of femininity as 'false refinement'; and of their refusal of the compromises which 'give a sanction to the libertine reveries of men'. Implicitly, through the obsessive epistolary confessions of passion in *Emma Courtney*, and explicitly through the powerful Gothic image of the madhouse/ prison in which the heroine has been incarcerated by her husband in *Wrongs of*

Woman, they expose those 'reveries' and the conventions they engender as, precisely, a form of psychic imprisonment.

This uncompromising sexual radicalism in Hays and Wollstonecraft was recognised by contemporary commentators: as Marilyn Butler points out, *Emma Courtney* 'attracted more remonstrance than any other individual revolutionary novel'.[23] Contemporary objections focused, inevitably, on Hays's 'free thinking and free speaking' heroine (Hays, *Memoirs of Emma Courtney*, p. xvii), whose 'active sensibility' leads her to offer herself to the man she has chosen (before even meeting him) as her 'ideal object' (p. 60). In Wollstonecraft's case, the publication of *Wrongs of Woman* alongside Godwin's *Memoirs of the Author of a Vindication of the Rights of Woman* brought vilification which, predictably, merged Wollstonecraft with her heroine. The *Memoir* revealed details of Wollstonecraft's sexual relationships, suicide attempts and the birth of her illegitimate daughter; combining the two, the conservative woman writer Hannah More, for example, can claim that in *Wrongs of Woman* 'a direct vindication of adultery was for the first time attempted by a *woman*, a professed admirer and imitator of the German suicide Werter'.[24]

The novels' refusal to compromise can be seen very clearly in their endings – or lack of them. The conventional happy endings of heterosexual romance make it particularly resistant to feminist rewriting. Given the limited possibilities available to Hays and Wollstonecraft within the sentimental novel of the time, this makes fiction a difficult form to turn to transformational effect, and particularly difficult as a way of imagining an achieved alternative order. Among the various endings sketched out for *Wrongs of Woman*, one gestures towards an alternative. By an act of narrative will, Maria's daughter is found to be alive after all, providing the motivation for a female community. Jemima, the prison warder and ex-prostitute, the radicalised middle-class wife Maria and the female child are left together as Maria exclaims: ' "The conflict is over! I will live for my child!" ' (Wollstonecraft, *Wrongs of Woman*, p. 203).[25] 'The conflict' refers to her attempted suicide. It might as easily refer to the novel's major narrative conflict: it seems uncertain whether to focus on Maria's developing relationship with Jemima or with Darnford, the fellow-prisoner with whom Maria falls in love. That conflict is potentially very positive, breaking the exclusivity of heterosexual romance by putting it into a wider context of other possible relationships. But from the point of view of the novel's projected endings, it is conceived as a binary choice between tragedy and separatism. The novel can find no lasting form for the *Vindication*'s heterosexual 'sympathy which unites hearts'.

The end of *Memoirs of Emma Courtney* is, if possible, even bleaker, a bleakness related to the novel's reflexive obsessive focus on its heroine's romantic obsession. Just before the end, Emma voices a desperate progressivist faith in the coming of a new order:

> But men begin to think and reason; reformation dawns, though the advance is tardy. Moral martyrdom may possibly be the fate of those who press forward, yet, their generous efforts will not be lost. (Hays, *Memoirs of Emma Courtney*, p. 199)

She clearly includes herself among those suffering 'moral martyrdom', and this effort to see her story in terms of a wider social process is given a very specific focus in the next paragraph:

> Ere I sink into the grave, let me behold the son of my affections, the living image of him, whose destiny involved mine, who gave an early, but mortal blow, to all my worldly expectations – let me behold my Augustus, escaped from the tyranny of the passions, restored to reason, to the vigor of his mind, to self controul, to the dignity of active, intrepid virtue! (*Memoirs of Emma Courtney*, p. 199)

As far as Emma, at least, is concerned, it is men who now have to be responsible for change. Her daughter, like Maria's in *Wrongs of Woman*, is dead, and this final moral exhortation is addressed to her adopted son, Augustus Harley – as is the novel as a whole: it opens with the words 'Rash young man!' (p. 3). He is the son and 'living image' of the Augustus Harley whose apparent indifference to Emma's passion for most of the novel dealt that 'mortal blow' to her 'worldly expectations'. The stress on the physical identity of father and son points up the threat that Emma's representative tragic narrative of female obsession and male indifference will be repeated endlessly. Her argument seems to be that a different masculinity would have responded positively to her advances, allowing reciprocated feelings to break the cycle of tyranny. The spectre of repetition in the private, sexual sphere threatens to undermine the already precarious faith in progress, and the novel ends at the level of individual history, with Emma asking only that a 'mild radiance' 'gild' her 'closing evening; before the scene shuts, and veils the prospect in impenetrable darkness' (p. 199). The novel can only gesture towards an imagined social/sexual alternative to present 'tyrannies'.

At a symbolic level, however, the resemblance of father and son does make the important political point that masculinity must change if social progress is to be achieved. What it also makes clear, at the level of psychic structures, is Emma's imprisonment in a destructive narrative of desire and dependence, one manifestation of which is her very belief that Harley the younger might be reformable. Earlier in the novel, she expressed the same view of his father:

> 'Could I have won him to my arms, I thought I could soften, and even elevate, his mind – a mind, in which I still perceive a great proportion of good.' (*Memoirs of Emma Courtney*, p. 147)

One of the most interesting aspects of this novel – and, indeed, of some parts of *Wrongs of Woman* – is the uncertainty as to how to judge its heroine. In the case of *Emma Courtney*, this is partly a straightforward function of the first-person epistolary form. But the comparison with *Wrongs of Woman* suggests a deeper uncertainty, engendered, I think, by sensibility itself, and the struggle for transformation in which the novels are engaged alongside their heroines. Thus both the preface to *Emma Courtney* and Emma herself stress her story 'as a *warning*, rather than as an example' (p. xviii) – and it is certainly painful to watch her bombarding Harley with letters trying to persuade him to love her. But the pain is partly to do with the representative power of her – at one level – absurd behaviour. Her passion is not simply, as her rationalist mentor Mr Francis claims, an irresponsible abandonment of reason, ' "the unnatural and odious invention of a distempered civilization" ' (p. 142). Francis reminds Emma that:

'The first lesson of enlightened reason, the great fountain of heroism and virtue, the principle by which alone man can become what man is capable of being, is independence.' (*Memoirs of Emma Courtney*, pp. 142–3)

But as Emma points out, his analysis underestimates the effect of ideology – what she calls ' "the habits acquired by early precept and example" ' (p. 86). And it underestimates particularly the gendered nature of rational ideals:

'Why call woman, miserable, oppressed, and impotent, woman – crushed, and then insulted – why call her to *independence* – which not nature, but the barbarous and accursed laws of society, have denied her? *This is mockery!*' (*Memoirs of Emma Courtney*, p. 146)

Following Wollstonecraft, Emma refuses Francis's gendered distinction of reason and feeling: ' "But do you not perceive, that my reason was the auxiliary of my passion, or rather my passion the generative principle of my reason?" ' (p. 145). The interchanges between Emma and Francis, here and throughout the novel, make sentimental fiction out of rational argument. They thus enact precisely that inextricable relationship between the two which Emma describes – as, of course, does Emma's destructive obsession with Harley, presented as the inevitable consequence of a 'superior' female mind which lacks, and therefore constructs, an ideal object:

'Hence the eccentricities of conduct, with which women of superior minds have been accused – the struggles . . . of an ardent spirit, denied a scope for its exertions! The strong feelings, and strong energies, which properly directed, in a field sufficiently wide, might – ah! what might they not have aided?' (*Memoirs of Emma Courtney*, p. 86)

The only 'field' officially available to women is that of romantic love, and *Emma Courtney*'s claims to be the history of, specifically, the formation of a 'mind' (p. 6) make clear the extent to which that is a generic as well as a personal and vocational restriction. Emma's (Hays's) sex excludes her from other possibilities: from scientific discourse, for example – the 'science of mind' (p. 5), which is a major referent in the text; or from aspiring to the epic form and heroic artistic identity of, for example, Wordsworth's *Prelude; or, Growth of a Poet's Mind*. Yet Emma, like Wollstonecraft, claims mental kinship with Romantic genius: 'the imagination capable of sketching the dangerous picture' (p. 82).

So the novel invites sympathy with its heroine, while maintaining a sense of her passion as tragically misdirected and therefore, importantly, arbitrary in its object. As a young girl reading novels, Emma 'sighed for a romance that would never end' (*Memoirs of Emma Courtney*, p. 12); as an adult, she feels that she loves 'an ideal object', 'however romantic it might appear to others, and did appear even to myself' (p. 60). But at the end of the novel, Emma is allowed a deathbed confession from Harley: it turns out that he has loved her all along, but has been prevented from telling her by Burkean chivalric codes – 'the dictates of a rigid honour' (p. 180). At this point, the novel briefly betrays a far less sceptical collusion with Emma's romantic fantasy, reinstating even 'rational' love as a private event beleaguered by social institutions.

In line with this uncertainty about the status of romance, the role of Harley shifts between a residual libertine identity, representative of Burkean social structures, and an emergent 1790s new man, victim along with the heroine of 'human institutions' (*Memoirs of Emma Courtney*, p. 180).[26] The 'human institutions' concerned are actually, of course, the demands of a wife, the victim of Harley's misguided libertinism, whose claims to liberation cannot be accommodated within the romance structure – a silencing of other women's voices which sharply differentiates *Emma Courtney* from Wollstonecraft's concern with the range of women's experience of oppression in *Wrongs of Woman*. Wollstonecraft's novel does, however, betray a similar uncertainty in its treatment of the hero, Darnford. Like Emma's love for Harley, Maria's for Darnford is explicitly the product of 'fancy, treacherous fancy', and Maria herself reflects 'how difficult it was for women to avoid growing romantic, who have no active duties or pursuits' (Wollstonecraft, *Wrongs of Woman*, pp. 86–7) – though we hear less of this line as she falls increasingly in love with his marginalia, and then with him. (Darnford lends Maria books in prison and, like Emma Courtney, Maria is in love with her 'ideal object' before she meets him.)

Like all the women characters in the novel, Darnford is given the opportunity to tell his life story, focusing particularly on a trip to revolutionary America. His account hovers between political correctness and libertine aestheticism. Having arrived in America as a British soldier, his 'political sentiments now underwent a total change' (p. 95), and, like Maria, he 'detested commerce' (p. 97); at the same time, he tries to excuse his philandering there by blaming the 'leaden' charms of the American women: ' "I found that I could only keep myself awake in their company by making downright love to them" ' (p. 96). The description of Darnford's eagerness to meet Maria is particularly ambivalent:

> Accustomed to submit to every impulse of passion, and never taught, like women, to restrain the most natural, and acquire, instead of the bewitching frankness of nature, a factitious propriety of behaviour, every desire became a torrent that bore down all opposition. (Wollstonecraft, *Wrongs of Woman*, p. 93)

To be the object of a torrent of desire that bears down all opposition is the dream of every romance heroine, and here that sexual fantasy is given political resonance: even 'bewitching' frankness is more attractive than the 'factitious propriety' instilled through repressive ideologies of femininity. But this Rousseauian identification of masculinity as nature is severely (though not wholly) qualified by the image of a potentially destructive 'torrent', an image connected elsewhere in the novel with insanity.[27] And in the plans for the end of the novel, of course, Darnford proves to be treacherous.

Although I think it does present a potential problem for the novel, the difficulty of imagining a new masculinity – the failure, in effect, of heterosexuality –

is less bleak in *Wrongs of Woman* than in *Emma Courtney*. Romantic love is just one of the novel's interests and paradigms – it is as indebted, for example, to *Caleb Williams* as it is to *La Nouvelle Héloïse* – and, as I have already suggested, the relationship between Maria and Jemima competes with that between Maria and Darnford. After Jemima's narrative, for example, we are told that 'active as love was in the heart of Maria, the story she had just heard made her thoughts take a wider range' (p. 120). Wollstonecraft's deep dissatisfaction with the sentimental novel as a vehicle of social transformation is evident at such moments, moments which shift our focus on to discourses of class as well as gender. It is evident, too, in the novel's experiment with a variety of narrative forms – from free indirect third-person narration, to personal testimony, to the public rhetoric of Maria's self-defence before the divorce court.

Nevertheless, in a classic sentimental moment, it is the love of Maria and Darnford which first inspires Jemima's willingness to tell her story:

> So much of heaven did they enjoy, that paradise bloomed around them; or they, by a powerful spell, had been transported into Armida's garden. Love, the grand enchanter, 'lapt them in Elysium,' and every sense was harmonized to joy and social extacy. So animated, indeed, were their accents of tenderness, in discussing what, in other circumstances, would have been commonplace subjects, that Jemima felt, with surprise, a tear of pleasure trickling down her rugged cheeks . . .
>   . . . the world contained not three happier beings. (*Wrongs of Woman*, p. 101)

This dangerously enchanting 'Elysium' is, explicitly, not 'the world'. At a less conscious level, the ideal of community is qualified by its class politics: the redemption of the working-class woman, Jemima, is dependent on her ability to respond to a middle-class sentimental ideal. And once outside the prison, which briefly becomes a private haven here, the relationship between the three breaks down. The passage remains, however, an importantly positive utopian moment, a brief realisation of Wollstonecraft's struggle to bring together personal and historical change, to make 'the sympathy that unites hearts' socially as well as personally effective. The effort of imaginative transformation is summed up in that phrase 'social extacy', with its conflation of public and private, communal responsibility and individual pleasure.

IV

At the present moment, holding on to some version of that utopian vision – for all its grand narrative dangers – looks particularly urgent.[28] Despite a belief in the possibility of changing both narratives and their political effects, I find that my analysis of these two revolutionary novels has tended to emphasise the difficulty, even the impossibility, of their project. To end with a positive reading of this moment from *Wrongs of Woman* is thus a willed political decision – as well as being, no doubt, evidence of my own residual romantic desire for happy endings. The possibility of turning that private pleasure to political effect is where Wollstonecraft, Hays, and this essay began. As Wollstonecraft and Hays recognised, though the terms would be unfamiliar, sexual preference is unavoidably a political issue. To locate it in a historical and discursive context is to go some way to avoid making it also divisive. My own strategy in this essay has been to focus on historical difference; I want to end with a comment which locates the problem of heterosexuality for contemporary feminism in the context of other differences. This is from Kadiatu Kanneh's contribution to a recent feminist reader on heterosexuality:

> I want to suggest that loving men – as well as women – is not an accident, a problem for feminist identification, but a valid move towards cultural or racial self-determination; another or temporary choice for full self-expression. We need to move beyond locating contradiction as a barrier to political organization. Heterosexuality needs to be recognized as another instance of standing in more than one place at the same time, when race, class, culture, nationality, go deeper than the skin. (in Wilkinson and Kitzinger [eds], *Heterosexuality*, p. 47)

Notes

1 Carol S. Vance (ed.), *Pleasure and Danger: Exploring Female Sexuality*, 2nd edn. (London: Pandora, 1992), p. xvi.

2 Michel Foucault, *The History of Sexuality. Volume One: An Introduction*, trans. Robert Hurley (Harmondsworth: Penguin, 1981), p. 157. The choice between heterosexual desire and freedom is offered by Sheila Jeffreys in *Anticlimax: A Feminist Perspective on the Sexual Revolution* (London: The Women's Press, 1990); quoted in Sue Wilkinson and Celia Kitzinger (eds), *Heterosexuality: A Feminism and Psychology Reader* (London, Newbury Park, CA, and New Delhi: Sage, 1993), p. 19. For a useful survey of the issues surrounding the politics of sexual preference, see Wilkinson and Kitzinger (eds), *Heterosexuality*, pp. 1–26. On feminist debates around pornography and the liberation of sexualities, see Gail Chester and Julienne Dickey (eds), *Feminism and Censorship: The Current Debate* (Bridport, Dorset: Prism Press, 1988); Lynne Segal and Mary McIntosh (eds), *Sex Exposed: Sexuality and the Pornography Debate* (London: Virago, 1992); and Vance, *Pleasure and Danger*.

3 Kate Soper, 'Postmodernism and its Discontents', *Feminist Review* 39 (1991): 106–7.

4 The context of Beatrix Campbell's phrase is her insistence, as long ago as 1980, that 'Heterosexuality has to feature in our politics as more than a guilty secret': Beatrix Campbell, 'A Feminist Sexual Politics: Now you see it, now you don't', *Feminist Review* 5 (1980): 1. For further discussion of the difficulty of 'altering one's desires when they appear to conflict with "feminist" political or moral principles', see Jana Sawicki, 'Identity Politics and Sexual Freedom: Foucault and Feminism', in Irene Diamond and Lee Quinby (eds), *Feminism and Foucault: Reflections on Resistance* (Boston, MA: Northeastern University Press, 1988), p. 180.

5 Angela Carter, *The Sadeian Woman: An Exercise in Cultural History* (London: Virago, 1979), p. 11.

6 Sigmund Freud, 'Three Essays on the Theory of Sexuality', in James Strachey (ed.), *Standard Edition of the Complete Psychological Works of Sigmund Freud*, Vol. 7 (London: Hogarth Press, 1962), pp. 147–8.

7 On the continuities between earlier and current forms of romance fiction, see Tania Modleski, *Loving with a Vengeance: Mass-Produced Fantasies for Women* (New York

and London: Methuen, 1982), pp. 15–34. On romance as 'pornography for women', see Ann Barr Snitow, 'Mass Market Romance: Pornography for Women is Different', in Ann Snitow, Christine Stansell and Sharon Thompson (eds), *Desire: The Politics of Sexuality* (London: Virago, 1984). Various contributors to Wilkinson and Kitzinger testify to the power of romance in their own fantasy lives (Wilkinson and Kitzinger [eds], *Heterosexuality*, pp. 41–2, 68–9). And for a particularly entertaining and articulate testimony to and analysis of the 'uncontrolled level of fantasy response' evoked by Colleen McCullough's *The Thorn Birds*, see Cora Kaplan, '*The Thorn Birds*: Fiction, Fantasy, Femininity', in *Sea Changes: Essays in Culture and Feminism* (London: Verso, 1986), pp. 117–46.

8 I am thinking particularly here of Carter's rewriting of romance in *Nights at the Circus*, but examples could be found in many other recent fictions by women.

9 Modleski, *Loving*, p. 104.

10 See Vivien Jones, 'Women Writing Revolution: Narratives of History and Sexuality in Wollstonecraft and Williams', in Stephen Copley and John Whale (eds), *Beyond Romanticism: New Approaches to Texts and Contexts 1780–1830* (London and New York: Routledge, 1992). In trying to forge connections between psychic narratives, political representations and revolutionary change, I have been influenced by Ronald Paulson's important study of the crisis of representation precipitated by the French Revolution. However, I would want to question his at times rather mechanical application of Freudian categories. Paulson suggests just two interpretations for 'the phenomena of revolution in this period or perhaps any period. One is oedipal and the other is oral-anal': Ronald Paulson, *Representations of Revolution (1789–1820)* (New Haven, CT and London: Yale University Press, 1983), p. 8.

11 Mary Wollstonecraft, *Vindication of the Rights of Woman* (1792), ed. Miriam Brody Kramnick (Harmondsworth: Penguin, 1982), p. 81. Where possible, references to Wollstonecraft's works are to readily available editions. Otherwise, references are to Jane Todd and Marilyn Butler (eds), *The Works of Mary Wollstonecraft*, 7 vols (London: William Pickering, 1989).

12 Mary Wollstonecraft, *Mary and The Wrongs of Woman*, ed. Gary Kelly (Oxford: Oxford University Press, 1980), p. 153.

13 Again, this is Wollstonecraft's term, used of Edmund Burke in her *Vindication of the Rights of Men* (Todd and Butler [eds], *Works of Mary Wollstonecraft*, vol. 5, p. 46).

14 Laura Mulvey, *Visual and Other Pleasures* (London: Macmillan, 1989), p. 19.

15 Edmund Burke, *A Philosophical Inquiry into the Origin of Our Ideas of the Sublime and the Beautiful*, ed. Adam Phillips (Oxford and New York: Oxford University Press, 1990), p. 100.

16 Edmund Burke, *Reflections on the Revolution in France*, ed. Conor Cruise O'Brien (Harmondsworth: Penguin, 1983), pp. 169–70.

17 Barbara Taylor makes an illuminating comparison between this aspect of Wollstonecraft's project and the third, deconstructive phase of feminism described by Julia Kristeva in her article 'Women's Time': Barbara Taylor, 'Mary Wollstonecraft and the Wild Wish of Early Feminism', *History Workshop Journal* 33 (1992): 201. For further discussion of Wollstonecraft's attempt to 'reconceive the culturally determined sexual division of reason and pity', see Frances Ferguson, 'Wollstonecraft Our Contemporary', in Linda Kauffman (ed.), *Gender and Theory: Dialogues on Feminist Criticism* (Oxford: Blackwell, 1989), p. 61. And for an eloquent example of that 'reconception' in a personal context, see Wollstonecraft's letter to Godwin of 13 September 1796: 'When heart and reason accord there is no flying from voluptuous sensations, I find, do what a woman can. – Can a philosopher do more?', *Collected Letters of Mary Wollstonecraft*, ed. Ralph Wardle (Ithaca, NY and London: Cornell University Press, 1979), p. 350.

18 For a very useful account of recent political responses to the commodification of

sexuality, see Jeffrey Weeks, *Sexuality and its Discontents: Meanings, Myths and Modern Sexualities* (London and New York: Routledge, 1985), chs 2 and 3. For critiques of the liberationist model, see Vance, *Pleasure and Danger*, p. xvii; Wilkinson and Kitzinger (eds), *Heterosexuality*, p. 171. For critiques of ways in which anti-pornography arguments produce the same endlessly repeated story, see Mandy Merck, 'The Fatal Attraction of *Intercourse*', in *Perversions: Deviant Readings* (London: Virago, 1993), pp. 214–15; Segal and McIntosh (eds), *Sex Exposed*, pp. 70–71, 77–8, and *passim*.

19 For a very valuable discussion of Wollstonecraft's fraught relationship with Rousseau, see Taylor, 'Mary Wollstonecraft'. I would, however, want to put a different emphasis on the role of sexuality within Wollstonecraft's political model.

20 Cf. Kaplan on men's 'roomier and more accommodating psychic home' (Kaplan, *Sea Changes*, p. 159). Kaplan, however, sees Wollstonecraft as perpetuating, rather than trying to break down, gendered psychic economies.

21 For an illuminating analysis of this passage, and of Wollstonecraft's concept of imagination more generally, see John Whale, 'Preparations for Happiness: Mary Wollstonecraft and the Imagination', in Robin Jarvis and Philip Martin (eds), *Reviewing Romanticism* (London: Macmillan, 1992), esp. pp. 171–3.

22 Mary Hays, *Memoirs of Emma Courtney* (1796; London and New York: Pandora, 1987), p. xviii.

23 Marilyn Butler, *Jane Austen and the War of Ideas*, 2nd edn (Oxford: Clarendon Press, 1987), p. 117. For further discussion of the reception of *Emma Courtney* and *Wrongs of Woman*, see Claudia L. Johnson, *Jane Austen: Women, Politics and the Novel* (Chicago and London: University of Chicago Press, 1988), pp. 15–16.

24 From Hannah More's *Strictures on the Modern System of Female Education*, 1799, in Vivien Jones (ed.), *Women in the Eighteenth Century: Constructions of Femininity* (London and New York: Routledge, 1990), p. 134.

25 On this female community as the 'by now conventional suggestion' in women's fiction of the period, see Janet Todd, *The Sign of Angellica: Women, Writing and Fiction, 1660–1800* (London: Virago, 1989), p. 251. For other important recent discussions of *Wrongs of Woman*, see Laurie Langbauer, who focuses on the novel's representation of the maternal body and the figure of the prostitute, in *Women and Romance: The Consolations of Gender in the English Novel* (Ithaca, NY and London: Cornell University Press, 1990), pp. 93–126; and Patricia Meyer Spacks, who argues that Maria escapes from her husband's plotting by 'acknowledging desire (to achieve "happy endings") and discovering rather than imposing the patterns of its fulfilment', in *Desire and Truth: Functions of Plot in Eighteenth-Century English Novels* (Chicago and London: University of Chicago Press, 1990), p. 189.

26 The critique of Burkean masculinity is made explicit at various points in the novel and is, in fact, associated most often with Emma's husband Mr Montague, described as 'a gallant knight, a pattern of chivalry . . . particularly calculated for the defender of distressed damsels' (Hays, *Memoirs of Emma Courtney*, p. 38). Harley, by contrast, is thus the more dangerous, unobtainable, version of traditional masculinity.

27 Earlier in the novel, for example, Maria contemplates the other inmates of the asylum:

What is the view of the fallen column, the mouldering arch, of the most exquisite workmanship, when compared with this living memento of the fragility, the instability, of reason, and the wild luxuriancy of noxious passions? Enthusiasm turned adrift, *like some rich stream overflowing its banks, rushes forward with destructive velocity* . . . (Wollstonecraft, *Wrongs of Woman*, p. 83; emphasis added)

28 The first draft of this essay was written in 1992, when the particularly right-wing Conservative government in Britain had just won a fourth term of office.

Chapter 13

The Pornographic Subject
Feminism and Censorship in the 1990s
Linda Ruth Williams

> Man in his lust has regulated long enough this whole question of sexual intercourse. Now let this mother of mankind, whose prerogative it is to set bounds to his indulgence, rouse up and give this whole matter a thorough, fearless investigation.[1]

This statement was written in 1853. In 1980 it was included as the keynote quotation for a collection of feminist essays against pornography. The connection is clear: 130 years later, women are still struggling to curb the evils of rampant male sexuality, this time in the form of photographic representations of women, and it is still women's role to act as the moral arbiters of our society, just as it was for Victorian angels in the house. The reproduction of what are essentially nineteenth-century arguments for femininity as the touchstone of moral purity, which will finally lead our sexually wayward society back on to the straight and narrow of authentic relationships, has formed a cornerstone of the feminist opposition to pornography since the early 1970s. The characterisation of male sexuality as the wolf has been a central move in the larger establishment of a feminist bestiary containing a variety of male images and types. Prime exhibit, and the subject of this essay (albeit read from a rather different point of view), is the voyeuristic consumer of images of passive women, the male pornographic subject. It is this man – as publisher or producer, cameraman, vendor and purchaser of the product – whose voracious and intrinsically *masculine* vision objectifies women on camera, and in so doing censors their behaviour in real life, for it is pornography which has made our streets unsafe and which has, therefore, 'censored' *us*. This essay offers a negotiation of this web of polemic, and of the arguments which have surrounded various feminist responses to sexual representations and to the Obscene Publications Act, in the light of changes in British censorship practices in the early 1990s.

Censoring the Censors

'Censorship is probably as old as society', writes Sigrid Nielsen, in a brief history which shows that almost as soon as texts could be printed, they could be censored.[2] A prototype form of the Obscene Publications Act was drafted in 1580, but the history of serious censorship law really begins with mass-market reproduction of images and texts which might, as Lord Justice Cockburn put it in 1868, have 'a tendency . . . to deprave and corrupt those whose minds are open to such immoral influences, and into whose hands a publication of this sort may fall'.[3] There is a long tradition of aristocratic porn collectors, and censorship law has typically emphasised 'protection' of the lower classes against depraving influences: 'pornography was born as a genre available to bourgeois men who could declare that their interest was scholarly. What defined it from the start was that it was forbidden to the general public.'[4] Even as late as the trial of *Lady Chatterley's Lover* in 1960, the prosecuting counsel was arguing against publication of the book because one wouldn't want one's servants reading it, yet the text had long been available to those intellectuals who had the means to get hold of it: 'One of the more surprising things to emerge at the Old Bailey trial was that all the "experts" had apparently contrived to read the ostensibly banned novel without any difficulty at all.'[5]

Feminism offers exemplary voices which speak for and against representations of perversion, fragmented sex and what our culture overtly condemns and covertly enjoys as sexually 'inauthentic'. The feminists who have forged an uneasy alliance with the avowedly right-wing lobby of pro-censorship campaigners, in both Britain and the USA, are hardly participating in the same sexual liberation movement as that of writer Susie Bright, performer Annie Sprinkle or photographer Della Grace. If 'masculine sexuality is like a bludgeon or a speeding train',[6] then female sexuality is – as the lesbian writer Susie Bright, one-time editor of *On Our Backs*, puts it – 'purg[ed] of anything aggressive, vicarious, and non-oval shaped'. Bright indignantly continues:

> The mainstream lesbian media mouthed sexist clichés about the 'nature of men and women' that could have come out of a fundamentalist pulpit. . . . Women . . . were lauded for our inherently sexual gentility and monogamous nature, equating our desire with romantic love, our sex with a nurturing, non-genitally-focussed sensuality. Sexual pleasure and liberation were absolute non-priorities for women. . . . Finally, women never used, produced or enjoyed pornography.[7]

Kimberly Leston's survey of pornography for straight women in a 1992 issue of *Options* magazine is written in the same spirit:

> How conveniently comforting it has been for men to believe that female sexuality has so little to do with juicy, dirty, actual sex – that we are turned on by nothing more than a sense of humour and a caring attention to detail in restaurants.

But despite this growing awareness, which is leading to a porn industry specifically geared to the as yet untapped market of both gay and straight women, there is a rather more vocal body of feminists who now consider the soft-core porn industry enough of a problem to require oppositional tactics, in order to expose the inadequacy of obscenity law, and to curtail further the circulation of sexist and sexual imagery. In Britain, the infamous vagueness of the Obscene Publications Act has allowed material some would deem obscene still to be sold. Despite its revision in the 1959 incarnation, the Act has maintained Judge Cockburn's nineteenth-century 'tendency to deprave and corrupt' criterion, a notoriously slippery term of judgement. Some censors, including the BBFC (British Board of Film Classification, which, despite its changed name, continues to censor as well as to classify, in that it will suggest cuts before a film or video is classified), have taken the lead from the 1979 Williams Report in substituting terms of obscenity and indecency for the unworkable 'tendency to deprave and corrupt' criterion, even though it is hardly easier to judge an image or text for its *intrinsic* offensiveness or obscenity than for its depravity or corrupting influence.[9] It is exactly this 'failure' in existing law which has spurred feminist anti-pornographers to contrive other ways of repressing certain images – the Act as it stands is so full of holes that it is not surprising that a wide range of images and texts which pro-censorship activists would like to catch have fallen through the net, and continue to be distributed. An example is the Paul Raymond publications (which include *Men Only, Men's World, Club, Escort*, and so on) – target of many a feminist campaign because they are so visible, but particularly marked out by the Campaign Against Pornography, which developed out of the movement that gathered in support of Clare Short's Page Three Bill. These publications, by the pioneer of the Soho sex industry and purveyor of the most widely 'consumed' girlie magazines, jump through a number of hoops before they reach the top shelves, but they do get there eventually. Raymond's lawyer, Carl Snitcher, outlines the process:

> Our magazines are produced within the guidelines that Paul himself lays down. Then they're read by me, and after that they go to a barrister who specialises in the subject, and then he gives his opinion. Next they go to the printers who wouldn't print them unless they're satisfied that they were perfectly OK legally. Then they go to the distributors and their lawyers look at them. So they're being scrutinised by lawyers throughout the whole process of production and distribution.[10]

So, before the magazine is let loose on the voyeuristic gaze of its punters, it is scrutinised by a series of legal gazes, a filter through which it passes before being deemed (legally speaking) pure of depraving or obscene images. Raymond is careful not to represent images of overt sexual violence, actual sex or anything illegal, and his magazines can thus generally avoid prosecution, if not the hostility of feminists. Sticking to the negative definition of acceptability implied by the Act, he states: 'As far as I'm aware, the magazines which I'm involved with do not deprave and corrupt and consequently they're not obscene.'[11]

This negative definition of obscenity in terms of cause and effect (if it doesn't do *this* then it can't be *that*) has, for some women, allowed a situation to prevail in which the Raymonds of this world still operate fairly efficiently within the law, yet still leap way beyond what they would find acceptable (as does Page Three). The terms of debate have shifted yet again to meet this problem; indeed, the terms have all but reversed: from a simple call for censorship to a redefinition of censorship as that which pornography 'does to' women. It is here that the argument that porn is itself already censorship, and consequently that censorship of it is only censoring the censors, begins to have currency. Thus women are not simply the obvious victims of porn in the sense implied by Andrea Dworkin's 'pornography is violence against women', or Robin Morgan's hardly more subtle 'Pornography is the Theory, Rape is the Practice'. In terms of this new twist to the tale, it is pornography that censors us (rather than the other way round), and if we then want to censor *it*, this is only because an initial 'censoring' of our rights and freedoms has already taken place.

The terms of this shifting of the question into one of civil liberties (from 'how do we censor pornography?' to 'how does pornography censor us?') have been largely marked out by Dworkin and feminist attorney Catharine MacKinnon, co-authors of a wave of proposed US anti-pornography legislation which claims not to be censorship legislation. They have been quick to round up the support of the moral majority and traditional right-wing pro-censors; so, by affiliation, the proposed legislation has become part of the censorship lobby's armoury. Dworkin may not claim to be a censor (the cry from anti-pornographers that they don't want to be agents of sexual repression is unbelievably regular), but that does not stop the censors from claiming *her*. And one effect has been that, ironically, feminism has given more in this way to actual censors, and to the right-wing censorship lobby which has deployed their arguments, than to women themselves.

While feminists may be unhappy with the current censorship laws, censors have been very happy with feminism, which has supplied them with a range of new arguments, and a level of street-credibility or political chic, to make their job more acceptable. Indeed, to some extent feminism has replaced the old range of moral arguments, in that the feminist criterion of political offensiveness has taken over from or supplemented criteria supplied by Christian moralism to mark out the unacceptable. Often the very same sexually explicit texts and images banned under the terms of the pre-1959 OPA on the grounds of intrinsic moral obscenity are now damned afresh by feminism on the grounds of political 'obscenity'. As film critic Chris Rodley writes, on a different censorship issue (concerning the limits of horror films): 'It is now commonplace for the British Board of Film Classification . . . to discuss its actions against certain films conveniently within a feminist discourse, somewhat belatedly appropriated.'[12]

Not surprisingly, this appropriation and assimilation of feminist terms in service of quite another agenda has been seriously divisive. In Britain, as Melissa Benn has written in *City Limits*, the Off the Shelf campaign embraced 'women as diverse as radical feminist academics/activists, members of the Townswomen's Guild, and Dame Jill Knight, initiator of Clause 28 and the name that has caused the most edgy reaction from OTS campaigners'. The wide exposure which Dworkin has received, particularly in the media coverage of the Minneapolis and Indianapolis ordinances, has itself had the curious effect of blotting out most opposing voices, so that it has seemed at times as if her position were the only possible feminist view, one which subordinates a variety of important feminist issues to one dominant cause. For Dworkin, pornography is misogyny made flesh, and her articulation of this view has had a profound impact on British feminism, which – unlike movements in much of the rest of Western Europe – is already working within a tradition of draconian censorship laws and illiberal attitudes to sexual expression.

The main body representing this view here is called (apparently paradoxically) the Campaign Against Pornography and Censorship, a contradictory name really made possible only by the argument that pornography is a form of censorship. Catherine Itzin, CPC's co-ordinator, argues that 'the existence of pornography actually censors women's rights and freedoms',[13] suggesting another spurious cause-and-effect relationship, the ironic reversal of that which Paul Raymond asserts. For Raymond, if it doesn't deprave and corrupt, it can't be obscene: unravelling or reversing the usual flow of the OPA argument, here, if there's no effect (corruption) then there cannot be an 'obscene' cause, and his magazines are consequently not deemed offensive. For the CPC, pornography is the prime censor of women's behaviour by restricting their freedom; therefore one must fight it on its own terms, censoring it as it has censored us.

This is an argument which has allowed campaigners the liberty to slide from one ill-defined term to another, and women on this side of the fence can be seen to make astonishing slippages from untested theories to pseudo-factual assertions. The 1976 Race Relations Act is frequently deployed as an example of legitimate curtailments of the circulation of inflammatory material which might serve as a model for anti-porn laws, even though it has had little impact on the ethnic minorities it claims to protect. However, despite the dearth of evidence linking pornography to actual sexual violence,[14] the point continues to be made. For example, Itzin again says:

> How much do you censor your movements in public places? Mine are tremendously restricted, I won't go lots of places after dark. We're protecting ourselves from sexual violence and where is it that sexual violence is legitimated and women are represented as targets and appropriate victims for that sort of behaviour? It seems to me that it's in pornography.[15]

Upon that little phrase 'it seems to me' much rests. It is pornography, not any other possible causative factor, which has made our streets unsafe for women; and the implication is that if we wipe out pornography we will, in one mighty gesture, reclaim the night. This *feeling* that the connection between porn and violence *must be there* is highly problematic, but it is characteristic of much of the debate.[16]

In similar terms, Ros Schwartz testifies to her experience as a juror on an obscenity case:

> I understood on a visceral level what felt like a wide intellectual leap, the connection between pornography and fascism, the ultimate degradation of human beings. Pornography isolates – individuals locked away, reading in secret. This is why I came to the conclusion that it has to be confronted. Similarly, I believe that extreme right wing organisations should not be granted free speech. Pornography, as I began defining it, threatens women in the same way as those organisations threaten ethnic and minority groups.[17]

No doubt this feels like a wide intellectual leap, because it is one; yet this slide from pornography to holocaust is a rhetorical device characteristic of a number of anti-porn writers, and it has a foundation in the precedent drawn upon in arguing the anti-porn case as a civil liberties issue. Dworkin and MacKinnon's work in America has been to try to shift the terms of debate and law so that, as I have argued, the issue is one not of censorship but of women's civil rights, and both CPC and CAP (Campaign against Pornography) in this country have emulated this move. It is argued that just as racist literature and representations can be prosecuted under the Race Relations and Public Order Acts as incitement to racial hatred, so pornography is 'incitement to sexual hatred', and laws should be passed to make this equally illegal. Catherine Itzin made the link in *The Guardian* in 1990: 'We have no difficulty as a society in banning race hatred literature. Why is there such a fixation about pornography legislation?'[18] She continued by arguing for a position which is 'antipornography and anti-censorship in equal measure', and for a campaign which is 'simultaneously against pornography as sex discrimination and for freedom of speech'. Pornography, then, is not simply a symbol but a graphic realisation of women's lack of freedom of speech in this country. Itzin thus advocates

> repealing the obscenity legislation and replacing it with a Freedom of Information Act and effective legislation against pornography. The US civil rights legislation is one model for English equality legislation, and the Race Relations Act's incitement to racial hatred is another model for legislating against pornography as 'incitement to sexual hatred and violence'.[19]

However, as the Feminists Against Censorship group point out in their 1991 text, *Pornography and Feminism: The Case Against Censorship*, the Race Relations Act has offered no protection to ethnic minorities;[20] but in terms of Itzin's preference for gut feelings over logical arguments ('it seems to me that [violence is legitimated] in pornography') the slippage over this significant point matters little.

Pornography and Multiple Identification

I now want to shift this discussion slightly to look at the theoretical perspective on pornography which, for the most part, grounds these censorship campaigns. It is the offspring of an uneasy marriage between, on the one hand, the commonsense image of pornography as the commodity in a market dominated by male consumption and distribution, in which women play only the part of passive victims of male gaze and packaging; and, on the other, early developments in feminist film theory, which analyse the act of looking itself as specifically masculine. The first point here – the notion that pornography is particularly pernicious because it is produced and purchased by men – needs to be reassessed in the light of the fact that many women are involved in the porn industry at a variety of levels – not just as objects of the camera's and the punter's gaze, but as editors and controllers of the product. Whilst it has traditionally been the case that male pornographers have placed women in the position of symbolic or nominal editors of magazines as a tactic to make punters feel more comfortable with what they are doing, more recently women have been taking control in guiding policy and developing the recent spate of porn for heterosexual women (*For Women*, the reissued *Playgirl, Ludus*, and in the video market, Candida Royalle's work as well as a growing range of male-stripper videos).

The second position which underpins much feminist objection to porn, the critique of the male gaze which rests objectifyingly upon the female body, has also come under closer scrutiny more recently. As Elizabeth Grosz emphasises in her helpful piece on Voyeurism in *Feminism and Psychoanalysis: A Critical Dictionary*, the conflation of looking with particular masculine positions of power and the desire to objectify is based on an unrecognised confusion of terms. The feminist critique of the male gaze is an amalgam of a range of contradictory sources: the Sartrean analysis of the phenomenology of the look in *Being and Nothingness* (or, more probably, its reworking through the existential feminism of Simone de Beauvoir's *The Second Sex*) mixed with Freud's and Lacan's anti-phenomenological accounts of voyeurism, exhibitionism and relationships of desire in the 'field of vision', often accessed via Christian Metz and Laura Mulvey.[21] Upon this mixture of incompatible concepts, a feminist critique of visual sexuality and its representations, identified as intrinsically masculine, was forged. Visual perception is thus always-already gendered: since the gaze is male, non-visual, tactile sexuality must be female. The perspective of our perception is determined by, and then reinforces, each sex's sense of gender identity, and what turns it on. But as Grosz writes:

> When they state baldly that 'vision' is male, the look is masculine, or the visual is a phallocentric mode of perception, these feminists confuse a perceptual facility open to both sexes to use as they are able with sexually coded positions of desire within visual (or any other perceptual) functions. . . . Vision is not, cannot be, masculine (nor the tactile or the auditory, feminine); rather, certain ways of using vision (for example, to objectify) may confirm and help produce patriarchal power relations.[22]

For anti-porn feminists who have bought into this notion of the gaze, however, the pornographic situation takes that which is inherent (for them) in all visual relationships to an extreme: pornography turns all viewers into voyeurs, and all voyeurs into men. Again, this is essentially a meeting of Freud on scopophilic perversity and more familiar (existential) positions on the gendering of activity and passivity, and the different relationships to the gaze experienced by men and women. Pornography is then simply the consolidation and logical conclusion of the male voyeurism inherent in all acts of seeing. Alongside Grosz's charge of philosophical confusion, psychoanalysis offers a further critique of this one-way, seer–object relationship, which I wish briefly to outline.

The feminist 'male gaze' position urges that the power relation between the looker and his object is clear, and only a few writers have countered this with an account of the pornographic scene on what are perhaps the most obvious grounds for analysis: with reference to fantasy. The psychoanalytic understanding of fantasy as the unconscious bedrock of subjectivity, as well as of creative acts and scenes, is rapidly gaining ground as an important concept in cultural analysis – particularly in American feminist film theory and, in Britain, in disparate collections including *Formations of Fantasy*, edited by Victor Burgin and others; and *Fantasy and the Cinema*, edited by James Donald; and in the work of Elizabeth Cowie. Much of this work takes its cue from an important essay by Jean Laplanche and J.-B. Pontalis, 'Fantasy and the Origins of Sexuality', as well as Freud; and one of its primary emphases is that fantasy 'allows' contradiction. Fantasy – as Cowie writes, paraphrasing Laplanche and Pontalis – is 'the *mise en scène* of desire, the putting into a scene, a staging, of desire'.[23]

Against feminism's one-way relation of visual domination, in which the porn punter is only ever one objectifying and objectionable thing, in these alternative analyses the fantasist can occupy a multitude of positions. The two most salient points which emerge from a range of psychoanalytic and aesthetic texts on fantasy are that first, as Freud writes, the exemplary form of fantasy is not unconscious (although he makes no real distinction between conscious and unconscious forms of fantasy); and second, that in fantasy the subject is split into multiple identificatory positions. As Laplanche and Pontalis write:

> Fantasy . . . is not the object of desire, but its setting. In fantasy the subject does not pursue the object or its sign: he appears caught up himself in the sequence of images. He forms no representation of the desired object, but is himself represented as participating in the scene although, in the earliest forms of fantasy, he cannot be assigned any fixed place in it. . . . As a result, the subject, although always present in the fantasy, may be so in a desubjectivized form, that is to say, in the very syntax of the sequence in question.[24]

Fantasy in its most exemplary form is, then, waking reverie consolidated in creative writing – nearer to consciously created pornographic texts than one might think. Yet this understanding of porn as a composite fantasy into which readers enter as spectators and participants, as characters who play important roles, as aggressors and passive parties, has been largely missed in anti-porn feminist critiques. In allowing multiple readings and encouraging multiple points of entry and identification, the fantasy scenario disrupts any sense that the fantasist is a unified subject observing or participating in his fantasy from only one position. As Stephen Neale writes, paraphrasing Laplanche and Pontalis: 'fantasies are marked by multiple and fluid identifications on the part of the subject, [and] fantasies constitute scenarios with multiple points of entry'.[25]

What this means for a reading of pornography is that we have to refuse a monolithic interpretation of it as straightforwardly misogynistic – its overt discourse on sexual difference and gender relations must often be problematised, in practice, by a covert identification across the gender lines. When men and women encounter porn, they enter into a situation within which, as identifying subjects, they cease to occupy *one position*. If one is male, for once one can indulge submissive or homoerotic desires (particularly when one is watching hard-core porn involving men) which may contradict one's active or aggressive social role. If one is female, one might use the position of voyeur (otherwise deemed a masculine position) to indulge pleasure in the spectacle of woman, or any active scenario which excludes oneself. The pornographic scene can be one in which desire cuts across 'normal' flows, since in pornography (as with other forms of fantasy) the position of the gaze is not fixed: as the central male 'cum shot', which is intrinsic to hard-core porn films, shows, the question of whose pleasure is facilitated by the image of male orgasm is not simply answered. Susan Barrowclough discussed this in an article in *Screen* some time ago (1982), but the point has yet to filter down into other feminist debates:

> Within these multiple readings is the possibility that the individual male spectator takes the part not of the male, but of the female. Contrary to the assumption that the male uses pornography to confirm and celebrate his gender's sexual activity and dominance, is the possibility of his pleasure in identifying with a 'feminine' passivity or subordination. . . . It may be that his gaze falls, not on the female genitals (which he may be accustomed to seeing elsewhere) but on the male, and that the chief part of his pleasure, which he may disown subsequently, is homoerotic rather than heterosexual. This ambiguity pornography permits.[26]

But this is not an ambiguity which certain feminisms permit. While Susie Bright, investigating women's own secret 'top shelves', has argued that many women do make use of images 'not meant for us'; this is relatively uncharted territory. ('I began my pursuit of women's erotica looking underneath my girlfriend's beds,' writes Bright. 'Stashed away, but within arm's reach, I discovered back issues of "men's" magazines, Victorian-era ribald short stories, trashy novels with certain pages dog-eared . . . and even serious critiques of pornography that were paper-clipped to fall open to the "good parts".')[27]

Much proposed feminist anti-porn legislation would not only ban soft heterosexual porn, but would take all types of gay pornography, including lesbian erotica, down with it. The idea that pornography could offer a site upon which individuals could challenge their own sexual identities is not admitted. In this sense the cross-gender identifications which pornography facilitates – and which some feminisms disallows – can be understood in terms similar to that of the cross-gender and cross-role identifications of s/m or B&D scenarios. In sadomasochistic practice the ambivalence which characterises the seat of power in Hegel's Master-Slave dialectic is lived, exploited and enjoyed – just who is in control in a voluntary domination scenario is not obvious (although many testify that it is masochists who have all the power). American performance artist and playwright Holly Hughes touched on some of this in a recent interview:

> For example, even though I'm a self-identified *femme*, when I'm fucking my girlfriend a lot of my fantasies are about *being a guy fucking a woman* . . . I've accepted that because it *works* for me – *I have a dick and I know what to do with it.* But there remains that critique in the lesbian feminist community: that there's *no language for female desire.* . . . And perhaps I'm so saturated by heterosexual images that I can't conceive of something that's uniquely my own *and* lesbian. That might be true, but my feeling would still be, '*So?* So can I still have my dick?'[28]

Video Views

The importance of pornography as one of the primary problems of patriarchy is not clear to me. The pornography industry is only as old as the printing press or the technological ability to reproduce photographs and moving images – in its current form it is only as old as mass culture; rape is as old as human society. Sex crime precedes pornography by thousands of years, and it occurs now in cultures in which pornography is banned. Besides the theoretical objections, outlined above, to the way in which porn is read by its feminist detractors, there is another argument to be made about the fact that anti-porn campaigns have constituted the key form of feminist praxis in recent times. One problem with the strong feminist investment in pornography as *the* issue is that – notwithstanding the regular scandalised tabloid outcries against violent horror films and so-called 'video nasties' – the situation with pornography is changing constantly, and the efforts and arguments of anti-porn feminists are fast being outstripped by what is available and 'publicly acceptable'. Horror may continue to be periodically deemed beyond the pale, but the movement towards greater liberalisation in pornography appears to be irreversible.

While in the 1980s gay magazine publisher Bryan Derbyshire was fined £2000 and given a three-month suspended sentence for publishing images of penises which *might* be erect; and, more recently, gay safe-sex campaigners could also be arrested for representing erections, even in order to demonstrate the use of condoms, by late 1992 much of this had changed. In *Seriously Sexy: Safer Sex for Young People* and *Getting It Right: The Safer Sex Video for Young Gay Men*, two of the three videos produced by Pride Video Productions in association with the Terrence Higgins Trust early in 1993, erections were definitely *on* the agenda, and the videos marry graphic, erotically charged images of real sexual situations (which include masturbation over porn magazines, mutual masturbation, oral sex and what appears to be penetrative sex) with insistent safe-sex messages. This is a significant break from the traditional sex education video – which, if it was not a porn film limply disguised by the presence of a man in a white coat offering a pseudo-medical gloss on the raunchier images, was simply a range of dull information. The past problem with erections had been bound up with the fact that in order to be erect you had to be actually aroused; consequently, any image was an image of a real sexual scenario, which was itself deemed unacceptable. Now, real sex on screen is entirely possible, and the Pride videos work on the assumption that people will listen to safe-sex messages if they are being turned on at the same time.

Both these videos were passed by the BBFC with 18 certificates, within a few weeks of the decision to refuse Quentin Tarantino's intelligently satirical hoodlum movie *Reservoir Dogs* a video certificate on the grounds of its violence. Within the rubric of the Video Recordings Act, sexual situations can be represented if they have some educational purpose. The Pride videos can essentially be argued to be safe-sex education vehicles; consequently they get away with representing images unseen in the mainstream video market until now. The scare concerning representations of actual sex performed by actually aroused people for the camera is no longer a problem for the BBFC, as long as the subtitles keep telling you to use a condom. Arousal has become eminently educational.

So how would anti-porn feminism fare with these images? No one could successfully argue that they constitute incitements to sexual hatred; indeed, considering their potentially life-saving educational role, to do so would be monstrously irresponsible. But given that they can also be easily categorised as semi-hard-core porn videos (there are no graphic penetration shots or 'cum shots', but plenty of erections, and the sexual contact is certainly not simulated), what of the argument that these films, as pornographic images, exploit women as sex objects, and fragment their bodies in a violent manner? Here an interesting new situation is highlighted, for the representability of certain body-bits has changed radically. Where women were once the things to be seen (as they still are in mainstream cinema), their bodies dwelt upon by a camera-eye reluctant to show any part of men's bodies more risqué than a naked torso, in this new spate of sex videos the male anatomy is not a problem – what *cannot* be seen is the female genitalia. So we now have a situation in which men and male arousal are foregrounded, while devious cinematography and *mise en scène* contrive to cloak the labia under all circumstances. It is the aroused male body which is undeniably the object of the gaze in these videos, not the passively available female body of mainstream soft porn.

Nevertheless, despite this new form of visual coyness, these films do constitute such a radical break with even recent codes of what is acceptable that it is unlikely that anti-porn feminism will have any place as a serious position in future debates. A curious crossover has taken place between what is now allowable on video (within certain strictures) and what can be done in the soft-core magazines I mentioned above. Magazines, marketed as solely recreational and consequently making no educational claim whatsoever, can show any number of female genitalia, but draw the line at erections. Videos can now get away with images of aroused men under the banner of education, but cannot show of women what even the softest of magazines will display, even in service of safer sex.[29] This situation, however, is changing rapidly, and it is likely that even as this book goes to press the examples of greater liberalisation will be even more numerous, especially in the wake of the 1992 dissolution of trade barriers, which promises to bring the availability of porn in Britain into line with the rest of Europe. In the light of this it is even more pressing that feminism ceases to put all its eggs in one basket, and rechannels its energies in the direction of real issues of oppression.

In taking the front seat, the porn question has displaced or overshadowed a range of more important issues which feminism could more productively address. No study has consolidated the link between pornographic representations and certain types of behaviour, so activists have had to rely on their feelings instead. The discrepancy between fantasy images and the real has been analysed in some detail, however, and not only by the psychoanalytically informed; as one critic has asked: 'Why do we assume that we, as feminists, can distinguish between fantasy and reality in pornography, but men can't?' – the answer being, perhaps, that through the pornography debate, women have succeeded in (what Alice Echols calls) 'demoniz[ing] maleness and heterosexuality'.

Feminism needs its demons, and through this fight – united against the common enemy of masculine sexuality – it has arguably striven to retain a coherence it was in danger of losing.[30] Unfortunately, this procedure has produced some extremely dubious readings – the need to say that pornography is essentially *one thing* is a strategy in the bigger process of forcing the feminist movement itself to be *one thing*. The hope that opposition to porn will act as glue to a dispersing and fragmented women's movement is then based on the agreed assumption that the pornographic subject is himself united by his one violent and objectifying gaze. The feminist anti-porn movement has consequently enforced unity on at least two fronts: in assumptions made about the viewer of the scene (the porn punter), who is understood as gazing in only one direction and with only one (misogynistic) intent; and in its attempts to gather together a united and unwavering response to that gaze.

But if we are beginning to understand the pornographic subject through theories of multiplicity and pleasurable self-division, then why should feminism itself not be accepted on these terms too? It has long been a movement which has celebrated its own diversity and productive incoherence, yet this argument has not carried much weight in the porn debate. Far from demonstrating that sisterhood is powerful, or even that it survives in a happy state of multiplicity, pornography is a site upon which the sisterhood is perhaps fatally divided against itself. The result has – ironically – been not unity but a bitter debate between pro- and anti-censorship feminists, and a cause which is swimming against the tide in terms of both what the BBFC deems permissible and EC conventions on visual acceptability. Women who do want to produce and market their own porn currently face severe difficulties in Britain (the existence of the third Pride video *Well Sexy Woman: A Lesbian Guide to Sexual Health*, notwithstanding), but, ironically, more from their sisters than from the law. In 1990, Sophie Moorcock, the editor of the erotic lesbian magazine *Quim* (which ran to two issues) pointed out:

> Although there is a great demand for *Quim*, we and other lesbians producing erotica have experienced enormous censorship in Britain, and for this reason half of *Quim*'s sales are in other countries. We distribute in the Eastern Bloc, but they won't stock us in Gay's the Word or in Sisterwrite in London. We are censored both by mainstream and by lesbian retailers. There are those who want to present lesbians to the straight world as more well behaved and more moral than everyone else. They have dissociated themselves from lesbian erotica because it's an overt expression of our sexuality.[31]

Moorcock's work is circumscribed by retailers rather than the law itself, but this also means that it is impossible to get hold of American publications such as the path-breaking lesbian porn magazine *On Our Backs*, even though these are produced by and for women in circumstances which ensure the complicity and pleasures of those involved.

Pornography has not necessarily thrived on women's opposition to it, although it is arguable that any mild moves towards censorship are good for it. What does not kill porn possibly makes it stronger: Paul Raymond argues for the relative inaccessibility of his magazines, on the grounds that 'if Smith's sold our titles in their shops it could drop sales! People might think that the titles were too tame if they saw them in Smith's, and one might lose sales as a consequence' – thus suggesting that the Off the Shelf campaign has had an effect it would hardly have wanted. More contentiously, it could be argued that feminism has certainly thrived on pornography, which it has constructed as a common object of hate, in an attempt to situate itself more coherently at a time of fragmentation and backlash. However, as Sophie Moorcock says: 'I don't believe you destroy the monsters of oppression by smashing the mirrors that contain their image.'

Notes

1 Letter from Elizabeth Cady Stanton to Susan B. Antony in 1853, quoted in Laura Lederer (ed), *Take Back the Night* (New York: William Morrow, 1980); and by Alice Echols, 'The New Feminism of Yin and Yang', in Ann Snitow, Christine Stansell and Sharon Thompson (eds), *Desire: The Politics of Sexuality* (London: Virago, 1984), p. 69.
2 See Sigrid Nielsen, 'Books for Bad Women: A Feminist Looks at Censorship', in Gail Chester and Julienne Dickey (eds), *Feminism and Censorship: The Current Debate* (Bridport, Dorset: Prism Press, 1988).
3 Quoted in Gillian Rodgerson and Elizabeth Wilson (eds), *Pornography and Feminism: The Case Against Censorship* (London: Lawrence & Wishart, 1991), p. 19.
4 *ibid.*, p. 18.
5 John Sutherland, *Offensive Literature: Decensorship in Britain, 1960–1982* (London: 1982), p. 11. Sutherland continues: 'A perverse construction was put on this by Colin MacInnes who argued that the trial was evidently redundant.'
6 Ann Snitow, quoted by Echols, 'The New Feminism', p. 72.
7 Susie Bright, *Susie Sexpert's Lesbian Sex World* (San Francisco: Cleis Press, 1990), p. 13.

8 Kimberly Leston, 'Sex, Mags and Videotape', *Options*, February 1992: 53.
9 *The Home Office Report of the Committee on Obscenity and Film Censorship*, 1979, known as 'The Williams Report'. In her introduction to an interview with James Ferman in 1982, Beverley Brown writes: 'the Williams report argued that offensiveness ought to be the main principle of intervention, demanding an end in particular to the "unworkable" tendency-to-deprave-and-corrupt test of the Obscene Publications Act': 'A Curious Arrangement', *Screen* 23, 5 (1982): 2.
10 Carl Snitcher, quoted by Mark Kermode and Julian Petley, 'Members of the Press', *Time Out* 1026 (18–25 April 1990): 21.
11 Paul Raymond, in Kermode and Petley, 'Members of the Press'.
12 Chris Rodley (ed.), *Cronenberg on Cronenberg* (London: Faber, 1992), pp. 107–8.
13 Catherine Itzin quoted by Maggie Mead-King, 'Should pornography come off the top shelf?', *The Guardian*, 15 February 1990: 38.
14 The direct connection between pornography and women's inability to do and be certain things is certainly not clearly causal. One of the strongest findings of the Williams Report was that still images and written pornographic material caused no tangible or demonstrable harm to those exposed to it. See also Chapter 5 of Rodgerson and Wilson (eds), *Pornography and Feminism*.
15 Catherine Itzin in Mead-King, 'Should pornography come off', p. 38.
16 As Alice Echols writes:

there is reason to be dismayed by the movement's assumption, despite the dearth of solid, confirming evidence, that pornography is a causative factor [in sexual violence]. And there is reason to be alarmed by its casual attitude towards ascribing causality. For instance, Kathleen Barry has cautioned us against getting 'bogged down in academic research' and urged us to 'rely more on our common sense, our own convictions, and what we see in front of us'. (Echols, 'The New Feminism', p. 70)

17 Ros Schwartz, 'A Question of Allegiance?', in Chester and Dickey (eds), *Feminism and Censorship*, p. 14.
18 Catherine Itzin in Mead-King, 'Should pornography come off', p. 38.
19 Catherine Itzin, *The Guardian*, 2 February 1988: 22.
20 Feminists Against Censorship write:

[S]ince 1979, when the first Thatcher government came to power, there have been no major prosecutions under the 'incitement to racial hatred' clauses of the Race Relations and Public Order Acts. After the murder of a black man, Kingsley Reid was able to say publicly, 'One down, one million to go', and not face charges. On the other hand, the Dowager Lady Birdwood is being prosecuted for distributing anti-semitic literature and she has told the press she welcomes the hearing in court as another public forum for her views. The legislation is not working. (*Pornography and Feminism*, p. 62)

21 See Elizabeth Grosz, 'Voyeurism/Exhibitionism/The Gaze', in Elizabeth Wright (ed.), *Feminism and Psychoanalysis: A Critical Dictionary* (Oxford: Blackwell, 1992), pp. 447–50; Jean-Paul Sartre, chapter on the Look in *Being and Nothingness* (Harmondsworth: Penguin, 1974); Simone de Beauvoir, *The Second Sex* (Harmondsworth: Penguin, 1980). Freud discusses the relationship between voyeurism/exhibitionism and both masculinity/femininity and activity/passivity in 'Instincts and their Vicissitudes' (1915), in James Strachey (ed.), *Standard Edition of the Complete Psychological Works*, Vol. 14 (London: Hogarth Press, 1957), pp. 111–40; and *Three Essays on the Theory of Sexuality* (1905), in James Strachey (ed.), *Standard Edition of the Complete Psychological Works*, Vol. 7 (London: Hogarth Press, 1962), pp. 123–245. See also Jacques Lacan, 'Of the Gaze as *Objet Petit a*', in *The Four Fundamental Concepts of Psycho-Analysis* (New York: Norton, 1978); and Jacqueline Rose's discussion of this in *Sexuality in the Field of Vision* (London: Verso, 1987). Christian Metz's *Psychoanalysis and Cinema: The Imaginary Signifier*, trans. Celia Britton, Annwyl

Williams, Ben Brewster and Alfred Guzzett (Basingstoke: Macmillan, 1990) was the first significant text to use psychoanalytic theories of the gaze in film theory; while Laura Mulvey's much-anthologised and important essay 'Visual Pleasure and Narrative Cinema', *Screen* 16 (1975): 6–18, picked up on Metz's neglect of the question of how the viewer is gendered in relation to cinematic spectacle.

22 Grosz, 'Voyeurism/Exhibitionism/The Gaze', p. 449.
23 See Elizabeth Cowie's two important essays 'Fantasia', *m/f* 9 (1984): 70–105 (from which this quotation is taken); and 'Pornography and Fantasy: Psychoanalytic Perspectives', in Lynne Segal and Mary McIntosh (eds), *Sex Exposed: Sexuality and the Pornography Debate* (London: Virago, 1992: 132–52), both of which refer to Jean Laplanche and J.-B. Pontalis's key essay 'Fantasy and the Origins of Sexuality', *International Journal of Psycho-Analysis* 49, 1 (1968): 1–18.
24 Laplanche and Pontalis, 'Fantasy and the Origins', p. 17.
25 Stephen Neale, 'Sexual Difference in Cinema – Issues of Fantasy, Narrative and the Look', in *Sexual Difference, OLR* 8, 1–2 (1986): 124.
26 Susan Barrowclough, 'Not a Love Story', *Screen* 23, 5 (1982): 36.
27 Susie Bright, 'Women's Sexual Fiction', *Libido: The Journal of Sex and Sensibility* 1, 3 (1989): 13.
28 Holly Hughes interviewed by Andrea Juno in Andrea Juno and V. Vale (eds), *Angry Women* (San Francisco: Re/Search Publications, 1991), pp. 100–01 (original emphasis).
29 Unless, that is, they are certified '18R', to be supplied only in restricted, licensed sex shops. These videos do show explicit images of the female genitals, although hitherto they have not represented erect penises.
30 Alice Echols writes: 'With the anti-pornography movement, cultural feminism has succeeded in mobilizing feminists regardless of sexual preference – not an inconsiderable task.' Her position on this becomes clear towards the close of her essay: 'Thus, when Judith Bat-Ada argues that to fight pornography "a coalition of all women needs to be established, regardless of race, color, creed, religion, or political persuasion," she abandons feminism for female moral outrage' (Echols, 'The New Feminism', pp. 69, 77).
31 Sophie Moorcock quoted in Kermode and Petley, 'Members of the Press', p. 22.

Chapter 14

Unsafe Sex?

Eliding the Violence of Sexual Representation

Joseph Bristow

February 1992 proved to be an exceptionally agitated month for public debates, court rulings, and advertisers' views on sexual representation in Britain. At almost one and the same time, gay male sadomasochism, satanic ritual abuse, and the emotive picture of David Kirby's death from AIDS in Benetton's characteristically shocking advertising campaign hit the headlines. Highlighting the disgust each of these contentious issues would instantly invoke in their readers, feature journalists, by and large, adopted a moralistic rhetoric which, once more, served to forestall any detailed analysis of these phenomena, let alone the possible connections between them. The use of pain in the name of pleasure, the occult sacrifice of children, and the use of a life-threatening syndrome to market sweaters undoubtedly share the same potential to animate the press into a queasy state of revulsion and fascination – where the desire to recoil from offensive materials discloses more than a little identification with them. Taken together, these particular acts and images point to the persistent problem that arises whenever one tries to understand the links between representation and sexuality in a climate where widespread responses of anger, outrage and contempt may be seen to rearticulate the violence and hatred attributed to what stands before the viewer.

At a time when both the popular and so-called quality press have borne sensational witness to the sexual field of vision, cultural theorists have had to face increasing pressure from two politically motivated lobbies that are currently seeking to ban from sight any materials deemed *either* obscene *or* offensive to women. Recurring throughout current debates about the need to regulate even further sexual images and sexual activities that appear harmful is the prominent place of the male homosexual body, a body that has had a long-standing capacity to undermine normative beliefs in what constitutes moral propriety.

Much of my argument concentrates on the contradictory place of gay male sexuality in the different, but not entirely separate, concerns of conservative and radical feminist accounts of pornography. In particular, I shall be discussing how the moral right's desire to strengthen indecency and obscenity legislation, on the one hand, and radical feminist campaigns to institute civil liberties ordinances giving women redress from being harmed by sexually explicit materials, on the other, have serious implications – not only for the expression of male same-sex desire, but also for the perpetuation of gay men's lives. By tracing the links between four seemingly discrete issues – the 1990 Operation Spanner trial, which sentenced sixteen men to jail for practising consensual s/m; the 1987 Cleveland child abuse case; the 1989 controversy regarding the public funding of Robert Mapplethorpe's photography in Cincinnati; and the 1992 Benetton promotion – I wish to explore where, in this panic-stricken era of AIDS, safer sex may figure within a representational regime that renders sex unsafe to parties who would, to all intents and purposes, appear diametrically opposed.

The most useful place to begin – since it orchestrates so many confusions about what appears to be sexually unsafe – is a report on the evidence of a satanically ritualised abortion. This report, which makes horrific reading, casts into very sharp relief how easy it is to mistake a piece of theatre for indisputable proof of appalling sexual abuse. This account of what appears to be satanic ritual abuse sets in motion a disturbing metonymic chain of meanings around sexual desire and sexual violence. Under these anxiety-ridden circumstances, it proved impossible for both the police and the public to make distinctions between the frightening harm inflicted on children and the agreed terms in which consenting adults play out an s/m scene.

I

On 16 February 1992 Eileen Fairweather, a researcher for Channel 4's *Dispatches* programme, described how she had called on the assistance of Jennifer Evans, a ritual abuse survivor, to help her interpret a video that had first come into the hands of the *Observer* newspaper, and was subsequently passed on to the Obscene Publications Branch at Scotland Yard. The first scenario Evans explains is an abortion at five months where, we are told, very small forceps are being used to pull the baby out. Apparently, it is between the ages of 20 and 22 weeks that ritual sacrifices occur. Claiming intimate knowledge of the staging of these gut-churning events, Evans assures Fairweather that this video, which frames gynaecological equipment with occult symbols, is the product of the satanic group that drew her into its lure when she was a teenager. Having foregrounded the authenticity of Evans's account (the young woman is, Fairweather remarks, 'either an incredibly good liar or incredibly brave'), the researcher turns to the opinions of two doctors, Stephen Hempling, who served for eighteen years as a police surgeon; and Wendy Savage, whose suspension and long-delayed reinstatement as a gynaecologist drew special attention to the misogynistic practices of the British medical profession in the 1980s.

Hempling recognises that a termination is being carried out, but he cannot comprehend why this is performed by another pregnant woman. Evans states that this practice ensures that the demonic spirits of the aborted child pass into the abortionist's baby. However, Savage, straining hard to see what is happening, is altogether less sure. 'It's obvious', she observes, 'that something is being stuck and stirred inside the vagina, but what and why I don't know.' Unclear whether she is actually seeing a baby's head emerge, Savage concludes: 'For all I know it could be an orange.'[1]

Even with Savage's hesitant comments in mind, this newspaper story caused me – and doubtless thousands of other readers – considerable distress, not to say bewilderment. Ritual abuse has surely taken the evidence of child abuse gathered by Marietta Higgs (a paediatrician), Sue Richardson (a social worker), and their colleagues in Social Services at Cleveland in 1987 to yet more terrifying heights. Subsequent investigations by doctors and social workers into ritual abuse in Rochdale, Nottingham and Orkney have led to increasing anxieties about the sanctity of the family unit, the fantasy life and sexuality of children, and the professional responsibilities of the police, doctors and Social Services. In the frenzy that such thoughts stir up, one may well feel at a loss to begin comprehending the psychic mechanisms, together with the social and geopolitical conditions, which bring about such acts of violence upon the minds and bodies of women and children.

More confusing still was the follow-up report in the next issue of the *Observer*. By now further information had come to light which proved that this video was not, in fact, the work of ritual abusers but a piece of performance art produced by Psychic TV, the group fronted by the rock musician Genesis P. Orridge, and filmed in 1979.[2] In its full-length version, the video is introduced by the gay film-maker Derek Jarman and the London-based body piercer Mr Sebastian. Since the late 1970s, Jarman's films, most notably *Sebastian* (1976), have tested the limits of what can and cannot be broadcast on even the most adult air time available on British television's Channel 4. Mr Sebastian, who is one of the best-known piercers in this country, has suffered considerable police harassment, including a case taken against him in 1990 on the basis of committing grievous bodily harm on clients using his services. Although this second article in the *Observer* links Psychic TV to some form of ritualism, it is probable, given Mr Sebastian's presence, that the video draws on the resources of piercing enthusiasts – some of whom are interested in forms of mutilation that result in the permanent alteration of the shape and size of the nipples and genitals.

Such practices often arouse revulsion, if not contempt, in the uninitiated. Having noted the attraction of piercing among members of San Franciso's gay community, anti-porn feminist Sheila Jeffreys makes the following observation:

> The degree of self-mutilation that gay male SMers are prepared to seek is very remarkable. Penises are not just tortured, they are even cut off for SM kicks. . . . Piercing, particularly in the realm of castration, is the SM activity that takes us nearest to the elision of sex with death.[3]

On this contentious view, there is barely any distinction to be made between erotic piercings and sexual abuse. Especially attentive to the murderous impulses of male sexuality – most luridly manifest, for Jeffreys, in gay male s/m – this interpretation is led to conclude that such self-mutilation may be the product of an internalised loathing of the body resulting directly from a virulently homo-phobic dominant culture. Any question of consent in such activities is – to use Jeffrey's telltale verb – elided in this analysis.

The meaning of consent was most certainly elided in a court hearing that took place the day before *Dispatches* broadcast footage from the Psychic TV video on 20 February. In an appeal against the brutal sentences served upon sixteen men involved in s/m practices in December 1990, three Appeal Court judges deemed, under the provisions of the 1861 Offences Against the Person Act, that consensual acts of s/m resulting in no permanent injury were unlawful, since such activities constituted assault. Sections 20 and 47 of the 1861 Act declare that no one shall 'maliciously wound or inflict any grievous bodily harm', or commit (in an oddly worded formulation) 'actual harm' upon any other person. On appeal, Lord Lane, the Lord Chief Justice, decided to shorten the sentences of the convicted men. None the less, he would not submit to the arguments put forward by Ann Mallalieu QC, who stated that since no physical damage had been done, it was not appropriate to charge these men with assault. The ac-tivities, the appellants emphasised, were consensual. Yet for the judiciary, such arguments were already too clouded by a veil of moralistic thinking of the kind that led Lord Lane to declare that 'the satisfying of the sado-masochistic libido does not come within the category of good reason'.[4] In other words, there was no way in which s/m could be regarded, either physically or mentally, as safe.

Under his original ruling, Justice James Rant had made a well-known distinc-tion between liberty and licence. This line of thought derives from one of the founding texts of the modern state, the second of John Locke's *Two Treatises of Government* (1690), where he asserts that humanity must conduct its affairs within a '*State of Liberty*' and '*not a State of Licence*'. Although, argues Locke, 'Man in that State have an uncontroleable Liberty, to dispose of his Person or Possessions . . . he has not the Liberty to destroy himself, or so much as any Creature in his Possession'[5]. With this formulation in mind, Justice Rant insisted that no appeal to consent in the name of liberty could subtract from the licence indulged by these sexual acts.

For ten years, this closely knit group of s/m-ers had been practising types of genital torture, including introducing heated wires and hot wax into the urethra, sandpapering and scalpelling the scrotum, and passing nails through the foreskin – all of which inflicted pain in the name of pleasure. In 1987 – when the child abuse cases in Cleveland were very much in the public eye, causing widespread fears about the collapse of the family unit – the police seized one of the videos made by members of this circle. This video had been produced exclusively for this sexual network, and was not made for commercial gain. At first, the Obscene Publications Squad assumed that this material was the work of ritual abusers. After interviewing those involved, the police were surprised to find that no one needed medical treatment. Glaringly unsafe practices that looked suspiciously like occult rituals turned out to be consensual and non-injurious.

And so began the punitive series of investigations that the police named Operation Spanner. In March 1993, when a further appeal was brought to the House of Lords by five of the men charged with assault, Justice Rant's ruling was upheld by three out of a committee of five law lords.[6] In making their appeal, the appellants this time relied on Article 8 of the European Convention of Human Rights, which guarantees respect for private and family life. In the face of these claims, Lord Templeman insisted that sadomasochistic encounters could be unpredictably dangerous, glorifying immoral cruelty and degradation. Likewise, Lord Jauncey declared that it would not be in the public interest that the deliberate infliction of bodily harm should be held lawful. Lord Slynn, by contrast, dissented from this view by stating that it was not for the courts to introduce, into existing statutory crime relating to crimes against the person, concepts that did not properly fit there. Another dissenting voice was that of Lord Mustill, who indicated that there was more than a little uncertainty here about the appropriateness of using the 1861 Act to outlaw what should be a case about the criminal law of private sexual relations.

It should be borne in mind that although the 79 sections of the original 1861 legislation, which has been variously amended and superseded in subsequent years, range widely over a great number of offences – including abortion, homicide, bigamy, child-stealing, and the 'abominable crime of Buggery, committed either with Mankind or with any Animal' (Section 61) – it is Sections 20 and 47 that are generally referred to when it comes to judging the medium offence of assault in a non-sexual context. A standard textbook on the criminal law by Glanville Williams notably situates its discussion of these sections in a chapter entitled 'Other Non-Sexual Injuries'. There was, to be sure, considerable incoherence in the reasoning behind the law lords' final judgement, since the s/m-ers were being sent down for committing acts of harm on moral rather than physical grounds – namely, those of grievous bodily harm and actual harm. On the one hand, the law lords, concerned as ever with the hypothetical public interest, adverted to the irrationality of the individual who is likely to be harmed (depraved and corrupted) by sexual actitivies. The s/m-ers, on the other hand, offered a rational explanation of consent to acts conducted in private, where limits of safety were carefully negotiated, and proper checks against harm (permanent injury) were maintained. In other words, the defence of rational consent was undermined by the apparently irrational brutality which is supposed to lurk beneath the civilised veneer of each and every human being – and which s/m so glaringly brings into focus.

So intent was Justice Rant in making his original ruling that he endorsed a sweepingly broad definition of illegal sexual acts that included love-bites inflicted by consenting partners. If it is unlikely in practice, it none the less remains the theoretical case that love-biting can now form the grounds for arrest. Until this ruling is contested, boxing and tattooing are still encompassed by the concept of liberty, while love-biting and piercing are now licentious, and so may be subject to prosecution. Since the law currently has no understanding of sexual desire other than that which it proscribes as depraved and corrupt under Lord Cockburn's test of the Obscene Publications Act in 1868, it is not surprising that Sections 20 and 47 of the 1861 Act, originally devised to prohibit permanent injury, should have inappropriately been deployed to eliminate a set of practices that could readily be elided with assault. After all, that is what these s/m activities appeared to be.

This severely confused state of legal affairs – where tattooing is permissible, while forms of body-piercing are not – has serious implications for specialist magazines interested in both types of adornment. The British journal *Body Art* advertises tattooists and runs a mail-order body jewellery service, but feels obliged not to list the names of piercers. Since many body adornments originate outside Europe, this magazine also contains visuals of the kind that would appear in *National Geographic*. Although *Body Art* has not, to my knowledge, been seized under the provisions of the Obscene Publications Act, a similar American journal, *Modern Primitives*, was impounded by HM Customs in 1990.

Eliding relations between sex and violence into the notion of sexual violence, the Appeal Court Judges and Sheila Jeffreys would, in their distinctive ways, seem to share a similar understanding of gay male s/m. Although it is now commonplace to point out that the moral Right and anti-porn feminism often occupy the same ground in considering the rights and wrongs of sexual representation, the origins of their mutual disgust at gay male sexuality are, it must be stressed, separate on several counts. The Appeal Court judges' ruling is a direct descendant of the final punitive clause of the 1885 Criminal Law Amendment Act, which prohibited acts of 'gross indecency' between males, even in private. Forming part of legislation mainly aimed at raising the age of consent – and thus protecting young women in particular from sexual exploitation – this eleventh clause, known as the Labouchere Amendment, was the final addition to the hard work undertaken by an unholy alliance of feminists and social purity campaigners to cleanse the nation of the sexual irresponsibility of men. In its singularly hyperbolic definition, gross indecency was seen, under these circumstances, as the most perverse form of sexual behaviour.

Varieties of radical feminist thinking share this belief, if for different reasons. Since gay men, according to British sociologists Liz Stanley and Sue Wise, 'revere "maleness" to the nth degree', it is not surprising that gay male subculture has shown an interest in the acts of domination that constitute s/m.[7] Gay men, rather than rejecting icons of violent masculinity, would seem on this model to have become fixated by them. Donning leather, rubber, boots and masks, inflicting pain on one another, acting out fascistic fantasies, gay men must be seen, in this formulation, more as an extension – if not the pinnacle – of a constitutively misogynistic patriarchy. It follows that since these sexual scenarios exclude women – who are, by implication worthless to all men (and especially to gay men) – gay male s/m-ers have indulged in glorifying the institutions of male violence to their highest power. In gay male s/m, radical feminism brings into focus the sexual hatred that lies at the root of masculinity, and destroys the lives of women and children.

Jeffreys is especially suspicious of libertarian defences of such practices – practices that implicitly derive their principles from John Stuart Mill's *On Liberty* (1859). (Mill, we must bear in mind, opens his influential discussion by stating that the desire to interfere with the liberty of another party 'for his own good, either physical or moral, is not sufficient warrant' for doing so.[8]) Where the Appeal Court judges point the finger at abstract notions of indecency, obscenity, corruption and – in the instance of Operation Spanner – Locke's opprobrium against licence, Jeffreys once again explains the cause as internalised homophobia: 'It is a real irony that theorists of gay liberation should espouse and promote as sexual freedom a practice which results from and recycles the hatred and oppression they experience from the straight world' (Jeffreys, *Anticlimax*, p. 224).

Such remarks could be read, in their own inflexible terms, to have resulted from and recycled the very forms of hatred and oppression that have traditionally condemned grossly indecent men to prison cells. In other words, such feminism would emerge as nothing less than internalised puritanism. But caution must be shown in reading Jeffreys's intolerant comments against the grain. Rendering radical feminist thinking as internalised puritanism would be to participate in nothing other than the relentless logic of cause and effect in which so much thinking about sexual representation remains locked, and in which, as we have seen, the gay male body figures so largely.

Male homosexuality, it hardly needs to be said, excites horror across the whole spectrum of current understandings of sexual representation, not just in specific relation to the minority practice of s/m. The meanings attached to the gay male body are often ascribed to acts and behaviours that do not involve gay sex. Although it is tempting to entertain the thought that the massive stigmatisation of gay male sexuality is in the main a product of a so-called 'moral panic' around AIDS, the very concept of a 'moral panic' suggests that the syndrome is entirely discrete, as Simon Watney observes, 'from other elements and dramas in the perpetual moral management of the home'.[9] Satanic ritual abuse, gay male s/m, and – as I shall point out in a moment – the act of sodomy come together in violent condensations of fear not just about male same-sex desire, but about sexuality in general.[10] The spectacle of the male homosexual body has such a hydraulic pull on the culture that the anxieties it induces would seem to be intimately connected with a disavowed knowledge of its enduring presence within the social forms and sexual categories which have sought to expel it.[11]

But this is no easy equation. Although a powerful psychic economy is at work whenever tabooed sexual practices come into view, it is difficult to know exactly what these activities are reflecting – either in the spectators or in the participants. Indeed, the very idea that some form of mirroring is in play, in which pornography can stand as the theory and rape as the practice, leads not so much to a behaviourist 'monkey see, monkey do' model of interpreting human sexuality, but more to an infinite and escalating vision where porn and rape become one and the same thing for ever – what Jeffreys calls 'the nearest elision between sex and death'. It is precisely this elision – which both the moral right and radical feminism believe to be occurring in apparently sexually violent acts – that rapidly and emotively enables categories to collapse, and crucial distinctions to be lost from sight. Similarly entranced by this elision, the dominant culture managed to mark out feminism itself as a source of sexual violence. The Cleveland child abuse cases, as my next section will show, aroused the fear that no less than a feminist paediatrician was engaging in practices that looked as sexually perverse as those of gay men.

II

When, by mid-1987, over eighty children were overrunning the wards of a major hospital in Cleveland, a scandal broke about the practice employed for identifying sexual abuse in these wards of court. In the course of diagnosing sexual abuse, Marietta Higgs used the technique of eliciting anal dilatation.[12] In her painstaking account of what happened in Cleveland, Beatrix Campbell makes an extremely important point about the historical forces shaping the outrage provoked by Higgs's close inspection of the anus: 'The evidence of buggery of young children not only challenged the notion that it was . . . "a rare form of perversion", but it also challenged the assignment of buggery to the gay community.'[13] Given that sexual abuse is mainly performed by men known intimately to the children (frequently their fathers), Higgs's revealing focus on the anus destabilised contemporary understandings of male sexuality within the family. Since notions of perversion have frequently set gay maleness and child abuse in the same mould, it is not surprising that the anus should form the focus of so much loathing.

In articulating the signs of abuse that could be interpreted by dilating this part of the body, Higgs was also entering one of the most unspeakable sites of sexuality and social control. For ever to be kept clean, the anus is, by inverse proportions, for ever marked as dirty. It is the place where, as the culture dictates, dirty homosexuals enjoy our dirty pleasures – where what should be regulated and evacuated is deregulated and inhabited. But it is also, as Freud's two essays on anal erotism remind us, where pleasure becomes repressed as parental control impresses itself on the routine contraction of the sphincter. Crowding in upon the anus are a multiplicity of antisocial impulses, impulses which the male homosexual – given his attributed attachment to this bodily part – would seem unwilling to repel. 'Defaecation', writes Freud, affords the first occasion on which the child must decide between a narcissistic and an object-loving attitude. He either parts obediently with his faeces, 'sacrifices' them to his love, or else retains them for purposes of auto-erotic satisfaction and later as a means of asserting his own will.[14]

Guy Hocquenghem takes this point even further by locating the troubling potential of the anus within the economic sphere. He argues that these pleasures, associated so strongly with hoarding and privacy, have much to tell us about capitalism: 'The anus is over-invested individually because its investment is withdrawn socially.'[15] In the light of such remarks, Higgs may well be thought to have been undoing the work not only of potty training but of the social and material organisation of the body itself. So: not only did anal dilatation imply that some family men might be committing buggery, it also – at a level of far greater abstraction – figured Higgs as a sodomite invading the safety and cleanliness of the family home.

So just as the doctor identifying abuse was seen by men to be an abuser herself, she also – at some imaginary level – changed genders. She turned into, as it were, a gay man – the kind of man who was supposed to have an interest not only in anal pleasures but also, according to traditional prejudices, in the sexual exploitation of children. Since she courageously retained her composure throughout the virulent press campaign fought against her, and then through the demanding inquiry headed by Justice Elizabeth Butler-Sloss, Higgs was represented not as a mother with vast domestic responsibilities, but – in Campbell's words – as 'a solitary figure, a woman without relationships, without networks, without a neighbourhood' (Campbell, *Unofficial Secrets*, p. 54). Higgs, then, was marked by the long-standing stigma which, as Jeffreys's earlier research demonstrates, has frequently been attached to spinsters, professional women and – most significantly – feminists.[16] In 1987, it was preferable for many to view Higgs as a sodomitical feminist invading the privacy of the family rather than as a highly principled gynaecologist upholding what is a traditional family value: the care and protection of children.

By 1990, when attention had turned to the 53 charges of incest committed by nine adults on over twenty children in Nottingham, there was a similar refusal to respect the evidence gathered by doctors, Social Services and foster parents. The children were placed in a variety of foster homes, and it was there that reports of satanic ritual abuse began to emerge. Although, in the light of events in Cleveland, a 1988 Home Office circular had laid down guidelines on how information concerning sexual abuse should be recorded by carers and social workers, Dan Crompton, Chief Constable of Nottingham, declared that he wanted, in a murderous-sounding injunction, to 'kill off once and for all' rumours that satanism played any part in these crimes. Nottingham police, claims Campbell, transgressed Home Office advice, and told foster parents not to take down details until they had arrived.[17] The police, the parents emphasised, never turned up. The narratives told by these children seemed so bizarre that the police found them unacceptable. Either the work of lively imaginations or, more likely, the product of low intelligence (the police insisted that these children came from poor backgrounds), such stories were thought to be perverted.

Just as the anus proved to be full of unspeakable signs of violence in 1987, so too did the memory of the working-class child three years later. But in the face of the law, it was proving impossible to understand what the children were saying. Doubtless the commonplace logic that deprivation causes depravation underwrote some of the responses to the children's stories. But surely there was also an unconscious acknowledgement here that polymorphous perversion is, under caring conditions, more readily expressed by children, and that the child is – in broadly psychoanalytic terms – a pervert. Since if – as Freud insists – childhood inhabits the unconscious, then the child is a danger to us all. Perhaps it is because of the anxiety that perversion subsists so multivalently in the figure of the child that titanic efforts are taken by the culture to ensure the innocence of children. It is discomforting, to say the least, to think that children's stories of abuse bring the law and the family up against the recognition that there is such a thing as children's sexuality. But as these cases prove, the feelings of children, their pleasures and their sorrows, are overlooked in the interests of silencing them – just in case the children become as grotesque as the abusers themselves.

Rosalind Coward has written: 'refusing to consider children's sexuality and sexuality in the family will reinforce a growing push to see men's sexuality as dangerous, and opportunistically amoral, ready to strike at the first opportunity'.[18] Such a view, which recognises that children and grown-ups alike express sexual feelings, will prove especially difficult to form when influential radical feminist arguments base male sexuality on the violence evident in pornography, child abuse and s/m. Coward believes that the 'mundane care of a small child is far more likely to break down men's bizarre sexual fantasies, than any attempt to push men back outside the family' (Coward, 'Innocent Pleasure', p. 14). In positing child-care as a practical remedy for child abuse, Coward suggests that the male fantasies of sexual exploitation will be transformed into clearer understandings of a child's pleasure in its own body, and in physical comfort. Signs of pleasure, she argues, are probably misread as sexual come-ons by abusers. Yet the motives for abuse are surely overdetermined, and it goes without saying that they involve making fantasies become realities. As I noted above, it is in gay male s/m that this elision is said to be most in evidence. But defenders of s/m – from the position of many sexualities – would claim that their practices constitute perhaps the safest form of sex, where the agreed terms of consent must be strictly obeyed, and where the possible transmission of bodily fluids carrying HIV can be minimised. Sex and violence here are to be expressly divided, not elided.

The same goes for the apparently fixed structure of domination and submission that characterises the pleasurable punishments of s/m. What looks like an abusive asymmetrical relation of power, where the dominant partner has full control, is far from what it seems. It is notable that apologists for s/m often emphasise the authority of the masochist in these erotic acts. For it is the 'bottom' who has control of the 'safe word' to bring the infliction of pain to an end – that is, at the point where pain can no longer be safely tolerated. Consenting to humiliation, the 'bottom', so to speak, masters the 'top'. Moreover, there is – according to Pat Califia – a scarcity of 'tops' in the s/m scene.

Califia's critical speculations on this topic are not in the least concerned with theorising the psychic drives and defences that make the majority of s/m-ers into submissives. Rather, she draws attention to the institutional organisation of role-playing and the opportunities afforded by the s/m scene, pointing out how this subculture organises its desires according to its own specific codes – codes that frequently appear entirely to invert common cultural understandings of pleasure and pain, worth and worthlessness. Being a 'bottom' is attractive because 'You don't have to do anything to be a bottom. Nobody will challenge you if you tell people that's what you are. You can have zero skills, zero experience, and zero energy and still be a credible bottom.'[19] Somehow, having less ability endows one with more more status in this environment.

From the entirely different perspective of a psychonanalytically informed film theory, Linda Williams insists that the wide range of s/m movies she analyses in her study of hard-core pornography indicate that the 'violence that has generated so much heated discussion in debates about pornography is enjoyed by male and female spectators alike'. Such viewers, adds Williams, 'owing to their different gendered identifications and object choices, find both power and pleasure in identifying not only with a sadist's control but also with a masochist's abandon'.[20] Her conclusion is that such films keep in play a range of identifications between active and passive, and male and female subject positions. I would extend this point by suggesting that the kind of spectatorial oscillation so readily engaged by s/m is in fact constitutive of most forms of visual pleasure. In other words, s/m narratives serve to accentuate the mobility of sexual identifications frequently solicited by the cinematic apparatus. The gaze lured by the camera, then, is not entering into a scenario where there are clear points of separation between subject and object. Nor is there a fixed hierarchy of power and powerlessness structured into these stagings of domination and submission. Considerations of this kind must surely be borne in mind if one is to avoid conflating the emphasis on the safety, consent and limits underwriting the pleasurable punishments of s/m with the non-consensual forms of assault legislated against on the grounds of grievous bodily harm.

III

In the public arena, apart from the videos thought to represent sexual abuse, gay male s/m has been most visible in art galleries, particularly in the work of Robert Mapplethorpe, whose photography stands as an important precedent for the kinds of imagery packaged in Madonna's highly commercial book simply entitled *Sex*. Mapplethorpe's early death in April 1989 came three months before a furore exploded in Cincinnati over an exhibition of his work. On 27 July that year, as a direct reflex to the public display of Mapplethorpe's photographs, the notorious Helms Amendment was set in train. Immediately prohibiting the National Endowment for the Arts from funding projects depicting 'obscenity', it was adopted as internal policy by the National Endowment of the Humanities.

Judith Butler, in an informative essay on this controversy, points out how the wording of the Helms Amendment is in part drawn from the MacKinnon–Dworkin Ordinance which was amended, subsequently adopted, and then over-ruled as unconstitutional in Minneapolis in 1984.[21] The Helms Amendment states that funds must not be used to 'produce obscene or indecent materials, including but not limited to depictions of sado-masochism, homoeroticism, and child molestation'. Although in its original formulation the Ordinance taken before the city authorities in both Minneapolis and Indianapolis aimed ex-clusively to defend the civil liberties of women, and so to prohibit 'the sexually explicit subordination of women, graphically or in words', Minneapolis amended it to broaden the remit.

The Amendment, appropriated by conservatives, stated that 'the use of men, children, or transsexuals in the place of women . . . is pornography for the purpose of this law'. Founded on the idea that pornography destroys women, the Dworkin–MacKinnon Ordinance was, therefore, rewritten to give more power to traditional views of obscenity, regardless of gender. In the first draft of his amendment, Helms, like the city authorities, took up the radical feminist position on pornography as an offence against the liberties of a particular con-stituency, and sought to extend it to outlaw material 'that denigrates, debases or reviles a person, group, or class of citizens on the basis of race, creed, sex, handicap, age or national origin'. Given the infamous looseness of British laws on obscenity enshrined in the 1959 Obscene Publications Act, as well as in the highly inclusive Customs and Excise Management Act 1979, it may well be that moves by the Campaign against Pornography and Censorship to introduce a radical feminist ordinance modelled on American precedents would, once more, create especially unsafe conditions for many types of sexual representation, in-cluding those which seek to interrogate the eroticisation of violence. The need to follow Dworkin and MacKinnon's joint lead is made by the majority of contributors to Catherine Itzin's *Pornography*. In Britain, we should remember, those of us who are Her Majesty's subjects, rather than citizens, have no re-course to the First Amendment.

One photograph by Mapplethorpe that has caused widespread offence is his 'Self-Portrait' (1978; Figure 14.1). How should we view this picture? Is it promoting sex as violence? Or eliding sex and violence? Is it a celebration of s/m? Or an exploration of it? If it is displayed, will it harm women and children? Such questions, which rapidly distort Mapplethorpe's careful staging of the cultural position of his gay male body, readily emerge from those anti-porn constituencies which invest their energies in collapsing images into acts. The photograph provides an exemplary instance of how sexual representation is not

Figure 14.1 Robert Mapplethorpe, 'Self-Portrait', 1978 Copyright © 1978 The Estate of Robert Mapplethorpe

directly expressive of a desire to do something, but a reflection on what that desire might be.

Dressed in leather chaps and cowboy boots, Mapplethorpe takes up that other item of the Wild West, the bullwhip, and relocates where the United States proverbially sticks its greatest insults – up his ass. Transforming the cherished appurtenances of John Wayne's masculinity into s/m icons, Mapplethorpe organises his body to affront the national sensibility. His photograph obviously disturbs the boundary between publicly reviled and privately perverse homosexuality. What he inserts into his anus for pleasure emerges from it like a sinuous faecal column, and so the picture opens itself up to a great many readings, including an obvious one concerning the anal-sadistic phase noted by Freud. Yet for all its hermeneutic possibilities, one thing is for sure: in this self-portrait, Mapplethorpe is in control of our gaze – all the more so when the bullwhip resembles an electric cable operating the camera. In other words, Mapplethorpe is both subject and object of this portrait. His reflexive look surely aims to encourage viewers to perform a double-take on what we are looking at. But the persistent horror of the gay male body, condensed in the countercultural rebelliousness of his anus, was enough for this picture to be declared obscene, and undeserving of public funds.

Whether they depict naked children, orchids or leather-bound s/m-ers, Mapplethorpe's photographs certainly provoke debates about the legitimate boundaries of representation. Even when he is detached from the calumny of obscenity, Mapplethorpe has been charged with perpetuating racist stereotypes, as in 'Man in a Polyester Suit' (1980; Figure 14.2). Ostensibly exposing fears of

Figure 14.2 Robert Mapplethorpe, 'Man in a Polyester Suit', 1980 Copyright © 1980 The Estate of Robert Mapplethorpe

rapacious Black male sexuality, this photograph may equally be seen to be entirely complicit with those fears. Reduced to his penis, this faceless man is – unlike Mapplethorpe in his 'Self-Portrait' – to be looked at. The arrangement of the white shirt-tail, the cut of the suit and the position of his hands construct a particular lure for our uninterrupted gaze, soliciting our ironic reflection on the grand proportions of the penis arranged by the cheapness of the garment.

Isaac Julien and Kobena Mercer emphasise the 'ontological reduction' at work within this image, asserting that there is an all-too-familiar form of racism informing the – albeit playful – framing of the genitals.[22] But it is notable that Mercer has shifted his focus on these representations in a highly charged climate where radical feminists and the moral Right make increasing calls for censorship. 'Under these conditions', writes Mercer, 'it is not inconceivable that a reading of Robert Mapplethorpe's work as racist, however well intended, could serve the ends of the authoritarian trend supported by this new alliance of social actors.'[23] Mercer's instructive remarks are exemplary in the way they demonstrate the importance of remaining flexible with the kinds of critique that are mobilised in order to achieve hegemony for a more democratic politics.

IV

I want to end this essay with another image, one in which the gay male body occupies a rather different field of vision – not as a reflexive s/m-er but as a suffering victim. Since the early 1980s, a genre of so-called 'AIDS victims' photography has emerged, most memorably depicting the horror-stricken and emaciated face of Rock Hudson. It has, of course, been left to the innovative direct actions of ACT UP, OutRage and allied organisations, such as the group of photographers contributing to the Ecstatic Antibodies exhibition in 1989, to create positive – indeed, sex-positive – countercultural images of men and women living with AIDS.

In February 1992, Benetton launched its £650,000 British advertising campaign. Having previously caused great offence with several earlier promotions, including a picture of a Black woman clutching a white baby to her breasts, Benetton used a gallery in the Royal College of Art to present that season's photographs. There were seven pictures in all. They displayed the following things: poor Blacks scrambling on to a truck loaded with waste; a bombed-out car ablaze on an Italian street; a Black guerrilla holding a human thighbone; women grieving before a shrouded but bloody corpse after a Mafia killing; thousands of Albanian refugees preparing to leave their escape ship; Asian people wading through a flood; and the death of David Kirby from AIDS in the care of his family.

This montage indicates that the break-up of Communism, the corrupt practices of the Italian Mafia, Third World poverty, dead homosexual bodies, and cannibalism all add up to the same thing, since each has an equal place in selling sweaters on a global scale. Several of these photographs were unacceptable to the Advertising Standards Authority, although the one representing the flood was tolerated because the people wading to safety apparently did not look distressed (they were, so to speak, simply wading). Oliverio Toscani, Benetton's creative hit man, remarked that his company had 'moved away from the mere promotion of products to the promotion of social awareness'.[24] Luciano Benetton was to make a related point in the interviews he gave at the time of the campaign. 'It's not my fault', he stated, 'if people in other countries [like Britain] don't like the ads or that we have become victims of censorship.'[25] Determined not to withdraw his company's use of these images, Benetton made this declaration: 'eventually we will be understood'.

Such promotional gestures would appear to be a wholesale disavowal of the fact that multinational economics have absolutely no ethics, yet the idea that commerce has a conscience won some highly vulnerable people over to its cynical cause. Benetton's 1992 campaign was endorsed by David Kirby's parents, who allowed Thérèse Frare's prizewinning photograph to be used in the Benetton campaign. Toscani claimed that this image functioned as a *pietà*, reworking the Roman Catholic iconography of the Holy Family. It is interesting to note that it was this image, not the others, that caused such outrage. Why? Arguably because thoughts of sexuality and understandings of sex-related images are somehow closer to home. Even though Black and Asian people featured prominently in the campaign, it is surely worth bearing in mind that there was no representation of AIDS in Africa.

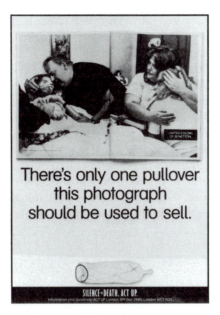

Figure 14.3 ACT UP poster, London (1992), © John Campbell

Within a matter of days, an ACT UP poster was pasted on bus shelters and walls across London (Figure 14.3). Making a witty and incisive reply, this impressive piece of direct action states: 'There's only one pullover this photograph should be used to sell', and underneath, framing the ACT UP slogan 'Silence=Death', there is an unrolled condom. This poster is significant for me in two respects. First, rather than stigmatise Benetton's campaign as 'obscene', it follows feminist interventions dating from the 1970s in countering sexism, brilliantly parodying advertising copy to rearticulate the politics of the image. But second, this poster omits one key element – the erect penis that should be firmly tucked inside the rather flaccid-looking condom. It is still not possible to circulate material featuring a hard-on in the name of safer sex, since such publications would be deemed unsafe by the law – and assaultive to women by some radical feminists. The only visuals allowed to represent erect penises are videos produced by campaigning groups such as the Terrence Higgins Trust, whose *Gay Man's Guide to Safer Sex* (1992) and *Getting It Right: The Safer Sex Video for Young Gay Men* (1993) have been able to produce exciting, imaginative, and ultimately life-saving images on the grounds of their educational value.

More troubling still, within weeks of the court appeal against Operation Spanner and the launching of Benetton's campaign, the Conservative Party of Great Britain entered its fourth consecutive term of office. In their election manifesto, the Tories promised to maintain the toughest porn laws in Europe. Meanwhile, Clare Short and Dawn Primarolo of the Labour Party have misguidedly been devising legislation, based on radical feminist principles, to restrict the location of pornography. That such campaigns are proving a distraction from a broader feminist agenda on sex, sexuality and representation is explained with exceptional clarity in a pamphlet by Feminists Against Censorship, and in several of the contributions to *Sex Exposed*, edited by Lynne Segal and Mary McIntosh. Many of the women involved with both these publications are activists within Feminists Against Censorship. One of their members, Elizabeth Wilson, insists that, in countering the fundamentalism of the anti-porn lobby, feminists must redirect their energies to 'attack sexism as a representation of male power, rather than attacking sexual material as a representation of male sexuality'.[26] With this singularly important point in mind, it is palpably clear that if women and men choose to believe that in pornography we are witnessing the elision of sex and violence, then it is more than probable that the state will enact laws which will elide silence with nothing less than death.

Notes

I should like to acknowledge the guidance offered on legal matters by Peter Vincent-Jones of the School of Financial Studies and Law, Sheffield Hallam University. Lynne Segal kindly offered advice on several points of argument. My thanks to her. Remaining errors of fact and judgement are necessarily my own.

1 Eileen Fairweather, 'Hidden Meaning Lurking in Every Sadistic Act', *The Observer*, 16 February 1992: 4.
2 See David Rose's report in *The Observer*, 23 February 1992: 11. Wendy Savage wrote to the *Observer* claiming that at no point did she believe an abortion was being carried out (*The Observer*, 1 March 1992: 54).
3 Sheila Jeffreys, *Anticlimax: A Feminist Perspective on the Sexual Revolution* (London: The Women's Press, 1990), pp. 220–21.
4 The information in this paragraph is drawn from the law report in *The Independent*, 20 February 1992: 3. Lord Lane, whose sentences had frequently caused controversy, announced his resignation on 25 February 1992.
5 John Locke, *Two Treatises of Government*, ed. Peter Laslett (Cambridge: Cambridge University Press, 1970), pp. 288–9.
6 Information regarding the law lords' judgement has been taken from Shiranikha Herbert, 'Law Report', *The Guardian*, 12 March 1993: 8; and David Smith and Gillian Rodgerson, 'Lawyers' Last Ditch Attempt to "Free the Spanner Men" ', *Gay Times*, April 1993: 8–9.
7 Liz Stanley and Sue Wise, *Georgie Porgie: Sexual Harassment in Everyday Life* (London: Pandora, 1987), p. 93. I have commented on the work of Stanley and Wise in 'Homophobia/Misogyny: Sexual Fears, Sexual Definitions', in Simon Shepherd and Mick Wallis (eds), *Coming On Strong: Gay Politics and Culture* (London: Unwin Hyman, 1989), pp. 54–75.
8 John Stuart Mill, *Utilitarianism, On Liberty, and Considerations on Representative Government* (London: Dent, 1972), p. 73.
9 Simon Watney, 'The Spectacle of AIDS', *October* 43 (1987): 75.
10 Gayle Rubin's thoughts on this matter, from her ground-breaking essay, are still relevant:

This culture always treats sex with suspicion. It construes and judges almost any sexual practice in terms of its worst possible expression. Sex is presumed guilty until proven innocent. Virtually all erotic behaviour is considered bad unless a specific reason to exempt it has been established. (Gayle Rubin, 'Thinking Sex: Notes for a Radical Theory of the Politics of Sexuality', in Carol S. Vance (ed.), *Pleasure and Danger: Exploring Female Sexuality* [London: Routledge & Kegan Paul, 1984], p. 278)

11 Jonathan Dollimore draws on the work of Freud and Foucault to identify a 'perverse dynamic' that 'signifies that fearful inconnectedness whereby the antithetical inheres within, and is partly produced by, what it opposes' (*Sexual Dissidence: Augustine to Wilde, Freud to Foucault* [Oxford: Clarendon Press, 1991], p. 33). Dollimore's writing is particularly useful in understanding how perversion stands in troublingly close proximity to normative categories which seek to banish it from view.

12 Anal dilatation is discussed in detail in the *Report of the Inquiry into Child Abuse in Cleveland 1987* (London: Her Majesty's Stationery Office, 1988), pp. 190–93.

13 Beatrix Campbell, *Unofficial Secrets: Child Sexual Abuse – The Cleveland Case* (London: Virago, 1988), p. 63.

14 Sigmund Freud, 'On Transformations of Instinct as Exemplified in Anal Erotism' (1917), in *The Standard Edition of the Complete Psychological Works*, ed. James Strachey (London: Hogarth Press, 1959), vol. 9, p. 130.

15 Guy Hocquenghem, *Homosexual Desire*, trans. Daniella Dangoor (London: Allison & Busby, 1978), p. 83.

16 Jeffreys's radical feminist historical method is exemplified at length in *The Spinster and Her Enemies: Feminism and Sexuality 1880–1930* (London: Pandora, 1985). The biases of Jeffreys's work are discussed in Margaret Hunt, 'The De-Eroticization of Women's Liberation: Social Purity Movements and the Revolutionary Feminism of Sheila Jeffreys', *Feminist Review* 34 (1990): 23–46.

17 Beatrix Campbell, 'Hear No Evil', *New Statesman and Society*, 5 October 1990: 15.

18 Rosalind Coward, 'Innocent Pleasure', *New Statesman and Society*, 19 October 1990: 10. Coward has been particularly attentive to the contradictory place that children have come to occupy within the popular imagination in Britain in the early 1990s. Her essay on the imaging of children within an angel/demon dichotomy, played out so violently in the light of the arrest of two boys, aged 10, for the murder of James Bulger, aged 2, in February 1993, identifies how 'the crisis around children is really a crisis about ourselves': 'Why Little Angels Become Monsters', *The Observer*, 28 March 1993: 55.

19 Pat Califia, 'The Limits of the s/m Relationship, or Mr Benson Doesn't Live Here Anymore', in Mark Thompson (ed.), *Leatherfolk: Radical Sex, People, Politics and Practice* (Boston, MA: Alyson Publications, 1991), pp. 223–4.

20 Linda Williams, *Hard Core: Power, Pleasure, and the 'Frenzy of the Visible'* (London: Pandora, 1990), pp. 216–17.

21 Information about the Helms Amendment has been taken from Judith Butler, 'The Force of Fantasy: Feminism, Mapplethorpe, and Discursive Excess', *Differences* 2, 2 (1990): 105–25. For details concerning the Dworkin–MacKinnon Ordinance, see Donald Alexander Downs, *The New Politics of Pornography* (Chicago: University of Chicago Press, 1989). Recent scientific investigations of causal links between pornography and sexual violence are analysed in Mike Baxter, 'Flesh and Blood', *New Scientist* 126 (1990): 37–41; and in Diana E.H. Russell, 'Pornography and Rape: A Causal Model', in Catherine Itzin (ed.), *Pornography: Women, Violence, and Civil Liberties* (Oxford: Oxford University Press, 1992), pp. 310–49. For an analysis of pornography which theorises the complexities of spectatorship, undermining causal links between what is viewed and what is done, see Williams, *Hard Core*, and 'Pornographies On/Scene, or Diff'rent Strokes for Diff'rent Folks', in Lynne Segal and

Mary McIntosh (eds), *Sex Exposed: Sexuality and the Pornography Debate* (London: Virago, 1992), pp. 233–65.

22 Isaac Julien and Kobena Mercer, 'Race, Sexual Politics, and Black Masculinity: A Dossier', in Rowena Chapman and Jonathan Rutherford (eds), *Male Order: Unwrapping Masculinity* (London: Lawrence & Wishart, 1988), p. 143.

23 Kobena Mercer, 'Just Looking for Trouble: Robert Mapplethorpe and Fantasies of Race', in Segal and McIntosh (eds), *Sex Exposed*, p. 109.

24 Toscani made this remark in an interview reported in *The Guardian*, 20 February 1992: 22. At the close of the 'Feminist Criticism in the Nineties' conference, at which this essay was first delivered as a paper, Jacqueline Rose drew attention to Patricia Williams's account of being debarred from a Benetton store in the SoHo district of New York City which used a 'screening device' to eliminate undesirable types. Williams recalls how, in 1986, she saw in a store window a sweater that she wanted to buy her mother:

> I pressed my round brown face to the window and my finger to the buzzer, seeking admittance. A narrow-eyed, white teenager wearing running shoes and feasting on bubble gum glared out, evaluating me for signs that would pit me against the limits of his social understanding. After about five seconds, he mouthed 'We're closed', and blew pink rubber at me. . . . No words, no gestures, no prejudices of my own would make a bit of difference to him; his refusal to let me into the store – it was Benetton's, whose colourfully punnish ad campaign is premissed on wrapping every one of the world's peoples into its cottons and woollens – was an outward manifestation of his never having let someone like me into the realm of his reality. (Patricia Williams, *The Alchemy of Race and Rights* [Cambridge, MA: Harvard University Press, 1991], p. 45)

It should be borne in mind that in the 1980s, Benetton, which had 7000 franchises worldwide, was the largest consumer of wool on earth.

25 Benetton made this statement in an interview conducted by Lesley White: 'Blood, Sweaters, and Designer Tears: Luciano Benetton', *The Sunday Times*, 16 February 1992: section 2, 3.

26 Elizabeth Wilson, 'Feminist Fundamentalism: The Shifting Politics of Sex and Censorship', in Segal and McIntosh (eds), *Sex Exposed*, p. 28.

Notes on Contributors

Christine Battersby is Senior Lecturer in Philosophy, and contributes to the Centre for the Study of Women and Gender, at the University of Warwick. She has published numerous essays on feminist philosophy, cultural history and aesthetics, and women in literature and the visual arts. Her *Gender and Genius: Towards a Feminist Aesthetics* was first published in 1989. She is currently working towards a book on feminist metaphysics.

Gargi Bhattacharyya is Lecturer in Cultural Studies at the University of Birmingham.

Joseph Bristow lectures in English at the University of York. Among his books are *Empire Boys: Adventures in a Man's World* (1991) and *Robert Browning: New Readings* (1991). He has edited *Sexual Sameness: Textual Differences in Lesbian and Gay Writing* (1992), and the forthcoming *Oxford Book of Adventure Stories*, and has co-edited (with Angelia R. Wilson) *Activating Theory: Lesbian, Gay, Bisexual Politics* (1993). He is currently researching a study entitled 'Effeminate England: Homoerotic Writing and the Nation State'.

Elisabeth Bronfen is Professor of English and American Studies at Zurich University. Her recent publications are *Over Her Dead Body: Death, Femininity and the Aesthetic* (1992) and *Death and Representation*, co-edited with Sarah W. Goodwin (1993). She has written articles in the area of psychoanalysis, contemporary culture and gender studies, and is currently working on a new book with the title *Beyond the Phallus: Hysteria, Representation, Interpretation*.

Derek Duncan lectures in the Italian Department at Bristol University, and publishes on twentieth-century fiction.

Maud Ellmann is a University Lecturer and a Fellow in English of King's College Cambridge. She is the author of *The Poetics of Impersonality: T.S. Eliot and Ezra Pound* (1987), and of *The Hunger Artists: Starving, Writing, and Imprisonment* (1993).

Rita Felski is Professor of English at the University of Virginia. She is the author of *Beyond Feminist Aesthetics* (1989), and has recently completed a book entitled *The Gender of Modernity* for Harvard University Press.

Vivien Jones is a Senior Lecturer in the School of English at the University of Leeds. She has published books on Henry James and Jane Austen, and articles on women and writing in the eighteenth century. She is the editor of *Women in the Eighteenth Century: Constructions of Femininity* (1990).

Kadiatu Kanneh is Lecturer in English in the School of English and American Studies at the University of Sussex. She has published essays on Black literature, and on questions of identity in postcolonial and feminist theories.

Sally Ledger is Lecturer in Literary Studies at the University of the West of England. She is co-editor of *Cultural Politics at the Fin de Siècle* (1994), and is currently working on a study of the New Woman at the *fin de siècle*.

Terry Lovell is the Director of the Centre for the Study of Women and Gender, and a Reader in Sociology, at the University of Warwick, where she teaches courses in women's studies and cultural studies. Her publications include *Pictures of Reality: Aesthetics, Politics and Pleasure* (1982), and *Consuming Fiction* (1987), a feminist history of the novel. She has edited the collections *British Feminist Thought* (1990) and *Feminist Cultural Studies* (1994).

Josephine McDonagh is Lecturer in the School of English and American Studies, and co-director of the Centre for Women's Studies, at the University of Exeter. She is the author of *De Quincey's Disciplines* (1994).

Laura Marcus is Lecturer in English and Humanities at Birkbeck College, University of London. She is the author of *Auto/biographical Discourses: Theory, Criticism, Practice* (1994) and is currently working on a study of the role of fiction in feminism.

Jane Moore is Lecturer in the Centre for Critical and Cultural Theory at the University of Wales, College of Cardiff. She is co-editor of *The Feminist Reader: Essays in Gender and the Politics of Literary Criticism* (1989), and has written essays on Mary Wollstonecraft and critical theory.

Lawrence Normand teaches in the English Department at the University of Wales, Lampeter. He has published on Shakespeare and twentieth-century poetry. He is currently working on the relations between history and literature in the early modern period, and is co-author (with Gareth Roberts) of a forthcoming study, *The Witch-Hunt in Early Modern Scotland: King James' 'Demonology' and the North Berwick Witches*.

Jane Spencer is Lecturer in the School of English and American Studies, and co-director of the Centre for Women's Studies, at the University of Exeter. She is the author of *The Rise of the Woman Novelist* (1986) and *Elizabeth Gaskell* (1993).

Lynnette Turner is Lecturer in English Studies at Cheltenham and Gloucester College of Higher Education. She researches in the area of late-nineteenth-century anthropology and postcolonial methodologies, and has published articles on gender and ethnography.

Linda Ruth Williams lectures in film and literature at the University of Southampton. She is the author of *Sex in the Head: Visions of Femininity and Film in D.H. Lawrence* (1993), editor of *The Bloomsbury Guide to Twentieth Century Literature* (1992), and co-editor of *The Body and the Text* (1990), as well as other works on feminism, psychoanalysis and modern fiction.

Bibliography

Ardis, Ann. *New Women, New Novels: Feminism and Early Modernism*. New Brunswick: Rutgers University Press, 1990.

Armstrong, Nancy. *Desire and Domestic Fiction: A Political History of the Novel*. New York and Oxford: Oxford University Press, 1987.

Battersby, Christine. *Gender and Genius: Towards a Feminist Aesthetics*. London: The Women's Press, 1989/Bloomington: Indiana University Press, 1990.

Bell, Diane, Pat Caplan and Wazir Jahan Karim. *Gendered Fields: Women, Men and Ethnography*. London and New York: Routledge, 1993.

Benjamin, Jessica. *The Bonds of Love: Psychoanalysis, Feminism and the Problem of Domination*. New York: Pantheon, 1988.

Bergman, David. *Gaiety Transfigured: Gay Self Representation in American Literature*. Madison: University of Wisconsin Press, 1991.

Boffin, Tessa and Sunil Gupta (eds). *Ecstatic Antibodies: Resisting the AIDS Mythology*. London: Rivers Oram Press, 1990.

Boone, Joseph A. and Michael Cadden. *Engendering Men: The Question Of Male Feminist Criticism*. London and New York: Routledge, 1990.

Boothby, R. *Death and Desire: Psychoanalytic Theory in Lacan's Return to Freud*. New York and London: Routledge, 1991.

Bowlby, Rachel. *Just Looking: Consumer Culture in Dreiser, Gissing and Zola*. New York: Methuen, 1985.

Braidotti, Rosi. *Patterns of Dissonance: A Study of Women in Contemporary Philosophy*. Trans. Elizabeth Guild. Oxford: Polity Press, 1991.

Bray, Alan. *Homosexuality in Renaissance England*. London: Gay Men's Press, 1982.

Bray, Alan. 'Homosexuality and the Signs of Male Friendship in Elizabethan England', *History Workshop* 29 (1990): 1–19.

Brennan, Teresa (ed.). *Between Feminism and Psychoanalysis*. London: Routledge, 1989.

Bright, Susie. *Susie Sexpert's Lesbian Sex World*. San Francisco: Cleis Press, 1990.

Bristow, Joseph (ed.), *Sexual Sameness: Textual Differences in Lesbian and Gay Writing*. London and New York: Routledge, 1992.

Bronfen, Elisabeth. *Over Her Dead Body: Death, Femininity and the Aesthetic*. Manchester: Manchester University Press, 1992.

Brooks, Peter. 'Storied Bodies, or Nana at Last Unveil'd', *Critical Inquiry* 16, 1 (1989): 1–32.

Buck, Claire (ed.). *Bloomsbury Guide to Women's Literature*. London: Bloomsbury, 1992.

226

Buck-Morss, Susan. 'The Flâneur, the Sandwichman and the Whore: The Politics of Loitering', *New German Critique* 39 (1986): 99–140.

Burgin, Victor, James Donald and Cora Kaplan (eds). *Formations of Fantasy.* London: Methuen, 1986.

Butler, Judith. *Gender Trouble: Feminism and the Subversion of Identity.* New York and London: Routledge, 1990.

Butler, Judith and Joan W. Scott. *Feminists Theorize the Political.* New York and London: Routledge, 1992.

Butters, Ronald, John M. Clum and Michael Moon. *Displacing Homophobia: Gay Male Perspectives in Literature and Culture.* Durham, NC and London: Duke University Press, 1989.

Campbell, Beatrix. *Unofficial Secrets: Child Sexual Abuse – The Cleveland Case.* London: Virago, 1988.

Carter, Angela. *The Sadeian Woman: An Exercise in Cultural History.* London: Virago, 1979.

Carter, Erica and Simon Watney (eds). *Taking Liberties: AIDS and Cutural Politics.* London: Serpent's Tail, 1989.

Chapman, Rowena and Jonathan Rutherford (eds). *Male Order: Unwrapping Masculinity.* London: Lawrence & Wishart, 1988.

Chester, Gail and Julienne Dickey (eds). *Feminism and Censorship: The Current Debate.* Bridport, Dorset: Prism Press, 1988.

Cixous, Hélène. 'The Laugh of the Medusa', in *New French Feminisms,* eds Elaine Marks and Isabelle de Courtivron. Hemel Hempstead: Harvester Wheatsheaf, 1981, pp. 245–64.

Crimp, Douglas (ed.). *October* 43 (1987). Special Issue on AIDS.

de Lauretis, Teresa (ed.). *Differences* 3, 2 (1991). Special issue: 'Queer Theory: Lesbian and Gay Sexualities'.

Derrida, Jacques. *Spurs: Nietzsche's Styles/Éperons: Les Styles de Nietzsche,* intro. Stefano Agosti, trans. Barbara Harlow. Chicago: University of Chicago Press, 1979.

Derrida, Jacques and Christie V. McDonald. 'Choreographies', *Diacritics* 12 (1982): 66–76.

Diamond, Arlyn and Lee R. Edwards (eds). *The Authority of Experience: Essays in Feminist Criticism.* Amherst: University of Massachusetts Press, 1977.

Doane, Mary Ann, *Femmes Fatales: Feminism, Film Theory, Psychoanalysis.* New York and London: Routledge, 1991.

Dollimore, Jonathan. *Sexual Dissidence: Augustine to Wilde, Freud to Foucault.* Oxford: Clarendon Press, 1991.

Donald, James (ed.). *Fantasy and the Cinema.* London: British Film Institute, 1989.

Downs, Donald Alexander. *The New Politics of Pornography.* Chicago: University of Chicago Press, 1989.

Duberman, Martin, Martha Vicinus and George Chauncey Jnr (eds). *Hidden from History: Reclaiming the Gay and Lesbian Part.* Harmondsworth: Penguin, 1991.

Faderman, Lillian. *Surpassing the Love of Men: Romantic Friendship and Love Between Women from the Renaissance to the Present.* London: Junction Books, 1981.

Felman, Shoshana and Laub, Dori. *Testimony: Crises of Witnessing in Literature, Psychoanalysis and History.* New York and London: Routledge, 1992.

Felski, Rita. *Beyond Feminist Aesthetics.* London: Hutchinson Radius, 1989.

Felski, Rita. 'The Counter-Discourse of the Feminine in Three Texts by Huysmans, Wilde and Sacher-Masoch', *PMLA* 106, 5 (1991): 1094–105.

Foucault, Michel. *The History of Sexuality. Volume One: An Introduction,* trans. Robert Hurley. Harmondsworth: Penguin, 1981.

Freedman, Diane P., Olivia Frey and Frances Murphy Zauher (eds). *The Intimate Critique: Autobiographical Literary Criticism.* Durham, NC: Duke University Press, 1993.

Freud, Sigmund. *The Interpretation of Dreams* (1900), in James Strachey (ed.), *The Standard Edition of the Complete Psychological Works of Sigmund Freud*, vol. 4. London: Hogarth Press, 1955.

Freud, Sigmund. *Three Essays on the Theory of Sexuality* (1905), *Standard Edition*, vol. 7. London: Hogarth Press, 1962.

Freud, Sigmund. *Beyond the Pleasure Principle* (1919), *Standard Edition*, vol. 18. London: Hogarth Press, 1955.

Fuss, Diana. *Essentially Speaking: Feminism, Nature, and Difference*. London and New York: Routledge, 1989.

Fuss, Diana (ed.). *Inside/Out: Lesbian Theories, Gay Theories*. New York and London: Routledge, 1991.

Gallop, Jane. *Thinking Through the Body*. New York: Columbia University Press, 1988.

Gerard, K. and G. Hekma (eds). *The Pursuit of Sodomy: Male Homosexuality in Renaissance and Enlightenment Europe*. New York and London: Harrington Park Press, 1989.

Gilbert, Sandra M. and Susan Gubar. *The Madwoman in the Attic: The Woman Writer and the Nineteenth-Century Literary Imagination*. New Haven, CT and London: Yale University Press, 1979.

Gilbert, Sandra M. and Susan Gubar. *No Man's Land: The Place of the Woman Writer in the Twentieth Century*. Volume 1: *The War of the Worlds*. New Haven, CT: Yale University Press, 1988. Volume 2: *Sexchanges*. New Haven, CT: Yale University Press, 1989.

Goldberg, Jonathan. *Sodometries: Renaissance Texts, Modern Sexualities*. Stanford, CA: Stanford University Press, 1992.

Greenberg, David F. *The Construction of Homosexuality*. Chicago: University of Chicago Press, 1988.

Greene, Gayle and Coppélia Kahn (eds). *Changing Subjects: The Making of Feminist Literary Criticism*. New York and London: Routledge, 1993.

Gunew, Sneja (ed.). *Feminist Knowledge: Critique and Construct*. London and New York: Routledge, 1990.

Harding, Sandra. *Whose Science? Whose Knowledge?: Thinking from Women's Lives*. Milton Keynes: Open University Press, 1991.

Hertz, Neil. *The End of the Line: Essays on Psychoanalysis and the Sublime*. New York: Columbia University Press, 1985.

Hocquenghem, Guy. *Homosexual Desire*, trans. Daniella Dangoor. London: Allison & Busby, 1978.

Irigaray, Luce. *Le corps-à-corps avec la mère*. Montreal: Les éditions de la pleine lune, 1981.

Irigaray, Luce. *Speculum of the Other Woman*, trans. Gillian C. Gill. Ithaca, NY: Cornell University Press, 1985; first publ. in French 1974.

Irigaray, Luce. *This Sex Which Is Not One*, trans. Catherine Porter and Carolyn Burke. Ithaca, NY: Cornell University Press, 1985; first publ. in French 1977.

Itzin, Catherine (ed.). *Pornography: Women, Violence, and Civil Liberties*. Oxford: Oxford University Press, 1992.

Jacobus, Mary (ed.). *Women Writing and Writing About Women*. London: Croom Helm, 1979.

Jacobus, Mary. *Reading Woman: Essays in Feminist Criticism*. London: Methuen, 1986.

Jacobus, Mary, Evelyn Fox Keller and Sally Shuttleworth (eds). *Body/Politics: Women and the Discourse of Science*. New York and London: Routledge, 1990.

Jardine, Alice. *Gynesis: Configurations of Woman and Modernity*. Ithaca, NY and London: Cornell University Press, 1985.

Jardine, Alice and Paul Smith (eds). *Men in Feminism*. New York and London: Methuen, 1987.

Jeffreys, Sheila. *The Spinster and Her Enemies: Feminism and Sexuality 1880–1930*. London: Pandora, 1985.

Jeffreys, Sheila. *Anticlimax: A Feminist Perspective on the Sexual Revolution*. London: The Women's Press, 1990.

Johnson, Barbara. *The Critical Difference: Essays in the Contemporary Rhetoric of Reading*. Baltimore, MD: Johns Hopkins University Press, 1980.

Juno, Andrea and V. Vale (eds). *Angry Women*. San Francisco: Re/Search Publications, 1991.

Kader, Cheryl and Thomas Piontek (eds). 'Flaunting It: Lesbian and Gay Studies', *Discourse* 15, 1 (1992).

Kaplan, Cora. *Sea Changes: Essays in Culture and Feminism*. London: Verso, 1986.

Kauffman, Linda. *Gender and Theory: Dialogues on Feminist Criticism*. Oxford: Blackwell, 1989.

Kelly, Gary. *Revolutionary Feminism: The Mind and Career of Mary Wollstonecraft*. London: Macmillan, 1992.

Krupnick, Mark (ed.). *Displacement: Derrida and After*. Bloomington, IN: Indiana University Press, 1983.

Lacan, Jacques. *Écrits: A Selection*, trans. Alan Sheridan. New York: Norton, 1977.

Lacan, Jacques. *Le Séminaire de Jacques Lacan. Livre VII: L'Éthique de la Psychanalyse*, ed. Jacques-Alain Miller. Paris: Seuil, 1986.

Lacan, Jacques. *The Seminar of Jacques Lacan. Book II: The Ego in Freud's Theory and in the Technique of Psychoanalysis, 1954–1955*, ed. Jacques-Alain Miller, trans. Sylvana Tomaselli. New York: Norton, 1988.

Leeds Revolutionary Feminist Group. *Love Your Enemy: The Debate Between Heterosexual Feminism and Political Lesbianism*. London: Onlywomen Press, 1981.

Licata, S. J. and R. P. Petersen (eds). *The Gay Past: A Collection of Historical Essays*. New York: Harrington Park Press, 1985.

Light, Alison. *Forever England: Femininity, Literature and Conservatism Between the Wars*. London and New York: Routledge, 1991.

Lovell, Terry. *Consuming Fiction*. London: Verso, 1987.

Marxist–Feminist Literature Collective. 'Women's Writing: *Jane Eyre, Shirley, Villette, Aurora Leigh*', in *1848: The Sociology of Literature: Proceedings of the Essex Conference on the Sociology of Literature, July 1977*, eds Francis Barker *et al.* Colchester: University of Essex, 1978.

Mercer, Kobena. 'Welcome to the Jungle: Identity and Diversity in Postmodern Politics', in *Identity: Community, Culture, Difference*, ed. Jonathan Rutherford. London: Lawrence & Wishart, 1990, pp. 43–71.

Merck, Mandy. 'Difference and its Discontents', *Screen* 28, 1 (1987): 2–9.

Metz, Christian. *Psychoanalysis and Cinema: The Imaginary Signifier*, trans. Celia Britton, Annwyl Williams, Ben Brewster and Alfred Guzzett. Basingstoke: Macmillan, 1990.

Miller, James (ed.). *Fluid Exchanges: Artists and Critics in the AIDS Crisis*. Toronto, Buffalo and London: University of Toronto Press, 1992.

Miller, Jane. *Seductions: Studies in Reading and Culture*. London: Virago, 1990.

Miller, Nancy K. *The Heroine's Text: Readings in the French and English Novel, 1722–1782*. New York: Columbia University Press, 1980.

Miller, Nancy K. *Getting Personal*. New York: Routledge, 1991.

Millett, Kate. *Sexual Politics*. London: Virago, 1977.

Mills, Sara. *Discourses of Difference*. London: Routledge, 1991.

Minh-ha, Trinh T. *Woman, Native, Other: Writing Postcoloniality and Feminism*. Bloomington and Indianapolis: Indiana University Press, 1989.

Minogue, Sally (ed.). *Problems for Feminist Criticism*. London and New York: Routledge, 1990.

Modleski, Tania. *Loving with a Vengeance: Mass-Produced Fantasies for Women*. New York and London: Methuen, 1982.

Modleski, Tania. *Feminism Without Women: Culture and Criticism in a 'Postfeminist' Age*. New York and London: Routledge, 1991.

Moers, Ellen. *Literary Women: The Great Writers*. New York: Anchor Books, 1977.

Morris, Meaghan. 'Things to do with Shopping Centres', in *Grafts: Feminist Cultural Criticism*, ed. Susan Sheridan. London: Verso, 1988.

Mulvey, Laura. *Visual and Other Pleasures*. London: Macmillan, 1989.

Murphy, Timothy and Suzanne Poirier (eds). *Writing AIDS: Gay Literature, Language, and Analysis*. New York: Columbia University Press, 1993.

Nead, Lynda. *Myths of Sexuality: Representations of Women in Victorian Britain*. Oxford: Blackwell, 1988.

Newton, Judith Lowder. *Women, Power and Subversion: Social Strategies in British Fiction, 1778–1860*. New York and London: Methuen, 1985.

Okely, Judith and Helen Callaway (eds). *Anthropology and Autobiography*. London and New York: Routledge, 1992.

Ortner, S.B. and H. Whitehead (eds). *Sexual Meanings: The Cultural Construction of Gender and Sexuality*. Cambridge: Cambridge University Press, 1981.

Piontek, Thomas. 'Unsafe Representations: Cultural Criticisms in the Age of AIDS', *Discourse* 15, 1 (1992): 128–53.

Ramazanoglu, Caroline. *Feminism and the Contradictions of Oppression*. London and New York: Routledge, 1989.

Rich, Adrienne. *On Lies, Secrets, Silence: Selected Prose, 1966–1978*. London: Virago, 1980.

Riviere, Joan. 'Womanliness as a Masquerade', in *The Inner World and Joan Riviere: Collected Papers 1920–1958*, ed. Athol Hughes. London: Karnac, 1991, pp. 90–101. 1st publ. *International Journal of Psycho-Analysis* 10 (1929):303–13. Also published in Burgin *et al.* (eds), *Formations of Fantasy*, pp. 35–44.

Rodgerson, Gillian and Elizabeth Wilson (eds). *Pornography and Feminism: The Case against Censorship*. London: Lawrence & Wishart, 1991.

Rose, Jacqueline. *Sexuality in the Field of Vision*. London: Verso, 1987.

Sedgwick, Eve Kosofsky. *Between Men: English Literature and Homosocial Desire*. New York: Columbia University Press, 1985.

Sedgwick, Eve Kosofsky. *Epistemology of the Closet*. Berkeley: University of California Press, 1990.

Segal, Lynne and Mary McIntosh (eds). *Sex Exposed: Sexuality and the Pornography Debate*. London: Virago, 1992.

Shepherd, Simon and Mick Wallis (eds). *Coming on Strong: Gay Politics and Culture*. London: Unwin Hyman, 1989.

Showalter, Elaine. *A Literature of Their Own: British Novelists from Brontë to Lessing*. London: Virago, 1978.

Showalter, Elaine (ed.). *Speaking of Gender*. New York and London: Routledge, 1989.

Showalter, Elaine (ed.). *Sexual Anarchy: Gender and Culture at the Fin de Siècle*. New York: Viking, 1990.

Showalter, Elaine (ed.). *Sister's Choice: Tradition and Change in American Women's Writing*. Oxford: Clarendon Press, 1991.

Silverman, Kaja. *Male Subjectivity in the Margins*. London and New York: Routledge, 1992.

Smith, Bruce R. *Homosexual Desire in Shakespeare's England: A Cultural Poetics*. Chicago and London: University of Chicago Press, 1991.

Smith, Paul Julian. *Laws of Desire: Questions of Homosexuality in Spanish Writing and Film 1960–1990*. Oxford: Clarendon Press, 1992.

Snitow, Ann, Christine Stansell and Sharon Thompson (eds). *Desire: The Politics of Sexuality*. London: Virago, 1984.

Sontag, Susan. *AIDS and its Metaphors*. Harmondsworth: Penguin, 1988.

Spencer, Jane. *The Rise of the Woman Novelist*, Oxford: Blackwell, 1986.

Spender, Dale. *Mothers of the Novel*. London and New York: Pandora, 1986.

Spivak, Gayatri Chakravorty. 'Love Me, Love My Ombre Elle', *Diacritics* 14, 4 (1984): 19–36.

Spivak, Gayatri Chakravorty. 'Three Women's Texts and a Critique of Imperialism', *Critical Inquiry* 12, 1 (1985): 243–61.

Spivak, Gayatri Chakravorty. 'Can the Subaltern Speak?', in *Marxism and the Interpretation of Culture*, ed. Cary Nelson and Lawrence Grossberg. London: Macmillan, 1988.

Stambolian, George and Elaine Marks (eds). *Homosexualities and French Literature: Cultural Contexts and Critical Texts*. Ithaca, NY and London: Cornell University Press, 1979.

Stanley, Liz. 'Feminist Auto/Biography and Feminist Epistemology', in *Out of the Margins*, ed. Jane Aaron and Sylvia Walby. London: Falmer Press, 1991.

Stanton, Donna (ed.). *The Female Autograph: Theory and Practice of Autobiography from the Tenth to the Twentieth Century*. Chicago: University of Chicago Press, 1984.

Steedman, Carolyn. *Landscape For a Good Woman: A Story of Two Lives*. London: Virago, 1986.

Thompson, Mark (ed.). *Leatherfolk: Radical Sex, People, Politics, and Practice*. Boston, MA: Alyson Publications, 1991.

Vance, Carol S. (ed.). *Pleasure and Danger: Exploring Female Sexuality*, 2nd edn. London: Pandora, 1992.

Walker, Alice. *In Search of Our Mothers' Gardens*. London: The Women's Press, 1984.

Wallace, Michele. *Invisibility Blues*. London: Verso, 1990.

Ward Jouve, Nicole. *White Woman Speaks with Forked Tongue: Criticism as Autobiography*. London: Routledge, 1991.

Watney, Simon. *Policing Desire: Pornography, AIDS, and the Media*. London: Methuen, 1987.

Weeks, Jeffrey. *Sexuality and its Discontents: Meanings, Myths and Modern Sexualities*. London and New York: Routledge, 1985.

Whitford, Margaret. *Luce Irigaray: Philosophy in the Feminine*. London and New York: Routledge, 1991.

Whitford, Margaret (ed.). *The Irigaray Reader*. Oxford: Blackwell, 1991.

Wilkinson, Sue and Celia Kitzinger (eds). *Heterosexuality: A Feminism and Psychology Reader*. London, Newbury Park, CA, and New Delhi: Sage, 1993.

Williams, Linda. *Hard Core: Power, Pleasure, and the 'Frenzy of the Visible'*. London: Pandora, 1990.

Williams, Patricia J. *The Alchemy of Race and Rights*. Cambridge, MA: Harvard University Press, 1991.

Wilson, Elizabeth. *Adorned in Dreams: Fashion and Modernity*. Berkeley: University of California Press, 1987.

Wilson, Elizabeth. *The Sphinx in the City: Urban Life, the Control of Disorder and Women*. London: Virago, 1991.

Wise, Sue and Liz Stanley. *Georgie Porgie: Sexual Harassment in Everyday Life*. London: Pandora, 1987.

Wolff, Janet. 'The Invisible Flâneuse: Women and the Literature of Modernity', in *Theory, Culture and Society* 2, 3 (1985): 37–46.

Wollstonecraft, Mary. *Vindication of the Rights of Woman*, introd. Barbara Taylor. London: Everyman, 1992.

Wright, Elizabeth. *Feminism and Psychoanalysis: A Critical Dictionary*. Oxford: Blackwell, 1992.

Index

MAKING MUSIC WITH SOUNDS

Making Music with Sounds offers a creative introduction to the art of making sound-based music. It introduces the elements of making compositions with sounds and facilitates creativity in school-age children, with the activities primarily for 11–14-year-old students. It can also be used by people of all ages becoming acquainted with this music for the first time.

Sound-based music is defined as the art form in which the sound, rather than the musical note, is the basic unit and is closely related to electroacoustic music and the sonic arts. The art of sound organisation can be found in a number of forms of music—in film, television, theatre, dance and new media. Despite this, there are few materials available currently for young people to discover how to make sound-based music. This book offers a programme of development starting from aural awareness, through the discovery and organisation of potential sounds, to the means of generating and manipulating sounds to create sequences and entire works. The book's holistic pedagogical approach to composition also involves aspects related to musical understanding and appreciation, reinforced by the author's online pedagogical ElectroAcoustic Resource Site (EARS II).

Leigh Landy is Director of the Music, Technology and Innovation Research Centre at De Montfort University, UK. He is an active composer, editor of the journal *Organised Sound* and co-founder of the Electroacoustic Music Studies Network.